# THE GARFIELD ORBIT

A  BOOK

BOOKS BY MARGARET LEECH

The Garfield Orbit (*with Harry J. Brown*)
In the Days of McKinley
Reveille in Washington: 1860–1865
Anthony Comstock: Roundsman of the Lord (*with Heywood Broun*)

*Fiction*

The Back of the Book
Tin Wedding
The Feathered Nest


BOOKS BY HARRY J. BROWN

The Garfield Orbit

*Editor*

Letters from a Texas Sheep Ranch
The Diary of James A. Garfield (*with Frederick D. Williams*), three volumes

# THE GARFIELD ORBIT

MARGARET LEECH

*AND*

HARRY J. BROWN

1817

HARPER & ROW, PUBLISHERS

NEW YORK, HAGERSTOWN

SAN FRANCISCO

LONDON

FIRST EDITION

*Designed by Sidney Feinberg*

*Civil War maps and genealogical chart by John Shimmin*

Library of Congress Cataloging in Publication Data

Leech, Margaret, 1893–1974.
  The Garfield orbit.
  Includes index.
  1. Garfield, James Abram, Pres. U.S., 1831–1881.
2. United States—Politics and government—Civil
War, 1861–1865.  3. United States—Politics and
government—1865–1881.  4. Presidents—United
States—Biography.  I. Brown, Harry James, joint
author.  II. Title.
E687.L43      973.8'4'0924  [B]      76-5140
ISBN 0-06-012551-9

78 79 80 81 82 10 9 8 7 6 5 4 3 2 1

# CONTENTS

# ILLUSTRATIONS

[ vii ]

The Garfield house in Hiram. *Courtesy of the Teachout-Price Memorial Library, Hiram College*

Eliza Arabella Garfield ("Trot," 1860–1863) (Oil painting by Caroline Ransom). *Courtesy of the Lake County Historical Society*

Officers of the Forty-second Ohio Infantry Regiment, 1862. *Manuscript Division, Library of Congress*

Brigadier General Garfield, 1862 or 1863 (Photo by Mathew Brady). *Prints and Photographs Division, Library of Congress*

Major General William S. Rosecrans. *U.S. Signal Corps photo No. 111 BA 1533 (Brady Collection), National Archives*

Committee on Military Affairs, House of Representatives, 1867–1869. *U.S. Signal Corps photo No. B 1447 (Brady Collection), National Archives*

James G. Blaine. *Prints and Photographs Division, Library of Congress*

Samuel Jackson Randall, Speaker of the House, 1876–1881. *Prints and Photographs Division, Library of Congress*

The Garfield house at Thirteenth and I streets, Washington, D.C. (J. M. Bundy, *The Life of James A. Garfield,* New York, 1881).

Mollie Garfield and her father, 1870 (Photo by Mathew Brady). *Courtesy of the Lake County Historical Society*

Edward Garfield (1874–1876). *Courtesy of the Lake County Historical Society*

Summer of 1874. *Manuscript Division, Library of Congress*

Isaac Errett, prominent Disciple leader. *Courtesy of the Western Reserve Historical Society*

Dr. John P. Robison (Crisfield Johnson, comp., *History of Cuyahoga County, Ohio,* Philadelphia, 1879).

The Dickey farm in Mentor. *Courtesy of the Lake County Historical Society*

William Cooper Howells (William Dean Howells). *Courtesy of the Rutherford B. Hayes Library*

Burke A. Hinsdale. *Library of Congress*

Jacob Dolson Cox. *U.S. Signal Corps photo No. 111 B 3260 (Brady Collection), National Archives*

Joseph Henry, Secretary of the Smithsonian Institution, 1846–1878. *Prints and Photographs Division, Library of Congress*

President Rutherford B. Hayes, 1879 (Photo by J. Landry, Cincinnati). *Courtesy of the Rutherford B. Hayes Library*

Home from Chicago, 10 June 1880. *Smithsonian Institution Photo No. 75-14928*

The Republican ticket, 1880. *Smithsonian Institution Photo No. 75-14933*

Lawnfield, 1880. *Courtesy of the Lake County Historical Society*

The candidate, 1880. *Courtesy of the Lake County Historical Society*

The office, 1880. *Library of Congress*

*Following page 200*

ton, D.C., 9:20 A.M., 2 July 1881. *Smithsonian Institution Photo No. 75-14931*

Waiting for news at the White House gates. *Smithsonian Institution Photo No. 75-14927*

On the train, Elberon, and the arrival at Francklyn Cottage, 6 September 1881. *Smithsonian Institution Photo No. 75-14930*

Remains of the President lying in state. *Courtesy of the Architect of the Capitol*

## MAPS

# PREFACE

When Margaret Leech died in 1974 she left unfinished a biography of
James A. Garfield on which she had worked for many years. Epilogue I
and the first eight chapters were in a near final form; notes and references were in a preliminary state. My own work on the book has been
that of both editor and writer. I have gone over her work carefully,
checked sources and quotations, incorporated in the text revisions that
she had indicated, and made other changes that seemed necessary or
desirable. In the notes and references I have departed from Miss
Leech's practice and have adopted the academic mode of using a su-
perscript number in the text to alert the reader to the presence of a
note in the back of the book. I have written Chapters 9 and 10 and Epilogue II. Although these serve to round out Miss Leech's narrative, I
have dealt with the last eighteen years of Garfield's life in a more summary fashion than she would have done. I have selected the illustrations from those collected by both of us, supervised the preparation of
the maps and the genealogical chart, and selected and edited the letters
of Garfield that follow Epilogue II.

— HARRY J. BROWN

The path of youth winds down through many a vale,
And on the brink of many a dread abyss,
From out whose darkness comes no ray of light,
Save that a phantom dances o'er the gulf,
And beckons toward the verge. Again the path
Leads o'er a summit where the sunbeams fall,
And thus, in light and shade, sunshine and gloom,
Sorrow and joy, this life-path leads along.

James A. Garfield, "Memory,"
*The Williams Quarterly,* March 1856

In the evening, Crete set me on a new line of thought, namely, the enumeration of the circles in which I had lived. There were these—1st, Orange; 2d, Chester; 3d, Hiram; 4th, Williams; 5th, Ohio Teachers; 6th, Ohio Senate; 7th, Army; 8th, Congress; 9th, law. My relation to each of these is something of a test.

*The Diary of James A. Garfield,*
Vol. III, November 16, 1875

# GARFIELD AND RELATED FAMILIES

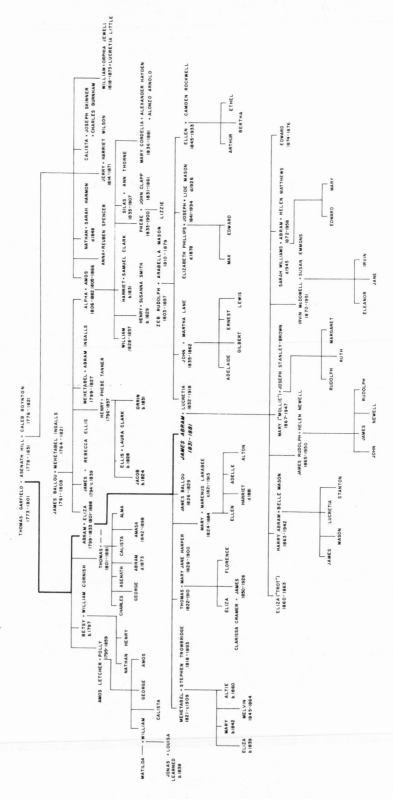

# EPILOGUE I

## A HOT SATURDAY MORNING
## IN WASHINGTON

IT WAS EARLY when the President awoke. A glare of summer morning bleached the walls. The stench of the Potomac flats drifted sourly through the windows. This was a morning that the President had eagerly anticipated. He was leaving Washington on the nine-thirty train, bound for a vacation in New England, and in two days he would rest among the noble elms of Williamstown.

He was alone in the lofty bedchamber that surveyed a heat-hazed prospect of the river and the distant Virginia heights. Crete's neat little head was missing from her pillow. She had remained at Long Branch, New Jersey, while he came back to Washington to wind up business connected with the close of the fiscal year. They were to meet at Jersey City that afternoon.

The pall of summer drooped over the White House. Congress was gone until December. The petitioners had fled. There was peace—or at least comparative peace, for it had been a busy enough week—in the President's office and the scuffed corridor of the east wing. The stillness of the family wing was, for a family man, less grateful. The main sources of uproar had been removed by Grandma's absence in Ohio and the departure of the little boys to join her. Mollie, his darling "Mollie-Whack," had stayed with her mother at Long Branch. Only Hal and Jim were on hand, keeping "bachelors' hall" with their father.[1] Dearly as he loved his "old boys," the President never felt much enthusiasm for keeping bachelors' hall. He needed his strong, steady little wife, so long his stay and counsellor; the experience of recent weeks, when for the first time he had had to consider and care for her, had in no wise diminished his dependence. His mood was too cheerful now for loneliness, and yet he was more than ordinarily anxious to be with

Crete again. They had been parted for five days, their longest separation since her serious illness in May, and he wanted to see with his own
eyes that she was still improving.

Crete's breakdown had been for her husband a calamity totally un-
foreseen; and, though it is hard to speak surely of the feelings of a
woman so talented in hiding them, it had seemed to take Crete by
surprise, too. There had been a sort of warning—a sense of malaise
and the first creeping fingers of a chill—after she attended the un-
veiling of the statue of Farragut, but the weather had been oppressively
hot; besides, a touch of malaria was a commonplace in Washington.[2]
Crete had dressed and gone down to her reception in the evening. It
had proved to be an exceptionally enjoyable occasion. The color had
risen in the President's tired, handsome face as, coming a little late into
the lambent gaslight of the Red Parlor, he marked the pleasant company that had gathered. General Sherman, his wrinkles twinkling with
vivacity, was casting the net of his charm over a shoal of admirers.
Another group had formed near Crete, who sat by the marble mantel,
hugging an unseasonable fire. The ladies, in jewel-colored silks and
coquettish little evening hats, lent elegance to the background of
scarred wallpaper and threadbare carpeting and upholstery; but, as
one caller remarked, the dominant character of the scene was its domesticity. The Garfields somehow contrived to make the decaying
grandeur of the mansion as homely as their farmhouse parlor at Mentor, Ohio.[3]

Mrs. Garfield had chatted animatedly with her friends, but before
morning she had a hard chill, and her temperature rapidly mounted.
The peculiar features of the case were the patient's extreme agitation
and fatigue. The family doctor, a homeòpathic practitioner named
Susan Ann Edson (labeled by the youngest Garfield, Abram, "Dr.
Edson, Full of med'cine"), did not limit herself to the expected diagnosis of malaria. She found a complication of nervous prostration,
brought on by overwork, and two consulting physicians concurred in
her opinion. The President was distressed by the mention of nerves
and overwork, but he was most sharply concerned about Crete's fever
and agonizing headache, which the minute homeopathic dosage did
not relieve.[4] "When you are sick," he had once quaintly written his
wife, "I am like the inhabitants of countries visited by earthquake."[5] A
terrible fear brushed Garfield's heart as he saw Crete's altered face. On
the sixth day one of the doctors dropped a hint of meningitis. The
President at once telegraphed for his first cousin, Dr. Silas Boynton of
Cleveland, a homeopath who would give strong doses in an emergency.
It was only an overnight train journey from Cleveland to Washington,

but Boynton was in Kansas when the telegram came, and he did not reach the White House for three days.[6]

The time of waiting for Boynton was the worst time of all. The President had lost faith in the remedies of the Washington doctors. Mrs. Garfield was in constant pain and was growing alarmingly weak. The mansion broiled in a heat wave, and a caved-in sewer in the south grounds made the rooms on that side so noisome that the exhausted woman was carried across the hall. The entrance gates were closed to traffic. The children's play was hushed. Dr. Edson, on the President's entreaty, moved in to act as nurse; until the Garfields' friend, Mrs. Lionel Sheldon, arrived from Cleveland, the President himself was Dr. Edson's assistant, taking the first watch of the night and once prolonging his vigil until dawn. Hour after hour, in the stifling, heavily curtained bedchamber, Garfield tended his wife and counted it "a sweet privilege" to serve her. He was "tearfully proud" when she praised his nursing to one of the doctors.[7] With searing clarity he had begun to see how selfish his love for Crete had been, how profound his absorption in his own pains and worries, his chronic insomnia. The concerns of self—even the despondency of his first months in office, with all their burden of ugly controversy and attack—had become insignificant. His mind was wholly possessed by the fear that he might lose the woman who lay feverishly tossing on the bed: the life of his life, the dear one.

After Dr. Boynton took charge, the cloud soon lifted. Crete's fever yielded to stronger prescriptions. Mrs. Sheldon went on duty in the sickroom (after two weeks her place was taken by the doctor's wife, Ann), and the President was able to turn his attention to the public business; but he was forewarned that his wife's convalescence would be slow and difficult. Still helplessly weak, she was quivering with morbid fears and fancies. It was hard for Garfield to realize how badly her nerves were shaken. When Garfield was gone for a few hours for a steamboat ride on the Potomac, she was anxious about his "non-return." The next day Hal and Jim gave up an excursion to Fortress Monroe with the Rockwells because she was fretful about it. "I wish you had let them go and not told me of it," she hinted ruefully to her husband. He quietly sent the boys off the next day. That same evening he kept from her the news that Irvin McDowell Garfield, aged ten, had sustained a badly sprained ankle when he caught his foot between the iron pickets of the White House fence and fell backwards while trying to scale it.[8]

The next week, Lucretia Garfield "commanded" the President to join a party going on a weekend trip to Fortress Monroe; Hal, Jim, and

Mollie went also.[9] The earlier incidents had been like a crisis in her nervous illness. On May 31, Dr. Boynton was able to say "with emphasis" that her illness was ended; she now needed "only care and strength."[10] Prostrated by weakness and fatigue, she became once more the selfless wife and mother. She was able to advise and comfort seventeen-year-old Hal when he blurted out his love for pretty Lulu Rockwell. It was only puppy love, of course, but Hal took it hard, and the Garfields were not the kind of parents to make light of youthful heartaches.[11]

It was a memorable day when Mrs. Garfield returned to the family dining room.[12] The President and Harry made a chair of their hands and arms and carried her downstairs. The little ones had missed their mother badly. There was joy on every face around the table. A week later—nearly seven weeks after her illness began—the President took his wife and the three youngest children to Long Branch. He had always loved the sea, holding a nearly mystical belief in its healing power, and he rejoiced to see the strength it gave to Crete. When he left her at the Elberon House with Mollie and Mrs. Boynton, she was wonderfully improved, able to enjoy a carriage drive and even to walk a little.[13]

The jaunt through New England would be quite another matter.[14] It might be best, the President thought, to settle Crete in some quiet place. Shy and retiring by nature, she found public appearances an ordeal at the best of times. She would not be fit for excitement for many months to come, and the President of the United States could not go anywhere without attracting crowds. This simple little trip, beginning with Commencement at Williams College, had expanded into a tour attended by a retinue of cabinet officers and punctuated with speaking engagements. In respect to seclusion, it would be more like a royal progress than a family outing. The President himself had no objection. He throve on crowds, delighted in excitement. Moreover, in its origin and opening feature, the trip was to Garfield a matter of profoundly personal importance. Williams had no alumnus more devotedly loyal. He had received many honors from his college. His student days were warm and living memories. Now Harry and Jim, aged seventeen and fifteen respectively, were about to enter Williams in their turn; to Garfield this Commencement of 1881, when the names of his eldest sons would be inscribed on the roll of incoming freshmen, was a day of crowning fulfillment.

Jim came in before his father was up, and after a while they both went to crawl into bed with Hal.[15] The President lay in the middle, talking about the responsibilities of his office. His limbs carried the weight of forty-nine years, his hair was thinning, and grizzle dimmed the brightness of his beard, but he was still a splendid figure in his shirt. Neither of these fine lads could match him in good looks. Hal, brown-eyed and stockily built, resembled his father in sociability and high-strung temperament, but he was a plodding student; deliberate in thought and action, he showed something of his mother's steadiness in his bearing. Jim, still a lanky adolescent, had the President's fair complexion and gave promise of his height, though not his massive frame. He was moody and quick-tempered, more resistant than Hal to correction, far quicker at learning. They belonged in the same category, in spite of their personal differences: average American youngsters of secure, middle-class background, more vitally interested in sports than study, lacking in any special aptitude or sharp prod of ambition.

The President regarded them with love and bafflement. Between him and his dear "old boys," there was a gulf that his own hardscrabbling youth had not prepared him to bridge. He had never understood that it was a gulf created by the effortless ease and privilege of their rearing. Their sojourns on the farms at Solon and Mentor had been holiday diversions, their chores a mimic labor. They loved and honored their father but did not speak his language. The President was in closer communication with his private secretary than his own flesh and blood. Joseph Stanley Brown, pulling himself up by his own shabby bootstraps, driving to get ahead, was the kind of young fellow whom the President understood.

Just back from an errand to London, Joe was to have breakfast with the President and receive his parting instructions; this, or some other prompting, reminded Garfield that he had things to do before he took the train. With a sudden change of mood, he broke off his serious conversation and began "pulling and hauling" the boys about, chanting as he did so a ditty from his favorite operetta, *Pinafore*—"I mixed those babies up." Jim broke away to execute a "flipflop" over the bed and threw a teasing challenge to his father. The President vaulted over the bed himself and landed his 200 pounds lightly on the other side. He then offered a challenge to the boys. "He knelt down on the floor, straightened himself out so that his body was parallel with the floor, his arms straight down and resting on the tips of his fingers and on the tips of his toes, and humped himself across the room." Hal and Jim tried to perform the feat but failed.[16]

Garfield hated to come off second best, even in the most unequal competition. His feat was a fitting climax to the mood of well-being with which he had lately been suffused. Only two months earlier he had been dejected and ill; Crete's sickness had cured him.[17] It was a paradox on which his thinking lingered, that forgetfulness of self could work this miracle of cure. The President had a mind hospitable to miracles, and not only those of the Gospels. Though an educated man could not own to superstition, he was susceptible to the signs of dreams and omens, coincidences and conjunctions of the planets.[18] It is not entirely fanciful to suppose that, at the outset of a journey, the grandson of "James the Astrologer" might have been mindful of the comet that was flaming nightly over Washington. But no trace of uneasiness has been noted. Garfield spoke of his personal miracle with abounding confidence in the future. The portents all seemed favorable on this morning of July 2, as the President put on his new light gray suit and went downstairs to breakfast, bubbling with plans for his vacation.[19]

# CHAPTER 1

# ELIZA

BEFORE CRETE there had been his mother, and she was with him still, a tiny, feeble, perverse woman of nearly eighty years. His home had been hers since he had a home to offer. It was his pleasure to treat her with an extraordinary courtesy. She had the best bedroom and the place on his right at table, and she had Crete to look after her comfort and nurse her when she was ailing. Garfield could never do enough to atone to his little old mother for the struggle of her early widowhood and the misfortune of her second marriage. The wrongs of that marriage lay in the distant past, but Garfield felt them keenly. Only a few weeks before his inauguration, he had known a swell of indignation at a mention of his stepfather, William—or was it Warren?—Belden. A newspaper item told that the man was dead. It was of no conceivable importance; the Garfields had buried him ages ago. Yet, even in death, this dim old enemy could stir Eliza Garfield's son with an anger that was hot and fresh, after all the years and the silence.[1]

The emotional bond with his mother was strong, but Garfield had long since slipped from the tentacles of her influence. Stephen Trowbridge, the erratic, land-speculating farmer whom Hitty Garfield married, once had the impudence to write Eliza that her word was law to all her children but James.[2] It was a mean thing for Stephen to say because it was the truth and Eliza hated to hear it. Ever since James had grown to manhood, she had been battling to hold on to him, and she was still battling when Stephen wrote, although James by then was forty years old and a prominent member of Congress. She would try to be meek and grateful, but sometimes her temper was poisoned beyond bearing. Then she would rail against the worldliness of life in Washington, lashing out at James and Crete for giving receptions—a word that

[ 7 ]

Eliza used as another might say "orgies"—and consorting with "vicious and ungodly company."[3] Or else she would remind James that she was about to die (he had been hearing this since childhood) and implore him to heed his mother's prayers, read the Scriptures to his family, fear God, save his soul, quit public life. These outbursts were worse than useless, but Eliza's frustrations were urgent. She had worshipped James ever since they had laid the big, cleaned-up baby, with his big, sandy head "like a red Irishman," on her bed in the cabin at Orange.[4]

Eliza had always been intensely jealous in her affections. She had been born at the dawn of the nineteenth century on a farm near Richmond, New Hampshire, the fourth surviving child of James and Mehetabel Ingalls Ballou. There were two brothers, James and Henry, and a sister, Mehetabel, whom they called Hitty. For more than four years, Eliza was the baby of the family. Then one day the father took the little girls up on his horse and left them with neighbors overnight. When they came home, there was a baby sister. Hitty was highly pleased at finding this small Alpha, but Eliza kept a vivid memory of her own indignation and the "improper" language she had used. "I suppose I was mad to be crowded out of the place I had occupied so long," she wrote Alpha when they were both old women. "I guess I vented all my spite then, for I have never felt any since." But it would have been hard for anyone to harbor ill will for Alpha, who grew up to be as mild and easy-tempered as Eliza was fiery and high-strung.[5]

The children's father was descended from a colonist of Norman French extraction who had come to New England in the middle of the seventeenth century and founded a goodly line not wanting in men of intellectual standing. The New Hampshire James—the Christian name was recurrent in the family—made a somewhat irregular claim to intellectual gifts of his own. According to family tradition, he was a remarkable mathematician who could calculate eclipses and the conjunctions of various planets and frequently spent the night in observation of the heavens. He was locally famed as "Ole Conjurer Blue," a fortune teller with the gift of second sight. So many people came to have him cast their horoscopes that he kept a public house to serve them. A sociable, lively man, high-colored and portly, he had a well-stocked bar and set a good table, and for a while he prospered. But, clairvoyant though "James the Astrologer" was reputed to be, he could not see the way to his own fortune. He wasted his substance on a losing business venture, and his sudden death in 1808 left his widow in financial straits.[6]

Mehetabel Ingalls Ballou was a plucky, red-haired woman, a skillful weaver who was not afraid of work and change. As soon as the lawyers had put her affairs in order, she sold the farm and took her five children to Otsego County in central York State, where she had kinsfolk

in the town of Worcester. The Ballous stayed there for more than four
years before moving farther still. By that time the two young boys were old
enough to look after themselves—it was said that her eldest, James,
was a soldier in the War of 1812—but all five of Mehetabel's children
were in the party of family and friends that traveled in 1814 to the
Ohio frontier.

Among the playmates whom Hitty and Eliza found at Worcester
was a boy named Abram Garfield, whose widowed mother had taken a
second husband, Caleb Boynton, and was raising a second family. The
lad's roots, like those of the Ballou youngsters, were deep in the soil of
New England. There had been Garfields in Massachusetts since the colony was founded, and men of both their families had fought in the
Revolution. (The name Garfield was pronounced "Gaffield." The New
England elision was evidently used by members of the family, since it
persisted in the West where "r's" were notably hard.)

Abram was a warm, open-hearted boy, stamped with the Garfield
pattern of exceptional muscular strength and little interest in book-
learning. When he was about fourteen, he was much in Hitty's company because she was "put out" with an aunt in whose house Abram,
too, was staying. He fell head over heels in love, and, though Hitty was
some months older, she responded to his passion and promised that
she would wait for him. Before the Ballous left Worcester, it was understood that Abram would come for Hitty as soon as he was grown.
Eliza, for her part, sniffed at Abram as "a green boy." She did not give
him a second glance while he was courting her sister.[7]

Abram's heart was faithful, but the romance grew dim for Hitty in
the strange scenes of Muskingum County, Ohio—"almost out of the
world," as Eliza thought—and she listened to the pleas of an enamored
Ingalls cousin who was old enough to take a wife. Abram, setting out at
seventeen to claim his sweetheart, was stopped short at Buffalo by a
man from Ohio who told him she was married. But so many of his
kinsfolk and friends were moving west—including his mother and stepfather and their children—that Abram finally went anyway, and three
years later, in 1819, he reached Muskingum County. He soon learned
that an uncle of Eliza's with whom he had once lived in Worcester was
in the neighborhood and set out to visit him. Eliza, who was living with
her uncle, was working for neighbors on the day that Abram came by
their farm and asked his way of the man of the house, who was
swingling flax in a field. When the man came in for his dinner, he told
Eliza he had seen her husband and would bet on their being married in
less than three months. His teasing implied that the eighteen-year-old
Eliza could have any man she fancied—and that she would fancy
Abram. Her features, perhaps, were already rather sharp and set, but

she had inherited her mother's bright coloring as well as her clever hands, and her fine singing voice made her welcome in any gathering. She was small and swift of foot, fond of company and chatter, and she was saucy, too, for she bridled at the mention of Abram Garfield, saying she never liked him. But, on seeing the fine big fellow that the "green boy" had become, Eliza changed her mind, and they were married within three months, just as the neighbor had predicted.[8]

Eliza doubtless loved to tell her children about their father, recalling his great strength and masculine beauty. When she was in her seventh decade she wrote it all out for James, describing Abram's broad shoulders and imposing height, his white, even teeth, and the full curve of his lips—"tolerable thick, but to me very handsome." Pressed by James she also wrote an account of her courtship, telling of Abram's earlier love for Hitty, of his disappointment at learning of her marriage, and of his arrival in Muskingum County. Did she, after so many years, feel a twinge a jealousy? At the bottom of her letter she wrote, "I want you to keep this private."[9]

Eliza left home with the light and callous heart of youth, not knowing why her mother wept to part with her, and rode pillion behind Abram to the Western Reserve in the north of the state. Abram farmed here and there in Cuyahoga County and then obtained a contract to build a section of the Ohio and Erie Canal, the great waterway that would connect the back country with Lake Erie at the little village of Cleveland. He made money on this contract, but a second and larger job of canal construction in Tuscarawas County proved to be a losing venture that wiped out nearly all his profits.[10]

For the first eight years of their marriage, the Garfields did not have a house of their own or even a fixed abode; they stayed off and on at Newburgh, where Abram's younger brother, Thomas, and their half-brother, Amos Boynton, had their farms. In 1826, Amos married Eliza's sister Alpha, and he and Abram presently bought adjoining parcels of land in Orange township. Amos built a log house and cleared his acres while Abram was still lotting on a big profit from the canal. After his failure, Abram decided to follow his half-brother's example. Farming was probably the occupation for which he was best suited. Inferior in mental capacity to his quick-witted little wife, Abram had skills that were valued in new settlements. Eliza bragged that "he could outlift anyone he came in contact with" and "do as much work in a day as any man would in two."[11] He was especially noted for his prowess as a wood-chopper. People would come from miles around to see Abram "Gaffield" wield the ax, gripping the handle by the end but striking true and deep.[12]

In Eliza's telling, her life with Abram had been a golden time but

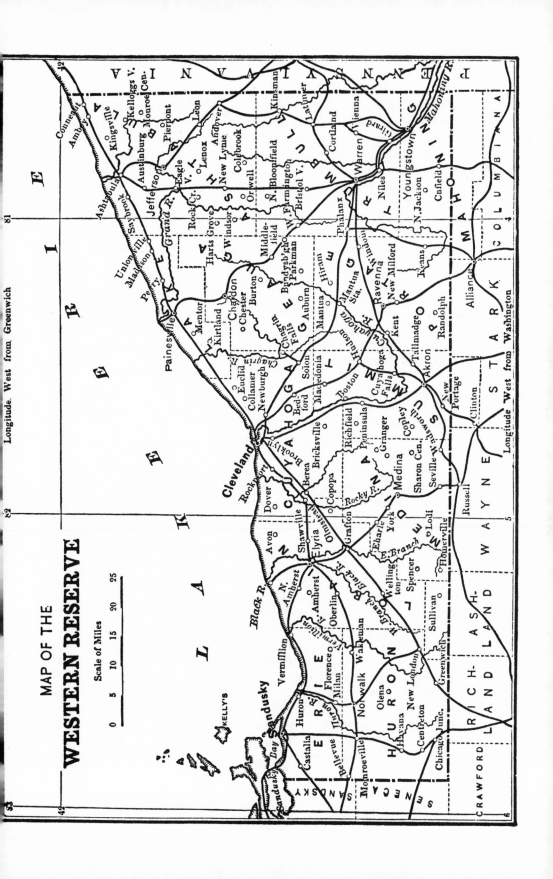

# MAP OF THE
# WESTERN RESERVE

Scale of Miles

0   5   10   15   20   25

Longitude. West from Greenwich

the years of wandering had been far from easy. Wherever they went, privation and toil went with them, and ague waited every fall in sodden river bottoms. Eliza slaved at the backbreaking chores of the frontier, besides bearing and nursing four children—Mehetabel, Thomas, Mary, and James Ballou—and on the canal she had to furnish board for a gang of twenty laborers. Perhaps such exertions did not touch her closely. She was small, but she was fit and wiry; a willing worker, so resilient that, after giving the laborers their supper, she would entertain them with her singing. In this remote world she was central and important, fulfilled in family love and management. "We enjoyed ourselves with our little Children as well as parents ever did," she wrote, and the words have a chime of simple joys remembered. Eliza had not faltered under hardship, but her courage failed when they lost their little Jimmy, the two-year-old who was their pet and darling.[13]

It happened without warning—or without such warning as people then could recognize—while Abram was building their cabin at Orange. Eliza, alone with the children at Newburgh, was sitting up late on a January night. Jimmy was restless and complaining and begged his mother to let him sit with her. After a while, she took him up, saying "kiss me and I will." He put his little hand in her bosom, kissed her, and sank back dying in her arms. Eliza could never tell about the rest of that night. She had to wait until morning before she could send for Abram—and then through all the dragging hours while the messenger toiled through the forest to find him and bring him back. When at last Abram came, he cried out, the Lord gave and the Lord hath taken away, Blessed be the name of the Lord. But Eliza could not speak the words with her husband. She was filled with rebellion against the will of God.[14]

"I could not be reconciled to the Death of my Child," Eliza wrote. "I almost frowned on my Maker."[15] But in empty days at Orange, where Amos and Alpha took the family in until their house was ready, Eliza longed for the healing certainty of faith. She and Abram haunted religious meetings and looked for help in prayer and preaching. Among the itinerants who roved the forest trails there were preachers who called themselves Disciples of Christ. The heralds of another Reformation, which would sweep away the differences of sect and unite all Christians in one communion, they exhorted their hearers to repent and be baptized and to imitate Christ's first followers in their daily course and conduct. The simple message prevailed with power among the pioneers, whose early church affiliations had been lost in the new country. Abram and Eliza and the Boyntons were among the many converts that the Disciples garnered in the townships of the Reserve.[16]

It was in their new house, their first house, that Eliza felt hope beat again in her breast; felt, too, the stir of another life; and prayed for another son. Her prayers were answered, and she was "made to rejoice," forgetting the pangs of her hard travail in the wonder of this "Man Child" and her secret intuition of his future. For Eliza knew from the first that this was a child of high destiny, born to be great and good.[17]

James Abram Garfield was born in the township of Orange, Cuyahoga County, Ohio, on November 19, 1831. The flood of migration from New England had as yet washed but thinly over the wide lands of the Reserve. The township of Orange was a wilderness dotted with lonely clearings. Near the log house that Abram had raised, his freshly slashed acres touched primeval forest. The first awareness that the baby had, when he began to look beyond his mother's breast, was of nature and love and play—and death. He had been given, as was then commonly done, the name of a child who had died. He bore also the name of his father, who died when the new James was only a year and a half. Abram was seized with a heavy chill after fighting a forest fire. When his breath came hard and short, some unidentified helper applied a blister to his laboring throat. There was no other medical aid at hand. So Eliza was left, in her turn, a desolate widow with a young family to rear. And little James grew up in the reflected light and the legend of a father he could not remember.[18]

Hitty and Mary, twelve and eight respectively, made themselves useful in the house, and light outdoor chores could be entrusted to ten-year-old Thomas, a dutiful boy, strong for his age, though afflicted by "fits" that were probably a mild form of epilepsy.[19] Eliza could not do the heavy work of the farm unaided, but she was not expected to stay there. It was customary for a widow to sell her land and go to work, moving in with relatives who would look after her young ones in her absence and "putting out" older children as farmboys or domestic helpers. This was the way in which the Widow Ballou had managed, but the Widow Garfield did not intend to follow her mother's example. She had decided that she would stay on the farm and keep her children with her. She sold all but thirty acres of land and began her struggle to feed and clothe her family with the help of God.[20]

Human assistance was obviously also needed. Thomas was robbed of his youth before his childhood ended, but he could not do a man's work or earn a man's wage for the next five years. Who farmed the widow's thirty acres in the meantime? Who was there but the double brother-in-law and only near neighbor? An exemplar of stern virtue, high-minded and devout, Amos Boynton was a second father to Eliza's children.[21] Occasional financial aid may have come from Abram's brother, Thomas, who profited intermittently from some business enterprise in Cleveland. An inveterate gambler, repudiated by the Disciples after his single attempt at conversion, Thomas scandalized Eliza—"he gambles with his own Boys," she once wrote James with horror—but she seemed to prefer him to the God-fearing Amos. Sinful though Thomas might be, he had the Garfields' hearty charm. He also had his ups and downs of fortune, whereas Amos was blessed with a steady prosperity that provoked Eliza to invidious comment on the Boyntons' concern with possessions.[22]

Many years later, when Eliza's reminiscences became a subject of national interest, she gave no credit to either brother-in-law. She presented her "struggle" as an independent effort; while insisting on its rigors, she denied that her family had ever needed help or wanted for anything. How she managed in the first years was never explained. She was a deft seamstress who could easily have found employment if she had consented to break up her home, but, with young children to look after, Eliza could not pay the long working visits that were the rule in scantily settled places.[23]

"When I think of days past," Eliza plaintively wrote James during his college years, "when I could sit around the fireside with my Fatherless children and know what they were all about and know they were comfortably clothed and fed, I could lay my head on my pillow and sleep soundly."[24] To "know what they were all about"—that was Eliza's recompense after Abram was gone. His loss had aggravated a morbid twist in her nature, opening the wound of her first Jimmy's death and recalling a train of earlier bereavements: her father, struck down in his prime; her mother, gone two years after their parting; her sister buried, too, who had been Abram's first sweetheart. The high rate of mortality in the new country was a constant reminder of the coldness of the grave and the "mouldering" of its occupants. Eliza always feared the worst in the sickroom, feared it volubly and hysterically when sickness touched her children.[25]

But Eliza was too high-spirited for the dullness of depression. She would often raise her sweet voice in the ballads of her girlhood or give forth, with the children chiming in, the hymns that made the rafters shake at Lord's Day meetings of Disciples. Her conversation crackled with old saws, tags of verse, borrowed scraps of rhetoric. She dramatized everything; death itself was not exempt. Such phrases as "Death loves a shining mark" and "she came down to the Grave like a shock of Corn" suggest the gusto of her speech. She was a sharp-tongued gossip, well posted on the doings of her neighbors and not averse to suspecting them of shabby motives and conduct. A remarkably graphic memory enlivened her store of reminiscences. Though her father had died when she was a child of six, she vividly portrayed his rosy, corpulent good looks and recalled his genius as an astronomer and mathematician and his great gift of clairvoyance. Her recollections of his prosperous New Hampshire farm betrayed a furtive respect for the worldly possessions she professed to scorn. Eliza talked of the treasures of heaven but pined for the treasures of earth—and envied those who had them. (As the old log houses became a badge of poverty and mean social standing, Eliza succeeded in getting a new frame house, painted red, like her father's.)[26]

Whatever performance Eliza might give, it held her children spellbound. Their little mammy was the source of entertainment and wisdom, as she was the fount of love. They would cherish the memory of her singing, her stories and her precepts—above all, her selfless devotion. With their mother and each other, they were quick to touch and caress, and the glow of early affection would never cease to warm them. Hitty and Mary, old women before they were fifty—worked out, wept out, burned out by poverty and grief—had known their only carefree hours under their mother's roof. Thomas, when he had gone to settle and fail in Michigan, would return in dreams to the little Orange farm, and one of his letters was blotted by homesick tears. James would always hold the name of "mother" sacred and keep in fond remembrance the lost Eden of his boyhood, the joys of pasture and rock and woodland, of wading in the brook and picking wintergreens on the hill. The very fabric of the dingy old cabin was so dear to James that he mourned years later over its ruins and sighed to find the broken back wall of the chimney, which his childish eyes had watched through leaping flames.[27]

It was natural that the Widow Garfield should take a particular pride in her baby. She could see her handsome husband in the fair, strong-shouldered little man who frolicked at her knee, with his full lips curving sweetly in a smile. He was good-natured and affectionate, an active young one "never still a minute at a time."[28] When he was only three, Hitty started carrying him to the district school at Chagrin Falls. He proved to be a clever student with an unusually retentive memory, and his mother busied herself with plans for his education. Chagrin Falls was three miles distant, a round trip of six miles. With three children of school age at the Boyntons' and a few others scattered over the township, Orange was entitled to a school of its own. The Widow Garfield offered a corner of her land and persuaded her neighbors to build a log schoolhouse on it. The arrangement meant a very short walk for James.[29]

Eliza loved all her children, and she never meant to be partial. But Hitty and Mary, after all, were girls, and her good, soft-hearted

"Thom" would not go very far in the world. It was around James that Eliza's fancies clustered, wreathing a future bright with his achievements.[30]

When Eliza sold the farm in 1853 and gathered her children for a good-bye visit, she did not sit with them at table but humbly asked to serve them at their last meal in her home.[31] The gesture touchingly commemorated the time when they had all been together; in fact, that time had not lasted very long. Only four years after Abram died, Hitty married Stephen Trowbridge and went to live in his ramshackle house at Solon. Not long afterward, Thomas began to work out for wages and was often away from home. During much of his boyhood, James lived alone with his mother and his sister Mary, seven years his senior.[32]

James ruled the house. His mother treated him as a privileged being. Mary, a sensitive girl, credited in the family with the gift of second sight, asked no greater happiness than to share her young brother's games or ramble with him through the high woods. By the age of eight, James was running wild. He disregarded his doting mother's wishes, took no interest in saving his soul, and was often rebellious and defiant. On the other hand, he was always a model pupil. Although frontier children were notoriously riotous in school, James held his teachers in respect and was submissive to their correction. He resented a reproof from anyone else. His gentle older brother surely did not risk incurring his displeasure. Pathetically eager to be friends, Thomas would join James in play, sledding down the hill in winter or "sporting" in warm weather beside the brook. James was plied with earnest advice to be a good boy, but he was unused to rebuke. He was offended by the counsel of that just man, Amos Boynton, and imagined that his uncle did not like him because he told him his faults.[33]

James later altered this opinion and condemned the lack of restraint with which he had been reared. He sometimes implied that it had developed his will power—"an aid to a thunderbolt of boy like me"[34]—but in dark moods he bitterly deplored the handicap of his upbringing. Writing on his thirty-first birthday to his friend Harry Rhodes, he described his childhood as a "chaos" in which he was denied inspiration and guidance, "allowed to catch up any or no chance habits of mind, body, morals and manners."[35] The fact that his mother was pinched for money was closely involved in Garfield's resentment. It has been said that poverty was of no consequence on the frontier, where all alike were poor; but there, as everywhere else, degrees and distinctions existed, and the Widow Garfield was keenly aware of them.

James learned at his mother's knee to feel the shame and enviousness of poverty, and he lamented his early disadvantages all his life.[36]

Worst misfortune of all, the basis of his rebellion, was the absence of a father. This was the cause of straitened means and neglected discipline, this was the oddity that set James apart from his fellows.[37] He depended on his orphan state to win forbearing treatment—but he also felt that the indulgence was humiliating. He was on the watch for slights and sneers from other boys, and he went through a truculent phase of fist-fights with his schoolmates. A striking contrast to his lopsided home was provided by the symmetrical Boynton family: father, mother, three boys, three girls. James often crossed the fields to their comfortable house, with its ample barns for the dairy herd. He liked his cousins—William and Henry, Harriet and Phebe and Cordelia, and the baby, Silas—and was sure of finding a welcome from his placid little aunt. As long as memory lasted, James would remember the taste of Aunt Alpha's Indian bread. He was not at ease with his uncle, but he respected the unfaltering constancy of his character; even a small boy could see how strictly, yet lovingly, Amos Boynton held his children to a high standard of conduct.[38] James thought of his own father with a persistent longing that fed on his mother's stories. He desperately wanted to know more, to make some contact with the dead man and penetrate his mystery. But there was nothing left, no likeness or keepsake, not even a letter.

Eliza's tales of "James the Astrologer" had given her children a leaning toward the occult. In 1851 the rampant spiritualist revival suggested an expedient to James. He had been made vividly aware of his father by passing through the sections of the canal which Abram had built near Newcomerstown. On arriving at Cleveland, James visited a séance and called for his father's spirit; after interrogating the raps that purported to represent it, he was half persuaded that they had been in communication.[39] Subsequent experiments made James sceptical, but, although he derided spiritualist beliefs, he never flatly denied the possibility of communication with the dead. His conduct closely paralleled that of his mother, who was obliged as a good Disciple to condemn the tenets of spiritualism in public but never lost her concern with the other world. One séance was actually held in Eliza's house, with her granddaughter, Eliza Trowbridge, as the medium.[40]

Garfield's desire to make contact with his father was still burning in maturity. When a political campaign took him to the Muskingum Valley in 1871, he sought out Robert Nugen, who had worked for Abram on the canal and was now its superintendent. Never, said Nugen, had he seen so powerful a man. He said also that Abram had had admirable control over his men. Others in the area remembered Abram too, speaking "in high terms of his manliness and honesty." James persuaded the Board of Public Works at Columbus to dig out from some musty file the original bid and contract for the job near Newcomerstown. In a few scrawled words and the painfully careful signatures on the two yellowing forms, Garfield felt that at last he touched his father. Abram had written on the bid: "If eny of them is struck to us, we will commence them soon." James liked the ring of that. Poring over the faded script, he felt a surge of pride at the assurance that his father had been manly and honorable in his dealings.[41]

The want of a father was an obvious factor in the emotional disturbances which James began to manifest in boyhood. Another important factor was the influence of his mother's twin obsessions: the hovering presence of death and the prominence that her younger son was destined to attain.

Eliza had informed James of her own prospective demise when he was still small enough to nestle sobbing in her lap. His fright did not deter her from a relentless pursuit of the subject; nor did she fail to add forebodings of "an early grave" for himself. The human crop that the settlers raised was in general a weedy yield. Born of exhausted mothers, undernourished and sickly, the pioneers' children offered little resistance to infections. They swallowed enteric diseases in impure water and tainted meat. Malaria shook and burned them in the fall, and every winter brought a train of grippy colds, abscessed ears, and lingering bronchial infections. Consumption was the great killer of the young, and over them all hung the dread of the cough that did not mend in spring. James was permanently saddled with all his childhood ailments. The most alarming were the blinding headaches which later led more than one doctor to suspect the dreaded "brain fever," but he was also subject to severe infections of the throat and chest. Boils and rheumatic pains recurred throughout his life, and he was chronically afflicted by an unstable digestive tract, vulnerable to emotional strain. James was always morbidly concerned about his symptoms, though he learned to hide his worry with a plausible show of indifference.[42]

Nursing James was Eliza's jealously guarded privilege. An experienced attendant on the sick, she plied James with poultices and infusions, liberally laced with caresses. She prided herself on her knowledge of roots and herbs and did not cease to value their remedial properties when doctors at length came riding with saddlebags filled with drugs. Medical practice on the Reserve was largely preempted by graduates of the homeopathic college that was founded at Cleveland in 1850. James was a devout convert to "little pills." He also adhered to

the principles of the hydropaths, bathed under waterfalls or cold douches, and lay wrapped in a wet sheet to reduce a fever.[43]

If James was apprehensive in time of sickness, his compensation was the leisure of convalescence. He read everything he could lay hands on, newspapers and history books included, but liked best to steep himself in tales of adventure and to indulge the romantic fancies that they stimulated. At night, beside the blazing hearth, he "traced a thousand fantastic figures of giants on fiery steeds, and hosts embattled for war. . . ."[44] To the amusement of his playmates, he was often lost in thought, "framing mighty plans and transactions" of which he was the hero. "O James! do you visit with yourself as much as you used to?" a favorite cousin, Phebe Boynton, once mockingly inquired.[45] But Eliza's prophecies of renown had dangerously stimulated James's tendency to daydream. In "the throbbings of youthful ambition, the laying of plans, and building of bright fabrics visionary and wild," he escaped from his humble condition to the brilliant future in store for him.[46]

Something more might seem needed to explain the severe emotional crisis of James's adolescence, and something more there was—his mother's second marriage. Occurring when he was ten years old, it was obviously an event of critical importance, but very little is known of it. The records of Cuyahoga County confirm that a marriage contract between Eliza "Guiffield" and Alfred Belding was solemnized on April 16, 1842, at Bedford, that Belding petitioned for divorce in 1848, and that the divorce was granted two years later. According to Belding's petition, his wife had left him a year after their marriage and refused all his appeals to live with him. These dry legalities supply the only information on the subject. The circumstances of the courtship, the adjustments necessitated by the marriage, the cause of disagreement—all are wrapped in mystery.[47]

The mystery was created by Eliza. Her way of facing down a mortifying mistake was to ignore it. The facts, however, could not be concealed from the large acquaintance she had formed through family and church connections; communications among the early settlers were as efficient as the tomtoms of African tribes. Roads might be bogged and houses scattered, but the gossip drummed through. The marital troubles of the Beldings would have been a resounding scandal in a dozen townships of Ohio and eastern Michigan; as an accomplished newsmonger, Eliza could not fail to know it. Yet she resumed without a quiver the status of the lorn Widow Garfield, alluding to this condition—even in letters to James—as though it had never suffered interruption. Her bold tactics were remarkably successful. James A. Garfield ascended to national reputation without a stepfather in his history. His

mother's expurgated account of their life at Orange was unquestioningly accepted by newspaper correspondents and biographers. Her second marriage was, by that time, an old story. People who knew of it had died or forgotten or did not want to offend the Garfields. Letters bearing on the matter had vanished. No whisper of rumor was published until 1881, when the newspapers reported the death of "William Belden," stepfather of the president-elect. Only one newspaper dug out the name Alfred Belding, and the unlikely tale did not reach a wide audience.[48]

The result has been to distort and obscure the record; the suppression is like a huge blot in the middle of a document. Most important is the blank in James's story. What was the emotional reaction and what the conduct of a boy so unfitted to tolerate either the rivalry or the authority of a stepfather? It is only clear that the experience was traumatic. No trace of it is found in Garfield's private papers until, at the age of forty-nine, he reads of his stepfather's death. His comment strikes the page in a splash of inaccuracies. He is confused about the year in which the "unfortunate" marriage occurred. He does not correctly remember his stepfather's name. He even mistakes the place of his death, calling it Bryan, although he has just read "Byron" in the newspaper, and this is a town in Michigan well known to him, the place where his Uncle Joseph and Aunt Calista lived for a time, near which his brother Thomas has had a farm for years.[49]

One other inference may be drawn: that the experience deeply complicated James's feelings about his mother. They were often alone together after Mary's marriage in 1845 to Marenus Larabee of Solon. James frequently hurt himself while chopping wood and had to stay home from school until his injuries healed. The fact that he was left-handed might in part explain his clumsiness, but the number of his accidents—"almost a score"—is astonishing, and he twice gashed his foot so severely that he was laid up for six weeks. His need to be close to his mother was so strong that he was miserably homesick for her when, as a big boy of fifteen, he worked for a month on a nearby farm.[50] At an age of independence for country boys, James was clinging to his mother. Then, the next year, he ran away from home.

Cuyahoga County saw spectacular changes while James was growing up. The frontier receded, and with it went the solitary, self-reliant life of the pioneer. Years before the overland rush to the California gold fields, throngs of "movers" brought the stir of trade and unfamiliar faces. In increasing numbers they pushed on to the rolling prairies of Iowa or the wooded wilderness of Michigan, but the population of the Reserve was swelled by those who stopped there. A good-sized village

sprang up at Chagrin Falls. Orange township, bypassed by progress, still saw strange neighbors and new frame houses, and improved roads brought the local farmers into the range of stores and mills and stagecoach stations. The greatest change was in Cleveland. A lakeside hamlet when James was born, it had been transformed by the canal into a bustling port before he was sixteen. The canal was still the main highway of the back country in 1848, but the railroad was coming. Branch lines would soon begin to draw the scattered villages together, and Eliza would exultantly announce, "The iron horse is beginning to snort in Solon."[51]

James started to keep a journal in 1848. Its laconic entries afford the first day-by-day account of his activities. The year begins quietly enough with a round of "schools," for, besides his regular lessons, James frequently attends a singing school in the evening and occasionally a spelling school. (He could benefit from the latter instruction—and also from a course in English grammar.) He has a rifle and a bosom friend, Orrin Judd, with whom he goes a-hunting. At sixteen, he is an able hand, commanding a wage of seventy-five cents a day; though he likes school and excels at his studies, he skips the spring term in order to work full time. Thomas is living with Eliza and working their small farm, and James sometimes helps him—hoeing corn, mowing and raking hay, grinding scythes—but more often he hires out away from home. Three times in the spring, he makes a trip to Cleveland, boating wood. He is away from Orange for days and even weeks at a time. There is no further word of homesickness at this period and, though James chops mountains of wood, no mention of accidents.[52]

The journal conveys the impression that a year has worked a miracle in James, but the impression is misleading. Under the facade of cheerful interest in work and social diversions, he was deep in the "chaos" of childhood. A diet of "nautical novels" had concentrated his fantasies on the adventurous life of a sailor. The sight of a passing ship on the vast blue waters of Lake Erie made him "almost insane with delight." When James left home in August, he was running away to sea.[53]

James was acting on a wildly unrealistic impulse, his flight compelled by a storm of feeling that he never understood. His subsequent comment that he "was rushing with both soul and body to destruction" probably contains an element of truth, though it was set down during a phase of exaggerated repentance. After he arrived in Cleveland, his plans collapsed with comical speed. He was frightened away from the first vessel he boarded by the curses of a drunken captain, and he decided that he was not ready to become "a real sailor."[54]

Retreating to the familiar environs of the canal, James applied to

Captain Amos Letcher of the *Evening Star*. His choice of this particular canalboat is easily explained. Amos Letcher was his first cousin, the son of Abram Garfield's sister, Polly. He offered to take James on as driver. The towpath was in sorry contrast to life before the mast. "As canaling was at the bottom of sailing," James once remarked, "so driving was at the bottom of canaling. I took the job." The *Evening Star* was bound for Pittsburgh with a load of copper ore. After traversing the canal by horse power, it was towed by steamboat up the Ohio River. James fell overboard fourteen times and recalled his escapes from drowning as almost miraculous, since he did not know how to swim.[55]

The life of the canal was a scandal to decent folk, but the innocent James did not shrink from the "degraded young men" among whom he found himself. He wanted, as always, to be liked, and he was favored by his convivial personality and well-developed muscles. He earned the respect of his mates by knocking down a deckhand who challenged him to a fight, and he mastered his duties so competently that he was promoted to bowsman at fourteen dollars a month. His wages were to be raised to twenty dollars in October, but his "apprenticeship" to the sea was interrupted before the second promotion took place. On returning to Cleveland after his fourth trip on the *Evening Star,* James succumbed to a severe attack of fever and ague. His cousin Charles—one of Uncle Thomas's sons—took him home to an emotional reunion with his mother.[56]

Throughout the autumn and winter James remained at home, sick in mind as well as body. His mental attitude at this time supplies an extreme example of the duality which frequently befogged his motives. Six weeks of free life had plunged James into a vortex of guilt, but he intended to return to the canal as soon as he was physically able.[57]

There can be no doubt of the severity of his breakdown. His mental agony went far beyond the depression which was the natural accompaniment of his recurrent bouts of malaria. For five despairing months James struggled with a deadening paralysis of will. His only comfort was his "good angel," his mother. Eliza uttered no reproaches. She tenderly cared for her erring boy and prayed for his repentance. Her entreaties persuaded James to pray himself, but he was not yet ready for conversion. Another year would pass before he was inspired by the eloquence of a Disciple preacher to make a public profession of his sins and in some chilly stream undergo the rite of baptism by immersion which was the Disciple's passport to salvation.[58]

Eliza awaited his change of heart with a singularly tactful forbearance. She did not argue the question of the canal but guilefully suggested that James might while away his convalescence by passing a term at a school. A projected Disciple academy at Hiram in Portage County had not gone beyond the planning stage, but a substitute was offered by Geauga Seminary, conducted by the Free Will Baptists near Chester Cross Roads. The teacher at Orange that winter was a Geauga student, and his enthusiasm for the school had persuaded a number of Orange boys, including Orrin Judd and Garfield's eldest Boynton cousin, William, to go there in the spring. James was easily induced to join them when Eliza produced seventeen dollars, the entire savings of the household. Supplied with unaccustomed wealth and laden with his mother's provisions of flour and salt pork, James set out in early March for a term at Chester Cross Roads.[59]

Remembering himself as he was at seventeen, James saw "an overgrown, uncombed, unwashed boy with the delicate japan of the soul tarnished past restoration . . . compelled to begin the work of exhuming my manhood from the drift and rubbish which every chance had thrown upon me." So James wrote in his most bitter outburst of self-revelation, the letter deploring the "chaos" of his upbringing.[60] But such gloomy thoughts were far from young Garfield's mind as he gaped at the spindly pillared edifice of Geauga Seminary and the crowd of boys and girls who were hurrying to and from it. Even by contemporary standards, Geauga was a second-rate school; but seminaries on the Reserve were few and far between, and more than two hundred students enrolled at Chester Cross Roads for the spring term of 1849.[61]

James was quickly swept into the current of new and exhilarating experiences. He was excited by his introduction to algebra and philosophy, by singing in a glee club, by joining societies with long Greek names and taking part in their debates. He was busy, too, with odd jobs of wood-chopping, for his fortune of seventeen dollars was quickly disappearing. As was customary the stated school fee covered tuition only. Lodging, including a charge for cooking provisions, cost each student about a dollar a week, and his budget was further depleted by the purchase of books and sundry items, sometimes unanticipated. The three Orange boys, for example, were obliged to buy a stove for the room they hired near the seminary building. The landlady agreed to accept their services at wood-chopping in partial payment of her charges, but they still had to look for other work in order to make ends meet.[62]

It was the end of March before James found time to write his mother. His letter, jointly addressed to her and Thomas and headed "First Epistle of James," bubbled with enthusiasm. He liked school better every day, he wrote. His bed had broken down, but he had bought flax cord and mended it. He had $1.48 left. He wanted his cashmere pants and some neck-handkerchiefs. He wanted an epistle.[63]

A change of scene had been the medicine James needed. His last trace of depression had vanished, his dependence on his mother was forgotten. Even his compulsion to return to the canal was subtly beginning to weaken in the wonderful novelty of boarding school.

As friendly as a puppy, James readily won the liking of his school-mates. He made them laugh by his odd remarks in class, and he gained the reputation of being original. Physically as well as mentally, he stood above the others. Grown tall and broad of chest, he was still a slouchy cub of a boy, with tousled fair hair and exceedingly pale blue eyes—"a gander eye," as the mocking phrase went—but some dignity was there, and a nascent power. Dozing off one day in class, James was wakened by a burst of laughter and found himself the focus of attention. The unabashed way in which he looked about him made Lucretia Rudolph, a Disciple girl from Garrettsville, think of a young lion abruptly aroused from sleep.[64]

Although there were more than a hundred girls at Geauga during Garfield's first term, he did not single out any for particular attention. But there is no doubt that he was enjoying himself (except during a period of illness). "Fine times" and "happy times" are phrases that ap-pear in his diary for those months. He had a "very pleasant time" on a June "pic nic" attended by "19 Couple of the students." When five couples went to Kirtland for an exhibition and did not get back until 11 P.M., he had "a fine time." As the term neared its end, he found the prospect of parting "very unpleasant." After a lonesome summer month he was back at Geauga. During the fall he was looking to books for guidance on sex. It is a sad commentary on the dearth of sensible information then available that James vastly admired two pamphlets by the popular phrenologist, Orson Squire Fowler: *Love and Parentage* and *Amativeness*. Fowler's advice to young men was unrealistic, minatory, and scientifically false, but James wished that there were ten thousand copies of *Amativeness* in every town in the United States.[65]

James was permanently marked by his search for a teaching job in the fall of 1849. It was his first experience of appearing before strangers as a suppliant. He found it so disagreeable that, after a few refusals, he gave up and went home to Orange. There he learned that a nearby school, in a section of Solon township known as "the Ledge," might be available to "Widow Gaffield's Jimmie." He made haste to call on the directors and succeeded in closing the bargain. The fact that he had been thought of was all-important to James. It was his steadfast—though not completely warranted—claim that he never again took the initiative in seeking any position. The small and not very striking chain of incidents became the basis of his conviction—"the law of my life"—that job-hunting was unlucky for him and even contrary to the will of God.[66]

In the elation of getting the school, James had bravely faced its "hard" reputation, but he expected trouble and soon found it. On his eighteenth birthday in November he reflected that he was rather young to have the care of a company of scholars some of whom were older than himself. Though flogging was common practice in the district schools, James thought it abused and was reluctant to resort to it. Unruly boys finally drove him to using the whip and even to rough-and-tumble fighting. The difficulties of preserving order combined with some inner turmoil to make James restless and despondent. It was a real triumph of will that, under such handicaps, he acquitted himself with credit. He wound up the term with an evening "exhibition" and bade farewell to "the Ledge" in the satisfaction of having done his duty. In those weary months a callow boy had taken a long step toward maturity. He had discovered that he possessed a true talent for teaching. In disciplining others he had been obliged to discipline himself, to hide his own rebellious moods and control his naturally hot temper.[67]

In 1850 James repeated the pattern of studying spring and fall at Geauga, but in these two terms the spell of the school was broken. James found much to criticize in Free Will Baptist doctrine, and he frequently returned to Orange on weekends to take part in Disciple meetings at "the little red schoolhouse" that had replaced the rude log structure of his early boyhood.[68]

A chief cause of Garfield's disaffection was his religious conversion, which occurred only a few days before the opening of the spring term of 1850. The Disciples, embattled against "sectarianism," had actually introduced still another set of quibbles over dogma, and James was bristling with objections to Baptist tenets, from which those of his own church differed only on niggling points. His conversion, in this first phase of excited feeling, was not an altogether beneficial influence. Transports of thanksgiving and storms of repentance may have brought James some emotional release, but his conversion also aggravated his rooted feelings of guilt. It aligned him with the most reactionary Disciples in tolerating the institution of slavery and doubting that any form of civic participation—even voting—was compatible with a Christian life. In obvious imitation of his bigoted little mother, James displayed a censorious prudery that was ill-suited to his youth and ardent temperament; as faithfully as a letterpress copy, he repeated Eliza's cant phrases and pious references to death. One of her phrases, "Remember Lot's wife," was his abrupt injunction to a female classmate

whom he caught turning to look back at him in the Geauga yard.
Lucretia Rudolph thought James a "strange mortal" and "the drollest
genius" she had ever seen.[69]

James's conversion, however, was not the sole reason for his dissatisfaction with Geauga. He was also painfully conscious of being thrown
on his own resources, without hope of financial assistance. Always embarrassed by limited means and taking odd jobs to meet his running expenses, he had nevertheless been encouraged to believe that he had
first claim on any money that Eliza and Thomas could scrape together.
But by 1850 a change had occurred: Thomas had married and was expecting a child. Egged on by his wife, he was planning to leave his
mother's farm and look for larger opportunities in Michigan. James
was made aware of his duty not only to look after himself but to begin
to repay his mother and brother for their past generosity.[70] He managed to get through the spring term by boarding himself on a monastic
diet ("not much meat, but pudding and milk, bread, butter, etc.") at a
cost of about fifty cents a week.[71] He spent the summer vacation working at carpentry at Chester, but he started the fall term with empty
pockets. In secret shame but outward defiance, James wore the garb
that advertised his straits: patched jeans, coarse boots, and common
rye-straw hat. He avoided social gatherings because he felt scorned for
his poverty and for his membership in a minority religious group, subject to "dry knocks" from the Baptists.[72]

James adhered obstinately to the belief that he had been treated
with contempt in boyhood. He would recall the "taunts, jeers, and cold,
averted looks of the rich and the proud," but he did not explain where
he met these high-toned beings.[73] They were certainly not among the
underpaid teachers and impecunious students at Geauga. On the point
of sectarian prejudice, James was equally disingenuous. There were
many Disciple students at the seminary. Two of Garfield's classmates,
Symonds Ryder, Jr., and Lucretia Rudolph, were the children of Disciple leaders. Among other friends of his own faith was Harvey
Everest, a serious lad from northern New York, with whom James
worked on one stint of carpentry. Moreover, in the middle of the
spring term of 1850, the Baptist trustees had appointed a Disciple principal, Professor Spencer J. Fowler, who took an interest in James and
included him in the list of those competing to speak at the Commencement exercises. James's composition "The Era of Universal Peace" was
among the winning entries, and he delivered his first formal oration on
Commencement Day in July.[74]

In the autumn Fowler's interest took the practical form of giving
James an opportunity to teach a class in mental arithmetic. But the very
kindness and sympathy of the new principal was a factor in increasing

James's irritation with the school. Fowler was embroiled from the start in difficulties with the board. His appointment, made at a time when the Disciples of the Reserve were about to begin building a school of their own, suggests that the Baptist trustees had been actuated by a desire to hang on to their Disciple students. They were unable to maintain their ostensibly liberal gesture, and their opposition made Fowler's position untenable. He resigned at the close of the fall term of 1850. James, applauding his "free spirit," took his own departure with few regrets.[75]

The Free Will Baptists soon gave up the school at Chester. Paying the place a sentimental visit before he went to college, James remarked the weed-choked flowerbeds and rotting steps and moralized over "the canker worm of religious sectarianism."[76] Yet, as he acknowledged in later years, Geauga had done much for his development. If he had acquired little Latin and less Greek, he had been imbued with a love of the classics; and a smattering of botany had awakened an enduring interest in science. More important, James had found his voice on the speaker's platform. While rehearsing the Commencement oration, he had been shaken by nervous fears, even with a dread that he might break down. In the end he had compelled attention and elicited applause. "I am no longer a cringing scapegoat," he exultantly wrote in his journal, "but am resolved to make a mark in the world. I know without egotism that there is some of the slumbering thunder in my soul and it shall come out!"[77]

For the first time the idea of getting a college degree took shape in Garfield's mind. He was beginning to think that education offered more than wealth could bestow. Education, from this time forward, became the path by which an obscure boy could "rise above the groveling herd" and attain "the fair temple of Fame."[78]

For Eliza, Geauga had been an answer to prayers. Once swept into the current of study and teaching, James had talked no more of returning to the canal. His feet were set on his destined path on earth, his soul was saved for all eternity.

Although James had renounced the canal, he would never forget the six weeks of adventurous living in which he had been "ripe for ruin," a "servant of sin," "ready to drink in with every species of vice."[79] He seemed to take a kind of shuddering pride in regaling his intimates with the soul-searing experiences of his "checkered life" and "strange, strange history."[80] The lure of the sea persisted as a romantic idea, but, in the light of his conversion, James condemned unsparingly the evil life of a sailor. He thanked God for his deliverance—and, after God, his mother. "In reviewing the varied scenes of my short yet event-

ful life, in examining the tangled web of circumstance and earthly influences," James wrote on his twenty-fourth birthday, "I can see one
golden thread running through the whole—my mother's influence
upon me. At almost every turning point in my life she has been the
moulding agent."[81]

Which was the true Eliza—the weaver of the golden thread or the
author of the chaos of childhood? James never frankly faced the confusion of his feelings. Their inconsistencies were obscured by a mist of
grateful affection as he gradually slipped beyond his mother's reach. It
was the irony of Eliza's triumph that it doomed her influence over
James. Education turned him into a supercilious young man, bored by
his family's "insipid commonplace talk"; with riper wisdom, he became
tolerant and detached, smiling indulgently at his mother's old-time,
countrified ideas.[82] Inheritance and early training had stamped Eliza's
brand on this youngest and dearest child, but (as her mean son-in-law,
Stephen Trowbridge, would remind her) her word was not law to
James.

CHAPTER 2

# THE ECLECTIC INSTITUTE

THE DISCIPLE SCHOOL had been in operation for two terms before James was enrolled among its students. In the winter of 1850–51 he had been engaged in teaching at Warrensville, but a trip to Muskingum County in the spring does not seem a cogent reason for further postponement of his studies. James had reached the age of nineteen; his years of preparation for college were running out. Yet he was diverted from his purpose by a wish to oblige his mother, enjoy a pleasure trip, and meet his Ballou relatives.

Eliza had not returned to the scenes of her girlhood since she had left with Abram thirty years before. Her brother Henry, the only remaining member of her family in the region, was a substantial farmer at Blue Rock, out of Gaysport on the Muskingum River, and a local officeholder highly respected in the county. He and his wife had cordially invited Eliza and James to stay with them, and Eliza was eager to accept. The interruption of James's studies did not appear to concern her. None of her immediate family had gone to college, and she had little conception of the usual age of college students. Perhaps both she and James had an unadmitted hope that this well-off Uncle Henry —though he had three sons of his own—might be of some advantage to a clever nephew who was striving to make his way.[1]

The journey of two and a half days was made by railway to Columbus, by stage to Zanesville, and finally by skiff to Gaysport. It was Garfield's first glimpse of a world outside the Reserve, and he savored every moment. Once comfortably settled in the Ballous' large brick house, he made friends with his two unmarried cousins, Orrin and Ellis, sharing their work on the farm and accompanying them to "frolics." Ellis, an earnest youth of marked literary talent, was an espe-

cially congenial companion with whom James went hunting and fishing
and rambled over the hills that were a delight to eyes accustomed to the
gently undulating landscape of the Reserve.[2]

There were obstacles to Garfield's complete enjoyment. Sundays
tried his patience because the Ballous were Methodists, whose noisy
services James unfavorably contrasted with the peaceful meetings of
Disciples. He was also shocked by the "pernicious" boldness of Muskingum County girls and felt ill at ease at "frolics" conducted in a spirit
of frontier jollification that was very different from the prayer-meeting
atmosphere of Disciple gatherings. Worst of all was the Blue Rock
school, which James was appointed to teach for the spring term
through Uncle Henry's influence.[3]

Although James had done well at "the Ledge" and, against lesser
odds, at Warrensville, his third teaching job was a fiasco. The smutty
old cabin, crowded with forward girls, big, fighting boys, and—to Garfield's intense disgust—little children, proved distasteful from the first,
but his ultimate humiliation was the discovery that elements of the
community resented the appointment of an outsider and refused in extreme cases to send their children to school. James was so embarrassed
at having been pushed in where he was not wanted that he demanded
and secured his release about a month before his contract expired.[4]

Nevertheless the visit had broadened Garfield's narrow horizons.
Enriched by travel, he escorted his mother to Orange and spent a labo-
rious summer in preparation for entering the new school on Hiram
Hill.[5]

The Western Reserve Eclectic Institute, as the Disciples called their
school, stood on the highest range of land on the plain of the Reserve.
The situation was commanding but bare. A "campus" existed that until
the preceding year had been a cornfield, reluctantly yielded by its
owner for the educational purposes of the church. The earth was still
ragged and shadeless, and Commencement exercises were held in an
adjacent orchard. The square, red-brick school was starkly new and
plain, from the basement of yellowish sandstone to the zinc-sheeted
cupola that housed the bell. Capable carpenters and masons on the
board of trustees had seen that the construction was solid, but there
had been no money to waste on adornment or fine furnishings. There
was not even a piano for the music students, who had to make do in the
first years with a crude melodeon called a "melopean."[6]

The rural isolation of the site—the nearest stagecoach route was
five miles away—had been a persuasive argument with farmer-trustees
who had a pious abhorrence not only of centers of commerce but of
thoroughfares leading to them. "Let us expose our children to the virus

of pestilence," the first catalogue of the Eclectic Institute exclaimed, "let them fall by the touch of the Asiatic scourge, rather than expose them to the moral effluvia that poison the great pathways of public travel." In their zeal for avoiding urban temptations, the trustees had over-looked the need of adequate living quarters; the few houses on Hiram Hill could accommodate only a fraction of the applicants for admission. Plans were belatedly made to erect several rooming houses with cook-ing facilities, but in the fall of 1851 most of the students were still living in crowded rooms, often inconveniently distant from the campus.[7]

It had at first been expected that the main burden of the higher classes (the school included a primary department for children of the neighborhood) would be carried by the principal, Amos Sutton Hay-den, with the assistance of one instructor. Brother Hayden, a pious, devious little man with the face of a pixie, had been the choice of the conservatives on the board of trustees; he was an educator only by strict Disciple standards. Possessed of scanty formal education, he had ap-plied himself to the Bible, which he expounded as an infallible histori-cal record as well as the source of "Eternal Wisdom." It was quickly evident that an unduly heavy load had been placed on the shoulders of his assistant, Thomas Munnell, an earnest, lantern-jawed graduate of Bethany, the Disciple college in western Virginia. Before James entered the Eclectic Institute, the faculty had been augmented by a graduate of Western Reserve College at Hudson, Norman P. Dunshee, who was considered the finest scholar at the Eclectic in its early days. Charles D. Wilber, a crippled Bethany student whose special interest was geology, had accepted an offer to act as instructor in natural science, and addi-tional classes were conducted by Almeda A. Booth, a frumpy spinster of twenty-eight who was the brainiest of Garfield's classmates. Full pay-ment of all the teachers' stipends was often long delayed. The Eclectic had no endowment but depended on the students' fees to cover its run-ning expenses. When debts were pressing or fees in arrears, the books were balanced by putting off the teachers.[8]

Although the school was avowedly nonsectarian, it was heavily slanted toward Disciple training. A central aim of its founders had been to prepare a new generation of preachers to replace the poorly edu-cated Disciple leaders, who were often tedious speakers. The chief em-phasis was placed on the Bible and on moral excellence, with particular reference to abstinence from alcohol and sexual misconduct. Each day opened with a lecture on Sacred History by Brother Hayden. It was fol-lowed by a public castigation, with names and misdeeds specified, of any students who had been caught in derelictions. This system, how-ever, was not entirely successful in eliminating "vice." There was no provision for patrolling the unlighted campus, and an unregenerate minority of the students ran the risk of detection in misbehavior under cover of darkness. Local storekeepers were sometimes not averse to selling liquor to students—a practice severely condemned by Disciples.[9]

The most important extracurricular activities were the meetings and exhibitions of the literary societies, and great importance was attached to their "lyceums," or debates. The female students had their own literary society whose members gave exhibitions and even delivered orations. The latter almost unheard-of practice—probably attributable to the influence of Almeda Booth—was disapproved by many strict Disciples, including Garfield himself.[10]

Except for the lyceums, which were often concerned with current public issues, the odor of piety permeated every licensed gathering. Bibles and hymnals played a part at the occasional "social evenings." Sports did not exist except for spontaneous contests of strength or skill. Dancing and games of chance were proscribed. So, in theory, was the drama, but in this case an evasion was countenanced. The so-called "colloquies" of the literary societies were actually talky, undramatic plays. Trustees and teachers winked at the colloquies because they did not bear the stigma of a curtain and they afforded practice in elocution as well as literary composition.[11]

Arriving on Hiram Hill with four Boynton cousins and Orrin Judd, Garfield breathed the air of Disciple faith and accorded the school an uncritical approval. Among his own people he was not ashamed to wear rough clothing, a cheap suit of Kentucky jeans, with calico sleeve protectors. His dedication to righteousness and pure living was mingled with a growing ambition for worldly honors. Professors Munnell and Dunshee quickened his desire for a classical education while on another level he was inspired by Principal Hayden's lectures on Sacred History. A leader in founding an outstanding new literary society, the Philomathean, Garfield took a prominent part in its lyceums and colloquies and turned out reams of flowery effusions in prose and verse. His oratorical and literary gifts were so exceptional that he was asked to deliver the valedictory address at the close of his first term.[12]

James gained wider recognition the next spring when he crossed swords with Joseph Treat, a freethinker and spiritualist of high reputation in the region. During one of Treat's lectures, James was so incensed by the speaker's atheistic jeers that he sprang to his feet and forcefully upheld the literal truth of the Scriptures. He then challenged Treat to a debate on "spirit rappings," and on the appointed evening he assailed the spiritualist position in a punishing attack. His oratorical power stirred the school, and the Disciple community echoed the word that one Eclectic student was destined for eminence in the pulpit and on the lecture platform. The courtroom was not mentioned, for the

Disciples looked askance at the legal profession. James was beginning to think that he was fitted for the law, and he regretted the difficulty of reconciling a legal career with the religion of Christ.[13]

Garfield continued to study at the Eclectic until he went to college in 1854. The school became his second home. There he had been encouraged to develop his latent talents; there he found love and comradeship and reveled in the diversions of rural life, chestnutting and apple-picking in the autumn, treats of "warm sugar" when the sap ran in the maples in the spring. Time and experience would modify his first undiscriminating approval, but his regard would never waver. The school, like a friend, had established a lasting claim on Garfield's loyalty that events were powerless to affect.[14]

Staying in school required more than study; it was necessary for Garfield to earn his way. For two terms he acted as janitor in the school, sweeping floors, making the fires, and ringing the bell. He took the winter off during his first year to teach again at Warrensville. The following summer he hired out to help build a house in Hiram. He took a course in penmanship, drawing, and mezzotint painting and thereafter offered instruction in these arts for a fee. After his first year as a student he regularly taught a wide variety of courses at the Eclectic.[15]

Garfield's attachment to the Eclectic had been firmly sealed by new friendships. The isolation of the school and its dearth of extracurricular activities forced the students to turn to each other for recreation and emotional expression. The presence of the opposite sex added a fillip of interest and frequently something more, but friendships between the inhibited young men tended to be fervent. They spent their leisure hours in vaporous philosophizing and in exchanging confidences and vows of eternal fidelity.

The climate of "soul communion" was ideally congenial to James.[16] Phrenology had taught him that he was highly developed in the faculty of "adhesiveness" (friendship and sociability) as well as that of "amativeness" (sexual and connubial love).[17] The exercise of the second faculty was forbidden to a bachelor, but sentimental relationships between men were sanctioned by the mores of the time and place. The words of a song, "Lay up nearer, brother, nearer, For my limbs are growing cold," tell much about the simple folkways prevailing at the Eclectic.[18] James gladly gave his "adhesiveness" free rein. His family had accustomed him to caresses—he took the sensual pleasure of a cat in having his head scratched—and it was natural for him to paw his friends with affectionate thumps and bearhugs. "I am so constituted," he wrote in his diary, "that I cannot enjoy a cold formal friend (a misnomer) but

must be as familiar as to a brother or a sister to enjoy them." [19] Famil-
iarity, in James's vocabulary, meant physical contacts that would have
been suspect in a more sophisticated environment. The erotic compo-
nent, however, should not be overemphasized; James and his friends
were not sexual deviates but men deprived, like prison inmates, of normal sexual expression. "Amativeness" was Garfield's ruling passion, fit-
fully checked by his submission to Disciple precepts and his dread of an
early involvement in marriage.

James was never without old friends at the Ecelectic. Several classmates—Symonds Ryder, Harvey Everest and others—had been at
Geauga Seminary. All six of the Boyntons attended the school at
various times, and Ellis Ballou came up from Muskingum County for
two terms. Dearly though James prized these established relationships,
he looked to untried fields for his explorations of "soul-communion." A
new friend, like a new place, gave him a thrill of discovery which he
could not resist. He was speedily drawn into particular intimacy with
his classmate, Corydon Fuller, and the crippled science instructor,
Charles Wilber.

Corydon, a year older than James, was a rather frail youth whose
pale, thin face wore a look of self-satisfaction. He plumed himself on
his talent for writing and produced a copious flow of literary composi-
tions. Having sized up James as "a perfect giant" of intellect, he attached himself to this towering spirit, matching James's effusions gush
for gush and bathing him in an admiration that was all but worshipful.
"Sycophant" is perhaps too harsh an epithet to apply to smug little
Corydon, but he had more than a trace of the self-serving deference
that makes the courtier and hanger-on. James saw in him the "twin
brother of my heart," ever ready to listen to his confidences and join
him in rhapsodies over literature and nature.[20]

Charles Wilber's approach to James was more critical. A moody intellectual, Wilber had no tolerance for adolescent transports. He
treated James, who was a year younger, as an overexcited and rather
tiring junior ("Don't rage, any more, James. Don't!") and briskly dis-
paraged his outbursts of frustration.[21] "Well James," he once wrote,
"either your cauldron is not large enough, else your fire is too hot. . . .
The world is not a fool—or an ash heap! If there is anything wrong,
depend upon it, it is you!" [22] Yet, in his punishing and ambivalent way,
Wilbur was strongly attached to James. He respected Garfield's mind
and valued their serious discussions of intellectual and religious matters. When Wilber had a mental breakdown in the autumn of 1852,
James was the only one who could manage him, and it was James who
escorted the wildly excited little man to his family's home at Auburn.[23]

Wilber's irrational behavior came as a stunning surprise to the school, but it was not interpreted as a sign of serious mental instability. Becoming "insane"—a misfortune by no means rare among the early settlers—was considered an accident as unrelated to the total personality as a broken leg. After a few weeks of rest Wilber was generally supposed to have made a complete recovery. But his aberration had probably contributed to the estrangement of his sweetheart, Laura Ann Clark, who fell in love with Ellis Ballou and gave Charles the mitten. Sutton Hayden, moreover, had promptly written Wilber off as a member of the teaching staff and asked James to take over his classes for the winter term. The arrangement was continued in the spring, and it led to Garfield's regular appointment to the faculty during his final year at Hiram.[24]

Two new boys enrolled at the Eclectic in 1853, both promising students. James Harrison Rhodes ("Harry") and Burke Hinsdale were boys of superior intelligence who were quite different in temperament and personality. Harry, the son of provident German parents, was a dreamy, vaguely motivated lad with a feminine craving for affection and an incongruous streak of Rabelaisian humor. Burke was a very serious (although not humorless), impoverished farm lad with long unruly hair, struggling to acquire a classical education in the face of his father's hope that he would become a farmer. Each in his own way, these students touched Garfield's deepest sympathies and won his lasting affection. The relation at first was that of bright students and admired teacher—both boys were several years younger than Garfield—but, after Garfield's return from college in 1856, the bonds became much stronger. Burke was to become closer to Garfield intellectually than any other man.[25]

Garfield's friendship with Dr. John P. Robison of Bedford was in a wholly different category, though it would prove no less enduring. Robison was a prominent figure in the church, an early associate of its leader, Alexander Campbell, and a zealous trustee of both Bethany College and the Eclectic Institute; but he was a far from typical Disciple. A blustering egoist of shrewd and aggressive character, he had given up the practice of medicine to engage in business, and by Disciple standards he was immensely rich. Many Disciples did not like Dr. Robison, but James thought that the people needed his prodding "to stir them up to duty." James had also been keenly interested in the lectures on phrenology which Robison had delivered to the students.[26]

While Robison was at the Eclectic for the 1852 Commencement, James applied to this comparative stranger for a phrenological examination. According to Robison's much later account—the only source of information on this meeting—he was to be the final arbiter of Garfield's decision whether to stick to carpentry for a living or strive for an intellectual career. Robison made a "commonsense" examination and assured James that he was mentally and physically fit to prepare for the career that he desired. Robison's account was blurred by fading memory as well as self-importance. James would not have thought of carpentry as the sole alternative to a college education; he had already prepared to escape from manual labor and the vexations of district schools by taking a course in Spencerian penmanship. But it is true that, before putting this new skill to use, he was hard-pressed for money—and he was involved in a love affair which threatened his plans for college. He regarded his impulsive appeal to Robison as a deeply personal matter; he did not allude to it in his diary or discuss it with his confidant, Corydon. But Dr. Robison evidently talked, for the Eclectic—always a hive of gossip—buzzed with a humorous report that James had asked to have his head examined. Though he must have been painfully embarrassed, James made light of the story and laughed it off as a "Munchausen tale." He bore Robison no resentment but responded warmly to his overtures of friendship.[27]

Modesty and tact were not among the Doctor's virtues, but he had a kind heart, and he had been touched by the boy's ambition to overcome the handicaps of indigence and obscurity. It can be confidently assumed that he was the "friend" who presently proposed to undertake the expenses of Garfield's education. Financial necessity had obliged James to go back to carpentering for the summer, but he proudly refused the offer. He would repay the Doctor's kindness with a lifetime of grateful affection.[28]

A constant factor in Garfield's years at Hiram was his friendship with the student and teacher, Miss Almeda Booth. The casual acquaintance of the classroom developed into a union of spirit so binding that, when James left Hiram for college, it was parting from Almeda that affected him most. "I can truly say," he wrote in his diary, "that I never met with any person, save my own dear mother, who has been of so much advantage to me in thinking, reasoning and living. . . . She is entwined closely around my heart, and can never cease to be held in fond remembrance." The words were set down in the emotional wrench of leave-taking, but James did not overstate his feelings. Through many vicissitudes he clung to Almeda's love and counsel, and her influence exceeded that of his wife in the early years of his marriage.[29]

For want of a better term, this peculiarly intense attachment must be classified as friendship. It was inevitably complicated by the difference of sex, but there was no element of romance in Garfield's regard for a dowdy woman nearly eight years his senior, coarse-featured, stout, and blunt in speech and manner. They had first been drawn together by their exceptional ability. They would pull away from the rest of the class like two matched runners, racing ahead. They were—often literally—in a class by themselves. James soon fell under the spell of the keen brain and fine character that gave Miss Booth great influence over her pupils and had prompted the Eclectic authorities to create for her the position of "governess" of the lady students.[30]

Miss Booth was making an advanced study of Greek and Latin with the aim of obtaining a college degree in a full classical course. James was struck by the discovery that her "turn of mind" was almost identical with his own.[31] His desire to explore the resemblance was cordially encouraged. She saw that the talented young man was sorely in need of guidance and readily adopted him as her favorite. He was not the last young man whom she would take under her protective wing.

They arranged to lodge in the same house, and they spent many evenings in Almeda's bedroom reading the Greek Testament. After taking an intensive course in Greek and Latin in the summer of 1853, they translated the "Epistle to the Romans" and an oration of Demosthenes, under the direction of their scholarly instructor, Professor Dunshee. They also found time for much general reading and for absorbing discussions of their ideas. Their talk increasingly turned to personal matters as James poured out his problems, amatory and financial, and bolstered his frequent infirmity of purpose with her firm standards of conduct.[32]

These personal conversations were the main source of the "advantage" which James derived from the relationship. It was Almeda who convinced him of the folly of acting on impulse and made him aspire to a life governed by reason; it was from her that he took his first lessons in acceptable social behavior and methodical habits of study. She was "more than a sister" to James—except for a deficiency that his diary did not mention: She denied him a sister's embraces and received his brotherly caresses with a spinsterish constraint.

Miss Booth had a strongly sensual nature, which she had taken extreme measures to suppress. She had abjured all feminine fripperies of dress and manner, and she ignored the liberal arts, which were considered the appropriate province of her sex. She was regarded as too sober and, in her flat-footed way, too masculine to feel a woman's normal impulses. The opinion of the school was partially justified. During years of strict repression, Miss Booth's face had come to resemble the mask she had assumed. Her maidenly reserve had hardened into prudery; her mind was no longer possessed by shameful desires. She believed that she had subdued them—yet she remained fearful of their recurrence.

One night early in March 1853, Miss Booth was closeted with James until an hour that scandalized Sutton Hayden, in whose house the two were staying. James was sternly reproved for failing to set "a good example." But what of the example set by the governess of the lady students? Almeda's reputation was above reproach, as free from stain as though James had gagged and bound her in her bedroom.[33]

It is impossible to fix the date when Almeda's fortress capitulated, but its fall may have been foretold on the June day of 1854 when James gave way to "an outbursting flood of tears" in bidding her farewell. It would be instructive to know how she responded. Surely she did not leave James bawling without a comforting caress. Perhaps she was blinded for a moment by a flash of desperate hope that James's love for her was deeper than he knew, more lasting than his infatuations with younger and comelier women.[34]

Garfield's first serious love affair had had its tentative beginning in the winter before he went to Hiram. It was born of physical attraction and died of waning passion.

Mary Louisa Hubbell had been one of Garfield's pupils at the school at Warrensville. A bright, warm-natured girl, sparkling with jests and coquetry, she had strongly attracted the susceptible young teacher, but James had been much embarrassed by the ill-tempered gossip that their flirtation provoked among the other girls. When he and Mary met again as classmates at the Eclectic, he was freed from jealous "slander" and surveillance—though not, as he naively supposed, from gossip. Their attachment, which Corydon Fuller described as "open and unconcealed," caused a hum of lively comment, and it was generally believed that they were engaged to marry.[35]

The progress of the affair was favored by the opportunities that the Eclectic afforded for private evening rendezvous. Strolling with Mary under the stars or lingering in the deserted halls and darkened basement chapel, James was thrilled by her fervid response to his advances. In this gay, provocative, yielding girl, he saw the sweetheart of his dreams. He was head over heels in love before the fall term was out.[36]

James was not Mary's first love. She had had more success in attracting men than in holding them. She was determined to hold James, and she knew no art more subtle than an assertive possessiveness. When he signed up for a second winter term at Warrensville, Mary arranged to go home and again attend his classes. She played her infatuated lover like a firmly hooked fish. James was readily persuaded to defy the hateful ordeal of gossip to which her presence would expose him.

Mary's parents were anxious to see their daughter settled in marriage. They made James part of the family circle, often inviting him to spend the night when it was not their turn to board the teacher, and they granted him and Mary a privacy not usually permitted to an enamored pair under such circumstances. Their attitude makes it hard to remember that Solyman and Lucinda Hubbell were devout Disciples, schooled in the strict Disciple prohibition of intimate association of the sexes outside of marriage.

The most flagrant instance of the Hubbells' obliquity was their behavior at Christmastime during James's second winter at Warrensville, when he was bedded down at their house with "lung fever." Nursing a man was then regarded by all respectable Americans as an improper service for any female except his mother, wife, or sisters. But Mary assisted Solyman in nursing James, and on Christmas Day she was left in solitary charge of the sickroom while her parents and younger sister went off to pay a family visit. Although James noted in his diary that it had not been a Merry Christmas for him (and mentioned that the doctor had been there again), he concluded his entry with a Latin notation to the effect that he had been well taken care of by a girl that day.[37]

The sick were expected to resume their duties as soon as they could stand, and James tottered back to his classes after five days. Thom, who had already paid him a solicitous visit, returned to drive his brother home for the weekend, and, on two other occasions in the early weeks of 1852, James came under his mother's inspection. It is clear that the all-knowing Eliza was worried, for in February she bounced over to Warrensville to size up the situation for herself. An overnight stay with the Hubbells convinced her that Mary was "not worthy" of James and would surely make him miserable if he united his life with hers. Eliza had shrewdly observed the Hubbells' desire to make a match. "You have got out of a nett that was spread for you," she later wrote her son—and undoubtedly spoke her mind to James on every visit he subsequently paid to Orange.[38]

James, in any case, realized that his affair with Mary was moving too fast and too far. Before leaving Warrensville he had a serious talk with her about his plans for college. He spoke also of his determination "never to hold out any false hopes or assurances" and warned that he had been fickle in previous attachments.[39] He might have maintained a firm stand if he and Mary had continued to see each other daily, but for the next five months they met only on occasional weekends. After her financially unprofitable winter Mary was obliged to spend the spring term teaching at Chagrin Falls; during the summer vacation, James was employed as a joiner at Hiram. Separation from a loved one was an emotional stimulant to Garfield. To pore over a letter or gaze upon a likeness—to recall, to yearn, to dream—moved him to raptures of sentiment. The alternation of fantasy and brief romantic encounters revived the first recklessness of his passion.

In April, greatly daring, James wrote a letter to Mary—his first to a lady friend—and was emboldened to continue the correspondence by the "afectionate little messenger of love" that she sent in reply.[40] Mary's letters have not come to light—they were probably returned and destroyed after the affair was over—but a number of Garfield's are preserved in his personal papers. These are very youthful letters, ingenuous in their ornate rhetoric and awkward versifying and touching in their gratitude for the love that Mary has bestowed on "a poor, penniless orphan-boy like myself."[41] James did not speak of marriage; he recalled his resolution to complete a thorough education. But, as the lonely weeks passed, his resolve was shaken, and he could not refrain from expressions of longing for a deep and abiding love.

Mary came to Hiram for the Eclectic Commencement of 1852, spending the night with her married sister, Leora. This visit brought James into contact with Leora's husband, Charles Kilby, and his older brother, Almond, who were building a new house and looking for an experienced hand. They promptly reached an agreement whereby James was paid a wage of seventy-five cents a day and lodged at the Kilbys' home for the term of his employment. He grew very friendly with his fellow worker, Charles Kilby, and spilled out to this willing listener the tale of his love for Mary and his dreams of a blissful future—without considering the likelihood that Charles would make a full report to Warrensville.[42]

In the heat of desire, James had yielded to dreams that took no account of his mother's advice or his own abhorrence of poverty and insignificance. His ardor reached a climax in mid-July, during one of his visits to Warrensville, when he and Mary "traded hearts" and talked for most of the night.[43] It had begun to cool by late August when they were reunited at the Eclectic. Once more engrossed by his classical studies and subject to Almeda's influence, he was dismayed by the unwisdom of committing himself to a promise of marriage before his education was well begun.

Yet James was already in some degree committed, and he felt the obligation keenly. He had a serious talk with Mary and thought that he spoke plainly, but he was not plain enough to alter her insistence that they were engaged to marry. By December, her tenacity had driven James to revolt. He appealed to Corydon to advise him in his duty.

"Shall the inconsiderate words and actions and affections of thought-less youth," he wrote, "fasten their sad consequences upon the whole of after life? Or is it right to shake them off . . . ?" Corydon's answer could be confidently foreseen; from the first, he had thought that Mary was "in no sense suitable" for James.[44]

In his distress James examined his character more honestly than he had ever done before—more honestly, perhaps, than he would ever do again—but he recoiled from the contradictions he discovered. His moral judgments were too rigidly patterned in black and white to admit the complexity of human motives. He had nothing but scorn for men who trifled with women's affections, and he could not endure the thought that there might have been an element of thoughtless trifling in his own behavior with Mary.[45]

Garfield's distress of mind was aggravated by physical fatigue. Though his health had not been good in the past year, he had taken on an excessively heavy program of teaching and study and had plunged into the distraction of overwork in disregard of his need of sleep and regular diet. His shredded nerves could not support the strain. His blinding headaches recurred, and, warned of imminent "brain fever," he gave up his studies for the rest of the winter term. He resumed teaching after a week's illness, but he was in acute depression, brooding over his personal dilemma and deprived of the will to deal with it. His avoidance of Mary's company had been uncharitably remarked. James was so sharply offended by the "slandering" of his classmates that for a while he largely absented himself from social gatherings. Even firm friends denied him an unqualified approval. Censure of his "familiar" manner with women brought James to acknowledge, in utter confusion, that the natural expression of affection was a fault.[46]

James oscillated for weeks between intolerable alternatives: to repudiate his ideals of Christian conduct and be branded as "a rake" or to bury himself in "a living grave" of marriage.[47] In his blackest moods he veered dangerously close to detachment from reality. He was obsessed by the idea that his actions were governed by some mechanical agency that he could not control. His being throbbed in time with the "ponderous and eccentric motions" of "an engine of fearful power" within himself. He was convulsed by an inward upheaval, as if he "were struggling to enter the chrysalis state."[48] But the approaching close of the term nerved James to escape from the maze of fantasy and face his inevitable decision. Adopting an argument advanced by Corydon, that marriage would be an injustice to Mary as well as himself, he informed her of this conclusion in an affectionate letter which warmly recalled the kindness she had shown him.[49]

James was aghast to learn that Mary was deeply wounded; his letter

had been a cruel blow. Her efforts to catch James had hooked the an-
gler more firmly than the fish. Like many another lovesick girl, she
hung on, blindly hoping, angered by her suitor's neglect and refusing
to admit its meaning. Marriage to James had become the reason for
Mary's existence. His rejection cast her adrift, bereft of hope and purpose. James contritely offered her his continued friendship, but Mary
was not consoled. His heart bled for his former sweetheart when she
returned, with gaiety sadly muted, for the Eclectic's spring term.[50]

Yet, as the school rallied strongly to Mary's cause, James was stung
by the injustice of public opinion and offended by the defection of
many valued friends.[51] Though he still suffered periods of self-castiga-
tion, he gradually appeased his conscience by dwelling on his good intentions and his careful avoidance of a formal promise of marriage. His
guilt for Mary merged in repentance for his failure as a Christian. He
reproached himself for having been indifferent to religion and vowed
himself anew to daily communion with God and devotion to His service.[52] With some trepidation he started to preach on Sunday to nearby
congregations. On a few occasions he prowled the Eclectic grounds at
night in search of "dissipation," and he seemed to take satisfaction in
the expulsion of four young men. "School goes better since the ex-
purgation," he wrote, "yet they have had a bad influence." But in spite
of the excesses of his penitence, James was on the road to recovery,
rejoicing in the power of his eloquence and the charms of female society. A summer passed in travel and in study of the classics completed
his return to normal.[53]

Mary was at the Eclectic in the fall of 1853 and the following winter.
She had grown vindictive—she had the effrontery to enroll in a class
that James was teaching—and her parade of martyrdom kept the
tongue of scandal wagging. She made friends among those who were
especially dear to James, but he had ceased to take offense at the sympathy that Mary's plight evoked. He did not feel resentment when her
friendship with Henry Boynton's intended, Susan Smith, drew Henry
into her circle, or even when his cousin, Phebe Boynton, became intimate with Mary. In the end, as James wryly observed, Mary "had
rather overacted her part in persecuting" him. Her rancor was merely
tolerated by those who loved James truly, and the gossips finally
wearied of the stale morsel of scandal. Early in 1854, a year after her
romance with James was ended, Mary left the Eclectic and took refuge
in her home at Warrensville.[54]

James was worried about his letters—those telltale love letters which
he wished to God he had never written.[55] The date of their return is
uncertain, but the Hubbells were still holding them in January 1855,
when Henry Boynton and his bride paid a call on Mary. Susan wrote

James of "the scorching flash" of Mrs. Hubbell's eye as she asked if
Mrs. Garfield blamed Mary for not giving up the letters. There was
enough in them, Lucinda Hubbell said, to prove all they wanted—and
enough, besides, in what James had told one of the Kilbys. By this time
it was common knowledge that James was again keeping company.
Some people thought that the Hubbells would "try to do something" if
he should get married.[56]

In time Mary stepped out with a Warrensville bachelor, William
Taylor, but she was greatly altered. She seemed, Henry Boynton reported, "anxious, restless . . . and rather too lively" for a woman of
her age.[57] Her merry disposition had soured; she had grown exacting
and perverse. She had been the first—though not the last—of the
women whom Garfield's touch had scarred.

The rest of Mary's story is quickly told. She married Bill Taylor in
1858, shortly before James himself was married. Their only child, a
frail baby girl, died in 1862, a few weeks after her birth. Mary herself
died on New Year's Day 1863, while Taylor was serving in Tennessee
as colonel of a volunteer cavalry regiment he had raised. Garfield was
also with the Union forces in Tennessee when the news reached him.
There was poignant regret in the letter he wrote to Phebe Boynton. "It
seems very strange and sad that Mary Hubbell is dead. It is a most sad
and painful thought to me that one has gone down to the grave with
feeling in her heart that I have wronged her. God knows I never intended to do her any wrong. . . . Nothing that she ever did or said
about me destroyed my kind feelings toward her." As long as he lived,
Garfield kept the little sheaf of his letters to Mary, enclosed in an
envelope on which he had written in his scholarly, Spencerian hand,
"*Epistolae ad Mariam tristis memoriae.*"[58]

James hated to end a way of life as he hated to lose a friend. But he
had awakened to his lack of general culture in literature and the arts
and wanted a college education. He would have preferred to stay at the
Eclectic if the school had succeeded in obtaining a charter to confer a
college degree. Failing that (the Eclectic did not become Hiram College
until 1867) his first choice was the Disciple college at Bethany, Virginia.
In the early summer of 1853 he went with Henry Boynton to attend
the Bethany Commencement and look the college over.[59]

It had been one of James's dreams "to sit at the feet" of the president of Bethany, Alexander Campbell, who had succeeded his aged father as leader of the Disciple church. A call at the Campbell home
confirmed Garfield's effusive admiration for the leader's intellect and
character, and he was awestruck by his introduction to the venerable
founder of the "Reformation," Thomas Campbell, decrepit but still ra-

diant with Christian faith. Bethany offered less exalted pleasures as well. James admired the fine situation of the college in the hills of western Virginia and enjoyed many congenial encounters with acquaintances old and new. The most joyful of these meetings was a reunion with his former teacher, Thomas Munnell, who had resigned from the Eclectic faculty because of illness.[60]

On the whole, however, Bethany was a disappointment. James felt a countryman's distrust of the "southern dandyism" of many of the students. He was scandalized by the presentation of a play, "with all the trappings" of the theater, as a feature of the Commencement exercises. The choice of *The Lady of Lyons* by Bulwer-Lytton was a further outrage. James's aspirations to general culture had not yet taken him very far. He indignantly remarked that the play "was tinged with obscenity, such as characterized all of Shakespeare's plays."[61]

A dispute was blowing up among the Ohio Disciples over the sympathy with slavery that was predominant at Bethany, but James appears to have been still indifferent to this disruptive issue, regarding it as a political matter of no concern to a Christian. Nearly a year would pass before he listed among his objections to Bethany the fact that it was "too Pro-Slavery."[62]

In spite of his dislike of worldliness and fine manners, Bethany seemed the logical place for James: the font of his religious faith and the college at which he could obtain a degree after a single year of study. Yet he became more and more opposed to going there. The arguments in favor of Bethany came to operate in its disfavor. James perceived that the Disciple college must be less highly accredited than colleges that required two further years of study. He was also becoming aware of the narrowness of his background and training—both in the humanities and in religious expression—and convinced that a truly liberal education should entail exposure to a variety of influences. He could, of course, have found a different climate at the hotbed of abolitionist sentiment, Oberlin College in Lorain County. Though both Almeda and Charles Wilber were planning to spend the next year there, James never considered Oberlin or any other of the several Ohio colleges he visited; his choice lay between the inspiration of Alexander Campbell and the Parnassian heights of New England. In the spring of 1854, with many misgivings about his finances, he wrote to Yale, Brown, and Williams for information about their terms and requirements for admission.[63]

During 1853 James worked harder than ever, and work took its toll, particularly on his throat. Professor Munnell's illness had obliged the student teachers to share his load. On April 20 James noted that he

had heard seven regular classes and commenced a writing class. During
the spring he also preached on several occasions away from home. At
term's end he agreed to continue teaching during the coming year—
with some reluctance, for he foresaw that it would cut down the time
he needed to study. But he dearly loved his classes, especially the
smaller groups in which he could establish an intimate rapport with the
students. And, with college in view, he could not resist Hayden's offer
of $300 for the school year. During the closing months of the year, al-
though a replacement for Munnell had been found, James was still
teaching seven classes on five days of every week. He also did some
studying and occasional preaching, and in December he began a series
of lectures to the Philomathean Society and started a penmanship class
with nearly seventy students. His throat caused him a great deal of
trouble; he was fearful that he might contract Munnell's dreaded
disease—bronchitis. After addressing a large congregation at Aurora
on Christmas Day, he wrote anxiously to Corydon, "my words are almost bloody." [64]

James had been reluctant to spare himself. His powerful build and
great muscular strength gave an impression of physical fitness in which
he took pride. But, fearful of permanent disability and possible death,
he was forced to admit that "to go on in this way" was "madness." On
New Year's Day he wrote in his diary: "In the first place I intend to
take special care of my health in order to save, if possible, my throat
and lungs for future use." He took advantage of the three weeks' vacation before the beginning of the spring term to rest his throat and to
"recruit and invigorate" his nervous system. The larger part of the time
was spent in accompanying his mother on another visit to their relatives
at Blue Rock. For the first time in years, James permitted himself a
long period of recreation. He "visited and sauntered," went "a gun-
ning," clambered over hills, attended a jury trial, and rode across some
forty-five miles of broken country to see Ellis Ballou, who was attending Ohio University at Athens. The return trip was physically strenuous, but he had accomplished his purpose; his throat was better and his
anxiety quieted during his final term at the Eclectic. [65]

It was nearly the middle of June before James decided on a college.
He had been disappointed in the three New England colleges to which
he had written. The letter from Yale had seemed to show "an aristo-
cratic face," that from Brown put him off by its "rigid sternness," and
no response at all had come from Williams. [66] A second inquiry, however, brought a reply from the Reverend Dr. Mark Hopkins, the president of Williams and an educator of national reputation. It was the
letter of a busy administrator, uninformed about an obscure applicant's
record and more than dubious about Garfield's lingering hope of com-

pressing two years of study into one. "I can only say," Hopkins concluded, "that if you shall come we shall be glad to do for you what the circumstances will admit." To James the noncommittal words seemed a hand held out in welcome from the East.[67] Persuading himself that the encouraging Dr. Hopkins might let him make up his studies in the summer and enter the senior class in September, he decided to leave at once. "The last link is broken," he elatedly wrote Corydon on June 26, "and I have snapped the last arrow upon the grave of my Fathers. . . . Next Thursday I start for the old Bay State."[68]

James put on a bold face, but his headlong flight from Ohio betrayed his deep anxiety—like one who advances the date of drastic surgery lest delay sap his courage to undergo it. At the age of twenty-two James was still not ready for the manly independence that the small, distant college would compel him to assume. "It matters not to the society in which I am to move," he plaintively wrote in his diary, "if I was an orphan boy, and battled the world alone. . . ."[69]

A man in years, an uncertain boy at heart, James bade farewell to Hiram, went to Solon, where his mother was living disconsolately with Mary Larabee, took her with him on brief visits to Orange and Bainbridge, saw her safely back in Solon, and started for Williamstown.

# CHAPTER 3

# LUCRETIA

HAD JAMES been reared a Moslem, he could have taken Almeda Booth as his first and most honored wife: the wise and loving woman on whose support he leaned, but from whom his fancy strayed when the dancing girls came on. In a strictly monogamous society, James was obliged to look elsewhere, and elsewhere he had begun to look before the ashes of his affair with Mary were cold. His gaze had come to rest on demure, dark-eyed Lucretia Rudolph, who had been his classmate at Geauga. Their acquaintance had been pleasant but casual; Lucretia had fallen in love with another classmate, a fellow named Albert S. Hall.

James happened to know that Albert S. Hall was unworthy of a pure girl's affections. The knowledge had its origin in his weeks on the canal. As the tale was told years later to Lucretia, it suggests one of the more farfetched coincidences of the Victorian novel.

While the *Evening Star* was passing through a lock (so James's story ran) he had seen "a dashing young man with dark eyes and raven locks" seated with a "Bacchanal group" in front of a "liquor doggery" on the bank and seemingly enjoying its rowdyism. Their eyes had met. That was the extent of their encounter. Several months later, when James arrived at Chester, the dashing young man had no difficulty in recognizing the pale convalescent from Orange as the weatherbeaten canal boy he had glimpsed on the *Evening Star*. Albert S. Hall—for it was none other—assumed that James was one of the "b'hoys" and hailed him with coarse jest and knowing wink. "From that hour," James wrote in 1856, "I knew the treachery of Albert S. Hall, and when I heard that Lucretia loved him, my heart was wrung with sorrow for her, but I knew that one so unknown as myself could do nothing to make the crooked straight."[1] After more than two years Lucretia decided that Albert was not the man she wanted to marry, and on the last day of the year 1851 she terminated the romance.[2] One may add that James had not been so disgusted with Albert's rakish behavior as his account implied. On the contrary, they had been on the best of terms at Geauga.[3]

Lucretia's parting with Albert had shattered her "fondest hope on earth." She had seen in her first suitor the lover of her daydreams, as virtuous and true as he was ardent. Her disillusionment had caused her a long agony of regret. With bitter tears she had knelt to pray for strength to subdue her "frenzied madness," but not for two despairing years did she find the resolution to suppress her "evil propensities" and yield her whole heart to God.[4]

In the early weeks of 1852 Lucretia was in the first anguish of her ruined hope, while James's fancy was fixed on Mary Hubbell, but they often saw each other at her father's house on Hiram Hill. Zeb Rudolph was zealously involved in the management of the Eclectic, of which he was a founder and trustee.[5] He had labored with his own hands on the school building, had built a house close by, and had moved his family from their home at Garrettsville in time for the opening exercises. James warmly recommended the Rudolphs as a good place to board. In calling on friends who stayed there, he frequently met the family, and he and Lucretia renewed the acquaintance that they had formed at Geauga.

In the spring of 1853 it chanced that James and Lucretia were brought into a closer relationship—that of teacher and pupil in the Greek and Latin classes that James took over as a result of Munnell's illness. The small Greek class was his particular favorite. With its seven sympathetic members he relaxed and expanded; the attendance of two young ladies gave a social character to the sessions, which were sometimes held in a corner of the basement chapel, sometimes beside the stove at the Rudolphs'. At Geauga, Lucretia had admired James's strange "genius." Now she was captivated by his vital, ranging mind and listened respectfully to every word he uttered.[6]

James, lonely and unsettled after his break with Mary, grew intensely aware of Lucretia's attentive presence. In person she was small and delicately made, with shining dark hair and a girlishly pretty face. Her soulful black eyes could glow with comprehension or flash with spirit, but the warmth was quickly hidden. Lucretia's habitual expression was pensive and reserved. James did not disapprove; the rising clamor about "women's rights" exasperated him. He detested aggressive females and would never have dreamed of marrying one of them.

It is significant that, from the first, James associated Lucretia with

marriage. Though his experience with Mary had made him wary of en-
tanglement, it had also made him realize his need of a woman's love.
He would have preferred to put off thinking about the matter; as this
seemed impossible, he determined to approach the "lottery business" of
marriage in a thoroughly rational manner.[7] As carefully as though he
were selecting a suite of parlor furniture, James began "studying" Lucretia's qualifications to last a lifetime.[8] The process, however, did not
prove to be as detached as he intended. When the "Grecians" and their
teacher sat for a likeness in April, James whispered to the artist to seat
Lucretia next to him.[9] He was chiefly responsible for the Commencement colloquy, *Mordecai and Haman,* in which he played King Aha-
suerus while Lucretia was cast as Queen Esther.[10] The mimicry of
marriage fluttered Lucretia, as James may have hoped but was not
allowed to know. Passing behind the stage at one rehearsal, she was
saved from a fall by strong, encircling arms. As she turned to meet
Mr. Garfield's eyes, Lucretia was pierced by "a strange wild delight."
She quickly freed herself and ran from the cause of such indecorous
excitement.[11]

Lucretia later said that she "forgot" the incident. She appeared, at
least, to have done so when she returned to Mr. Garfield's classes in the
autumn. But her prim little presence bemused him with the fancy that
there was "but one to recite, and only one book."[12] James would miss
Lucretia sorely when she left to spend the winter in teaching a village
school.

James and Lucretia had been shaped by the same religious faith
and regional environment and schooled in the same regard for book
learning and family solidarity, but in all else their early influences had
been utterly dissimilar. Lucretia's background had been one of stability
and comfort. Both of her parents came of pioneer families who had
planted vigorous roots in the wilds of Portage County. Zeb Rudolph, a
thrifty farmer and master carpenter of German extraction, was esteemed by the Disciples of the Reserve for his services to the church.
He had already been rising to leadership among them when he married Arabella Mason, a young convert whose family had migrated from
Vermont. Four children—Lucretia, John, Joseph, and Ellen—came to
bless the peaceful union. Their home at Garrettsville was embraced by
a large circle of kinsfolk, notably by the united clan of Masons, who
were fond of getting together for visits and celebrations. Families of
comparatively long and prosperous residence were the elite of the still
shifting population of the Reserve; such social standing as existed in
the unworldly and equalitarian Disciple community belonged to the
Rudolph children by right of their father's prominence in the church

and the no less influential position of their uncle, Carnot Mason.[13]

Lucretia had not suffered the wounds of want and insecurity, but she bore the scars of another deprivation. The Rudolphs had denied their children the endearments that warmed the Garfield cabin. Zeb Rudolph was inarticulate in all but selfless conduct. Even his fervent religious faith had no other utterance; his preaching was dull and tongue-tied. His family could not look for greater eloquence than his unfailing kindness. The gentle, motherly Arabella was scarcely more demonstrative. She reverenced the dry New England virtue of "self-government" and impressed it on her young ones. Their home was a haven to which they turned for shelter. If they longed for fondness, they learned to do without it.[14]

Crete, as her family called her, had been treated with especial solici-tude because of her delicate health. In early youth she had developed a weakness of the lungs, and her parents dreaded the racking cough and painful right side that disabled her in winter. Yet it was on this cherished firstborn that their austerity bore most harshly. As an aging woman, Crete would still wistfully recall the rarity of her mother's kisses, given on such occasions as leave-taking or meeting after a sepa-ration. She could not remember that her father had ever kissed her.[15]

Her longings were beyond her parents' comprehension, but Crete had a "spunky" disposition that stood in need of correction. It had not been hard to tame a loving and sensitive spirit, and Crete had grown up in the family image, a model of passive compliance. But "self-government" had exacted a heavy price. Crete was locked in a desolate repression which found relief in daydreams of an ideal lover. She was an exemplar of Christian faith, but her moral judgments had sharp-ened into severity, and religious dedication sometimes fell short of Christian charity. The only confidant to whom she had intimated her rebellious feelings was her dear friend, Lizzie Atwood. Albert Hall surely had small knowledge of the passions he inspired. The romance had left Crete still the prisoner of her fancies, as repressed in outward conduct as before. Her sexual immaturity is graphically portrayed in the picture of the "Grecians" and their teacher. Crete's likeness, taken when she had passed her twenty-first birthday, is that of a bashful little girl shrinking from the pressure of Garfield's brawny thigh.[16]

Thus was Lucretia, as she sat in Mr. Garfield's classes, blind to his yearning glances, and thus she might have remained if James had not engaged her in a rather formal correspondence and, on Mary Hub-bell's departure, proceeded to open courtship.

As long as he was subject to Mary's spiteful comment, James avoided personal contact with Lucretia, but he did not succeed in hiding his new attachment. Everyone at the Eclectic saw that he was in love—everyone but Lucretia. The idea never entered her mind (or so she said) until people began quizzing her and dropping pointed hints. She did not believe that the gossip had any basis, but she could not help thinking about it. Even if it was true that Mr. Garfield cared for her, Lucretia told herself, she could give him only a sister's regard. She was fond of Mary and disapproved of the way in which he had treated her, and she was half persuaded that her own romance with Albert had drained her of love. Still the feeling would spring up that she might love Mr. Garfield if she knew that she was loved. The fall term passed without a sign from him. Then, in November, after the close of the term, Lucretia received a letter from Mr. Garfield.[17]

James had availed himself of the short autumn vacation to pay a flying visit to Niagara Falls. After a day of sightseeing, he "felt like" writing to Lucretia, "and *did* so." "Lucretia, My Sister," his letter began, "Please pardon the liberty I take in *pointing* my pen towards *your name* this evening, for I have taken in so much scenery today I cannot contain it all myself." James regarded his travel-talk as a test of Lucretia's regard; if she did not reply, he meant to put her out of his mind forever.[18]

The unexpected overture took Lucretia by surprise. She did not know whether to answer this exciting letter or not; she had never written to a gentleman. Since her school was so near to Hiram that she came home every weekend, she supposed that she and James would shortly meet. At length, as she heard nothing further from him, she composed a sedately sympathetic reply, addressing James as "Very Kind Brother" and enclosing her translation of an ode of Anacreon. James wrote again and requested an answer. Though somewhat mystified to find herself in correspondence with a Hiram neighbor, Lucretia was compliant, and several letters passed between them in the course of the next months. James confessed that he missed Lucretia and suggested a possible visit to her "winter's empire," the village school. But their correspondence was chiefly concerned with literary subjects and with the study of "Dead Languages," a topic introduced by James for the evident purpose of sounding Lucretia's interest in the classics.[19]

In his search for a perfect mate James was looking for a younger and more alluring embodiment of Miss Booth, but Lucretia failed to meet this lofty standard. She had no genuine desire to continue a classical course. Though she left the question open and asked James for advice, he perceived that her interest was superficial and decided that her mind was lacking in depth and ambition.[20]

James was also dubious about Lucretia's views on relations between the sexes—in other words, her recognition of masculine ascendancy. The undoubted cause was her approval of orations by the Eclectic ladies. If he was interpreting this as sympathy with the crusaders for women's rights (all man-haters, in James's opinion) he had misjudged Lucretia's feminine character. He was, however, correct in concluding that she was a true and conscientious Christian. Satisfied on this most important point, he ventured to think that he might love Lucretia and unite his destiny with hers, if only he were certain of her sentiment for him and assured that she possessed the "warmth of feeling" that his happiness required.[21]

James was dangling—by mail—before Lucretia like a big, ripe plum ready to fall at the first breath of encouragement. But encouragement was not forthcoming. Lucretia's friendly letters did not hint at the hope that thrilled her as the ghost of Albert grew pale in the sunrise of her love for Mr. Garfield.

James's suspense became urgent as the winter term ran by. In February he finally made a definite plan to call at Lucretia's school, only to learn that she had fallen ill and was back in Hiram. Still racked by a tearing cough, she attended the farewell gathering of teachers and students at the close of the term. Except for a sleigh-riding party on New Year's Eve, this was the first time that James had seen her since the autumn; he had to talk with her that very evening or leave for the three-week spring vacation in continued uncertainty. After the farewells were spoken James and Lucretia held their first private conversation.[22]

Records of the interview by both James and Lucretia survive. In his diary James noted that they had "found a mutual desire to become better acquainted, and agreed to cultivate a more intimate acquaintance" because they were "still comparative strangers" though there was "a reciprocal attachment" between them. In a letter written a year after the event, Lucretia made clear that the cultivation of "a more intimate acquaintance" had begun at once. James had taken her in his arms and kissed her, and there were professions of love. Then, lulled by the music of his voice, she had rested on his bosom in "holy calm."[23]

Yet James started on his vacation with a somewhat troubled mind. He feared his impulsive behavior had again raised expectations that he might be unable to fulfill. "I hope, by the assistance of My Heavenly Father," his diary noted, "to move cautiously and judiciously in reference to the sacred subject of matrimony." From Muskingum County, he wrote Lucretia a long, confiding letter, which glowed with his "heart's warmest affections" and his joy at knowing that his love was "in some degree" returned. But he also mentioned his poverty and homelessness and dwelt on his determination, since his affair with Mary, to "do nothing without due consideration." They must both be sure, he solemnly enjoined Lucretia, that their attachment would endure the test of time.[24]

Lucretia's diary gives but a dim reflection of her relationship with James during the spring of 1854. The entries were mainly concerned with events at the Eclectic: the music lessons she had begun to take and the social activities in which she became involved. She participated in reviving the ladies' literary society and accepted, with an independence that may have surprised James, an invitation to deliver an oration at the Commencement exercises, choosing the theme of "Commerce" suggested by her favorite "Grecian," Philip Burns. With a new appreciation of "the sacredness of a true social life," Lucretia eagerly renewed old friendships and tried to overcome the distant manner that made strangers think her cold. In these preoccupations James played little part. There are incidental mentions of a few meetings spent in "pleasant" chat and attending a concert and a lecture on phrenology at which they had their heads examined. She enjoyed "the pleasure" of reciting to him alone but seemed to be escaping from his influence in deciding that classical lore was "musty" and "like living among the tombs." There is one implication that the "chats" touched personal matters. James showed her a letter from Corydon, in hopes of altering her adverse opinion of his loyal friend. Although she was impressed by the tone of the letter, it did not persuade her to take a more charitable view of Corydon's character.[25]

By the testimony of her diary, Lucretia usually saw James in public or when other callers were present, but their subsequent correspondence tells a different story. James seems to have dropped in at the Rudolphs' more frequently than the diary suggests. The promised lovers (as Lucretia's parents confidently assumed them to be) sat in her tidy little bedroom, the only semi-privacy that the crowded house afforded. There they watched the sunset flush the blossoming peach tree at Lucretia's window or read aloud from Longfellow's poems and the romantic tale, *Hyperion*. Sometimes, too, they "walked upon" their "lengthened shadows" down the hill sloping eastward from the Rudolph house. In these hours James came to know that he had found the ideal of Christian womanhood, the image of his noblest sentiments and highest aspirations; yet Lucretia's sympathy stopped short of the rapture James expected. Her soulful black eyes did not fulfill their promise of an intimate communion, gaze locked on yearning gaze, heart joined to quickened heart.[26]

Any of their common friends could have told James that in "outgushings of soul" he and Lucretia were mismated—and one, Philip

Burns, was presently to do so. But, weeks before Philip's letter was written, James had begun to sense a deeper incompatibility. Lucretia's love was all tenderness and sentiment. Her chaste embraces aroused him to "no delirium of passion." James did not know that there should be this "overwhelming power of feeling," but its absence inclined him to be cautious.[27]

James had fairly judged Lucretia's limitations, but the cooling of his desire was a telltale repetition of his retreat from Mary. The imperfections of his men friends and his "elder sister," Almeda, did not alter his constant attachment. He was critical only of the two women who, in their vastly different ways, had threatened him with the bondage of the marriage vow.

Shortly before Commencement he and Lucretia had a long talk in the music room of the Eclectic. Lucretia noted in her diary that their "attention was directed to not the most agreeable subject possible" and added that she trusted that their fears as then expressed might prove groundless. Only two days earlier she had written that the evening had found her "most dismally sad." She had had an intimation, it would seem, of James's restlessness.[28]

This was a private matter which she and James must settle for themselves. But she was not prepared for the dreadful possibility that others might have noticed the change in James. The knowledge struck without warning at the Commencement celebration on Thursday.

Commencement was a great day at the Eclectic, crowded with prideful relatives and friends who had come to congratulate the students and applaud their "exhibitions," and this Commencement should have been an especially great day for Lucretia, who was listed among the gentlemen orators as one of the principal speakers. She had persisted, though James laughed at her, in upholding a lady student's right to voice her opinions in public, and she had written and rehearsed her oration on "Commerce." But Lucretia's little achievement was spoiled by the "bitter draught" of gossip that Commencement morning brought her. Her diary makes plain, though not by explicit statement, that the Eclectic was again astir with rumors of James's fickleness. They were "such *awful words*," Lucretia raged. "True I believe—and may say *know* them—*false, base lies*. Yet to know such words should ever be spoken is enough to mantle my very brow with deepest blushes and pain my heart most torturingly. . . ."[29]

James and Lucretia met on the two days following Commencement. On Friday afternoon he was one of "a pleasant little company" calling on Lucretia. On Saturday he went to visit her "for about two hours." In his diary entry for this day he summed up their relation: "We love each other, and have declared it, but are both determined to let our judgment rule in the matter. I talked plainly with her upon the matter and she said she dare not say or do anything that would bind herself nor did I urge it. It seemed not best. Time which changes all things may make changes in us or in our circumstances." They agreed to correspond and write their thoughts freely. At the parting, Lucretia—as she later wrote in her diary—"turned away to hide the falling tear." James's tears were shed when he said good-bye to Almeda.[30]

Lucretia buried James's cooling ardor along with the campus gossip. She could not, would not distrust him. Months of loneliness stretched before her, a road without escape; "yet it is my wish and determination to be happy," Lucretia wrote in her diary.[31]

There was comfort to be found in the serenity of home and the familiar life of Hiram. A humdrum village round was all the diversion that Crete had ever known or needed—more, indeed, than her strength at times permitted, for her cavernous cough hung on until late summer, and overexertion at housework put her in bed with a torturing pain in her side. While events flowed peacefully around her, Lucretia dwelt in the treasurehouse of her memories and her bright-hued dreams of the future. Insofar as happiness consists of habit and illusion, she was able to achieve it.

# CHAPTER 4

# WILLIAMSTOWN

MEANTIME JAMES had torn himself from his mother's arms and set off on his adventures. The pangs of parting with all he loved were soon forgotten in the great diversion of travel. He journeyed through the fabled "East" like Marco Polo gaping at the marvels of Cathay and stored up every detail to put on paper.

A second inspection of Niagara ("the Great Watering Pot of the West") was followed by a visit to Butler, a center of Disciple missionary endeavor in western New York. There James stayed over July 4, spending much time with Corydon at the home of one Mary Watson, whom Corydon had wooed and won by correspondence. When the holiday was over, James and Corydon left for Albany to take the nightboat down the Hudson (the "Rhine of America") to New York. After a round of sightseeing and a weekend at the New Jersey village where Corydon was teaching school, James had a phrenological examination at the New York office of Fowlers and Wells before proceeding to Troy for the last lap of his journey.[1]

From the stagecoach James gazed ecstatically on Williamstown, "a diamond in an emerald casket," but he soon learned that there were disappointments among the casket's riches. Having taken a number of examinations, he was accepted—with a reservation about mathematics, which he was "to bring up"—as a member of the junior class that would enter in September. The senior class was out of the question; James would have to spend two years at Williams if he was to obtain a diploma. There was a more immediately pressing problem: he had come nine weeks too early and must pass an idle summer at a ruinous depletion of his funds.[2]

These facts had been known to James in the way that facts are known to a mind unwilling to accept them. Even now he had times of believing that he could somehow "leap a year" of college. He attended classes of the closing term—the Williams Commencement did not take place until the middle of August—but the superior educational advantages of his future classmates dimmed his hopes of easily surpassing them. Lashing himself to excesses of study, he grew nervously ill. He had "taken cold nearly every night," his temples drummed with headache, he could not sleep; in loneliness and suffering, he succumbed to the homesickness that travel had deferred. He broadcast appeals for letters to every acquaintance, male and female, he could think of. Most poignantly, he wanted Lucretia's presence, longing to lay his head on her dear bosom and listen to the beating of her heart. "Lucretia, dear Lucretia," James wrote, "my arm is round you now, my cheek is pressed to yours, here is my kiss." He drew the outline of a mouth on the paper, to show the place his lips had touched.[3]

Soon after writing this letter Garfield had an attack of headache so severe that, "nearly insane with the pain," he called in a doctor. Again warned of "inflammation of the brain" and advised to take a rest, he decided to pay a visit to certain Garfield connections to whom he had made his coming known before he left Ohio. Harriet Garfield, a school teacher who lived with her father and brother at Monterey in Berkshire County, had invited him to stay at their farm, and, when the Commencement ceremonies were over, James went there for two weeks. He was cordially received by Harriet, her brother Henry, and their stout, jolly father, Daniel. Under Harriet's escort, James took a three-day carriage drive to meet the many Garfield families in Berkshire County. For the remainder of his stay he rested in the peaceful valley, rode and fished, or idly feasted on the summer beauty of the hills. He had been warmly welcomed by his kinsfolk, yet to James these plodding farmers were "stranger Garfields." Old Daniel, in particular, was as bigoted as he was good-natured. An adherent of the blatantly nativist Know-Nothing party, he was perhaps the model for "Sam," a rhymed satire on the Know-Nothings, with which James regaled Williams College the next year. Though Harriet plied her "Dear Coz" with repeated invitations, he returned only once to Monterey.[4]

James had a closer feeling of kinship with the Disciples of West Rupert, Vermont, where he spent the last week of his vacation. A series of religious meetings made him well acquainted with the members of the local congregation and especially with the "settled speaker," Myron J. Streator of Ohio, who had recently buried his wife. Garfield's warm sympathy for his bereavement led to a closer intimacy than Streator's reserved nature usually permitted.[5]

His travels had put an end to Garfield's homesickness. Williams-

town, on his return, was a place already known, already, in the grandeur of its scenery, beloved. An old friend, moreover, was to join him
in his exile. James had not at first placed much reliance on Charles Wilber's talk of going to Williams, but Wilber had meant it, and James had
reserved a room for them on campus. He passed the last days before
college opened in dealing with the correspondence that had piled up in
his absence. There was a solicitous letter from Lucretia and her likeness. Her rapturous response to his letter of love and longing had gone
unanswered. James had not thought of writing her during his vacation.[6]

Lucretia was distressed by the long silence. Day after day she
awaited the letter from James that did not come. Her diary was the
confidant of her anxiety as the weeks went by. She believed he loved
her, she wrote; she could not believe that it was indifference that stayed
his hand. She became fearful that he was ill, then sure that disease was
"bending him low." At the same time she spoke of seeking her pillow
"with a doubting heart." Doubts of her lover's constancy mingled in-
sidiously with her apprehensions for his health.[7]

When, after four weeks, a letter came at last, James made no excuses but seemed to assume that an outing was a sufficient explanation
for not having written.[8] It might have occurred to Lucretia that he had
wanted her when he was sick and lonely, forgotten her when he was
well and befriended; but she was melted by the kindness with which
James banished for good her bugbear of a classical education and
called up visions of marriage based on interests congenial to her tastes.

James had become persuaded that "the mind and especially the
female mind should be ornamented, as well as strengthened," and advised Lucretia to "bring up" French and German, the natural sciences,
and the fine arts. "Dear one," he fondly asked, "if it shall ever be ours
to enjoy the same home should we not endeavor to be able to make that
a spot around which our affections may cling. . . ." Lucretia answered
Yes with all her heart. She was inspired to compose a poem, which she
posted off to James in a letter that made light of her "*womanish* fears"
for his health, and eagerly agreed that "Woman's province is her
home."[9]

A few considerate words had atoned for a month of misery. Back
on her pillar of confiding trust, Lucretia was without remembrance that
its foundation had been shaken.

By the spring of 1855 Lucretia had withdrawn into a "sort of
dreamy calm." She had wanted to take a school, but she was not physically strong, and her parents would not hear of her leaving home. She
had numbed her restlessness by studying and teaching at the Eclectic

and by taking piano lessons, as James wanted her to do. His letters were the events that starred her calendar. The receipt of a letter was often noted in her diary. When a lapse occurred during James's winter vacation, she commented on three occasions on the nonarrival of a letter. On the whole, James was a faithful correspondent. During the twelve months following his departure from Hiram he wrote two dozen letters to Lucretia; they were lengthy, affectionate, and newsy.[10]

Williams College in 1854 was still a sheltered grove of academe, secluded from the clash and scuffle of the American scene. New Englanders formed the majority of the 231 students, many of whom intended to enter the ministry. Though nonsectarian, the college was permeated with religious feeling. Attendance was compulsory at morning and evening chapel during the week and at two church services on Sunday. The Theological Society was one of the most active and important groups in the college. President Mark Hopkins, an ordained Congregational minister and a teacher of great personal force, himself took charge of indoctrinating the seniors in the various branches of philosophy. The president's brother Albert was largely responsible for a series of revivals that struck the campus during his forty years as a professor.[11]

In spite of outbreaks of high spirits, the dominant tone was one of serious purpose. Many students were working their way, and a six-week vacation—the longest of the year—was designed to enable them to take jobs in country schools. The most important contests, in the total absence of organized athletics, were those of the Commencement orators, who were chosen on the basis of scholarship. Rivalry was also incited by the elections of the two literary societies and, though with less involvement in college politics, by the five editorships of the literary periodical, the *Williams Quarterly*.

In academic scope and freedom Williams was not yet abreast of the intellectual progress of the century. The methods of instruction remained conventional and rigid, the faculty was for the most part undistinguished, and the college library was utterly inadequate; but Garfield's innocent eyes saw only the riches of the banquet spread before him. He fell in love that first year with the German language and culture and with geology and astronomy. Released from the demands of daily teaching, he devoured history and biography, discovered the beauties of Shakespeare, and kept pace with current publications in poetry and fiction. His boyhood addiction to novels, nearly forsworn since his conversion, was renewed by Cooper, Dickens, Thackeray, Scott, and many lesser authors, most of whose books were available to him in the library of the Philologian, the literary society

which he had lost no time in joining. He quickly demonstrated his outstanding ability in debate and delivered his first oration—on "Chivalry"—a few weeks after college opened. He also became affiliated with
the Theological Society and with an "anti-secret" society which en-
deavored to counteract the influence of the six Greek-letter fraternities
at Williams.[12]

James did not form these associations without meeting some prejudice at the outset. Most of his forty-five classmates were prepared to
regard a man from Ohio as little better than a freak. They stared in
wonder at a big, muscular backwoodsman with rough clothes and
hearty manners and with speech which, however diligently cultivated,
still carried some twang of frontier homeliness. James suffered at first,
moreover, from his initial identification with Wilber. There was a ludi-
crous contrast, as they moved about the campus, between Garfield's
massive frame and the awkward little figure that limped along beside
him. Somewhat older than the average junior, they were further set
apart by their ignorance of college ways, and the indictment was completed by the report that this particular pair belonged to an outlandish
sect called "Campbellites."

The supercilious Wilber never made a place for himself at Williams;
in time his intellect earned respect, but he made few friends. He dismissed collegians as mere "boys" and was in turn disliked for his con-
ceit. James, in time, gained wide liking and respect. Members of the
Theological Society who aspired to be Congregational preachers
learned that a "Campbellite" could be a sincere Christian, and they welcomed Garfield's help in conducting a campus revival. The "anti-
secrets"—in all but basic purpose another fraternity—valued "Gar" as a
loyal brother and friend. He quickly made his mark as a writer of prose
and verse and became an editor of the *Quarterly* in the spring of 1855.
He was chosen to appear as the official "Poet" of the Philologians at the
annual exhibition of the two literary societies, and he was elected, over
the opposition of a fraternity coalition, to the coveted post of president
of the Philologians during the first term of his senior year.[13]

Garfield's eloquence alone was a passport to acceptance. A public
speaker of seasoned experience, he brought to debate and declamation
a style that was far above the undergraduate level. Like many self-
doubting people, he gained power when he faced an audience. Physically removed from his hearers and usually set above them, he assumed
like an actor the role of expositor, guide, or critic. He never read his
discourses. Throwing back his fine head, he let his voice roll out in
fluent periods or passionate exhortations, plentifully strewn with gems
of rhetoric and classical allusions. A moralizing and embellished speech
was the fashion of the day, and the faculty and students of Williams

were struck as forcibly as any Ohio congregation by the power of Garfield's oratory.[14]

As James moved into a wider range of college interests, his dependence on Wilber inevitably slackened. Intellectually he owed much to his erratic friend—it is notable that Charles was his earliest mentor in geology (which remained a lifelong interest) and that he anticipated and stimulated James in the study of German and Hebrew—but their differences of disposition were highlighted at Williams, and their intimacy gradually declined. The second year they roomed apart, and James was glad to be alone. But there was no disagreement, and James could say in the spring of 1856 that he had never been on better terms with Charles. When Charles was in an increasingly nervous state during their last months at Williams, James was his only confidant. But socially, after their junior year, they went their separate ways without regret.[15]

The separation was beneficial to James in hastening his adaptation to a more casual and fun-loving masculine society than he had previously known. His new companions were not inclined to maudlin vows and confidences, and there was a limit even to their tolerance of "earnestness," particularly when allied with self-conceit. There was good talk at Williams, but it was interspersed with banter and clowning, and sometimes horseplay. At heart Garfield was one of the "boys" whom Charles despised. He loved letting off steam in shouts of laughter, guffawed at practical jokes, was convulsed by "college humor." He would always need and value intimate friendships with men, but he gradually moved away from the mawkish sentimentality of his boyhood (in middle life he remarked on the "gush and slush" of his early diaries). His years at Williams marked the beginning of the change. "The Charge of the Tight Brigade," a parody by James which commemorated a practical joke played by the freshmen on a sophomore beer party, shows how far he had advanced at college in shedding the prissy attitudes of the Eclectic.[16]

James's success at Williams had not been without cost. He once described himself as a "a sort of College Statesman," and statesmen have adversaries as well as friends. His aggressive and forthright manner alienated some of the students. This he came to regret. About three years after his graduation, he confessed to Harry Rhodes: "I would exchange all the praise for belligerent success which I gained in College for the friendships which I marred and which otherwise might be redolent with happy memories today." He added, "I am glad you are doing less at the strife and more at the social life."[17]

In the new year of 1855 James was sporting a set of luxuriant chestnut whiskers, grown to protect his sensitive throat from the rigors of the New England winter. Thus adorned, and attired in his "long calico

study-gown," he would sit of a March evening, reading Tacitus. There
is a new impression of ease in the picture of the bearded man of learning lounging in bachelor comfort on the Parnassian heights he had
scaled. Some sense of achievement was not wanting. Distinguished student at an eastern college, honored graduate soon to be, James was the
cynosure and pride of all whose humble lives had touched his own. His
reputation had traveled, like a legend, through Ohio and Michigan.
There seemed no limit set to what he might attain. From the wilds east
of Grand Rapids, his brother reported that Uncle Joseph Skinner was
saying James would be President some time.[18]

A stranger in the East, James had not succeeded in getting a district
school in the long vacation. He barely squeezed through the second
term on the proceeds of two writing classes and a Disciple revival and
on a few small sums received for contributions to various newspapers.
The first of the writing classes had grown out of a lecture engagement
at Pownal, Vermont, where he had gone at the invitation of one of his
classmates. The other and more important connection was made
through Myron Streator, who had gone from Vermont to the old
Dutch village of Poestenkill, New York, which lay a short distance east
of Troy and twenty-one miles from Williamstown.[19]

James was already due at college when the second writing class was
over, but he was persuaded to spend another week at Poestenkill to
help Streator with a series of meetings. The melancholy widower had
become ill and listless, and it was uphill work to make converts in an
eastern community where existing church ties were traditional and
strong. James unexpectedly found himself conducting the revival. The
local Disciples were so well pleased with his success that they insisted on
his staying for a second week of meetings, and they made up a purse of
$20 in token of their gratitude. James was also showered with gifts of
clothing by his hostess, Mrs. Edmond Cole, and her sister and next-
door neighbor, Mrs. Charles G. Learned. Although he missed three
weeks of college, he was glad that he had stayed; at Poestenkill he had
found another home, the tender care and "heart-gushing" affection
that he needed.[20]

James loved Lucretia, but he was a healthy male of twenty-two, condemned to a present of sexual abstention and a future of monogamy,
and he was vibrating in tune with every attractive woman he saw. One
fraternity brother remarked in him an "insatiable desire of *conquest*"
and cautioned him facetiously against the dangerous indiscretions of
"casting peculiar eye glances" and "quietly passing the arm about the
delicate *waste*."[21] But these were risks too pleasant to forswear. As a
Gospel preacher, James made no secret of his interest in women. Many

of them responded kindly to his affectionate manner and organ-toned consolation or counsel. Sister Mary Cole was one of the kindest and James was suitably grateful, but it was with Sister Maria Learned that sparks began to fly.

Maria Learned was so fragile and refined that she scarcely seemed a being of this earth. Her bosom fluttered and her clear blue eyes often glittered with fever, for Maria was consumptive. Few souls were attuned to her exquisite sensibility. She was uncongenial with her sister and bored with her attentive husband, a lumber dealer in Troy. Between visits from her intimate friend, Miss Rebecca Jane Selleck of Lewisboro, New York, Maria was starved for sympathy. She fell in love with James at their first meeting. A frequent caller at the Learneds' comfortable old house, he often lingered to talk or pray with Maria and Charles and their two surviving children. Jonas was an impressionable boy of fifteen who would be converted to the Disciple faith and immersed a few months later. Five-year-old Mary Jane was one of those precociously pious little invalids who figure in moral tales of the period. She loved to have James "tell her about the Savior" and was sad when he went away. After bidding him good-bye, she said, "Mama, it seems to me I shall never see him again. I love him so much."[22]

Myron Streator called Mary Jane a "second edition of the mother," and she had undoubtedly contracted the mother's disease. She sank rapidly in March. After her death her prophetic words about James were poignantly recalled. He was deeply moved by Myron's account of her sainted passing and her affection for him.[23] James had never cared for little children, though he made the proper gestures. He seemed to realize for the first time that a child, too, could give love and reach and touch the heart.

Yet James was curiously tardy in condoling with the bereaved mother. During the next two months, he did not visit Maria or even write the distraught woman—in spite of Myron's repeated hints that she needed him. It was a neglect so uncharacteristic as to suggest that James feared a more serious emotional involvement than he could handle. When he finally went back to Poestenkill in the spring vacation, he professed to believe that he was joining Myron for a trip. He had, however, been forewarned that the ailing preacher was about to retire to Ohio and had loaded James with engagements that he felt unable to fill himself. James spent the last three weeks of May in substituting for Streator at Poestenkill. He conducted another revival and accepted an offer to preach there every other Sunday until the Williams summer vacation.[24]

Financially the employment was a stroke of luck for James. The emotional rewards were generous, too. As James sat close beside the grieving Maria or knelt with her in prayer, he did not withhold the comfort of a brother's tender caresses. At the end of the journey from Williamstown—usually made on horseback, once on foot—Maria's clinging arms were waiting. James would have been outraged by the suggestion that these sacred embraces had a tinge of sexual feeling, and he must have been relieved to find that the situation was not "misunderstood" by Charles Learned, who regarded James as his own particular friend. Charles was surely unaware of the excesses of Maria's fancy as her passion for the young preacher mounted. James made her house his second home. The Prophet's Chamber, a cozy back guest room, was reserved for him. In his absence Maria would weep over his letters and kiss the place his hand had pressed. After a visit from him she would leave his napkin untouched on the table and forbear to smooth his bed. She showed an increasing tendency to magnify his relationship with her children over that of their real father, longed to place Jonie under James's immediate influence, and wildly exaggerated the slight connection he had had with Mary Jane. "Let none ask why I love you," she wrote James four years later. "Was there no bond but her blessed love, it would be stronger than death."[25]

The perfervid meetings in Maria's sitting room were interrupted in mid-August by the closing exercises of the college year and Garfield's preparations for the vacation. He was detained for a few days after Commencement by his duties as editor of the forthcoming *Quarterly*. Then, having extracted from Brother Hayden a draft for a sum due him, James set off on his long-anticipated trip to Ohio.

For Lucretia June seemed to bring the time of fulfillment within reach. She began to count the days and anticipate the joys that lay in store. She was "all hope," she later said, "expectant only of perfect bliss." Charles Wilber, who went back to Ohio in late July, saw her happy face as "an index to a glad heart." But the impression of radiant confidence was not borne out by Lucretia's conduct; soon after the meeting with Charles, she impulsively accepted an offer from the district school at Ravenna. After fourteen months of waiting for James, she left Hiram a week before his return.[26]

Lucretia had been driven by a little gust of panic and needed to be comforted and reassured, but James was far too deeply occupied with his own complexities to understand those of other people. He had slightly more than three weeks to spend in Ohio, and he had filled the time chock-a-block with plans. Two practical matters were weighing on his mind: He needed to borrow money for the expenses of his senior year and he was giving thought to the question of employment after his graduation. The Eclectic, embarrassed by debts and declining morale, was in need of energetic leadership. A number of Garfield's admirers looked to him to save the school, and he was interested in conferring with them, especially with Almeda and Phebe, and examining the situation at first hand. The personal concerns of the visit were scarcely less important. He had to spend some time at Solon and Orange, and his program was much complicated by his insistence on including his brother in the family reunion. If Thomas could not come home, James intended to travel to Michigan to see him.[27]

Though Lucretia was not at the center of any of these plans, she was definitely in the offing. With masculine arrogance, James had expected her to hover near at hand, ready to gather up any crumbs of attention he could spare, and he had been dashed to learn that she would be in Ravenna, tied all week to a classroom. He went to Ohio with a sense of grievance. After seeing his family he proceeded to Hiram and there embraced a host of friends, notably Almeda, who had returned to teach at the Eclectic with a brand new degree from Oberlin, and Harry Rhodes, who was now doing part-time teaching at the Eclectic while completing his course of study there. In Hiram, Garfield found opinion against Sutton Hayden's administration of the Disciple school. He also saw Lucretia, who came home to spend Sunday; early on the Monday, he escorted her back to Ravenna on his way to the annual meeting of the Disciples at Warren and Euclid.[28]

"Oh guide me, guide me," Lucretia had prayed, "that I may prove worthy of one so good and true, if he may be mine." The meeting was evidently a cycle of disaster. Lucretia was hurt and shy, James distant and self-centered. Lucretia withdrew behind her wall of reserve, sinking into "blues." She tried to pretend that all was well, but her defenses were crumbling as they walked desolately through the quiet streets of Ravenna and stopped at last before the house where she boarded. When James turned away, "how my spirit sank," Lucretia wrote—"oh! into one of those strange, indescribable, horrible depths of gloom which sometimes overwhelm the soul." Later in the day a little note from James stirred a flicker of hope, but he did not write again; and while for two full weeks she watched and waited, he did not come.[29]

Lucretia summoned all her strength and went on with her life. She resolved to have faith in James and could believe that she was "perfectly calm" after ten days without a sign from him. "All will be right, Father in Heaven," she wrote in her diary, but the words are less an assertion than an agonized prayer. In bed that night she suddenly burst into a flood of tears. The next day she bravely faced the certainty that she would not see James again before he left. She did not blame him for the pain his silence caused her but tried to analyze her feelings to determine whether she could master her "selfishness" and sacrifice her own desires to James. "With a warm large heart overflowing with love," Lucretia wrote, "at times he almost overwhelms with affection, and then he turns and in his own intellectual greatness and strength seems unapproachable, and everything must yield to his lofty ambition. Now I ask myself can I reciprocate that unbounded affection, or maintain sufficient dignity to stand beside him in his power . . . can I bear with . . . that almost neglect with which I shall be treated when he turns within himself. I begin to hope I can. I feel a power to do this that I never knew before."[30]

Lucretia was thinking primarily of James, and so was James himself. He was stunned by the disappointment of their meeting. His former doubts of Lucretia had all come surging back. He made an effort to be fair—"My wild passionate heart demands so much"—but he really did not think himself at fault or consider Lucretia's feelings. He would apparently have left Ohio without seeing her again had it not been for a chance meeting with a former classmate, Oliver P. Miller, a preacher in Ravenna, who had recently seen Lucretia and remarked that she seemed "very unhappy." The words were like a charm; they started James from his apathy and sent him rushing to Ravenna, remorseful and distraught.[31]

Happily for Lucretia, she was at home and alone on the evening James came to the door of her little room. Happily, too, his unexpected appearance shattered her guard of composure. "It stung me to the soul," James wrote, "to think that my manner had been such as to give her such suffering." Nevertheless he did not spare her a recital of his reproaches. In despair at being charged with coldness, Lucretia thrust her diary into his hands, trusting—like some poor voiceless creature— that her written words might tell him what her tongue could not express. James turned the little pages, absorbed, gratified, utterly melted by their record of devotion. "For months . . . her heart was constantly pouring out its tribute of love," he marveled. "When my letters did not reach her, her heart was tortured with fear lest I might be suffering with sickness and pain. From that journal I read depths of affection that I had never before known that she possessed. A new light had burst in upon my soul, and I felt as if the vail which had hung between our hearts was [lifted]."[32]

He took her on his knee, and she clung to him, her arms around his neck. He called her darling and kissed her when she smiled. There was a new ardor in Lucretia's caresses. The lovers said good-bye in a joy that transcended parting. They were to meet in their letters, in daily thoughts, and in prayers; James included Lucretia in a little ceremony he had arranged with his mother, to join him in reading a specified chapter of the Scriptures at a given hour each evening.[33]

Faith and rapture shone in the next letter that Lucretia wrote to James. "Is it *true,* dearest, that you *did come again?* . . . that we talked . . . looked into each other's eyes, and . . . down into the very depths of our hearts? . . . The darkness, doubt and cold distrust which made us both so miserable formed but the background on which was brought out so clearly, so vividly that beautiful brightness. . . . And now my own, my loved, my noble James, am I not happy? . . . What a new world I am living in. All my life before has been in a mist—a cloud. . . . O how beautiful to live in such a world of light and love. . . ."[34]

Garfield's visit to Ohio had renewed his "endearing ties," but he did not clutch at their support as he turned eastward for the second time. East and west, all was right with his world. He stopped off at Syracuse to take part in a Disciple meeting, at which he joined a party from Troy and Poestenkill, and arrived at Williamstown somewhat late but overflowing with ambition and high spirits. Stimulated by the vigorous personality of Mark Hopkins, his idol, James was soon "reveling in metaphysics" and other branches of philosophy. As though he could never have enough of learning, he also took up Hebrew and ranged over spacious areas of English and American history. It was a time of glorious freedom to study, without care for ways and means. During his vacation, James had resorted to the expedient of having his life insured for a sum sufficient to cover the expenses of senior year. The inveterate gambler, Uncle Thomas Garfield, had taken the policy as security for a loan, and James was resting confidently, though mistakenly, in the expectation of soon receiving the money.[35]

This fruitful autumn of 1855 was more than a grind for James, more than the additional labors of writing, editing, and public speaking. Politically a success, he presided with grace over the Philologian meetings. He took a trip to New York City to buy books for the society and attend a meeting of the Bible Union. He went on a jaunt of three days over the hills with the senior class to fraternize with the seniors of Amherst. There are lively glimpses of James, rolling on the grass in spasms of laughter, tramping over mountain trails, spouting Longfellow's new poem, "Hiawatha." But the most illuminating picture is that of James at a political meeting in November, transfixed by the speech of a man who had been abused and threatened in Kansas Territory for expressing opposition to slavery. The extension of slavery to the territories had been a raging sectional issue since the passage of the Kansas-Nebraska Act a year and a half before. James now seemed to hear of it for the first time. "This subject is entirely new to me," he said to a friend as they left the hall. "I am going to know all about it." In a private note, made the same night, he avowed, "At such hours as this I feel like throwing the whole current of my life into the work of opposing this giant evil." And he added a comment that foretold his early divergence from the antipolitical views of the Disciples: "I don't know but the religion of Christ demands some such action." [36]

Through all the varied experiences of that autumn, James drew faith and inspiration from the memory of his parting visit to Ravenna and from Lucretia's letters. "My every thought goes westward, singing," he wrote in his first letter after his return to college. And again, "Darling one, I shall walk in the light this year. . . ." In her letters Lucretia was no longer a dreaming girl but a woman of great and giving heart who fought to strip away her armor of reserve and bare the treasures of love that it concealed. The ardent letters kindled Garfield's flammable heart: "Your two dear letters express no wish, no thought, no emotion that my own soul does not fully respond to with the full tide of my affections. How inexpressibly blissful would it be could I but take you to my arms tonight and feel the throbbing of your own heart against mine, and the thrill of your ardent kiss." He was fast wearing out the glass of her likeness as his thoughts sped over the months until Lucretia should attend the Williams Commencement, over the years until they could begin to spend their lives together. [37]

James seemed, in this fortunate season, to have attained a new unity of love and purpose. Then, at Thanksgiving dinner in a hospitable house at Troy, he met Maria's friend, Rebecca Jane Selleck.

# CHAPTER 5

# REBECCA

"MY LOVE ALSO to the young lady there whom you say you 'like,' " Lucretia wrote James in December, in care of Mrs. Learned at Poestenkill; "why did you not say *love*, dearest?" Some feminine instinct had obviously been alerted, but it had no place in a world of perfect trust. "For I know you do love her," Lucretia's pen ran playfully on, "and surely you may, and every other lady who is good, whether she is like me or not. I wish I could find someone here like you. . . . I am sure I should love them."[1]

Her letter earned a prompt and appreciative response. "I should have said '*love*,' " James admitted, "if I had written a few days later, for I found that young lady (Rebecca J. Selleck) truly a noble and lovely spirit. No, true love is not that selfish, jealous, exclusive affection which is willing to recognize no merit but its own, but the expansive and generous expression of that affection which the honest heart must confess it cherishes for all congenial and loving hearts. Yes, you are all the more dear to me when I know that you love noble men and women. . . . In Rebecca I find another dear loved sister for us both. . . ."[2]

James was not quite as ingenuous as all these fine phrases implied. He was well aware that the charming Miss Selleck, twenty-four and still unattached, had been invited to Poestenkill expressly on his account. Maria wanted them to know and love each other, and James had been primed for another romantic friendship. Beyond that point, however, his conscience was clear. His Poestenkill friends knew that he was engaged to marry, and he could afford to smile at their belated attempts at matchmaking.

But, just as the temperance tracts said, it was the first misstep that counted. A taste of romantic friendship with Rebecca made James crave more and more. They read aloud from Tennyson's poems and from Kingsley's novel, *Alton Locke*. Rebecca's expressive fingers would sometimes toy with his beard. "Very early in our day, you gave it to me as a plaything," she once recalled.[3]

Maria's frequent presence exerted little or no restraint. It was as natural then for Rebecca to perch on Brother Jamie's knee as if they were alone. Their beloved sister smiled benignly on their caresses and told them their love was holy. She was always careful to speak affectionately of "dear Lucretia," but it is unlikely that Maria ever thought of James's engagement as anything but an unfortunate involvement that would surely be corrected in due season.

Never had James dreamed of such an affinity as the three of them enjoyed, not jealous and exclusive, but freely shared. They called themselves a triangle—a brother and two sisters, contiguous each to each and joined in "reciprocal oneness" by an equal love. Yet there was in fact an important difference between the "sisters" and the regard they felt for James. With Charles Learned's return each evening from his lumber business in Troy, Maria became once more the attentive wife (while Rebecca and James operated a "pedal telegraph" beneath the dinner table), and, when Charles signified his readiness, Maria retired to their double bed upstairs. Her love for James was a very passionate and dominating emotion, but it was never permitted to jeopardize her domestic security.[4]

It taxes belief that, at this sober time and place, James should have found a respectable woman who sympathized with his artlessly polygamous impulses. But James had done something still more extraordinary; he had found two such women.

Charles Wilber, who also visited Poestenkill and well knew of James's attachment to Rebecca, called her "that beautiful sister," and a photograph, taken when she was forty, does not belie the description. Dulled by time and disappointment, the heart-shaped face is still lovely. Its delicacy suggests the transparently fair complexion that western men admired in the gently nurtured ladies of the East. There is a quiet elegance in the arrangement of the hair and the choice of dress and ornament.[5]

Nineteenth century America afforded no society more decorous and tradition-bound than that in which Rebecca had been reared. The Sellecks of Connecticut, who traced their descent from an early seventeenth century immigrant from England, were of ancient and honorable lineage in the new nation. One Ebenezer Selleck, born in 1775, had been left some fifty years later a widower with grown children. He had taken as his second wife a lady eighteen years his junior, and

Rebecca was the elder of two children born to this autumnal union. Their home in the township of Lewisboro, New York, was set on a high ridge close to the Connecticut line. Socially as well as geographically, the family looked toward both states and in either direction encountered the genteel and well-to-do company to which their breeding entitled them.[6]

Rebecca, known to her intimates as Rancie or Ranca, never relinquished her position nor outwardly defied its code of conduct. Nevertheless, at twenty-four she had acquired some highly unorthodox opinions on the subject of love. Two powerful influences had been at work. The first was that of her wilful brother, Ebenezer, for whom she had an unusually fond affection. With maturity their love had grown in intensity, but Eben's jealousy and ill-temper caused Rancie much unhappiness. On the death of their aged father in 1852, the unstable youth had become the tyrannical head of the household. The mother, fading into invalidism, submitted to his exactions for the sake of peace. Rebecca's attempts to reason with him provoked angry scenes and sullen estrangements, during which Eben denied her his kisses. This overwrought relationship may partly explain the fact that an attractive and highly sexed woman had bypassed the normal destinations of marriage and motherhood.[7]

If Eben had supplied the primary deflection, Maria was responsible for the course it followed. Her ascendancy over the younger woman was complete, and she had undoubtedly inspired the daring ideas which accorded so oddly with Rancie's conservative background. Far from disowning the ambiguous implications of the "triangle," Rancie glorified it as the "holy trinity." The softness of Brother Jamie's beard against her cheek made her think of "the head of a girl love," and she often alluded lightly to her "triple" or "triune" nature. The affair with James was quite openly planned and promoted by Maria. Rancie responded to his ardent advances without any of the hesitations and reticences which modesty then required and—the most flagrant flouting of the proprieties—without expectation of marriage. For at first Rebecca, like James himself, respected his promise to Lucretia and regarded their love as an episode, radiant but brief.[8]

It was Maria who arranged the time of fulfillment on a night of late December, shortly before James ended his stay at Poestenkill. "When the good-night hour came," as Rancie naively expressed it, "our beloved sister dismissed us with her blessed smile of approval." That smile was the only sanction Rancie needed. Timid but docile, she went upstairs with James to the Prophet's Chamber. She was grateful to Maria for the happiness she found there. "Had we never have met afterwards," she wrote James a year later, "I should have thought that I had caught up the whole of love and garnered it in my heart in those few passing hours."[9]

A starving man before whom a feast had been spread, James returned to college invigorated and refreshed. By every canon of his moral code he had behaved in a reprehensible manner, but he gave no evidence of guilty feeling. On the contrary, he was bursting with good spirits. "I have accomplished more this term than I ever did in any term before," he wrote to Corydon in March. He was reading Hebrew and was "delighted with that noble old language." He had also done "a great deal of miscellaneous reading." To the March issue of the *Williams Quarterly* he contributed a poem, "Memory," and a long review article. His health was good, he assured his mother; he weighed 197 pounds. The expected loan from Uncle Thomas was delayed, but he shrugged off the disappointment and briskly arranged other loans to meet his college bills. Though undecided about his future, he was cheerful as he considered it. He leaned towards the approved fields of teaching and preaching, but the law was among the possibilities. He was receiving letters from Ohio that suggested a return to Hiram. He rejected a tempting offer of $1,000 a year to take charge of the schools in Troy (acceptance would have meant missing the spring term at Williams). Even the "terrible winter" of 1856 did not dampen his spirits; he loved to sit at his window in early morning "and drink in the beauty of the scene without."[10]

James seemed to have reached a new plateau of confidence, but he was not standing on safe and steady ground. Nothing in his narrow indoctrination had prepared him for Rancie's surrender to love. While enchaining his senses, it had confounded his standards and dazed his reason. He could not face his conduct squarely; above all, he could not admit that he was unfaithful to Crete. "I am already, in spirit, *your husband*," he wrote her in March, "and you *my darling wife*." When Crete anxiously asked if she filled up all his heart, he hastened to reply, "Yes, dear *little* creature, (and dearer because little,) you fill it *all* up, and leave no blank space." The blinding illusion for James as the hocus-pocus of pure, triple love. Bent on possessing both Rancie and Crete, he convinced himself that all would be well if they loved each other too. He was impatient to bring them together and sighed for Crete to join them when he went to Lewisboro during the spring vacation.[11]

Early on the morning of April 10 James left Williamstown, traveling by stage to North Adams and thence by rail "along the beautiful valley of the Housatonic" to Bridgeport. In that city, while he waited for another train to bear him on his way, he visited the residence of P. T. Barnum, modeled after a Chinese pagoda and "said to be the most

magnificent private dwelling in America." It was evening when he
reached the Norwalk station, where Rebecca was waiting. She drove
him home—a distance of twelve miles—in the sweet chill of the northern April.[12]

James was charmed by the Sellecks' quaint old house guarded by
two venerable elms; by the moss-covered stone walls that enclosed the
fields; by the distant view of the blue waters and twinkling sails of the
Sound. In the cozy chamber prepared for his use, a wide easy chair and
a stand for the lamp and his books were drawn close to a crackling fire.
All this was his to enjoy with Rancie for three enchanted weeks—except
for three days spent in New York buying books for the Philologian
Society. Maria had been invited but could not get away. Rancie's jealous
brother had caught the gold fever and sailed for California. Her
mother hovered in the background, but the chaperonage of an elderly
invalid could sometimes be eluded. The young people drove about the
countryside or rambled among the rocks. They read much together
—Tennyson, Scott, Whittier, Kingsley, Shakespeare—sometimes at
night in James's room in the cozy glow of the lamp and the fire. For
Rancie it was to become a room redolent with memories. When she
came back to the house after seeing James off at the end of the month,
she did not linger below stairs but went up to "our room" as she put it in
a letter written to him on the same day. "The ashes are cold on the
hearth," she wrote, "and every passing breath of air makes them its
sport. They do not symbolize the joys that glowed in their ruddy blaze
through the holy hours of last Sabbath Eve. No, those are deathless joys
that will bloom in perennial beauty. . . ."[13]

James sang Lucretia's praises and lamented her absence with a persistence that might have been irksome, but Rancie could not seem to
hear enough. "Not an hour passes but that she speaks of you," James
wrote his Ohio sweetheart. On one of their rambles, shortly before he
left, they picked the first hepatica for Crete. When he carelessly forgot
it, Rancie herself sent on the pressed spray of flowers enclosed in an affectionate note. She kept Crete's grateful reply, along with a letter from
James, "rocked in the snowy cradle" between her breasts. Desperately
lonely for his love, she was consoled by his promise to return in July
and make her home the scene of his reunion with Crete.[14]

Before going back to college, James stopped at Poestenkill to see
Maria. That subtle sister gave no sign of annoyance on learning that a
second triangle had been formed behind her back, but her alarm was
disclosed by strenuous efforts to reassert her influence over both James
and Rancie. She beguiled James with such loving sympathy that he
lingered at Poestenkill for ten days and returned for another "very
dear good visit" in June. In the interval, Maria went to Lewisboro,

reduced Rancie to a state of abject adoration, planted in her mind the seeds of rivalry with Crete, and canceled the plans for a Lewisboro reunion in favor of a gathering at Poestenkill. Maria made no progress in a new campaign to hold James in the East—he had all but decided to spend the next year teaching at Hiram, and he disregarded plans that the principalship of the fine Troy high school, which he had rejected the year before, would be once more available—but she had reason to hope that she and Rancie, between them, might succeed in drawing him back.[15]

Maria's machinations could scarcely affect the outcome; there was unhappiness in store for James and Crete and Rancie wherever they might meet. The new plan, nevertheless, was cleverly devised. Rebecca was to arrive at Poestenkill in late June, more than a month before the Commencement exercises. The Prophet's Chamber would afford an unusual degree of freedom and privacy to the infatuated pair before the arrival of Lucretia. It was more than likely that James would view with mixed emotions the arrival of his promised bride.

The change of plan added its grain of desolation to the disquiet with which Crete regarded her approaching journey. She had looked forward to a loving welcome from Rebecca, but Maria was a forbidding stranger on whose hospitality she was reluctant to impose. Overwrought and fearful, anxious to prove to James her warmth and trustfulness, Crete had become extravagantly emotional about Rancie. She made the unknown girl her closest confidante, writing her with pathetic candor of her worship of James and her nervousness over seeing him again. Crete actually invited Rancie to come home with them and spend the winter in Hiram—an invitation which, fortunately for all concerned, Rebecca did not accept.[16]

Crete's trepidation increased as the day of her departure neared. She was to travel under the escort of Albert Pratt, a lawyer at Bryan, Ohio, who had married Crete's school friend, Lizzie Atwood, and was taking his bride on a visit to his native Massachusetts. But at Troy Crete would leave the protection of her friends and move with James into the unknown. She trembled to think that their estrangement might be repeated. "My own Darling One," James reassuringly wrote on June 29, *"I have no such doubts or fears.* I look back upon that terrible experience of last year as perfectly natural under the circumstances—and from the very nature of the case it cannot occur again. It was the rending of the vail . . . between our hearts."[17]

James was "deceiving" Crete, but the deception was no more crass than he practiced on himself. To see him as lightly false and fickle is to miss the point of James. He was bound to Lucretia by the noblest aspirations of his nature. "The love that fills my soul," he wrote her in that same letter of June 29, "is not a wild, delirious passion—a momentary effervescence of feeling—but a calm, strong, deep and resistless current that bears my whole being on toward its object." Here is a nearly scornful mistrust of the profane love which his passionate body had been unable to refuse. In some immutable center of his being, Garfield knew that the joys of the flesh were fleeting and that his soul was linked to Crete's in a union that was sacred and eternal.

But this did not mitigate the shock of Garfield's disappointment when the flesh-and-blood Crete again stood before him. In the roar and grime of the Troy railroad station, he must have seen at last how grievously he had erred. The intricate harmony of his dreams changed to a harsh jangle amid which he bowed in guilty confusion, betrayed by his great capacity for self-deception and his imperative need for love.

Crete was trapped in the nightmare that James had told her could not come again. Suddenly, inexplicably, the warmth expressed in his letters had vanished; he was taciturn and constrained. During her stay of two and a half weeks—all spent at Poestenkill, save three days at Williamstown—he made no explanation of his change of heart. His silence caused Lucretia the sharpest pain she suffered. "How many many times have I felt that if you would only love me just enough to come and tell me all," she later wrote him, "I could endure to know the worst; but to see you shrink away from me as though you could not endure my presence, and hide from me the truth, was almost more than I could bear."[18]

An impassive manner, as usual, hid Crete's feelings, but she could not muster a pretense of happiness. Her gravity impressed young Mary Maxon Hyde, daughter of a leading Disciple in a nearby village where James had often preached. Mary and her sister Abigail attended the Williams Commencement and heard James deliver the Metaphysical Oration, and the two girls were also present at a social gathering at Poestenkill—probably a farewell gathering, for Mary recalled that James was distributing lithographs of his likeness to his friends. Abigail Hyde, in paying her compliments to the preacher's intended, congratulated Lucretia on possessing "the substance" while the rest of them had to be content with "the shadow." "It may be all that I shall get," Lucretia unsmilingly replied. The dry and ambiguous remark stuck in Mary's memory.[19]

In a confusing succession of strangers, Crete had not one friend to lend her support. Williamstown was no better in this respect than Poestenkill. Wilber, threatened by another mental breakdown, had fled the college a month before. The single familiar face at the Commencement exercises was that of Corydon Fuller, whom Crete had never liked. She was pierced with regret that she could not be close to the "darling sister" whom she had longed to love. The fault was not Rebecca's; she treated Crete with affectionate kindness. And, at least at Williamstown, where Maria did not accompany them, they were often alone together, sharing a room and bed. Crete thought that Rebecca was a good and noble girl; she made her a parting gift of Tennyson's poems, but she could not respond to her sisterly advances. Later, from Hiram, Crete wrote Rebecca a letter of bitter self-reproach, saying that she had behaved like "a rock" or "an iceberg." Rebecca replied that it had never entered her mind that Crete had been "cold and unloving"—a statement that was perhaps not quite candid in view of all the circumstances.[20]

For both women the great event of Commencement Day was the Metaphysical Oration. Garfield was in the depths of depression—a "steady, crushing weight of vain sorrow," Rebecca quoted him as saying—but he did not disappoint the expectations of his friends when he stepped forward to make his address on "Matter and Spirit." His presence had never been more commanding nor his tongue more eloquent. The close of his peroration was hailed with swelling applause, and a rain of bright bouquets fell around the orator's feet. Garfield's triumph sustained him, but he flagged visibly after the return to Poestenkill and, as the hour of departure for Ohio neared, he appeared as limp and sickly as a man coming down with fever.[21]

The triangle shuddered apart in stolen interviews, snatched embraces, whispered promises. Garfield vowed that, if he lived, he would come back the next summer. Then the last farewells were decorously spoken, and he and Crete boarded the train for Cleveland. It was not a journey of renewal and reconciliation. Two weeks after his return home, James wrote to Rebecca "those words," as Rebecca herself put it, "that revealed the agony of that trial through which" he was passing.[22]

Crete could not fail to guess some part of the reason for James's gloom and uncertainty, but her comprehension was clouded by lofty standards and tight repressions. It was impossible for her to suspect James and Rebecca of less than shining purity and honor. So great was Crete's trust in Rebecca that, a month later, she poured out her heart to the girl in a letter of wild grief—a confidence all the more pitiable since Rebecca had by this time become her aggressive rival.[23]

Although bound to stifle the base emotions of anger and jealousy, Crete came to realize that she could not maintain a friendship darkened by the unhappy associations of Poestenkill. In November she told James that she was convinced that there had been "somewhere a great wrong" and that "this separation of spirits, once so entirely one," was "no *natural* result." The next month she wrote to Rebecca of "a consciousness of her inability," as Rebecca quoted the letter to James, "to be to me the sister that she would." It was still far from Crete's thoughts that Rebecca had ever behaved toward James with less than perfect decorum. Later, when she was given some intimation of the truth, her resentment was not visited on her errant lover but on the sister who had pledged her love and loyalty in the very hour of betrayal.[24]

Garfield went back to Hiram in black despondency, hopeless of ever finding happiness in love. His heavy mood was not relieved by the situation at the Eclectic. It had become generally recognized that either Principal Hayden or the school must go. Slack administration and mounting debts had lost him the backing of even the most unprogressive trustees. The overworked faculty had grown discouraged and on edge. But Hayden obstinately stuck to his place. Garfield, closely in touch with Hiram affairs, was averse to working under him and had apparently expected that Hayden would shortly be forced out. On the contrary, the fall term of 1856 found Hayden still entrenched and still blandly impervious to hints that he should resign (although he had at least once suggested the possibility himself).[25]

Two years at an eastern college had diminished Garfield's former respect for the pious little principal, and he had undoubtedly been influenced by Wilber, who thought Sutton Hayden sly and scheming; but there was another factor in Garfield's disaffection. The warm opinion of his Hiram friends had given him an inflated conception of his importance to the Eclectic. His interest in the principalship had been so obvious in the spring that Lucretia had written to caution him against rushing things, explaining that both she and Almeda were fearful of his causing unpleasantness. James had airily disclaimed any thought of becoming principal, but his relations with Hayden were strained from the first. Beneath a show of civility, antagonism flashed between them. The old father-and-son relationship was over.[26]

The teachers were frequently left in charge of the school while Hayden traveled around on ineffectual fund-raising trips, but his absence did not remove all occasion for discord. James speedily clashed with another fatherly figure of his schooldays—his once esteemed instructor in the classics, Norman Dunshee.

Dunshee was senior member of the faculty in years and length of service, and he had long been regarded as Hayden's logical successor. Though his teaching methods were conventional, he had some pretensions to scholarship; as a hyperorthodox Disciple, safely limited in his ideas, he appealed to conservatives on the board of trustees. Garfield's opposition to Dunshee looked like an attempt to eliminate the leading contender for the principalship. In emphatically denying any personal interest in the position, Garfield may have convinced himself, but he convinced no one else. There was an element of dedication in his return to Hiram, a sentimental impulse to rescue the dear old school and set it on the path of liberal education. But, even on this high level of motivation, how was he to succeed except as principal? No other member of the teaching staff was eligible, in his view. His old friend, Harvey Everest, was nearly as dry as Dunshee; like the youngster, Harry Rhodes, he had not yet obtained a college degree. Almeda Booth, though admirably fitted to take charge of the school, was disqualified by her sex. Garfield showed no disposition to recommend an outsider; this was a strictly intramural contest between Dunshee and himself. The faculty split into factions, Almeda and Harry Rhodes supporting Garfield on every question of policy or method, while Everest aligned himself with Dunshee.[27]

When the dissension burst into the open in a clatter of rumor and controversy, Garfield proved to have an astonishing number of enemies. Conservative church leaders denounced the ambitions of a young man who had been contaminated by "eastern" ideas. Hiram gossips combed over tales of Garfield's philandering, past and present. With the approach of the trustees' meeting in May 1857, he was the target of more scurrilous gossip than had been provoked by the Mary Hubbell affair. Lizzie Pratt, paying a visit to Hiram, heard that people had told James to his face that his personal conduct would prevent his becoming principal. "The air is foul with slander," James wrote. "Alvah Udall tells me that the two fountains whence flow these aromatic rivulets are the Hayden family, and the Woods of Perry. They are trying to throw me into the cesspool thus formed as Falstaff was tumbled into the Thames."[28]

James, of course, had partisans who rallied to his defense. The students were mostly on his side; so were broadminded church members who wanted to see the school forge ahead and attain college status. With him, too, were Harry and Almeda, a host in herself. The board of trustees included Alvah ("Squire") Udall, who was not a member of the Disciple church, and who had no sympathy with bigots and scandalmongers; William Hayden, Sutton's brother, who was a supporter of Garfield; Isaac Errett, a very able Disciple preacher who became one of the foremost leaders in the history of the church; and Zeb Rudolph, Lucretia's father. When the board met, with Hayden's resignation at last before them, the strength of Garfield's case was apparent. Telling arguments in his favor were his influence over the students and his popularity with congregations and lecture audiences in many towns and villages on the Reserve.

Still there was enough reluctance to make Garfield principal to necessitate a compromise. Hayden himself proposed a solution. The board passed a resolution asking the five teachers to take over the administration of the school for the coming year. The teachers agreed provided satisfactory arrangements could be made. Arrangements were soon concluded. The teachers, composing a Board of Education, met promptly and elected Garfield chairman. Dunshee had gone down in defeat, and James was in charge of the school.[29]

Several months later Garfield gave his version of the "crisis" in terms that disclose his elation over the outcome and his keen resentment of the opposition he had encountered.

> There was much dissatisfaction, as you know, with the Principal, [James wrote Corydon Fuller late in August 1857] and when my enemies feared I might be placed in the chair, they commenced the most unholy warfare that one can well imagine, against me. All the lies of ancient and modern date were arrayed and marshaled against me, and yet I had never by word or action manifested the least desire to gain the Presidency of the Eclectic. However, the Trustees were urging me to take charge of the school, and after a long time I determined to do so, partly to hold it up and partly to stop the mouths of the barking hounds around me. I have taken it, and I am determined that it shall move for *one year*. A score are looking on with vulture eyes and longing for me to fail, and I am resolved that they shall not be gratified, if work and nerve and backbone can avail anything.[30]

When this letter was penned, the new school year was in its fourth week, with "250 students (no primary), as orderly as clock-work, and all hard at work." The "government" had been remodeled, rules published, and a new catalog brought out. The curriculum underwent some changes. Lectures on Sacred History, so dear to the heart of Sutton Hayden, were less frequent as topics such as "Teaching," "Self-Reliance and the Aims and Purposes of Life," and "The American Revolution" were introduced. Physical improvements were in order also. Those attending Commencement in June 1858 observed a new board fence, painted yellow, enclosing the grounds, and trees on the hitherto bare field. In spite of antagonism and friction, Garfield's performance as "chairman" was so impressive that, when the trustees met in the spring, he became principal in name as well as in fact. That same day he was forced in a teachers' meeting to answer a charge brought by Dunshee and Everest that he "had plotted to get the leadership of the school."[31]

During the three years in which the Eclectic was Garfield's major interest, he made an outstanding record as educator and administrator.

Yet the little victory at Hiram seems scarcely commensurate with the cost. Garfield, with his inordinate need for approval, provoked ugly attack and lasting enmity—for the small end that he might stand first in a merely temporary employment. The interlude at the Eclectic illustrates the mounting power of his ambition: To have the leading part thrust upon him—to yield in modest acquiescence to the wishes of his friends—had become the boldly legible signature of Garfield's public conduct.

From the beginning Garfield's speaking engagements afforded his greatest distraction from his personal troubles. Taking trains, meeting strangers—Brother This, Sister That—losing himself in the ebullition of his eloquence, he gained temporary surcease from tearful brooding over the past and shrinking dread of the future. He entered new fields, was active in organizing "Teachers' Institutes" that offered concentrated courses in pedagogy, lectured on scientific and literary subjects, and made his mark in the presidential campaign of 1856 as an effective speaker on the Republican side. His weight fell off, his throat grew hoarse and sore, he was repeatedly on the verge of physical breakdown; but he found it impossible to rest. He fled from the worried eyes of his mother and sisters. Almeda and Harry Rhodes were the only people in whose company he could at first find some measure of relief.

Harry, the German student whom Almeda had called "tremendous smart," had become a full-time teacher at the school in 1856. He was like Garfield in many ways: brilliant, self-doubting, ambitious, brimming with misty sentiment and idealism. A youth of contagious enthusiasm, he lacked Garfield's capacity for hard work. Forceful and overvehement in the pulpit, he was an uninspiring teacher who was unable to conceal his boredom with routine and even dozed off in class. But he was never bored with James. Although they now met as colleagues, Rhodes still regarded his former teacher with a boyish hero worship (he would follow Garfield's example by going to Williams to get his degree) and Garfield warmly loved him in return. They roomed together, sleeping in the same bed, and often talked until late of life and letters and their own fervent plans for the future.[32]

As Harry satisfied Garfield's need for intense masculine friendship, so Almeda was the loving woman on whom he leaned after his return to Hiram. Boarding, as often before, in the same house as James, she stood ready to mend his clothes or scratch his head, play chess or nurse him through a bout of fever. Her mind was wise, her talk was stimulating; it was with her that James found comfort for his abject loneliness.

Few people suspected that this stout, coarse-featured woman, devoid of grace or coquetry and indifferent to her dress, possessed a strongly passionate nature. To her pupils she seemed old—she was thirty-three in 1856—and dissociated from life outside the classroom or the study. It was told that she had been promised to a sweetheart who died, but the story does not appear to have been widely known, and it was perhaps too implausible to be believed. Lucretia, one of Miss Booth's most devoted pupils, thought it laughable to connect her with marriage and domesticity. While still young, Almeda had accepted the world's estimate, crushed back her vehement emotions, and compromised on motherly intimacies with men students. There was always some confused and confiding youth to spill out his woes and plead for advice. She had not been entirely unhappy before she met James.[33]

Almeda was hopelessly in love with James by the summer of 1855, and probably earlier. When he turned to her after the disappointment of his meeting with Crete, she had refused to advise him, but there must have been a flash of hope in her breast. Years later she wrote him of her "dreadful agony and abandonment" when he rushed off to the reconciliation with Crete at Ravenna. A year later he turned back to her in despair. She did not want to be broken down again, but she grasped at every chance to see him, to read with him or play chess. A change came over her. She appeared more feminine in manner, took more pains with her dress, and cultivated artistic interests. Inwardly she was on fire. She suffered humiliations because she was consumed, as though she had suddenly gone mad, with suspicion and jealousy. At least twice she was unwise enough to follow James to the room of another woman teacher. She vexed him with scenes and spells of coldness. He sometimes grew impatient and spoke sharply, but they always made up in the end. James could not do without Almeda; she had a place in his life that no one else could fill. He thought of her as another self.[34]

Inevitably there was talk—so much talk that it quickly reached the lonely Larabee farm where Eliza seldom saw her gossips. It touched Almeda lightly. Scandal glanced away from the image of a high-minded spinster, leaving it unscarred; but not in the eyes of Eliza Garfield. She credited Almeda with the wiles of Circe and advised James to change his boardinghouse, mend his own clothes, comb his own head. Eliza never forgave Almeda for her designs on James and never could stand the sight of her.[35]

James was incapable of deliberate cruelty to one who loved him, but his treatment of Almeda was blindly selfish; he indulged his need for her love without heed of the stormy emotions he aroused or the pitiful hopes he inspired. When things went wrong between them, he smugly ascribed Almeda's jealous outbursts to an illiberal conception of "friendship." It is obvious that James did not give his full attention to poor Almeda's heartaches. He was absorbed by a dilemma in which she had no part—the clash between his dreams of Crete and Rancie, the sacred love and the profane.[36]

Letters from Rancie showered James and kept him in a fluster. Coldly viewed, they are wearisome, even at times repellent. Rancie's normally effusive style gushes with fancy endearments, of which "Dearest vein of my heart" is perhaps the most bizarre, and there are frequent evocations of erotic images and sensual acts. Much of this suggests Maria's tutelage, and the impression is deepened by the scornful dismissal of Lucretia as a mistake of Garfield's "undisciplined heart." Rancie has become openly bent on marrying James herself. The knowledge that all is not right in Hiram—knowledge imparted generously by both James and Crete—has kindled her hopes that the graduation of James at Williams has not spelled the end of his romance with her. Her passionate letters are a desperate effort to cling to the source of the greatest happiness she has known.[37]

In the first months at Hiram Crete was too crushed by grief to face the future. "I take no note of time now," she wrote Rebecca in October. "The hours come and go . . . I am only conscious of being whirled along in this great maelstrom of life. . . . Oh, Ranca, how your last letter made me weep. It seemed that my heart must break—that I could not endure this dreadful life another hour." She and James did not meet, but they could not avoid occasional encounters. In the small social round of Hiram, each day must have brought its added wounds, stabs of pitying eyes, and tactless questions. Yet Lucretia appeared cheerful. Her mother, aching for her, took pride in her firm character. "I have often wondered at your self-control . . . when I knew your heart was sinking within you," Arabella wrote, after Crete had summoned the courage to leave home.[38]

Crete's courage began to revive when she ceased to struggle against her love for James and resolved to remain faithful to their engagement, however much he had changed. In the last year she had come to see him with clearer eyes, to admit his treacherous volatility and romanticism, and to recognize the drive to self-destruction that might bring his talents to shipwreck. Yet she felt bound irrevocably to this complex man, striving, suffering, potentially great. At length, on a Saturday in early November, James came to her home. Although she locked herself in her room and cried after he had gone, Sunday was for her "a strangely happy day." She wrote him a letter, at the close of which she invited him to call and sit by her and read on winter evenings. Hiram, however, was an unfortunate place in which to patch the delicate fabric of a reconciliation. Its mores demanded that James and

Crete should either marry or avoid each other. Friendship between them was frowned on as an affront to the proprieties. The desire to remove one ground for unpleasantness and gossip surely influenced Crete's decision to go to Cleveland and teach at a district school in the spring term of 1857. Criticism of James was growing clamorous; while Crete had private reservations about his conduct at the Eclectic, she was up in arms at a disparaging word from anyone else.[39]

Hours of loneliness and trial were in store for Crete at Cleveland, but she was compensated by the cultural opportunities offered by the ambitious young city. She took painting lessons, heard instructive sermons and lectures, and finally, shaking off a prohibition of her Disciple training, began to attend the theater. On weekends she frequently saw James. Like new friends for whom neither past nor future existed, they strolled about the city or stayed indoors to play chess or chuckle over *Pickwick*. Sometimes Crete's pride rebelled against passively waiting for James to make up his mind, but she could not resist the pleasure of being with him. "When I see you seemingly *not miserable* in my presence," she told him, "I count every moment . . . a treasure."[40]

James had slowly come to realize that his involvement with Rebecca had been unwise and wrong. By his own statement, he had never thought of marrying her, but he could not forget the fascination of their love affair. As the time approached for the promised reunion in Poestenkill, he talked earnestly to Crete of his divided feelings. She was grateful for his confidence and eager to forgive. His highflown parting words, *"courage* for my sake," did not ring ironically in her ears but gave her a little strength. In spite of herself, Crete was beginning to hope. "James dearest," she wrote him, "do not leave me here long to suffer. Almost I feel like pleading with you to *know your own heart.*"[41]

Maria and Rancie called James eastward with an equally desperate need. Soon after his departure the summer before, Maria's illness had taken a turn for the worse, and reports of her health had been ominous ever since. Late in April she had sent James a letter filled with loneliness and longing. "More than at any time before is my heart now begging for your blessed living presence. . . . If you were only here, I am sure I should be quite well."[42]

Such an appeal was potent to stir James to the depths, but his slow and crablike approach to Poestenkill revealed his misgivings. Though he made a trip to Virginia, he did not start for the East for nearly three weeks after the Hiram Commencement; having at length set out, he tarried at Philadelphia to visit the historical monuments. Left in ignorance of his plans, Maria and Rancie had despaired of his ever coming. At the last moment Rancie sped from Lewisboro to the rendezvous—a fact which James did not mention to Crete—and the triangle was reunited for the better part of the next two weeks. On an excursion to New York in late July he took Rebecca with him. She accompanied him to another consultation there with the phrenologist, L. N. Fowler, and made notes of a further analysis of his "bumps." They did not go to Lewisboro, perhaps because Rebecca's brother Ebenezer had come home the previous autumn, cured of the gold fever by two weeks of roughing it in California.[43]

Reality, for once, did not fall short of Garfield's dreams. At Poestenkill the days passed in an ecstasy all the sweeter because it was fated to end. James was frank in stating that he must keep his promise to Crete, but he deplored the duty that constrained him. Perhaps Crete's image grew blurred in the supercharged atmosphere of triune love. Maria, her health wonderfully improved, was in exalted spirits. She had decided to send her boy, Jonas, to the Eclectic and was sustained by anticipation of this link with James. Rancie clung to James without hope or consolation. She had written down Fowler's advice to Garfield: "You want a wife—refined, genteel, graceful, of a philosophic mind, sharp, lively, sprightly, forehead high and broad." The description fitted Rancie, but she knew—and was withered by the knowledge—that James would never be hers.[44]

Garfield's resolution faltered when the hour of parting came. "In those awful parting moments" he whispered to Rancie a doubt that he could take his marriage vows. The house, after his going, was like an empty shrine. His chair stood at the table, his napkin was untouched. His pillow kept "the marks of its last pressure." *Hyperion* and a fan lay abandoned on the bed. The desolate women let them lie there.[45]

Garfield took up his duties as chairman of the Eclectic in moody discontent. Memories of Poestenkill clustered thick about him, and the arrival of Jonas Learned (bearing the gift of a dressing gown made by Rebecca) stirred "a restless, homesick longing." On an early visit to Cleveland, James unbosomed himself to Crete. His account of his connection with Rebecca was drastically edited, but he did not minimize the tenacity of his attachment. Crete had no word of blame or bitterness. They went on seeing each other as before. When a series of preaching engagements took James to Cleveland and Newburgh during the autumn of 1857, he always dropped in at the cozy room which Crete was then sharing with an old friend, Mary White; he sat companionably with the two girls beside the grate or carried Crete off to take a walk or attend some church service. On one memorable Saturday evening, he took her to the theater. *Ingomar the Barbarian* ended Garfield's long prejudice against the stage and opened to him a new world of stimulation and delight.[46]

Crete had made clear to Garfield that he was free to marry Rebecca without reproach on her part. Many weeks later he told her that he had never wished a release from their engagement. Bachelorhood, not Rebecca, was his alternative to their marriage. "I must either pass my life with you or pass it alone," he wrote Crete in October. He admitted the "terrible power" of the fears that sometimes overcame him. "But most of the time," he went on, "I feel as if we had strength enough of mind and heart to live together and bless each other. . . . May God grant to give us peace and a life together." Some earnest assurances were plainly due to Crete; Hiram had learned the name of Rebecca Selleck and was buzzing with a report that Professor Garfield intended to marry her.[47]

The report had its origin in the rambling talk of poor, unstable Charles Wilber, who had come home on a visit after a year spent in retirement on an uncle's farm in Illinois. He knew more about Garfield's complicated love affairs than anyone but Garfield himself—he had seen the situation at Poestenkill and probably read some of Rebecca's incandescent love letters—and he had worked himself into a state of morbid concern about Lucretia. On learning that James was still vacillating, Wilber became greatly agitated. In some twisted way he was himself in love with Crete (as her mother suspected after hearing him rattle on), but his solicitude caused Crete much distress that autumn.

On his way back to Illinois Charles called at Crete's boardinghouse. It is likely that she received this old friend warmly and at first talked openly of her unhappy situation. The remark that Charles ascribed to her, "I could die for James, but it is an event not likely to take place," has a ring of sad irony that is characteristic of Crete. But she became indignant when Charles spoke ill of James and dropped dark hints about Rebecca's letters. The interview left Crete badly upset. Charles returned to his uncle's farm in a state of maudlin admiration of her loyalty and presently resolved to come to the noble girl's assistance. In the character of her trusted confidant, he sent an emotional appeal to Maria Learned, asking that she and Rebecca give James up and end Lucretia's suffering. Deeply offended, both women protested to James. Lucretia learned with abject humiliation that she had been represented as a suppliant for his love.[48]

Her pride stung and her temper high, Lucretia wrote Charles a severe letter, breaking off their friendship. James felt only a passing annoyance. Charles, though repeatedly proven unreliable, was his friend and hence was to be forgiven. A lull came over Garfield's tempestuous spirit as the winter set in. He had raved intemperately against his enemies, but now his anger calmed. He became absorbed in preparing and delivering a lecture on his beloved Walter Scott. He pursued a private study of the law begun the winter before. He enjoyed the worshipful affection of many of his pupils, in particular Jonie Learned and a second cousin on the Garfield side, Louisa Letcher. Her father, William Letcher—brother of Captain Amos of the distant days on the canal—had entrusted his "girl" to Professor Garfield's care. James saw much of Louisa and took her to spend the weekend after Christmas with his family at Solon.[49]

The Eclectic had no Christmas vacation, but Crete came home for the holidays, and James spent most evenings at the Rudolphs' hospitable house. There he watched out the old year of 1857, reading aloud the mournful stanzas of Prentice's "The Closing Year." His thoughts, as 1858 came in, were earnest and contrite. "Oh my God," he prayed, "may the sins of this closing year be blotted from the great book of thy remembrance, and my soul be fitted for heaven."[50]

Promptly on New Year's Day, as though to test the strength of Garfield's resolution, word came that Maria Learned was near death. Jonas left at once for home. James waited out a week in racking suspense. Then, on hearing from Rancie that Maria was calling for him, he canceled all his engagements and started for Poestenkill. The crisis of Maria's illness—lung fever—had passed before he arrived. On the night of his coming he sat with Rebecca beside the sickbed until two o'clock. The next day—Sunday—he spoke twice in church; during the rest of the day and all that night he sat with Maria. After a couple of hours of sleep and a few more with his two friends, he took his leave. "How strong the cord that binds me there! God help me! and bless them," he wrote in his diary. Rebecca was left desolate. "Before you had passed through the outer door," she wrote to James, "I sprang after you and caught one little glimpse of your precious form, and then I went to the window, where I could watch every movement—as if you were going from me forever." On Wednesday James was back in class; Rebecca stayed on with Maria.[51]

Shuddering over the "finalities" and "isolating effects" of marriage, James finally arranged with Crete in April to "try life in union before many months." They began to make plans for a home. Should they build or rent a house—or take rooms and board? They both wished to build, but time and money were short. Crete did not envision a small cottage for the two of them. "I have no idea of opening a *boarding establishment,*" she wrote, "still I would like to have a few of the choice ones with us." She desired "a nice little place" for Eliza, and room also for her Cleveland music teacher, who was being considered for a position at the Eclectic, and for Almeda. Good houses for rent were hard to find in the tiny village, and James did not want to leave the hill. Early in June, Crete told him that if he would be satisfied she would consent to board for a time, and she suggested the chamber of Mrs. Northrop.[52]

Meanwhile Crete had completed her course in art and gone to Bryan in northwest Ohio to stay with Lizzie Pratt and teach a drawing class. Soon after the Eclectic Commencement, Garfield took his mother to visit Cousin William Letcher in the nearby town of West Unity. He and Crete had several unsatisfactory meetings, from which James abruptly rushed away. She was hurt to see that he did not like to be with her, but in fact James could not find contentment anywhere. His vacation was an odyssey of frantic unrest. He dashed about Indiana, calling on relatives, visiting colleges, and looking into business opportunities. He was hurrying his business wherever he went, he wrote Crete from Indianapolis at the end of June. A tour of Illinois with Wilber followed the same pattern. The high point of this trip was an hour's visit in Chicago with Stephen A. Douglas, who was running for re-election to the United States Senate and was soon to debate a backwoods lawyer named Abraham Lincoln. James stopped at Bryan to see Crete on his way home. It was another miserable meeting, and she cried after he left.[53]

James was like a condemned man who panics as he nears the prison gates. In full flight from marriage, he wrote Rebecca yearning letters and went with Almeda to visit friends. He had given Crete to understand that he was marrying her from a sense of duty; she had proudly vowed that she would not marry without his love. Now, with a breaking heart, she assented to her fate. Having lost faith in their future, these two seemed to lack the strength to draw apart. They bowed to the inevitable and set the wedding day.[54]

On November 11, 1858, a goodly company gathered at Zeb Rudolph's dignified white house. James, for some reason, had asked a Presbyterian minister to officiate instead of one of his Disciple brethren. Crete's young sister, Nellie Rudolph, and a bevy of other maidens dressed in white attended the bride and helped to serve the refreshments. So Garfield's long struggle against monogamy came to an end at last, and he and Lucretia were made man and wife.[55]

# CHAPTER 6

# TRANSITION

THE NORTHEAST corner bedroom at Mrs. Northrop's boardinghouse had a walnut cottage bedstead, draped in white, and a marble-topped bureau with an oval glass above it. A stove and a wash-sink served comfort and convenience; nor had the reigning taste in furnishings been neglected. A walnut teapoy (where had Crete learned the word?) was placed beside the bed. There was a gaily patterned carpet, and the walls were brightened by sketches in crayon or oils. On a shaded crimson mat on the center table, the lamp stood among the emblems of domesticity: the newspaper, the account book, Crete's sewing things, the inkstand, a little glass hat filled with matches. This was the place where the Garfields sat to talk or read or work; the place where Almeda sat with them. Her room was right next door. James often sat there, too. "We live in the same room most of the time," he wrote to Harry Rhodes.[1]

Though amply forewarned about her husband's friendships, Crete could not have expected to see quite so much of Almeda. At home and abroad, she was their nearly constant companion. People accepted them as a threesome and included Miss Booth in their greetings and invitations to the new Mrs. Garfield. Shortly after his marriage, James enlisted Almeda's help in preparing for a debate with one William Denton, a popular lecturer on scientific subjects. This project occupied their every spare hour for several weeks. Moreover, since Harry had gone to complete his studies at Williams, Miss Booth was Garfield's mainstay at the school. In the previous spring Dunshee's hostility had gone from bad to worse. He and Everest had publicly accused Garfield of plotting to get the principalship. Their opposition again flamed up in the winter when it was learned that some students were playing chess. The two teachers—"as unreasonable and incorrigible as bulls," James wrote—joined Father Ryder and his Hiram faction in demanding that chess be prohibited at the school. Almeda was Garfield's stanch defender in the "chess war" as in every other dispute. He leaned on her judgment. When she praised a sermon or speech, his spirits soared. Her approval was "the end of criticism."[2]

Before her marriage, Crete had overheard Miss Booth say to Mary White that James was "one of that class of men who did not want a wife for society." She had not then believed that this was true, but she came to think that it might be. She was cruelly hurt—"it has pierced my heart like an arrow"—by the thought of sharing "only the commonplace things" with her husband. Above all else, she longed to be his wife "in the truest, noblest sense," and sometimes his inattentiveness made her cry or speak sharply, and sometimes she would try to draw him into the emotional discussions that husbands learn to dread. By some miracle of discipline and good feeling she and Almeda remained friends; but Crete often wished that Harry were there to make "a family together," Harry paired with Almeda and James left to his wife.[3]

Almeda thought that James seemed contented and happy. The accomplished fact of marriage had at first dispelled his gloom and armed him with resolve to make the best of things; but, in the depths of his being, he was no more happy than Crete. In lovemaking he thought that his sensitive little wife was cold and unresponsive. They were back in their old spiral of misunderstanding, failing, and hurting each other.[4]

Her great love for James would one day teach Crete how to make him happy, but that time did not come during the three years that they spent at Mrs. Northrop's.

The debate with William Denton marked a rise in Garfield's reputation throughout the region. An English spiritualist and freethinker, Denton was a dramatic orator and a man of some scientific training, reputed to be a graduate of Oxford. His theory of creation by "Spontaneous Generation and Progressive Development" had gained wide attention in American lyceums and other forums. This was his fortieth debate on the subject, and he met the Hiram schoolmaster in confident expectation of victory.[5]

It is hard for people of a scientifically oriented age to comprehend the alarm with which the churchgoing public of the nineteenth century learned of the new discoveries in the field of natural science. The battle over Darwinism was not yet joined at the time of the Denton-Garfield debate—the *Origin of Species* was published nearly a year later—but heralds of an evolutionary creation were already vocal among students of geology, botany, and zoology. The revealed truths of the Bible were threatened by the discovery of fossil remains of immense antiquity and by increasing knowledge of the vast multiplicity of plant and animal species and their far-flung distribution. Creation as an act of God, immutable and fixed, became a doubtful concept, and the limitless capacity of Noah's Ark was open to derision. With Genesis under attack, the whole firm structure of the Bible seemed to tremble, and Christians in dismay turned to their religious leaders for guidance. This was the mood of uncertainty in which men thronged to Chagrin Falls in the last week of December 1858, packing a large hall twice a day, for five days, to hear a preacher challenge a self-styled scientist.

Though Garfield was popularly regarded as the champion of the Bible, he in fact declined to stand on the shaky ground of Genesis. A month of intensive preparation, during which he and Almeda had scanned the recent scientific publications—especially those on geology—had opened Garfield's eyes to views and principles of which he had never heard in college. He resisted Denton's efforts to lead him into a general discussion of the Bible and hammered insistently at his opponent's "development" theory. Denton was not a Lyell or a Darwin, and he had not produced a theory which could withstand an adroit, closely reasoned attack. The climax of the debate was for Garfield a profoundly stirring experience. "Then for the last two days and evenings, it was a fierce, hand-to-hand fight," he reported to Rhodes. "I felt my whole soul rise up when he came out in his strength, and I may say to you that in almost every encounter I felt the iron of his strength bend in my grasp. . . . On the whole, it was by far the most momentous occasion of my life. For none was I ever better prepared, and on none did I ever succeed better." [6]

With a sure instinct for the contemporary, Garfield had appropriated a live intellectual issue. He proceeded to make vigorous use of it as invitations to speak piled on his desk. His lecture course on "Geology and Religion" became widely popular and did much to blunt the adverse criticisms of his conduct which continued to echo from Hiram. The tale that he kept a barrel of beer in Mrs. Northrop's cellar—a tale that, to Crete's regret, was based on fact—was exaggerated and exploited in the telling. He was accused of sympathy with slaveholders because he refused to join the hue and cry of the extreme abolitionists, among whom Dunshee and Everest were locally prominent. The angriest outbursts against Garfield were provoked in May 1859, when the Eclectic trustees dropped Dunshee from the faculty and offered his place to Rhodes. Garfield protested his ignorance of the action, but it had followed his earnest wish, and certain remarks in his letters to Rhodes—particularly the assurance, given in April, that the trustees would "dispense with Norman"—put it beyond question that he had come to an understanding with his friends on the board. It is fair to say that Garfield's patience had been sorely tried and that he was entitled to cooperation from the teaching staff. For a time Dunshee attracted some sympathy by posing as a martyr to his antislavery convictions, but he was intemperate in his charges of plots and politics, and interest in his wrongs gradually dwindled. A shabby, defeated figure, he vanished from the Hiram scene, leaving behind a lingering sense that he had been unfairly treated.[7]

The greatest effect of the debate with Denton and the ensuing lecture program was to recommend Garfield to local Republican leaders as an eligible candidate for the Ohio legislature. He had usually appeared to ignore suggestions that he was fitted for public life. Though an active Republican campaigner since 1856, he had confined his affiliation to opposing the spread of slavery. He had continued to take a supercilious view of party methods and to despise politicians in general as a reprobate and alcoholic crew.

Yet it was toward a career in politics that Garfield, in his ambivalent and crablike way, had all along been treading. No one had made him a bona fide offer, and that was an operative deterrent to a man who dreaded the posture of self-seeking. His debate over studying law had masked the basic ambition, but it was exposed, in this same spring of 1859, by Garfield's project for a political foundation at Hiram. The plan was altruistic. Garfield and Rhodes, with Almeda as their counselor-in-chief, were to use teaching as a stepping-stone to a beneficent political influence, local at first, but ultimately far-reaching. This utterly silly proposition—too visionary even for Harry to entertain—seemed to indicate that Garfield was hopelessly unadapted to practical politics. Yet the first practical overture found him alert and receptive. With his nomination as a candidate for the Ohio senate, Garfield prepared to play his first small part on the stage of his future career.[8]

Before the nomination was made, but not before feelers had been put forth, Garfield took a three-week holiday with Crete and Almeda. An invitation to deliver a Master's Oration at the Williams Commencement had fitted conveniently with his desire to attend Harry's graduation and to make a tour of new scenes on the way. Two student-teachers from the Eclectic went along on the first part of the tour, of which the high points—after the inevitable stop at Niagara Falls—were Montreal, Quebec, and the White Mountains. Garfield's love of the sea was gratified by two steamer trips, from Portland, Maine, to Boston and from the old Connecticut port of Stonington to New York. The students then returned home, and the others—including Harry, who had joined the party at Montreal—paid a visit to West Troy, where the Learneds now made their home, with Rancie as their frequent guest. Harry had become an intimate friend of Rancie and Maria and a link between them and James, and news had also traveled back and forth through Jonas Learned and occasionally through his father, who stopped at Hiram when his lumber interests took him to the West. But James had not notified the women of his marriage, nor had he communicated directly with them since, and he had hesitated to propose a visit with Crete and Almeda in tow. After sounding out Jonas, however, he had written Maria and received ecstatic assurances that they would all be welcome. Jonas had not been able to say what Rebecca's attitude might be, but he had warned James, "It could hardly be expected of her that she should be *just* as when you was here a long time ago." This was surely one of the most doleful of reunions. Maria had been very ill with fever and ague; she was, she had written James a few weeks earlier, "very weak and sallow and old." Rebecca, who had been sent for to care for Maria, had been ill too, her lovely face disfigured by the marks of erysipelas. But these dear ones loved James desperately still, and he would not wholly cut himself off from them again.[9]

The final event of the outing was the Master's Oration at Williams. Garfield had obviously wanted the honor, but he had been reluctant to work up a speech and had listlessly appealed to Harry to suggest a suitable theme. Since the students had recently formed an art association to collect paintings and engravings for the college, Harry had advised that a discourse on aesthetics would be timely. The recommendation was unfortunate. Like most of his countrymen, Garfield was naively ignorant of the fine arts. His ignorance must be pardoned—there was nothing to be seen in America except second rate paintings and sculpture or copies of famous works—but less excusable were the sanctity with which he invested these objects and the pretentiousness of his claim to a close communion with "Art." A mostly undistinguished flow of verbiage entitled Garfield to affix the letters "M.A." to his name.[10]

More mundane concerns awaited him at Hiram. A few days after the Eclectic opened, Garfield was requested by a group of Ravenna citizens to permit his name to be placed before the Ohio Republican convention as a candidate for the vacant seat of senator from the district comprising Portage and Summit counties. Having conferred with trustees and teachers, Garfield gave his consent. He stipulated that he would make no pledges or exert himself to obtain the nomination, and he stressed the point that he was not running of his own notion but at the instance of his friends. Though Garfield had some nervous doubts of his prospects, all went well at the preliminary caucuses and he was duly nominated by the convention, at which he put in a modest appearance. To succeed the zealously antislavery Governor Salmon P. Chase, the Republicans named a conservative businessman, William Dennison of Columbus. At a meeting at Akron a week later, Garfield met Chase and occupied the platform while the Governor held forth for nearly three hours. Garfield's own speech was short on this occasion, but Chase did not forget him.[11]

The news that Garfield had entered the arena of politics was grimly received by the local Disciples, already headshaking over rumors that he was studying law. "I always thought he'd go to the D——l *anyhow*," the embattled Father Ryder was quoted as saying, "and if he goes to the *Capitol I am sure he will*." But Garfield was by no means ready to burn his bridges behind him. He regarded himself, in the event of his election, as a school principal taking a leave of absence during two consecutive winter terms. Obviously Garfield could not afford to give up the position which was his main source of support, but the financial motive is insufficient to explain the tenacity with which he held on to his Disciple connections. Except for the three summer weeks in the East, he was indefatigable in preaching at annual meetings, and every autumn weekend found him addressing his devoted congregations. Clinging to the old life, Garfield seemed bent on proving—possibly to himself— that its direction had not changed. Nevertheless, in the course of the campaign, he made some thirty political speeches averaging two hours each. They were concerned with the overshadowing question of limiting the extension of slavery; and, since Summit County was safely Republican, they were mainly made on the more doubtful ground of Portage County.[12]

Garfield could talk movingly of the slaves and make men feel their wrongs, but he was still the advocate of gradual legal methods of redress. Early in the campaign he took an unpopular stand in a phase of the controversy that was peculiar to Ohio. Judge Joseph R. Swan, a Republican member of the state supreme court, had come under hot attack for sustaining the conviction of certain Oberlin citizens who had obstructed the arrest of an escaped slave. Garfield did not like the Fugitive Slave Law, but he thought that the judge was bound by it and by the legal precedents based on it. His published statement to that effect antagonized the radical Republicans, and for the rest of the campaign he was roundly abused by them as well as by the Democrats. Garfield's conservatism, however, was rudely jolted by John Brown's raid in October. When the old man was hanged a few weeks later, Garfield was torn by an inner conflict, unable to justify Brown's violent acts but feeling that he died a hero in the cause of the oppressed. He listened with strong emotion to a fiery speech made by Albert Gallatin Riddle, a prominent antislavery lawyer of Cleveland and a newly elected congressman. At this moment Garfield was ready to follow the abolitionists all the way. "Now as of old," he wrote Riddle in tones of evangelical fervor, " 'without the shedding of blood there is no remission' of so great a sin."[13]

Some weeks before this letter was written, Garfield had won his own election, carrying his district by a slightly larger majority than the head of the ticket. The New Year of 1860 saw him settled at Columbus, sharing a room with another Republican state senator, Jacob Dolson Cox, and preparing to take part in the inaugural ceremonies of the incoming governor, William Dennison.

Garfield had left the Hiram circle with a full heart, unable to restrain his tears as he read the loving note that Harry had stuck in his hat. He sent back a stream of lonely, longing letters, some of them jointly addressed to his Hiram "trinity," but from the first he was swept into the current of new friendships and experiences at Columbus. Promptly on New Year's Day he called at the Chase mansion and was effusively received. (Chase was a candidate for the United States Senate.) Garfield enjoyed the company of his roommate, Cox, and another senator, Professor James Monroe of Oberlin, both of whom had married daughters of Charles G. Finney, the noted revivalist and educator. He was delighted also with the warmhearted Bascom family with whom they boarded. They were surrounded by petitioners and "nearly killed with kindness," and Garfield was besieged by a special lobby of scientists who knew of his lectures and wanted him to sponsor a bill for a new geological survey of Ohio.[14]

At twenty-eight Garfield was the youngest member of the legislature. Against an unfamiliar background, eager and trying hard, he appears not only young but juvenile. He was boyishly impatient to get started, to don the legislative armor and attract attention on the senate floor and in the press. Cox, a self-contained lawyer of thirty-one, marveled at Garfield's boisterous spirits and was appalled by his demonstrative manners—especially the rib-cracking hugs in which he was prone to envelop his roommate in the street. William Dean Howells, a young poet who was working on the *Ohio State Journal,* remembered a morning when Garfield came into the busy newspaper office with a volume of Tennyson and declaimed "The poet in a golden clime was born" in his rich orator's voice. In the senate one day, Garfield impulsively sprang up to support a joint resolution inviting the members of the Tennessee and Kentucky legislatures to extend a projected trip to Cincinnati into an official visit to Columbus. The resolution passed, and Governor Dennison made Garfield the chairman of a committee charged with delivering the invitation. Before January was out, Garfield found himself at Louisville, attending a grand banquet in honor of the two legislatures and, with thoughts of sin and bloodshed laid aside, making an impassioned plea for the Union and asserting that the West could not be divided.[15]

The official visit was promptly paid, with more speeches and receptions, but Garfield was not heard from on this occasion. Perhaps he recognized the futility of his gesture, or perhaps he was merely exhausted after the excitement at Louisville. While spending the next weekend at Hiram, he succumbed to the pain of "brain fever," more agonizing than ever before. He dragged himself back to Columbus to vote for Chase, whose candidacy for the United States Senate he had supported against the "weak backed Republicans"; but he was for some days longer limp and dizzy with the persistent diarrhea from which he habitually suffered as a result of nervous strain.[16]

The mission to Louisville had attracted attention not altogether favorable. Garfield was blamed for spending the taxpayers' money on junkets and—by extremists of his own party—for consorting with slaveholders. His speech, however, had been well received at home. Whatever their differences on the subject of slavery, Ohioans shared a common alarm over southern threats of secession. Garfield had been a true spokesman of his state when he declared the indivisible unity of the West and denied that a boundary could ever be drawn across the Mississippi Valley. The applause for these sentiments must have been some consolation for his inability to arouse a similar enthusiasm at Columbus. He had relied on oratory to make his mark, only to learn that the Ohio senate had an aversion to "set speeches." His friends, he knew, were disappointed in his showing. Harry plainly intimated that Garfield had not taken the place that they expected, that there had been a lack of outspoken conviction and solid legal knowledge.[17]

Garfield would make a more substantial contribution the next winter, but his service at Columbus was largely an apprenticeship in which he learned "the run of Legislative business" and formed valuable connections with Ohio politicians. The most prominent of his new friends was Salmon P. Chase. With his eye on the Republican nomination for President, the former governor had been exceedingly anxious to demonstrate his strength in Ohio, and Garfield's allegiance in the successful but hard-fought contest in the legislature won Chase's lasting gratitude.[18]

Consistently loyal support also brought Garfield close to the able Governor Dennison, and they became personally devoted friends in 1861. A well-to-do banker and financier who had been trained in the law, Dennison was an early forerunner of the Republican businessman-

in-politics. Garfield rightly judged that his "aristocracy" would not en-
dear him to the people. Dennison served only one term in elective office but remained influential in national Republican councils.[19]

Dolson Cox's legal training and practical judgment did much to
direct and stabilize the inexperienced Garfield at the outset of his legislative career. He was especially useful as Garfield's mentor on questions
of law and parliamentary procedure. Their differences of temperament did not impede a strong reciprocal liking and respect. They were
basically in agreement on most political issues and stood together in opposition to Democrats and timid elements of their own party, former
Democrats and "fossil" Whigs. Cox was strongly antislavery in sentiment, and his influence, with that of Professor Monroe, may be credited in some part for Garfield's steadily increasing firmness on the
slavery issue. Their half accidental arrangement to share a room at the
Bascoms' was a stroke of good fortune for Garfield. William T. Bascom
was chairman of the Central Republican Committee of Ohio and also
acted as secretary to Governor Dennison. Familiar with personalities
and close to newspaper publishers, he was an admirable guide in the
intricacies of state politics. He grew very fond of both Garfield and
Cox, recognized them as men of strong ambition, and desired to promote their interests; but he was not a little puzzled by Garfield's lim-
petlike attachment to Hiram. "Bascom says," Cox wrote Garfield
shortly after the close of the session, " 'we must get him out of that
place and start him on another tack . . . it is not his sphere for life.' "[20]

During his first winter at Columbus, Garfield was a dual personality—a politician on weekdays and a preacher on Sundays. Disciple congregations hummed with rumors that he had been seen drinking in
public. To take a social glass was normal for the weekday Garfield, but
for the Sunday evangelist it was a cause of scandal. He had to arrive at
a choice, one way or the other, and indecision made him tense and nervous. He was also upset by the overwrought state into which Almeda
had fallen; she wrote him passionate letters and wildly resented his
request to be more discreet. Her agitation may well have been caused
by signs that Crete was expecting a child.[21]

Both James and Crete were trying bravely to make a success of their
marriage, but they were often engulfed by what he later described as "a
sadness almost bordering on despair." Garfield's edginess was marked
when he introduced Crete and Harry to Columbus in the late winter.
Crete, who had been hurt by his indifference to having her with him,
was rebuffed when she tried to talk over their troubles, and was informed that their marriage had been a great mistake. Harry thought
that James was "shattered and unsettled" by ambition and new inter-

ests, and he taxed him with "estrangement" from his old friends. Nor were things much better when the session ended and James returned to Hiram. He took an extra room at Mrs. Northrop's and shut himself up with his law books, preparing to take his bar examination the next winter. In May he was off to Ravenna and Warren to share with Republican friends the excitement over the nomination of Abraham Lincoln, a westerner and a conservative on the slavery question. He agreed to deliver a Fourth of July address at Ravenna and labored over its composition. Crete's longing for her unborn baby betrayed her loneliness. A fanciful letter, written at the end of May to "My darling child," spoke with a nearly hopeless melancholy of the anguish that life must often bring the little one.[22]

The Ravenna speech was Garfield's first political address in the grand manner, with polished references to classical antiquity, the venerated founding fathers, and the genius of the American people. He brushed aside southern threats of secession as a mere dispute of politicians; it was his firm belief that the Union would not be severed. Three weeks before delivering these pronouncements—which he would later describe as shortsighted—Garfield unexpectedly captured public attention. A delegate to the Ohio Republican convention at Columbus, he enlivened a rally with a rousing little speech that was noticed throughout the state. The oration at Ravenna was praised, quoted, and printed as a pamphlet, but it was the impromptu talk at the Columbus "Wigwam" that started a demand for Garfield's services on the stump. Bascom, pleased and astonished, signed him up for the campaign.[23]

Unfortunately, Garfield had to fill his Ravenna engagement on the day after Crete was delivered of a girl. He spent the next three weeks at home, then started on a tour of the Great Lakes with Harry and Almeda. Crete had not yet recovered from a hard confinement; she had had to give up nursing the baby and had developed a painful breast. It abscessed after the pleasure party left. Garfield was out of communication for a week, enjoying the wild scenery of the lakes and inspecting iron and copper mines. He went home at once on learning of Crete's illness, but to have left her in the first place was a callously selfish act. Garfield's upbringing had disposed him to regard his own wish and will as all-important, and he would not be the first man, or the last, to weary of the disabilities of a delicate woman's childbearing. Besides he had never cared for little children and was slow in adjusting himself to the unknown role of father. He had a bad case of the *"Blues"* after his return.[24]

Another conspicuous instance of lack of consideration for Crete occurred in October. Maria and Rancie spent a few days in Cleveland after accompanying Charles Learned on a trip to Port Austin, Michigan, where he was soon to settle and establish a lumber mill. Garfield's meetings with Rancie always caused Crete bitter unhappiness, and on this occasion he was frequently with his former sweetheart. He made trips to Cleveland at the height of the political campaign, and Crete apparently received the visitors at Hiram.[25]

The campaign offered Garfield a legitimate escape from Hiram and its problems. "No man in my recollection," Bascom wrote in September, "has sprung so suddenly into favor as an orator." There were many more invitations than he could accept. Because of his duties at the Eclectic, preference was generally given to engagements within a short radius of Hiram, and Garfield acquired a horse and buggy to free himself from dependence on railroad timetables.[26]

These autumn journeys followed a road that Garfield had often traveled, speaking in tents and leafy groves, starch-white churches and prim town halls. In 1860 he did not carry the gospel message, but he was preaching all the same—fulminating against the spread of slavery, denouncing the "squatter sovereignty" doctrine of Senator Douglas, the candidate of the northern Democrats. The crowds saw a fair, massively built man, a little overweight but with sturdy limbs, who conveyed a sense of strength and confidence. His dress was like a farmer's, loose and plain; his bearing, in repose, was still a trifle "lopping"; but his full-browed, Jovian head gave him a look of mastership and intellectual power. He spoke freely and forcefully in the grandiloquent style that was a politician's greatest asset, especially in the West. The families of rural America, flocking in thousands to hear speechmaking of every description, were looking for drama as well as guidance, hoping to find in the licensed emotionalism of the orator some release from lives that were always hard and often starved and barren. Good-looking young "Gaffield," with his throbbing voice and impassioned rhetoric, repaid his hearers for the hardships of a long outing: the backbreaking jolts of the wagon, the chill contents of the lunch baskets, the clamor of the restless, strident children.

Garfield made more than fifty speeches before the momentous election day of 1860. He went to Ravenna to receive the returns and at midnight of November 6 praised God that Lincoln and Hamlin were elected.[27]

Almost at once Garfield and Rhodes joined two other men on a trip to the town of Mecca in Trumbull County. Long on the outlook for profitable investments, Garfield had been infected by the enthusiasm for oil lands in that vicinity. The booming petroleum industry in western Pennsylvania had introduced a cheap new illuminant and turned attention to similar commercial possibilities in various parts of Ohio.

From canal boy to President.

Eliza and her children, summer, 1855. Front, from left: Mehetabel, Eliza, Mary; rear, from left: Thomas, James.

The Boynton cousins, c. 1855. Front, from left: Silas, Henry, William; rear, from left: Cordelia, Phebe, Harriet.

The Western Reserve Eclectic Institute, 1858.

The first faculty at the Western Reserve Eclectic Institute, 1850. From left: Amos Sutton Hayden (37), Thomas Munnell (27), Charles D. Wilber (20), Almeda Booth (27).

Almeda A. Booth. (A later photograph.)

Garfield's Greek class at the Eclectic, spring, 1853. Front, from left: Philip Burns, Jennie Gardner, Lucretia Rudolph, James A. Garfield; rear, from left, E. S. Pike, Joseph King, George O'Connor, Sterling McBride.

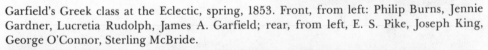

Zeb and Arabella Mason Rudolph, c. 1850.

Henry Boynton, left, and James A. Garfield, spring, 1853.

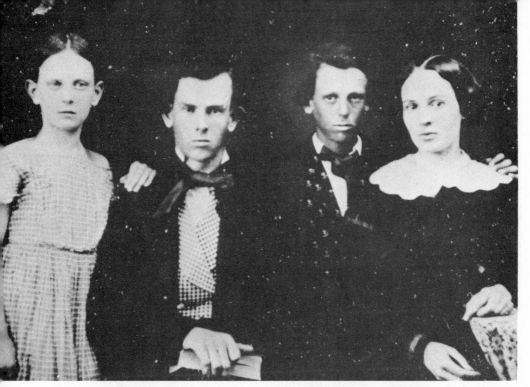

The Rudolph children, c. 1855. From the left: Ellen, Joseph, John, Lucretia.

Rebecca J. Selleck, 1872.

James A. Garfield,
Williams College senior, 1856.

"Poestenkill, New York—Winter," 1868.

The Garfield house in Hiram, showing alterations made by the Garfields. Bought by the Garfields in 1863, sold to Burke Hinsdale in 1872, now the home of Phebe Boynton's great granddaughter.

Eliza Arabella Garfield ("Trot," 1860–1863).

Officers of the Forty-second Ohio Infantry Regiment, 1862. Center front, Colonel Garfield; left front, Major Don Pardee; right rear, Lieutenant Colonel Lionel Sheldon.

Brigadier General Garfield, 1862 or 1863.

Major General William S. Rosecrans.

Committee on Military Affairs, House of Representatives, 1867–1869. Front center: Chairman Garfield.

James G. Blaine.

Samuel Jackson Randall, Speaker of the House, 1876–1881.

The Garfield house at Thirteenth and I streets, Washington, D.C. Built for Garfield in 1869, occupied by the Garfield family until 1880, sold by Mrs. Garfield in 1895, demolished in 1964.

Mollie Garfield and her father, 1870. "I am glad you like the picture of Mollie and me. I wish you were in it also." Garfield to Mrs. Garfield, 29 April 1870.

Edward Garfield (1874–1876). "And when the struggle was over, all the sweetness and beauty of his dear face came back and the thought of it will dwell in our hearts forever." *The Diary of James A. Garfield,* III, p. 370 (25 October 1876).

Summer of 1874. Photo taken in front of the Zeb Rudolph house in Hiram. Children in foreground, from left: Harry, James, and Mollie Garfield. At left: Eliza Garfield and James A. Garfield. Seated in doorway and on the step, from left: Lucretia Garfield, Mrs. Joseph Rudolph, Irvin Garfield, Joseph Rudolph. Standing in the doorway: Carry Will, a neighbor. At right: Zeb Rudolph, Arabella Rudolph, Mary McGrath, the Garfield nursemaid, holding Abram Garfield.

Isaac Errett, prominent Disciple leader.

Dr. John P. Robison.

The Dickey farm in Mentor, bought by Garfield in October 1876.

William Cooper Howells—the very best *man* I have ever known" (William Dean Howells).

Burke A. Hinsdale.

Jacob Dolson Cox.

Joseph Henry, Secretary of the Smithsonian Institution, 1846–1878.

President Rutherford B. Hayes, 1879.

Home from Chicago, 10 June 1880. Photo by pioneer Cleveland photographer J. F. Ryder, taken two days after Garfield's nomination for President at the Republican national convention.

The Republican ticket, 1880.

Lawnfield, 1880—the Dickey farm improved and renamed.

The candidate, 1880. Photo by Horace W. Tibbals, young Painesville photographer for whom Garfield sat in July and September.

The office, 1880. Building behind the Mentor residence used as a telegraph and general office during the presidential campaign. Photo shows Garfield in front of left window, the telegraph operator, and visitors.

Around Mecca, which lay directly west of the Pennsylvania diggings, the dark oil soaked the ground and puddled on surface rocks. Investors were thronging in with laborers and equipment. Garfield bought a claim while he was there and became the moving spirit in a company formed to handle deals in land and begin boring operations. He would not make his fortune at Mecca, but his hopes were bright as he ordered steam engines from Pittsburgh for the pumps.[28]

Somewhere along the way, Garfield had come out of the doldrums and reverted to his normally good-natured if mercurial self. He had his dearest Harry, fizzing with enthusiasm over Mecca oil, and he also had Burke Hinsdale, the awkward, thoughtful farmboy whom he had befriended as a student-teacher. Burke was now a student-teacher himself, rooming with Harry and boarding at Mrs. Northrop's. His dry humor contributed to the merriment of the supper table. Crete was in better health, and Almeda had calmed down. They were called by teasing nicknames, "the Lady Kensington" and "Queen Ann." Garfield would sometimes keep them all in peals of laughter with his flashing wit and his sallies at "Queen Ann's" expense.[29]

They were "a family together," as Crete had hoped, and it was still more wonderful to her that James had come to delight in their little girl. They had named her Eliza Arabella for the grandmothers, but she was always called "Trot," a nickname conferred by Garfield in some unexplained allusion to Aunt Betsy Trotwood in *David Copperfield*. Six months old when he left again for Columbus, she was a beguiling, pretty baby, with a round, dimpled face and her mother's large black eyes. Garfield liked to toss her high in the air, while Crete trembled for her darling, yet was proud, too, to see her sitting straight and "as fearless as a young eagle" on her father's uplifted hand.[30]

Their joy in Trot drew the parents closer and thawed the channels of tenderness that often froze between them. Crete missed James desperately after he went away. She had a fine leatherbound notebook in which she wrote letters to Trot. They were a journal of Trot's babyhood, to be read in later years, but they were also a record of Crete's pent-up feelings. Whatever his faults, James was still a great man in her eyes. "I want you to know very soon," she wrote Trot, "how rare is the treasure you possess in his love."[31]

Settled once more with Cox at the Bascoms', Garfield was no longer the unsure novice of the previous year. The secession of South Carolina and the agitation elsewhere in the Deep South had fired his patriotism, and his confidence had been hardened by advice from his political friends that he should run for Congress. He vigorously upheld Governor Dennison's message on the Union and assumed with Cox the lead-

ership of the resolute Republicans in the state senate. Casting aside all
thought of compromise, Garfield again saw slavery as a sin for which
bloodshed was the only remission. The impotence of the Buchanan administration filled him with anger and disgust, and he awaited with
mounting impatience the inauguration of Abraham Lincoln.[32]

On February 13 the president-elect arrived at Columbus on a circui-
tous progress from Springfield to Washington. He was received by the
governor and the legislature of Ohio, and he delivered one of the casual and enigmatic little speeches that concealed his grave anxiety over
the national crisis. Already in six seceded states the federal government
was defied, federal property seized, and the flag of the Union insulted.
Lincoln's assurances that nothing was going wrong rang hollowly in the
ears of loyal citizens. But Garfield did not share the disappointment
that was general in the East. Under this other westerner's homely awk-
wardness, he sensed honesty and purpose. He rejoiced that Lincoln's
tour was effective in "strengthening the hopes of the Union men and
the back-bones of 'Emasculates.' "[33]

Garfield's approval, however, was dashed by Lincoln's conciliatory
inaugural address and by the month of inaction that followed. A political defeat did not improve his spirits. The Ohio legislature had again
been charged with electing a United States senator when Chase resigned his seat to enter Lincoln's cabinet as secretary of the treasury.
Garfield and Cox campaigned strenuously for Dennison's nomination,
but the prize went to John Sherman, a cold, capable politician who had
served three terms in the House of Representatives. Adjournment was
postponed as secession spread, and Garfield marked time in anxiety
over the inaction of the North and his own plans for the future. He
and Cox resolved that, if necessary to rouse the loyal states, they would
raise companies and go into the army. Again under the guidance of
Cox, who was a purely theoretical general in the Ohio militia, Garfield
read works on military science and studied the campaigns of Napoleon
and Wellington. News of the attack on Fort Sumter startled them from
their books. On Sunday morning, April 14, they were called to the governor's office. Fort Sumter had surrendered, and Dennison showed the
two state senators the message he had drafted, asking the legislature
for men and money. Then and at a later conference, they mapped out
the plans for Ohio's part in the war. Monday brought the President's
proclamation calling out 75,000 militia for three months. The legislature rushed through the emergency measures, including a million-
dollar state loan for raising and equipping the militiamen, who were already crowding into Columbus.[34]

Garfield had promptly offered his services to Dennison, leaving the
nature of the appointment to the governor. On fire with patriotism and

eager to distinguish himself, he was obviously looking for a military commission. Friends expressed the flattering opinion that he would make a brigadier general, and Dennison at this time would have given him a colonelcy had he felt able to do so. However, in contrast with procedure in other states, where such commissions were handed out freely, the Ohio three-months men elected their own colonels as well as other officers. Dennison promised to make Garfield a colonel as soon as he could; meantime he sent him on a short trip to aid in organizing two regiments that were encamped near Cleveland.[35]

Volunteer companies from Portage had been ordered up at the urging of Erastus B. Tyler of Ravenna, a businessman and a brigadier of militia. These and other companies from the Reserve were soon organized as the Seventh Infantry Regiment. Tyler himself was chafing for active service and looked to Garfield for help. He wanted to be called to Columbus, apparently in hopes of obtaining one of the volunteer brigadier generalships, and had appealed to Garfield's influence for this object through Halsey R. W. Hall, who, with his father Lyman, owned a Republican newspaper at Ravenna. The order to Tyler came a few days later, just after Garfield was dispatched to Illinois to procure arms from Governor Richard Yates and to obtain his assent to a proposed consolidation of the state forces in the Mississippi Valley under the Ohio general George B. McClellan.[36]

Meantime Garfield had spent two days at Cleveland and had formed high hopes of being elected colonel of the Seventh Regiment. He was encouraged by a number of officers and men with whom he talked, and it was his understanding that Tyler was pledged to help him. Among the Clevelanders who offered their assistance was John H. Clapp, a clever, rather pushing lawyer who had married Garfield's cousin, Phebe Boynton. When Garfield went away, Clapp and other friends looked after his interest.[37]

On returning to Columbus from Illinois, his missions accomplished, Garfield found that Tyler had emerged as a strong competitor for the colonelcy. Garfield had broken a cherished rule of conduct in putting himself forward as a candidate. Upset by what he regarded as Tyler's perfidy and by news that the officers of the regiment had held an informal election in which Tyler was the winner, he decided to fight. But it was too late. Ill-feeling and suspicion of intrigue had been generated against Garfield, particularly in Ravenna. Some of this was the result of a report that John Clapp, a Republican, had denounced Tyler, a Democrat, when he electioneered for Garfield at Camp Taylor. When the entire regiment voted on May 7, Tyler won by a large majority.[38]

Tyler's conduct may have been as treacherous as Garfield maintained, but he was in fact a favorite with the men, and they were impressed by his record of twenty-three years' militia service. These were factors that Garfield refused to recognize. He acrimoniously charged that, in his absence on the public business, Tyler had used "bargains and brandy" to gain the favor of the regiment.[39]

Garfield had been unusually sure and straightforward in making a bid for command in wartime, but his confidence disintegrated in the rancor of rivalry and the mortification of defeat. He was not helped by those who loved him best. Crete, always jealous of his good name, had reported the disapproval of his home circle. She apologetically spoke of "too great anxiety for a desirable place in the army" and "the odium due to an office seeker" and even hinted that Garfield might appear not to have taken "the *most* honorable course." Garfield stoutly defended himself, but these criticisms touched him at a vulnerable point. Greatly though Crete loved him, she could not understand that passive conduct and "purity" of intention were incompatible with masculine aggressiveness. Garfield needed to make peace with the drives of his ambition and the mixture of his motives. Crete's rigid standards tended to confirm him in the feelings of guilt and frustration that were basic in his depressions.[40]

Almeda, with her old maid's harping on nobility and decorum, was as much at fault as Crete. Harry also had a good deal to say about ideals and honor and service to country, but he was a realist about James when the chips were down. Since war had come he saw that James must improve the occasion to distinguish himself. Dreamy, ingenuous Harry did not forget that Dennison had said to Garfield that they would be ruled by military men for the next twenty years at least.[41]

Garfield himself shied away from taking further initiative. He called off Clapp and was deaf to Bascom's pleas to contend for another colonelcy. An appointment, of course, was a different matter; the call for volunteers for three years' service had placed a large number of commissions at the disposal of governors. Dennison remembered his promise to make Garfield a colonel but had become fearful that the appointment of a totally untrained civilian would be criticized. In June he finally offered Garfield the commission of lieutenant colonel assigned to one of the new regiments under a West Point graduate. It was an excellent opportunity, but Garfield's pride rebelled; he had been promised the command of a regiment, not second place under some arrogant professional soldier. Though his dislike of subordination was excessive, his feeling is understandable in this case. Most colonels of the volunteer army had no more experience than Garfield, and frequently they possessed far inferior qualifications. Moreover it was inevitable that Garfield should contrast his lot with that of his former roommate, Cox, whom Dennison had made a brigadier general. Having asked for a few days in which to make up his mind, Garfield went to western Virginia with his blustering old friend, Dr. Robison, who was now a trustee of the Eclectic. Virginia was on the brink of secession, but the counties beyond the Alleghenies were loyal. After visiting the deserted campus of Bethany College, the travelers made a stop at Wheeling, where delegates of the western counties had convened in defiance of Richmond and were laying plans to set up a separate state. Their display of patriotism may have diverted Garfield's eyes from the fateful disaffection of the rest of Virginia; he persuaded himself that the army was not in need of his services and declined Dennison's offer.[42]

Garfield offered as reasons for refusal the condition of his "personal affairs" and his relations to those with whom he was "in business connection"—and he left the way open for an army commission in the future. But he did not conduct himself like a prospective soldier or a man with pressing business concerns. Leaving Hiram with his family in mid-July, he spent the next three weeks in travel in the West. The first stop was at Princeton, Illinois, where Crete's brother, John, was struggling to make a livelihood for his young wife and two small children. There James deposited Crete and Trot while he set forth via Chicago and Milwaukee on a roundabout tour of Michigan that included a visit to two Boynton uncles at Byron. He had arranged to meet Robison and Harmon Austin at the frontier settlement of Muir, the home of Isaac Errett, one of the most dynamic of the Disciple leaders. Their errand was to persuade Errett to head a projected department of theology at the Eclectic. He declined the offer, but the Ohioans spent a congenial weekend fishing and hunting with their host and another visitor, the rugged Disciple preacher, Jefferson Harrison Jones. By the end of July James had circled back to Detroit, where Crete was to meet him for the boat trip to Cleveland, but he kept her waiting in Illinois for another week while he traveled to Port Austin, on the edge of the Huron County wilderness, to see Maria and Rancie.[43]

These wanderings had not isolated Garfield from the war—the rout of the Union militia at Bull Run had shocked the northern states and set off a fresh fanfare of recruiting—but they had effectively cut him off from Columbus. An urgent letter from Dennison, proffering another appointment as lieutenant colonel, had been delivered at Hiram more than a week before Garfield reached home. Garfield wrote to the governor at once, inquiring whether the lieutenant colonelcies were all disposed of and indicating that he hoped he could accept an appointment if he would not be needed for a few weeks. The governor responded through his secretary, William T. Bascom, that he could appoint Garfield to a lieutenant colonelcy if Garfield could enter on his duties soon. Not long after the receipt of the letter, Garfield left quietly for Cleveland to communicate to the governor by telegraph his willingness to enter the army at once. On the evening of the day after the dispatch of the telegram he was in the capital, and on the following day he was ordered to report to Camp Chase near Columbus. An understanding concerning rank seems to have been reached with the governor. After three weeks of camp duty, study, and practice in horsemanship, Garfield was appointed colonel of the Forty-second Ohio Volunteer Regiment. When in December the governor issued a commission for three years, the date given for Garfield's appointment as colonel of the Forty-second was August 14—the day on which Garfield had telegraphed the governor from Cleveland.[44]

Two able lawyers, Lionel A. Sheldon of Elyria and Don Albert Pardee of Medina, became respectively lieutenant colonel and major of the still nonexistent regiment and helped to raise it. In recruiting Company A, largely made up of students and recent graduates of the Eclectic Institute, Garfield also had the assistance of Frederick Augustus Williams of Ravenna, a popular student-teacher who was elected captain of the company. Except for a second tour of recruiting duty and a few brief absences on military or personal errands, Garfield remained at Camp Chase until the middle of December. He engaged two Negro servants: a hostler named Green who looked after his horses, Billy and Harry, and a cook known as "Professor." Once an officers' mess was in working order, Garfield invited friends to visit him—Crete and Almeda stayed for a week—and proudly showed off the bachelor comforts of camp life. He spent many congenial evenings with Sheldon and Pardee, chatting over an after-supper cigar or hotly contesting a game of billiards, but the daylight hours were busily employed in learning and discharging his duties. As cheerful and devoted an officer as the loyal states could boast, Garfield was engrossed by the care of his command, seeing that the men were clothed, equipped, and fed and, like a tutor one page ahead in the lesson-book, putting them through their military paces. He had an expert drillmaster in Don Pardee, who had spent three years at the Naval Academy at Annapolis and barked out orders with a gruffness that awed the young recruits.[45]

Garfield had kept up his church activities until he entered the army, but he was conscious that military service was not entirely consonant with Disciple principles. Toward the end of October he paid a brief visit to Cincinnati, where the American Christian Missionary Society—a national association of the Disciples of Christ—was holding a convention attended by delegates from various states. He was present during a session at which his friend Dr. Robison offered a resolution of sympathy for the Union government. It was voted down after a stormy debate. The meeting was then adjourned and a "citizens' meeting" organized in its stead. The disaffected delegates withdrew or kept silence, and the resolution was promptly adopted.

An impressive figure in his blue uniform, Colonel Garfield rose to his feet at the close of these proceedings. With biting sarcasm he remarked that he was glad a way had been found by which—as men, not as Christians—they could express sympathy for their struggling countrymen. For himself, he blessed God that we had a country we could live and die for. The challenging words caused a sensation. It was correctly understood that Brother Garfield was dissociating himself from the semipacifist leadership of the church. He did not willingly preach again.[46]

CHAPTER 7

THE WAR: 1862

ON A FINE DECEMBER Sunday the Forty-second marched smartly into
Columbus, with its big Belgian muskets glinting in the sun and its band
clanging through the noise of cheers, and formed in a hollow square at
the depot for the presentation of a fine stand of colors given by the ladies of Portage County. Governor Dennison did the honors with a suitable little speech, Colonel Garfield appropriately responded, and the
regiment stormed two trains bound for Cincinnati. Proud father of a
thousand men, Garfield was gratified by the governor's comment that
this was the best regiment yet raised in Ohio.[1]

Late the night before the dispatch had come from General Don
Buell's headquarters, ordering the Forty-second to proceed with all
possible dispatch to Prestonburg in the Sandy Valley of eastern Kentucky. Garfield had impatiently awaited such an order, but it meant a
distant removal from home and dear ones, and the pain of severance
mingled with his bold desire for action. His parting from Crete and the
baby had been tender. With sadness drifting back from his own or-
phaned boyhood, he had reflected that Trot would not remember him
if he should not return.[2]

Not all of the old Disciple life was left behind. There were well-
known faces in the cars: manly young Captain "Gustus" Williams; Lieutenant Will Clapp, a clerkly boy who was acting as Garfield's adjutant;
Sergeant Charlie Henry, lively and black-bearded; the mettlesome
preacher, Harrison Jones, who was going along as chaplain. Harry
Rhodes was going, too—as far as Cincinnati. He had evinced a fitful
wish for a captaincy, but his only real interest was in staying close to
James, and he had not summoned the energy to raise a company. An
idling bystander of the war, Rhodes was content to enjoy the applause

that followed the Forty-second—people were out with coffee at every stop on the line, cheering crowds lined the march through Cincinnati—and to muse over the turbid Ohio, "sleeping so satisfied in the warm rich sunshine of a December summer," as the regiment moved up river the next morning.[3]

Garfield, meanwhile, had worked half the night loading gear and provisions, tents, wagons, horses, and 150 wild mules on two wretched little steamers. It worried him that his men were crowded in to sleep on decks and cabin floors. He was not to be with them on this stage of their journey; on getting off the cars, he had been handed a dispatch from General Buell ordering him to report to army headquarters at Louisville.[4]

Don Carlos Buell, recently appointed commander of the Department of the Ohio, had a minor but vexing problem on the eastern verge of the territory under his jurisdiction. General Humphrey Marshall, like himself a graduate of West Point and a veteran of the war with Mexico, had wormed a Confederate brigade through a gap in the Cumberland Mountains and encamped in the Sandy Valley on the Kentucky side. It was a question whether he could sustain his troops there, but as long as he stayed he presented a threat to Buell's left flank, and Buell had to try to drive him out before the Federals moved on Nashville.

A chase through 6,000 square miles of desolate foothills remote from the main column of the army entailed appalling problems in logistics and might well prove utterly futile. The task had aroused no enthusiasm in an ambitious young West Pointer, Colonel William B. Hazen, with whom Buell discussed it. But Hazen had had a suggestion to offer. By a curious educational transition, he had gone to West Point from the Eclectic Institute. He was a warm admirer of Garfield and urged him on Buell as the best man for the expedition. Buell, of course, had no use for volunteers, but he had evidently decided that Garfield might do, and he was evidently not disappointed in the big, soldierly officer who presented himself, freshly scrubbed and neatly uniformed, wearing the splendid sword that had been a parting gift from Dr. Robison. Garfield was straightway informed that he was to take command of a brigade and drive the rebels back from eastern Kentucky.[5]

Buell was noted for a stiff, taciturn manner, but his conduct of this interview was tactful, even persuasive. He flattered the green colonel with references to the territorial extent and the independence of his command and mentioned the chance it offered for distinction. He even threw in a word of regret that he could not have Garfield with him in

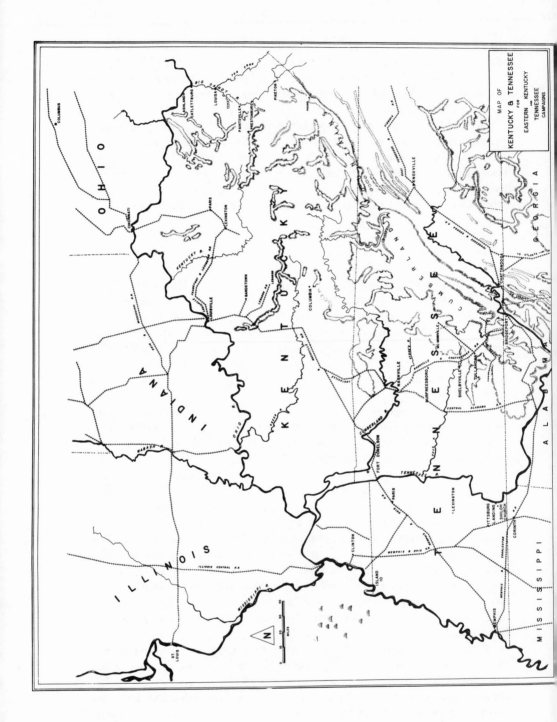

MAP OF
KENTUCKY & TENNESSEE
FOR
EASTERN KENTUCKY
AND
TENNESSEE
CAMPAIGNS

the grand column. Garfield was disposed to regret it, too. Independence appealed to him almost as much as distinction, but he was momentarily staggered by his new responsibilities. He was to operate, he gathered, in "a horrible country," with a brigade comprising two additional Ohio infantry regiments and one squadron of Ohio cavalry and augmented by a few elements—admittedly raw and poorly equipped— of Kentucky volunteers. The plan was to divide this force into two columns that would close on the Confederates from opposite directions. Garfield was to develop all details of the operation. He spent a sleepless night in studying maps and working out his recommendations. Buell's face was disappointingly blank as he scanned the report next morning, but at a final interview he assured Garfield that the conduct of the campaign was largely committed to his discretion. Only a request for artillery was, to Garfield's great disappointment, refused.[6]

After arranging for outfit and stores, Garfield went to Lexington and Paris to take command of his two new Ohio regiments, the Sixteenth and Fortieth. Holding the former as a reserve, he ordered the Fortieth, Colonel Jonathan Cranor commanding, to march eastward with the view of cooperating in the projected pincers movement. Garfield then hurried to Cincinnati, where he boarded a steamer for Catlettsburg at the mouth of the Big Sandy. The Forty-second had already moved ahead. Disturbed by the thought that brigade command might break up his familial relationship with his own regiment, Garfield thankfully rejoined it at the ragged hamlet of Louisa some thirty miles upstream. Although nominally in command of 3,000 men, he had not half that number with him. The reinforcements present on his arrival shortly before Christmas consisted of the Ohio squadron, a remnant of used-up Kentucky cavalry, and "a well-disposed, Union-loving mob" of survivors of the Fourteenth Kentucky Infantry.[7]

Garfield found himself in a grim, isolated mountain region of bloody feuds and archaic speech and folkways. The difficulties of the expedition had not been exaggerated. The winter weather was cold and foul, and every mile of his advance would carry him deeper into a tangle of winding creeks and harsh, mine-scarred ridges. To obtain subsistence there was out of the question. The river roads at this season were channels of half-frozen mud that were impassable for wagons. All provisions, as well as other impedimenta, would have to be carried by small steamboats and push-boats on the narrow, treacherous Sandy. To maintain a supply line far from its mouth might not be practicable, but Garfield's dash was too impetuous to be checked. On the second day after his arrival, he advanced. Most of his Kentuckians were left to await their equipments. Mounted on his horse Billy, Garfield led the rest of his force to encamp on George's Creek, only eighteen miles from the Confederate position at Paintsville.[8]

Quickly informed by scouts that Marshall was entrenching a strong, elevated position beyond the village and that he had artillery with which to defend it, Garfield sent an express messenger to Colonel Cranor with orders to hasten the Fortieth Ohio toward Prestonburg, in the Confederate rear, and join him in a concerted attack. The return of this messenger, his errand accomplished in spite of many obstacles and delays, sent Garfield's spirits soaring on New Year's Day 1862. Communication seemed to promise combined action, and he could not help hoping that he was on the point of capturing Marshall's entire brigade. Cranor, however, was incapable of rendering prompt aid of any sort; toiling through the mountains west of Prestonburg, he did not reach the Sandy Valley for a week.[9]

Meanwhile Garfield had reluctantly taken the advice of Sheldon and other officers who urged a few days' delay. When he next advanced, he had been joined by his "mob" of Kentuckians and some better disciplined units of the Twenty-second Kentucky. Moreover, from January 6 to 8, he had the services of 300 highly efficient troopers on loan from General Cox, who was operating in the Kanawha Valley of western Virginia. General Marshall was persuaded that he faced a superior force. Instead of making a stand, as Garfield expected, he abandoned his fortified camp to the Federals. A second surprise was in store for Garfield next morning when he found the Fortieth Ohio ensconced in the village of Paintsville. Mistaking the enemy's retreat for an advance, Colonel Cranor had judged it the part of wisdom to join the main column.[10]

Thus fortuitously united, Garfield's brigade roughly equaled Marshall's in numbers, but a shortage of provisions at Paintsville forbade pursuit with his whole force. Sending his cavalry on a dash at the enemy's rear, he ordered 1,100 picked men—many Hiram boys among them—to take hard crackers in their haversacks and set off on a roundabout march toward Prestonburg. The rest of the brigade was temporarily detained under command of Lieutenant Colonel Sheldon. Groping that night through a cold drizzle of rain, Garfield discovered that he was within striking distance of the enemy and sent an order to Sheldon to follow with every man who could march.[11]

Near midday on January 10, Garfield and his little infantry force came out on the forks of Middle Creek, which here wound tortuously through a huddle of heavily wooded, boulder-crowned hills. The indications were that the enemy lay concealed among the trees and rocks of a crescent-shaped ridge across the creek, and this impression was confirmed by a fleeting sight of rebel cavalry on a little plain that stretched before another curving ridge on the Federals' side. The plain might have been more unexpected than the cavalry; it was the first level ground that Garfield had seen in eastern Kentucky. With an effrontery scarcely warranted by his situation, he set his troops wheeling and forming in a battalion drill while he waited for his scouts to report. Having ascertained that the nearer ridge was unoccupied, he stationed his force on it.[12]

Garfield was now impatient to learn the exact whereabouts of the enemy and to launch an attack. By all the rules, he should have curbed the impulse, but his military reading had persuaded him that the great commanders of history—Napoleon, for instance, at Wagram—had succeeded by boldly flouting the rules. Though his cavalry had failed to come up, his column had been followed by some mounted citizens who took the side of the Union in this biggest feud of all and who readily lent themselves to a charge across the plain with the Colonel's mounted escort. Having drawn the enemy's fire, Garfield climbed on a crag that towered above the Union position and from this vantage point coolly directed the attack, sometimes under a hail of fire, with Chaplain Harry Jones acting as his aide.[13]

Captain Williams led two companies plunging through the icy, waist-deep creek. Shells began screaming overhead. As the Federals scrambled up the opposite steeps, flame burst from trees and rocks, and rebel soldiers plunged yelling down on them. A force under Don Pardee dashed to support their comrades. Under a rolling fog of smoke, the struggle lurched up and down the narrow ridge. Garfield threw in detachment after detachment. The Confederates slowly gave ground, but the Federal reserve was almost exhausted and the winter light was failing. Garfield had a moment of panic. In agony of mind, he prayed to God for Sheldon's reinforcements—and, turning, saw the colors of the Forty-second come sweeping into view. Shouts of joy resounded from the ridges and the advancing column, and Garfield threw in the last of his reserve. As night closed down the Federals drove the enemy over the crest, and the dark sky soon was lighted by the burning baggage of their camp.[14]

Shortly after the firing ceased, a Negro boy was brought to Colonel Garfield—an odd figure, dressed in Confederate uniform and fully armed and equipped. The servant of a Virginia colonel, Jim Rollins had slipped away near the close of the fight and come to the Union commander to give himself up. Garfield was touched by his trust. His thinking about slavery was changing; to limit its extension no longer seemed enough. He was coming to believe that the war to save the Union would inevitably carry nationwide emancipation in its train. It added a personal warmth to Garfield's intellectual conclusion that he stood to this Negro boy as the representative of protection and freedom.[15]

The talk with Jim was a fitting climax to a glorious day. The bold attack had not been costly to the Union force; most of the whizzing bullets had missed their mark, the screaming shells had all been duds but one. Garfield had a supper of coffee and hardtack and lay down amidst his men on the freezing, forested slope.[16]

Garfield had worn out himself and his brigade by hard marches and exposure. The problem of subsistence, moreover, had become acute. Prestonburg proved to be a dismal town, stripped of everything but mud. Piketon, twenty miles farther up the Sandy, was equally destitute. The uncertainty of transportation decided Garfield to return to Paintsville to rest and accumulate supplies. This movement gave Marshall a pretext for claiming, in one of the most misleading reports in military history, that the Federals had retired "well whipped." The fact was that, while Marshall's brigade soon disintegrated, leaving only a small force on the Kentucky side of Pound Gap, Garfield reentered Paintsville as a conqueror, issuing a Napoleonic address of thanks to his soldiers and publishing an offer of protection and amnesty to the inhabitants of the Sandy Valley.[17]

Apart from having put Marshall out of action, Garfield had abundant reason to consider himself a victor. His jubilant officers and men lauded his achievement, and he was extravagantly admired by the local Kentuckians. Official commendation came to him from General Buell and from General McClellan, general-in-chief of the Federal armies. The newspapers of the Union were glowing in their plaudits. Garfield's small success had been without bearing on the main currents of the war, but the North had long been starved for heartening news, and a rugged volunteer colonel was a hero that Americans could appreciate. Audacious and resourceful, Garfield was a worthy son of pioneers, and it added no little lustre to his popular reputation that he had outfoxed a professional soldier. From Ohio came a vociferous demand that he be made a brigadier general. Chase, Dennison, Bascom, and Dr. Robison were among the friends who worked for Garfield's promotion.[18]

Not long after his return to Paintsville, Garfield enriched his reputation with another exploit. The river became so high and turbulent that boats ceased to come up and commissary supplies ran dangerously low. Garfield went posthaste to Catlettsburg to order the captains to move. When they flatly refused, he took personal command of a steamboat loaded with provisions—and, standing at the helm by night and day, brought it through the raging waters to a safe landing. "So you see I have turned sailor at last," he wrote Crete. The adventure held for him more than an ordinary significance. Garfield had been giving much earnest thought to "special providences" and his place in the divine plan. To have been able to serve his soldiers in time of need seemed to give meaning to the otherwise incongruous weeks he had spent on the canal in boyhood.[19]

The rest of Garfield's stay in the valley was anticlimax. His major worry was the spread of sickness among his troops. In spite of rheumatism and a severe cold, he himself kept going until, after exposure to smallpox in February, he was given one of the formidable vaccinations of the time. Miserably ill, he contracted the prevalent camp fever and was laid up for two weeks, though he continued to manage the affairs of the brigade. As sufficient stores were obtained, he moved his men to Piketon. He was hoping for permission to push on "through the gates of the Cumberland Mountains" and strike at the Tennessee and Virginia Railroad. The Army of the Ohio was beginning a ponderous advance to the south, and Garfield, who always thought about the war in a grand design of strategy, was eager to cooperate with the main column in giving the death blow to the Confederacy.[20]

On proceeding to Piketon, however, Garfield's drive was checked. The Big Sandy, swollen with heavy rains, overflowed its banks, inundating the town and most of the camp on the very evening of his arrival. It took more than two weeks to clear up the wreckage and procure fresh supplies. The sick list of the brigade began an alarming rise. Hundreds of cases were shipped to the hospital at Ashland on the Ohio, and many died before they could be moved. Garfield grieved for boys whom he had persuaded to enlist and dreaded the thought of meeting their parents. With a heavy heart he received the official notice that he had been commissioned brigadier general. He had desired and confidently expected the promotion, but he was always shaken by change, and it saddened him to relinquish the command of his dear Forty-second. There was a particular solemnity in his protestations that he had done nothing to bring about his advancement. "Had I done so," he wrote Rhodes, "I should feel I was marring the plans of God, and should not succeed."[21]

Now Garfield's first thought was to complete his task in the "God-forsaken valley" and get his brigade into a healthy camp, away from hardships and shortages and the feuding Kentuckians whose folkways deeply shocked him. With a few hundred men he proceeded to Pound Gap in mid-March, in weather thick with rain and snow. Having surprised and scattered the remnant of Marshall's brigade, the Federals burned their huts and stores and slogged back through the mud to Piketon. It was the last and dreariest experience of the campaign. On his return, Garfield received orders to move his command to Bardstown in central Kentucky. In late March a small fleet of steamboats bore virtually the entire expedition to the broad waters of the Ohio. Garfield had Augustus Williams, seriously ill with typhoid fever, in his especial care. He stopped for a mournful visit to the Ashland hospital but took Augustus on to Cincinnati where his family could easily reach him. Having placed the sick man in a good private house, Garfield stopped overnight to transact some business and await the steamboat carrying the last detachment of the Forty-second, then continued downriver to Louisville with that regiment and two others. He was to relinquish the Forty-second to the immediate command of his good friends Sheldon and Pardee, whom he had recommended for promotion to colonel and lieutenant colonel respectively, but he would always be close to his men. He was anxious to be granted a few weeks in which to rest and drill the brigade before entering a broader field of operations.[22]

Reaching Louisville in the middle of the night, Garfield was stunned by orders to turn over his regiments and report to General Buell at Nashville or in the field. He was to be assigned a new command, presumably in the forces concentrating to join General Ulysses S. Grant (the hero of the Union since his capture of Fort Donelson in February) for an attack on the Confederate position at Corinth, Mississippi. Sheldon and Pardee were sleeping, and he aroused them for a hasty, emotional good-bye. He dared not take leave of the rest of his regiment. "It seemed," he wrote Augustus, "like leaving all in the army that I loved or that loved me."[23]

Forty-eight hours later, after riding all night on a hard-trotting horse from Columbia, Tennessee, Garfield caught up with Buell in the field. At dawn on April 4, he assumed command of the Twentieth Brigade of the Sixth Division of the Army of the Ohio. His regiments, the Sixty-fourth and Sixty-fifth Ohio, the Thirteenth Michigan, and the Fifty-first Indiana, were already under arms. Mounted on another borrowed horse, without staff or servants or baggage, Garfield started for General Grant's headquarters on the Tennessee River. Even as he rode, the Confederates were advancing for a massive attack on the unsuspecting Federal army that lay encamped between a dock called Pittsburg Landing and a bare little backwood meetinghouse that was known as Shiloh Church.[24]

There was small glory for anyone on the field of "bloody Shiloh," and Garfield had a chance at none of it. Even Grant's fame was dimmed by his unreadiness. The vanguard of Buell's army helped to avert a Union disaster, but the Twentieth Brigade did not reach the front until midafternoon of the second day of fighting, when Grant had rallied his forces and regained his lost positions. Except for a sharp engagement with the enemy's rearguard cavalry, Garfield's regiments did not see action. Theirs was the hideous aftermath of battle, the burial of miles of bloating dead. In the horrors of that field there lay revealed a vaster and more terrible conflict than any of which Americans had ever dreamed, a fury of war beside which the contest at Middle Creek seems as remote and romantic as a clash of knights in armor.[25]

For a week Garfield had been nearly a stranger to shelter, dry clothing, and hot food. Fatigue and exposure, though stoically borne, had reduced his resistance to the vanishing point. He came down with a violent dysentery, followed by a severe case of hemorrhoids (ridiculed in the Union armies as "the cavalryman's complaint"). Garfield still found it hard to ride when, at the end of April, the army started its advance on the enemy's works at Corinth.[26]

Grant did not lead the advance. The high command in the West had been assigned to Henry Wager Halleck, a paunchy armchair general of forty-seven who had returned to the army in 1861 after an absence of seven years. He desired to conduct the Corinth campaign in person, and presently came on from his headquarters at St. Louis to organize his forces. Grant, his fame as the hero of Fort Donelson badly dented, was to act as second in command. General John Pope, who had recently captured Island Number 10 in the upper Mississippi, was ordered to augment the column with his force. When all the brigades of three armies had been gathered in, Halleck had 120,000 men.

Corinth was less than twenty miles from the Shiloh battlefield. It took Halleck—"Old Brains" the impatient troops began to call him—about a month to get there. Warily feeling his way, he kept his troops laboring to remove felled trees and build corduroy roads and, at every halt, entrench. For most of the crawling advance Garfield was without either servants or horses. The cook, Professor, had gone home. The hostler, Green, when last heard of, was at Louisville with Billy. Jim Rollins, for whom Garfield felt personally responsible, had been left with the Forty-second. Garfield made himself as comfortable as he could. He finally got his trunk and enjoyed the luxury of changing his shirt. He gradually met friends he had known: his cousins, Ellis Ballou and George Garfield—Ellis was the brigade postmaster—and a dozen old acquaintances, former students at Hiram among them. The members of Garfield's staff were all from northern Ohio. His adjutant general, David G. Swaim of Salem, was picked from the Sixty-fifth OVI and became a close friend. Garfield also arranged the transfer of two aides who had been with him in Kentucky, Ralph Plumb and Jacob Heaton. Plumb, a capable captain in the quartermaster's corps, went to

Cincinnati in May to settle the Sandy Valley accounts and visited Hiram at Garfield's request. His easy, pleasant manner disarmed Crete's shyness—he reminded her of Augustus——and Garfield took great comfort in receiving firsthand reports and brand-new likenesses of his wife and little girl. Plumb brought along Harry, a spirited stallion that had been sent to Elyria for the duration of the Sandy Valley campaign. He also brought Billy and the hostler, Green, and a French cook to replace Professor.[27]

Garfield found his aides congenial, loved his horses, and took immense satisfaction in the new cook's soup; his health had improved in spite of heat and coarse army rations. Yet he was seething with angry dissatisfaction. The trouble went much deeper than his persistent sighing for his "dear old regiment." He had lost faith in the moral purpose of everyone concerned with the conduct of the war, from his divisional commander, peppery little General Thomas G. Wood, all the way up to the President. Since entering the Deep South, Garfield had become agitated by the sight of the grievous injustice of slavery and by its usefulness to the enemy. The "black phantom," as he once called it, met the Union army everywhere. "Before God I here record my conviction," he wrote Harry Rhodes, "that the spirit of slavery is the soul of this rebellion, and the incarnate devil which must be cast out before we can trust in any peace as lasting and secure."[28]

The principal targets of Garfield's indignation were his superior officers, particularly the West Pointers who dominated the western armies. He blamed the Washington government for weakness in evading the slavery question, but the tolerant attitude of the regular officers seemed to him close to treason.[29]

It is obvious that Garfield's judgment was colored by resentment of the military hierarchy in which he had lost status and independence, but his criticism of the West Pointers was not altogether baseless. With some outstanding exceptions, they were men of limited background and narrow education, and almost all of them reflected the southern influences that had long governed the military establishment. Halleck and Buell, natives of New York and Ohio respectively, were as solicitous as the Pennsylvania-born McClellan to preserve the existing relations between the races. The time was already late. Winds of change were sweeping through the northern states and the rank and file of their regiments. The Union soldier had come to hate slavery and identify it with rebellion. Garfield observed the change and pondered its implications. He was beginning to think that the ballot box was a more effective instrument of public policy than the sword.

Congress was not a new idea to Garfield—his friends had been talking about it for more than a year—but the autumn elections pressed on his mind with insistence. By a recent act of the Ohio legislature, the Nineteenth Congressional District had been reorganized to include Portage and Geauga with the three neighboring counties of Trumbull, Ashtabula, and Mahoning. The redistricting seemed favorable to the choice of a new Republican candidate. The first of Garfield's letters on the subject came from Harry Rhodes, who reported that Hall (presumably Lyman or Halsey) had recently remarked that Garfield would be spontaneously elected should the war be over by October and Garfield free. Garfield was not going to do anything about getting the Republican nomination—there was no possibility of that—but he wrote Harry that, if the people should see fit to call him, he would be greatly pleased.[30]

Military life had lost its charm for Garfield. In that steaming month of May he burned with impatience for the war to end and set him free. He dreamed of the coolness of the shores of Lake Huron, of taking a quiet midsummer holiday at Port Austin and then bearing his friends off to the Williams Commencement. Garfield missed his wife and little girl and longed to hold them in his arms again, but other fancies teased a badly frustrated man—a brigadier lost among brigadiers in the great, faceless army that inched toward Corinth.[31]

Though Garfield despised the West Point officers, he covertly respected their attainments and had relied on Halleck to bring off a decisive battle. The Union dared to hope, in May 1862, that the end of the war might be in view. McClellan had at long last moved the Army of the Potomac to Virginia and stood confronting Richmond. Farragut had captured New Orleans, thereby opening up the lower Mississippi as far as Port Hudson. The destruction of Beauregard's army at Corinth would deal a heavy stroke to Confederate power in the West. Not until the very last did Garfield comprehend that Beauregard would not wait to be destroyed, that he was moving off his army and leaving the Federals the empty shell of the Corinth defenses. His final illusion gone, Garfield derided the campaign with savage ridicule of "the lubberly bungling of General Halleck" and "this wonderful mystery of West Point known as scientific military strategy."

Having completed our fortifications and brought scores of siege guns where they could have filled the streets of Corinth with shell, [Garfield wrote] we lay ten days ingloriously skirmishing with the enemy's outposts, while they, with their locomotive whistles in our ears, were moving off their heavy stores night and day, and preparing to crown us with the emptiest of honors. . . . For two days before the evacuation was complete there was a general skirmishing along our lines. We fired into the bushes with light artillery. The enemy answered with musketry only.

Men of only *common* sense inferred that the enemy's artillery was gone. Men of scientific military sense seemed to make no inference at all. At last the enemy's pickets did not fire at all. A black smoke rose from Corinth, and it was not until the magazines had exploded that our Napoleon ventured to let us go and see for the first time the works of the rebels—not nearly so strong as our own.[32]

Halleck took no interest in pursuit but speedily dispersed his army, pulling it apart as though its usefulness had ended with the capture of a railroad junction. The Army of the Ohio was started on the march to Chattanooga with orders to repair the Memphis and Charleston Railroad on the way. Garfield again had a bad diarrhea—brought on, he himself wryly suggested, by disgust with Halleck's management—and he was laid up with fever at Iuka after three days' marching in intense heat. The surgeon advised a month's leave, but Garfield had made it a point of pride to stick out the campaign and stoically decided to remain.[33]

Buell was scarcely more inclined than Halleck to an expeditious advance. His army lumbered across northern Alabama, mending tracks and rebuilding bridges and holding courts-martial for the trial of erring officers. Garfield had been looking forward to a meeting with the Forty-second in Tennessee, but in the lagging progress all momentum and objective seemed lost; he saw, with deepening disillusion, that the overextended Federal lines were vulnerable to attack. At times, in his weak and depressed condition, Garfield felt ready to resign his commission. He resented more bitterly than ever the policy of cooperating with the slaveholders, and on one occasion he flatly defied an order to have his camp searched for a fugitive. Though it was now evident that the war would drag on, he was persuaded that the big battles in the West had all been fought. He confidentially admitted to Rhodes that he would prefer to serve in Congress rather than remain in the army.[34]

Garfield was receiving a number of letters from political friends in his district, asking him to permit his name to be presented at the approaching convention, and he did not know how to answer them without betraying his interest. He was anxious not to risk rejection and badly wanted the counsel of a man who could assess the effect of the redistricting and its bearing on the chances of the incumbent, John Hutchins of Warren. Providentially, toward the end of June, Garfield received a letter from his friend of a decade, Harmon Austin, a businessman of Warren, a Disciple, and a member of the Eclectic board of trustees. Austin had a minute, undercover knowledge of the politics of northern Ohio. He was discreet to the point of secretiveness, and always ready to manage a friend's affairs. Garfield wrote him immediately to ask his help in determining whether he should allow his name to be presented. He acknowledged that he would "esteem it a mark of high favor" should the people "of their own motion," without any suggestion from him, choose to nominate him. At the same time he let Austin understand that he did not "feel any impatient anxiety on the subject." Austin understood him perfectly and was soon cautiously "sounding" the sentiment for Garfield in Trumbull County and elsewhere in the district.[35]

The talk back home concerning him as a possible candidate for Congress only confirmed Garfield's reluctance to ask for leave. To return at this crucial time would, he thought, appear as a stooping to self-advancement that would cast suspicion on the patriotic motives with which he had entered the army. In July he became enfeebled by progressively severe attacks of dysentery and the drastic purgative and emetic medicines that were the prescribed treatment. As his health deteriorated his scruples hardened. During most of the month, he acted as president of the court-martial of Colonel John B. Turchin, a former Russian officer, who was on trial for depredations committed by the Illinois regiment under his command. The confinement in a stifling room told on Garfield's flagging strength, and he fell seriously ill, with fever and vomiting. Too weak to sit up, he persisted for ten days in presiding over the trial from a cot but was forced to give up and, accompanied by Captain Swaim, started on the journey to Ohio.[36]

The reverses that Garfield had expected had already begun. While Buell tarried, Confederate cavalry had overrun Kentucky and Tennessee, dashing at will through the tenuous Federal lines and cutting off their communications. It was a slow and painful journey that Garfield made in Swaim's devoted care. On arriving at Louisville, he telegraphed Crete that he was sick and asked her to meet him at Cleveland, bringing Harry and Almeda.[37]

In the preceding autumn, Crete had given up the rooms at Mrs. Northrop's and gone with Trot to live with her parents. The younger Rudolphs were seldom at home—Joe was in the army and Nellie was teaching school—but John had brought his family back from the West in the winter. Discouraged and in debt, he seemed at twenty-six already marked for defeat. He wanted to enlist, but he had Mattie and the two small children to think of; soon it was apparent that Mattie was pregnant again. At last John got a job breaking mules for the army and left in early June for Kentucky.[38]

Trot was always with her mother. In other respects, Crete's life differed little from that she had led as a girl. Outside the family circle, Almeda was her frequent companion. They went on painting expeditions and occasionally paid visits to friends. Crete appeared busy and cheerful, but her heart was desolate. She did not feel the patriotic excitement that sustained her mother-in-law. At first Eliza Garfield had been frantically opposed to James's enlistment, but then the war had braced her up. She avidly followed the news, calling down Biblical execrations on the rebels; she made bandages, knitted socks and mittens, and wrote letters on garish Union stationery. To Crete the war seemed remote from peaceful Hiram. She scarcely thought of it, apart from James. Yet she was a Spartan wife, proud of her husband's stern devotion to duty. Even after she grew concerned about his health, she hesitated to urge him to come home. Some remarks from Harry had implied a "congressional purpose" in his pressing James to ask for leave. Crete wrote James in June that she would rather not see him for a year than have his return give rise to questions and suspicions.[39]

In July, however, Crete grew so anxious that she urged James to come as far as Cincinnati—a discreet distance from his district—to recuperate. Her anxiety was soon sharply stimulated. While staying at the Larabees' farm, she was shocked to hear that Augustus Williams was dead. He had seemed to have won a long battle with typhoid fever when he attended the Eclectic Commencement with his sweetheart, Adelaide Robbins. His unexpected relapse and death lighted up Crete's fears for James, and she soon wrote again, suggesting that he come at least as far as Cincinnati for his health's sake.[40]

Another blow struck Crete still more closely—the news that her brother John was gravely ill with typhoid fever at the hospital in Lexington. Mattie was tied down by twins, only four weeks old. Crete left Trot in the care of Eliza and Mary Larabee and went with her mother to Kentucky. Unknowingly she had been near James when he arrived at Louisville in early August and telegraphed her to meet him at Cleveland. On finally receiving his message, she rushed back to Ohio. They went to Solon to see his family and get Trot, and then by easy stages they traveled home.[41]

James was the shadow of the hale and handsome man from whom Crete had parted eight months before. The skin hung loose on his big bones, and his wasted face was jaundiced. He needed rest and quiet but could find neither in the week he spent at Hiram. Austin's "sounding" had discovered a strong sentiment for Garfield in Trumbull County and elsewhere in the district. Judging that the time was ripe for a further step, Austin, Rhodes, and Wallace Ford—Garfield's "self-constituted guardians," as Almeda called them—prepared a letter for the *Cleveland Herald*, "purporting to be one of Wallace's ordinary letters" as correspondent of the paper, in which it was said that it was being remarked everywhere that General Garfield was the most suitable man to represent the district in Congress—and that it was more than probable that he would be elected if nominated. The timing of Garfield's return was politically opportune; but, even if his scruples had permitted, he was physically unequal to greeting the many visitors who flocked to the Rudolph house. He could not leave at once, for word came that John Rudolph had died and that poor Arabella was bringing the body home.[42]

As soon as the funeral was over, James took Crete and Trot to a farmhouse at Howland Springs near Warren—a retreat that had been recommended by the Austin family. He had worried lest a visit to Trumbull county be interpreted as "a political maneuver," but the farm proved to be a haven of peace after callers from Warren had been discouraged. The commodious house was set among trees on a hill. There was a medicinal spring and a green alley in which James played at bowls as his strength returned. Idle and purposeless as he had not been since boyhood, he passed quiet days with his wife and child. In a neat dress and apron, with her dark hair shingled, Trot had grown into a beguiling two-year-old girl, sociable, affectionate, and always in motion. She was disarmingly like her father; in spite of his belief in stern discipline, Garfield adored her independence and self-will.

There were changes also in Crete. James's unexpected return, closely followed by her brother's death, had shaken her composure. Her emotional defenses were down and, in relief that James was alive and in her arms, she responded passionately to his embraces. These weeks were the turning point in their marriage. Crete forgot her prim desire to be a wife "in the truest, noblest sense" and, with awakened insight, perceived how desperately James needed a woman who loved him with body as well as spirit. His reponse was overwhelming. It was significant that he at once began to talk of getting a home of their own. On their return to Hiram, he told Crete to rent a house and gave her money for the furnishings. He must have known before leaving for Washington that she was again pregnant. Many letters, after he had gone, breathed his love and gratitude and his joy in "the fragrance of the 'alabaster box,' which, so long sealed, has been broken at last."[43]

After four years of marriage, Garfield fell in love with his wife. It would, of course, be folly to pretend that his personality was transformed; Garfield would always be mercurial and restless—he began to be chafed by inactivity before they left Howland Springs—and his moodiness and self-indulgence were too deeply rooted to be entirely altered. The very month after leaving home he deeply hurt Crete by going to visit Rebecca at Lewisboro. He refused to surrender his independence. But, with humility and honesty of purpose, he asked Crete to be patient. "I hope *strongly* and *happily*," he wrote her on their anniversary in November, "that we have passed through the valley and shadow of that death which for so long a time we 'died daily.' But I here pray you to be still ready to bear with me if at any future moment my heart should for a time go down again into the deeps."[44]

With passing years, Garfield's doubts were wholly dispelled. He and Crete came to believe that theirs was an ideal union. As an elderly woman, Crete once diffidently told her oldest son of the "sacred" happiness they had known. "Again and again did he say to me, 'Was there ever such perfect love as ours?' " she wrote. "A favorite quotation with him was 'Great Son of God, Immortal Love'; and in it we did live and move and have our being." Garfield's romantic extravagance, with its tinge of religious sentiment, should not be accepted quite literally—in common with other human beings, he and Crete had their troubles— but the belief that their marriage was perfect uplifted and sustained them. In this faith, a difficult and divided man gave his wife a lasting devotion and gained a healing emotional fusion that calmed and irradiated his existence.[45]

On September 2, while Garfield was still secluded at Howland Springs, he was nominated for Congress by the Republican district convention at Garrettsville. As far as possible, he ignored the matter. As he put on a little weight and the yellow faded from his skin, he longed for the army, missing the "happy family" of his staff and the challenge of active service. He had received two dispatches from the secretary of war. The first conveyed an assignment to Cumberland Gap, which he had been too ill to accept; he was anxious to respond to the second, which instructed him to report at Washington as soon as he was able. It was rumored that he was to receive an important command. He wrote Captain Plumb that, if elected to Congress, he might "prefer to resign the seat and keep the saddle."[46]

The opening of the new Congress was more than a year away, but as the smoke cleared from the battlefields of late August and early September 1862, it was no longer said that the war would soon be ended. Two summer months before, the Union had held the key to Richmond, Chattanooga, Vicksburg; now the Confederates, their armies still intact, had seized the initiative on both western and eastern fronts. General Braxton Bragg had come pounding up through Tennessee into Kentucky, forcing Buell into a racing retreat to defend Louisville and Cincinnati. Pope had been crushed in two days of terrible fighting in Virginia at Second Bull Run, and the victorious General Robert E. Lee had crossed the Potomac to invade Maryland. Soon after returning to Hiram, Garfield began to make impatient preparations to depart. Still too weak to take the field, he was intent on summoning his aides and getting his horses and baggage in readiness for his new assignment. He reached Washington on September 19, just after the Army of the Potomac had turned the Confederates back from Maryland in a furious encounter along the Antietam Creek.[47]

Garfield entered a capital city poisoned by suspicion and fear. Three weeks earlier, McClellan's corps commanders had been tardy in supporting Pope, who blamed them for the rout of his army. In spite of the victory in Maryland, McClellan was distrusted, and doubts of his loyalty fed on the ease with which the Confederates were making good their retreat. Garfield saw only one gleam of "light in the midst of the darkness"—the President's announcement of his forthcoming Emancipation Proclamation.[48]

Though cordially received by the President and by secretaries Stanton and Chase, Garfield was checked in his desire for an independent command. His illness had lost him the assignment to Cumberland Gap, and he was plainly disappointed by Stanton's alternative suggestion of western Virginia. The secretary of war expressed the most cordial intentions but added, as Garfield wrote Crete, that "it would be difficult to give me any place that would save me from West Point." Chase was tireless in seeking patronage for his friends, but his influence at the War Department had declined. Nor was the formidable Stanton himself all-powerful. In July, General Halleck had been made general-in-chief of the Federal armies. He shunned active service—he had not even gone to the Bull Run battlefield, only a few miles from Washington—but his military knowledge was respected, and the President placed reliance on his counsel. Garfield's impulsive rush to the capital met a prospect of delay.[49]

Week after week, in growing vexation of spirit, Garfield tarried in Washington. At times he believed he was on the brink of an assignment. There was a scheme for the colonization of Florida by a loyal population, with Garfield figuring as military commander of the department. This imaginative plan came to nothing in the end, though it brought Garfield into touch with a number of the leading Republican extremists, including Horace Greeley and his associates on the *New York Tribune*. There was also a proposed expedition to Port Royal, on which Garfield was to serve as second in command to General David Hunter, a stout opponent of slavery in spite of his West Point training. Elated by their plans for an attack on Charleston, Garfield was champing to start and was keenly disappointed when an outbreak of yellow fever in South Carolina caused the expedition to be postponed.[50]

Outwardly, Garfield's stay in Washington had many agreeable aspects. From the day of his arrival, he had an attentive patron in the secretary of the treasury. On the invitation of Chase and his daughter and official hostess, Kate, Garfield soon left a solitary and expensive room at Willard's Hotel for the luxury of a fine mansion at Sixth and E streets. To obtain the Republican nomination for President in 1864 was Chase's dearest wish. He was assiduously cultivating useful friendships, and Garfield would in all likelihood be a member of the Ohio delegation in the next Congress; but Chase's liking for the younger man went beyond the practices of expediency. He treated Garfield as an intimate friend and admitted him to a confidential view of important matters of state. Garfield naturally saw much of the beautiful Kate, whom he described rather coolly to Crete as having "a nose slightly inclining to pug." He may have found Kate too worldly and ambitious for his taste, but the susceptible Garfield was certainly not indifferent to the charms of the reigning belle of Washington. An especially pleasant experience was a weekend visit he and Kate paid to Fairfax Court House as the guests of General Carl Schurz, then serving as a divisional commander under General Franz Sigel. Garfield's political convictions had led him to admire some very second-rate soldiers, and Sigel ranked high in his esteem. Two musical evenings at Sigel's headquarters confirmed Garfield's enthusiasm for the cultured, romantic, slavery-hating Germans who had enlisted in the cause of the Union.[51]

Kate was an accomplished hostess, and in her father's mansion Garfield encountered a hospitality more opulent and a company more distinguished than he had previously known. He was often stimulated and impressed, but he became uneasy as his stay in Washington dragged on. He had moods in which he felt himself an outsider in these elegant surroundings, and later he confessed to Crete that he had sometimes suffered from a "morbid fear" of intruding. Almeda believed that "the polish of Washington life" had aggravated Garfield's resentment of his own early lack of advantages.[52]

Garfield was usually able to conceal his feelings of inferiority, but they stirred painfully beneath his genial manner. The Chases obviously wanted him to remain with them. A lonely widower, Chase enjoyed having a congenial friend with whom to converse and play chess. He lived on such an extravagant scale—he was running deeply into debt— that the presence of an extra guest was of no practical consequence. Garfield's intelligence and exuberant warmth made him popular in any company; and, after the Ohio elections in October, he had the status of an incoming congressman, chosen by a comfortable majority in a year of widespread reaction against the administration and the war. But his "morbid fear" prevailed. In mid-November he made the arrival of his staff an excuse for ending his visit.[53]

In October Garfield went to New York City with Eli Thayer in connection with the scheme to colonize Florida. During his absence from

Washington he spent a couple of days in Lewisboro with Rebecca, whom he found convalescing from a severe illness—and threatened, he thought, with consumption. Crete was saddened when she learned (in a letter from him) that he had been with Rebecca. Garfield hastened to reassure her; the visit had been pleasant and sad—"pleasant because I was glad to revisit the scenes of six years ago and was enabled to do so without having my horizon clouded, or having the thorns again pierce me; pleasant because I am more than ever assured that he that is true to his own virtue is happier and better in being so, and I can say in truth that I love you none the less for having seen Rebecca again and she is no less dear to me from the fact that the sunshine has sweetly dawned upon your life and mine; pleasant because I took pleasure in telling her that I had passed a very happy month with you and that henceforth my life with you was full of promise of sweet peace and sunlight." The sadness came from Rebecca's condition and from finding her surrounded by people contributing little to making her life agreeable and seemingly unworthy to be her companions. Rebecca continued to be an occasional threat to Crete's peace of mind. But it was a needless worry on Crete's part; never again would Rebecca be to James more than a dear friend of his college days.[54]

"Mr. Chase is the only live, strong, earnest man in the Cabinet," Garfield wrote Burke Hinsdale at the end of October. In the course of their intimate association, Garfield had fallen under the spell of the big, solemn, authoritative statesman. Chase's patriotism, alloyed though it was by personal ambition, was highminded and devout. Long experienced in public affairs, he was a leading actor in the somber drama that was unfolding in Washington. Garfield did not question his version of the events and personalities behind the scenes.[55]

Not all of Chase's influence was negative. His discussions of the great financial questions that the war had raised kindled Garfield's enthusiasm for a subject that was to be a major interest of his own public career. But the heaviest immediate effect of their private talks was to accentuate Garfield's already marked trend toward distrust of Lincoln and to deepen his dislike and suspicion of northern Democrats.

In that depressing autumn, the President had few defenders from the charge of weakness and timidity—and Garfield was at the burning core of disaffection. The allies of Chase and Stanton were the anti-Lincoln radicals of Congress. Embattled leaders in the fight against McClellan, they decried him as a traitor to his country, the center of a spreading conspiracy, inside the army and out, to make a soft peace that would preserve the institution of slavery. McClellan's cause was championed by those who opposed a vigorous prosecution of the war.

Democrats flocked to his defense in 1862; Democratic platforms and orators praised him in the midterm elections. He was hailed as the next Democratic candidate for President and, when Lincoln at length removed him from command in early November, his political power remained a vivid menace.[56]

After Chase, the man who most forcefully affected Garfield's thinking at this time was a West Point officer, Major General Irvin McDowell. Cruelly assailed and slandered since Second Bull Run, this honorable, unfortunate soldier had been relieved of his command and was awaiting a court of inquiry for which he had applied. As an Ohioan and an intimate friend of the Dennison family as well as of Chase, McDowell had a claim on Garfield's sympathy. A warm liking developed between them during frequent meetings at the Chase mansion. Though ordinarily reserved to a fault, McDowell was anxious to justify himself to this kind, new friend. In the course of two long sessions with Garfield, he poured out the story of his wrongs, documenting it by his military orders and correspondence and the entries in his private journal. McDowell censured Lincoln for refusing to sustain him but charged his calamities chiefly to the jealous enmity of McClellan and his clique, especially the corps commander, Fitz-John Porter. This account, with its "correct views" of the men involved, was accepted by Garfield as "almost the whole history of the Army of the Potomac." It seemed to him so important that he wrote out a detailed report of the two interviews with McDowell, adding a few opinions and observations of his own, and mailed the bulky manuscript to Crete with the admonition that it should not be made public.[57]

Garfield's temperament was emotional rather than judicial. He felt a genuine regard for McDowell—he would name a son for him—and his loyalty swept aside his critical faculty. It was true that McDowell was an honest, patriotic man who had been savagely maligned; but his very grievances impaired the value of his testimony. A casualty of the passions and confusions of the war, desperately anxious to clear his name, he was unavoidably biased in his judgments. He was presently to appear as one of the most damaging witnesses at the court-martial of McClellan's close friend, Fitz-John Porter.

Not long after Garfield had sent his manuscript to Crete, he was unexpectedly appointed to the McDowell court of inquiry. He was well aware that the document disclosed a prejudice that unfitted him for this duty, and he wrote Crete to lock the papers away for the time being, but he made no move to disqualify himself. As it happened, he did not serve. He was transferred to a trial on which he was no less prejudiced, the court-martial of Fitz-John Porter. It was to end, after several weeks, in the condemning and cashiering of one of the most able soldiers in the Army of the Potomac. Garfield's part in the proceedings was veiled in military anonymity, but there can be no doubt of his prejudice. Seventeen years later, when a board of general officers reversed the findings of the court and recommended that its sentence be remitted, Garfield was "stung" by the action and spent a large amount of time preparing to debate the question when it came before the House.[58]

In the heat of conflict, political and military judgments had become commingled; yet a man of high principles had taken a long step in acting as an impartial judge at a trial on which his opinion was privately formed in advance. Doubtless Garfield did so in keen apprehension for the future of his country. In the face of Federal defeats in the field and "the painful weakness and uncertainty of the administration," he had despairingly foreseen the possibility of the Republic's going down "in blood and ruin" and had declared that he had no wish to survive it. He had come to believe that the discomfiture of disloyal men was a patriotic duty, dictated by the highest patriotic motives.[59]

Garfield had followed with great interest Lincoln's pronouncements in regard to emancipation. Although he had been elated by the announcement in September that on the first of January all slaves in states or parts of states then in rebellion would be "then, henceforward, and forever free," his hopes were dashed in December as he listened in Congress to the reading of the President's annual message. The President proposed constitutional amendments providing for compensated emancipation by 1900—a scheme that seemed to Garfield weak and absurd. And Garfield could scarcely credit his ears when he listened to the whole message "and heard no word or sentence that indicated that the administration intended to push the war to a triumphant conclusion." The Emancipation Proclamation of January 1 buoyed him up; he wanted to get back in the field "to help in carrying out the Proclamation." But he could not resist a dig at Lincoln. "Strange that a second rate Illinois lawyer should be the instrument through whom one of the sublimest works of any age is accomplished."[60]

Garfield's four months in Washington added nothing to his military reputation or experience, but they were immensely important for his political future. Active service in the Union forces had made a man of moderate views an abolitionist. His stay in Washington completed Garfield's transformation. He had become a Republican extremist, partisan in his opposition to northern Democrats and intent on crushing the legions and the political leaders of the rebellious South.

# CHAPTER 8

# THE WAR: 1863

WHILE THE PORTER court-martial ground to a close in January, Garfield requested and obtained an assignment to the Army of the Cumberland (as the Army of the Ohio had been rechristened when Buell was replaced by Rosecrans in the autumn). To remain in Washington had seemed an "almost personal debasement" after the shocking defeat of the Army of the Potomac at Fredericksburg. "I would infinitely rather die on the Rappahannock," Garfield wrote Burke Hinsdale. He had chosen Stone's River instead. The recent desperate fighting near Murfreesboro, Tennessee, had created vacancies in the high command as well as in the ranks, and Garfield was hoping that Rosecrans, an Ohio man who was close to Secretary Chase, might give him a division.[1]

After months of futile waiting Garfield was going back to his old army, back to the domination of West Point, possibly back to the mere command of a brigade in spite of his cabinet backing. He was ready to take his chances. His sweeping indictment of West Point had been modified by his experience in Washington and by his friendship with Irvin McDowell in particular. He liked what he knew of Rosecrans's bold leadership and antislavery convictions. Garfield had done nothing worthy of notice since the Sandy Valley campaign, an incident all but forgotten in the fiery holocaust of recent months. If he was to take his seat in the next Congress—he was not always certain that he would—he had less than a year in which to distinguish himself on the battlefield.

The assignment to active service restored Garfield's self-respect. Shame had kept him away from Hiram during his months of idleness. He had longed to see his family and the new home that Crete had prepared for them, but he had refused to ask for leave even during the holidays. Now a soldier bound for the front, Garfield confidently faced the critical eyes of the Hiram townsfolk before proceeding to Tennessee.

After much delay and dickering, Crete had rented a small, two-story house across from the Eclectic campus, or cricket field, as it had become during the Garfield regime. The situation was pleasant and there was a yard with thriving fruit trees in the back, but it was not the house of which Crete had dreamed. The rooms were cramped and inconvenient, the stairway and part of the second story were unfinished, and the niggardly owner stinted on badly needed repairs. Crete made the best of it as a temporary expedient until James was able to build. Her slender strength was reduced by a miscarriage in late October, but she managed a trip to Cleveland to buy furnishings. With the help of Harry and Almeda she had the first floor ready for Thanksgiving. The whole house was in shining order for Christmas. Her sister Nellie came to help with the housework. Eliza Garfield elatedly moved in. Still there was no word that James was coming.[2]

Crete had longed for his presence and had been hurt and indignant when she thought that he had been neglectful in writing. She had repented long before he came at last, stepping out of the January night into warmth and lamplight and rapturous welcome. His little Trot was taken up to hug him and marvel at the "chickens" on his buttons. The tiny parlor, with its glowing stove, was bright with his books and prints and Crete's new furnishings. Garfield was entranced by the coziness and sense of home. Since the sale of his mother's farm he had never had a home or supposed that he much desired one. The door had opened on another charmed and sacred center of family life—and stirred again the tender vines of sentiment that had twined about the cabin at Orange.[3]

It was Crete's happiness to please him, but her success was greater than she had intended. Garfield demanded the pride and possession of ownership. During his brief stay he arranged to buy the house for $825, scraping up outstanding loans to help pay for it. The contract was drawn before he left for the front.[4]

With some objections to further outlay, Garfield finally yielded to Crete's pleas for enlargements and repairs, and they were carried out in the fall of 1863. For the next nine years, as long as the Garfields remained in Hiram, they made their home in the little house across from the Eclectic campus.[5]

Less than a week after leaving Hiram, Garfield entered the town of Murfreesboro, a teeming military base girdled with camps and earthworks. He was weak and weary from rough travel and a recurrence of dysentery when at dusk he entered the galleried brick mansion in which General Rosecrans had his headquarters and was admitted to the big first-floor parlor which served the commanding general as combined office, bedroom, and mess hall. The ornate wallpaper contrasted oddly with the simplicity of the furnishings and the military bearing of the occupant. Rosecrans was convalescing from lung fever, but his manner was bright and genial. He received his new officer kindly and asked him to come back the next morning.[6]

Major General William Starke Rosecrans—"Old Rosy" to his troops—was at the height of his fame as a Union commander. Marked from the first as a daring fighter, he had gained immense popularity by his gallant attack at Stone's River and the subsequent occupation of Murfreesboro. Stone's River had in fact been perilously close to a Federal defeat. Its important effect was political rather than military; the chain of Federal reverses in 1862 had weakened morale in the loyal states and emboldened the advocates of compromise with the South. Rosecrans's narrowly won success earned him the thanks of Congress and the lasting gratitude of the President.[7]

In the military view the objects of the Federal offensive were still to be attained. Thirty-odd miles southeast of Murfreesboro the Confederates lay entrenched at Tullahoma, guarding the mountain route to Chattanooga. In replacing the dilatory Buell with the aggressive Rosecrans, the Washington authorities had designed to inflict a decisive defeat on the rebel commander, General Braxton Bragg, and push on to capture Chattanooga, the key to Atlanta and the heart of the South. The question in Garfield's mind was whether Rosecrans would promptly launch a second offensive or whether he might, after all, prove to be another Buell or McClellan, protesting a hundred reasons for delay. But Garfield's doubts vanished on his first day at army headquarters. He found Rosecrans "perfectly unlike McClellan" in his definite opinions and resolute decisions. He was impressed by "Old Rosy's" singularities, by the Spanish cast of his narrow, florid, scarred face with its aquiline nose and short beard. Rosecrans was a Roman Catholic convert—Garfield noted the cross attached to his watch and the worn rosary beads in his pocket. He swore like a mule-skinner, but he did not misuse the name of God. Garfield was struck by the distinction he made between profanity and blasphemy.[8]

The new officer became Rosecrans's constant companion. On the very night of Garfield's arrival he was awakened by a visit from the ailing commander, who lingered in animated talk until his Negro servant came to lead him back to bed. Rosecrans took a fancy to have Garfield sleep in his room; when Garfield rented a room of his own,

Rosecrans sent a written order that he was to sleep and eat with the commanding general until assigned to duty. Rosecrans needed little rest and was indifferent to countrybred notions of bedtime. He talked until the small hours about war, government, literature, business, and theology. The last was his favorite subject. His religious faith was thoughtful and devout. He had a priest at his headquarters and knelt in prayer before he slept. As an incidental result of this association, Garfield lost some of the anti-Catholic prejudice that was rampant among Americans of the day. Although the Roman ritual was peculiarly obnoxious to Disciples, he sometimes joined Rosecrans at services; later, when Garfield had his own quarters, Mass was sometimes celebrated in his room.[9]

An intimacy sprang up between the two strange roommates. Garfield had never become so well acquainted with a man on such a short acquaintance. He responded warmly to Rosecrans's overtures, but he grew restive as the general repeatedly evaded the question of his assignment and kept him dangling about headquarters in idleness. He recognized, however, that he could not get down to serious work until the arrival of his horses.[10]

By day as well as night Rosecrans talked, snapping out orders and lectures on military science, genially chatting and bantering, angrily protesting. He never lacked an audience, for he surrounded himself with people. With a cigar clutched between his nervous fingers or crushed between his teeth, he was as accessible as a politician to his daily file of callers. At his hospitable table there was always room for newspaper correspondents, to whom he expatiated on the situation of the army and his troubles with the War Department. A large staff of young officers hovered about him, alert and deferential as courtiers. His general officers were frequently detained in conference or familiar conversation. In a din of cheers for "Old Rosy" he often rode along the lines, stopping now and then to question a soldier or offer a word of fatherly advice.[11]

Rosecrans had daily evidence of his authority and popularity, but it was not enough. He had need of a friend to whom he could open his mind and heart and take counsel in his problems. His chief of staff, Colonel Julius P. Garesché, had fallen at Stone's River, his head slashed off to the lower jaw by an unexploded shell. The grief that Rosecrans felt was greater than a soldier cared to show. Garesché, a fellow Catholic, had been a friend since West Point days. They had received communion together in a little tent a few hours before Garesché was killed. A devoted staff member, Lieutenant Colonel Calvin C. Goddard, had replaced Garesché as chief of staff, but Rosecrans felt "almost alone in regard to counsel and assistance." While Garfield disconsolately idled around headquarters, he was being measured as a successor to Garesché.[12]

In the middle of February Rosecrans at last told Garfield that he had a division for him, but he proposed the alternative of his staying on at headquarters as chief of staff. Garfield hesitated. He was flattered and strongly tempted, but he was also perplexed. It is likely that he had begun to suspect that Rosecrans was more erratic than he had at first appeared. He could scarcely have failed to remark that Rosecrans had a blazing temper and was quick to take offense, that he talked intemperately about the War Department, that his slight stammer became marked in moments of stress. How enduring, Garfield wondered, was this sudden confidence in a new acquaintance? How much voice would Rosecrans allow his chief of staff in army decisions—that of a mere clerk or "a kind of *alter ego*" to the commander? "By taking that position, I should make a large investment in General Rosecrans," Garfield wrote Harry Rhodes, "and will it be wise to risk so much stock in that market?" Garfield wanted to serve the Union cause, but he was also —admittedly—thinking of his own military reputation.[13]

A series of searching talks with Rosecrans convinced Garfield that he would be given the important part he desired in shaping army policy and movement. It took time to clear the assignment with Washington, but at the end of February the matter was settled. Goddard was relieved with the explanation that Rosecrans wanted a general officer for the position; five weeks after reaching Murfreesboro, Garfield took his place at a crude little pine desk in a small room adjoining the parlor.

During his seven months' service as chief of staff, Garfield did all that could be done by efficiency and unsparing effort and zeal for aggressive action, but his path was mined with frustrations.[14] The favoritism shown the new volunteer officer would inevitably have created jealousy and antagonism, not only in Rosecrans's worshipful entourage but among the professional soldiers who dominated the western armies. It is all the more creditable to Garfield's goodwill and tact that, casting off the last remnants of his bias against West Point, he worked harmoniously with stiff-necked regular officers and won the respect and liking of some of the finest commanders in the Army of the Cumberland. Rosecrans made exigent demands on his chief of staff, sometimes loading him with larger responsibilities than he wished to assume; but Garfield's hope of becoming the commander's *"alter ego"* was never truly fulfilled. He was repeatedly checked by the limitations of his position—privileged but subordinate—and, though long assured of his paramount influence over Rosecrans, he came at last to recognize in him a basic instability that eluded counsels of steady action. Greatest disappointment of all to Garfield, he never realized his supreme ambition of taking part in a great Federal victory.

Soon after receiving his assignment, Garfield obtained his own quarters and, having been joined by his old cook, Professor, set up an independent mess that included his dear friend, Captain Swaim, now assigned to Rosecrans's staff in charge of the scout or intelligence department. Harry Rhodes, a recent bridegroom, arrived in late February for a week's visit, but there was little opportunity for confidential conversation. With improved health, Rosecrans had reverted to his custom of working at night. His energy flashed like fireworks as he sparked out plans and orders and teased his sleepy young aides. On May 4 Garfield noted that he had "not retired, on an average, before two o'clock for the last two months and a half." [15]

Reinforcements and matériel had been accumulating at Murfreesboro, and the early weeks were largely occupied with army reorganization. Garfield was also deeply concerned with arrangements for a preliminary operation in central Georgia. An officer formerly under his command in the Twentieth Brigade, Colonel Abel D. Streight of the Fifty-first Indiana, had proposed a raid on one of Bragg's main supply lines, the railroad between Atlanta and Chattanooga. Garfield's imagination was fired. He impulsively requested permission to go himself. Rosencrans refused to spare him but authorized the expedition with Streight in command and Garfield in charge of the entire planning and preparation. Garfield's thoughts went with the little force when it vanished into enemy country in April. His heart was set on its success; but early in May it became known that Streight and his men, their mission unaccomplished, had been captured by Nathan Forrest's dashing troopers. [16]

Garfield never admitted that the enterprise had been rash. He had taken a gambler's chance, and he buried his disappointment in preparations for the spring offensive. Letters of early May disclose his eagerness for action. "Nothing but hard blows that will break their armies and pulverize them can destroy the Confederacy," he wrote Secretary Chase. "I am, therefore, for striking, striking, and striking again till we do break them." Having expressed himself similarly to Corydon Fuller, he went on to say, "These views lead me to hope and believe that before many days we shall be in a death-grapple with Bragg and Johnston." The Army of the Cumberland had a numerical superiority over the forces of Bragg, though it had the disadvantage of an inferior force of cavalry. Bragg had advanced his lines to Shelbyville, due south of Murfreesboro. Raids and outpost skirmishes multiplied. Rosecrans repeatedly approached the point of ordering a Federal advance but time after time postponed it.[17]

The War Department was calling with increasing insistence for a movement in Tennessee. The gloomy news of Chancellorsville, another crushing defeat in Virginia, had heightened the disaffection to the Lincoln government and the war and threatened to impede the enforcement of the new conscription act. Military exigencies were no less compelling. Grant, after months of doggedly prodding the approaches to Vicksburg, had crossed the Mississippi below the city. Reinforcements would inevitably flow from Tennessee to its defense unless Bragg's army was engaged. But Rosecrans was deaf to the anxious appeals of General Halleck; he had no wish to cooperate with Grant's campaign. On the contrary, he argued the advantage of deferring his own movement until the fall of Vicksburg should release reinforcements for the Army of the Cumberland—"our last reserve" he called it in one dispatch to Washington. When he was entirely ready, Rosecrans intended to thrash Bragg and finish off the rebellion. Meanwhile he squabbled with the War Department about his need for more cavalry and for horses and light revolving rifles with which to mount and arm them.[18]

Rosecrans had an arrogant resistance to superior authority. While serving under Grant in the Corinth campaign of the previous autumn, he had angered that general by disobeying his orders and then replied to a reprimand with hot reproaches, as though they had been engaged in a private quarrel. His dispatches to the War Department had the same wrangling, personal tone. Halleck was his long-suffering friend, but Stanton had small patience with temperamental generals and had already the year before crossed swords with Rosecrans for exceeding his instructions in Virginia. As recently as January, Rosecrans had been reminded of Stanton's "senseless but strong prejudice" against him by his former chief of staff, General George L. Hartsuff, who was then on duty in Washington. Hartsuff wrote that he had repeatedly told Stanton that Rosecrans would belie his opinion if given "half a chance." He thought that the secretary had yielded up his prejudice—but admitted that it was "a rare thing for him to do."[19]

The belief that he was in disfavor with the War Department aggravated Rosecrans's natural refractoriness. His criticisms of Stanton and Halleck embarrassed Henry Villard, a twenty-eight-year-old German emigré who came to Murfreesboro in May as correspondent for the *New York Tribune*. The first interview convinced Villard that Rosecrans had no thought of an immediate advance. Murfreesboro appeared to be fortified for a siege; the camps had a look of permanence. Fighting the Confederates seemed to be less on Rosecrans's mind than battling the War Department.[20]

Villard judged that Stone's River had left a mark on Rosecrans— that heavy casualties and near defeat had damaged his once confident aggressiveness. Altogether the correspondent formed a poor impression; he stiffly regarded Rosecrans as a publicity-seeker who tried to "work the press" and thought that Garfield was "far more commanding and attractive" in appearance.[21]

Fine weather had brought the army a throng of visitors, not all of them primarily interested in the military situation. The inner circles of the Republican party were restive with the radicals' opposition to Lincoln and desire to prevent his renomination in 1864. Various men in public life were privately backed and canvassed, and Secretary Chase was frantically using the vast Treasury patronage to advance his own claims; but some of the dissidents thought that a right-minded Union general would make the strongest candidate. Horace Greeley of the *New York Tribune,* a severe critic of Lincoln, was impressed by Rosecrans's military record and popular following, especially in the West, and his interest was purportedly shared by an important group of party leaders. As an emissary to Murfreesboro, Greeley had selected James R. Gilmore, a former shipping and cotton merchant who had latterly devoted himself to antislavery propaganda and formed a desultory connection with the *Tribune* during the war. A series of fictional sketches based on observations made on business trips to the South and replete with dialect and incident had made Gilmore's pseudonym "Edmund Kirke" well known throughout the Union. He was instructed by Greeley to observe Rosecrans with a particular view to his antislavery convictions and, if the verdict proved favorable, to sound him on the subject of the presidential nomination.[22]

If Greeley's important associates were in fact as united on Rosecrans as Gilmore said, the popular author was a nearly laughable choice for their representative. He was a harmless opportunist, delighted with all the prominent men he met and eager to win their confidence. He liked and was liked by the President himself and did not want to work against him; still he went to Murfreesboro and began observing Rosecrans. He was soon on friendly terms with the commander—and with Garfield, who loved meeting authors and was charmed with "Edmund Kirke's" company and his latest volume of sketches.[23]

A fortnight at headquarters satisfied Gilmore that Rosecrans was the very man for Greeley and his friends. By his own account, the writer first disclosed the true nature of his errand to Garfield, whom he was nursing through a bout of fever. He recalled that Garfield was "greatly pleased" with Greeley's proposition. Rosecrans, however, declined to entertain it and expressed his complete trust in the President. Gilmore soon left for Washington with certain unrelated communications, one of them concerning a peace mission, which Rosecrans desired him to present to Lincoln in person.[24]

That Garfield wanted Rosecrans to accept was undoubtedly a figment of Gilmore's unreliable memory. Rosecrans's assurances had persuaded his chief of staff that an army movement was imminent. The desire to encourage a political involvement would have been utterly inconsistent with Garfield's absorption in the military situation. Garfield in fact came to deplore political overtures to Rosecrans because they played on the commander's vanity and made him regard himself as an important public figure.

"If the President-hunters had left him alone," Garfield wrote in a private letter in 1867, "he might have been at the head of our armies today. But in the fatal summer of 1863, he was enveloped in clouds of incense, and visions of the Presidency were constantly thrust before him. I think that this made him a little over-cautious and increased the delay in beginning the campaign of Middle Tennessee. . . ."[25]

In early June, with still unclouded confidence, Garfield received instructions to draw up a plan for a move on the Confederate works at Shelbyville and Tullahoma. He speedily prepared a draft and outlined a detailed order with time schedules fixed. His plan was promptly approved, and the army concentrated. But, on the eve of the departure, Rosecrans decided to ask the advice of his commanders; the operation was held in abeyance while seventeen general officers composed written opinions. They were unanimously opposed to an immediate or indeed an early advance. The three corps commanders, Thomas J. Crittenden, Alexander McD. McCook, even the redoubtable George H. Thomas, pulled back from the verge of action. The daring young general, Phil Sheridan, went along with the rest. Rosecrans postponed his movement indefinitely, dispatching the consensus of his generals to Halleck in justification of further delay.[26]

Garfield was appalled and bewildered. The Army of the Cumberland was at its maximum strength, as fit and eager as a boxer at the peak of his training. Bragg's army had been weakened, according to expectation, by the detachment of reinforcements for Mississippi. Yet, in this propitious hour, an epidemic of cautiousness had paralyzed officers whom Garfield knew to have been as restive for action as himself. He was naively unobservant of the obvious echoes of Rosecrans's views in the submitted opinions. "I know the General desires to move," he wrote Crete, "but it is hard to go with so many unwilling men in high places."[27]

Mingled with Garfield's discomfiture was a "mortification almost akin to shame." He had written good-bye letters, steeled himself to face danger and possible death, commended himself and the cause to God. His solemn commitment had ended ludicrously in anticlimax. But Garfield did not yield to disappointment; having obtained permission from Rosecrans, he submitted a formal letter of his own that summarized the opinions of the generals and undertook to contravene them in a cogent statement of the reasons, military and political, for an immediate, full-scale advance. It was the most presumptuous and perhaps the most effective act of Garfield's military career. Shortly after receiving the paper Rosecrans again took up Garfield's plan of campaign. Two weeks later, on June 24, the Army of the Cumberland was at last in motion. Unfortunately, however, the postponement had launched the movement in a spell of heavy rains that soaked men and equipment and turned the roads into swamps.[28]

Once in the field, Rosecrans became the audacious and skillful commander. In nine days of hard campaigning he outflanked the rebels at Shelbyville and Tullahoma and sent them flying into the Cumberland Mountains. The mired mountain roads forbade immediate pursuit with artillery and wagon trains, and the army's tents were pitched on the former Confederate camping ground at Tullahoma. The elated toops soon cheered the news that, without fighting a battle, Rosecrans had regained the whole of middle Tennessee. Bragg's army had crossed the mountains and the Tennessee River to take refuge behind the defenses of Chattanooga.[29]

Rosecrans throve on compliments and congratulations, but his pride was punctured by the great Federal victories at Gettysburg and Vicksburg. In the tumult of national rejoicing, his brilliant but indecisive campaign carried on with little bloodshed was almost ignored by the press and the Washington authorities. "You and your noble army now have the chance to give the finishing blow to the rebellion," Stanton telegraphed Rosecrans in announcing the fall of Vicksburg. "Will you neglect the chance?" Rosecrans dispatched a hotly sarcastic reply. Affronted by the slight to his own achievement, he reverted to a mood of sullen grievance. His nagging requisitions produced only an increasingly exasperated pressure to advance. The War Department's vision was bounded by a single imperative—that Rosecrans confront Bragg's army before it received reinforcements released from Mississippi. Rosecrans saw only his crying need of cavalry, the problems of supplying his army for the trek across the barren Cumberlands and the Tennessee, and the eventual difficulties of bringing supplies from the main base at Nashville. The angry dispatches crossed without communication, like hostile people passing in the street. Toward the end of July Halleck sought to soften the austerity of his official dispatches by personal letters—to which Rosecrans responded in kind.[30]

The success of the Tullahoma campaign belonged to Garfield as well as Rosecrans, and Rosecrans generously acknowledged the fact, praising his chief of staff in his official report as possessing "the instincts and energy of a great commander." But success had been spoiled for Garfield by Bragg's escape in the rains and Rosecrans's relapse into contumacy and temporizing. In the weeks after Tullahoma, Garfield began to have the first tentative doubts that Rosecrans was capable of persistently aggressive leadership.[31]

Garfield's physical endurance was flagging when in mid-July he accompanied Rosecrans on a tour of inspection preparatory to the new advance. His nerves were frayed by the painstaking thoroughness with which they examined the forts, camps, hospitals, and supply departments at Nashville. His digestion fell badly out of rhythm as Rosecrans, with a perverse assumption of leisure, drew out their stay for two weeks, sending for his wife and little girls (Rosecrans invited Crete and Trot also, but Crete was six months pregnant and did not come) and holding grand reviews and sociable meetings. Especially irritating to Garfield must have been Rosecrans's enthusiasm for a proposal, advanced by General Lovell H. Rousseau, which was entirely without bearing on the impending movement.[32]

Rousseau, a Kentucky politican who commanded one of Thomas's divisions, wanted to go to Washington to get permission from the War Department to raise a corps of 12,000 Union veterans, 10,000 of whom would be "infantry or riflemen" mounted on mules and the rest cavalry. The autumn elections were coming up in Kentucky, and Rousseau was angling for an opportunity to take part in them on his way to Washington; his chosen companion, Lieutenant Colonel John P. Sanderson, a Pennsylvania politician and journalist, was to interview a number of public men in his home state. Rosecrans was delighted to approve their plans for the trip to Washington—and presumably the side trips on the way. He sat for several hours one Saturday in Sanderson's hotel room, conferring with him and Rousseau and enjoying the old brandy and good cigars with which Sanderson regaled him; on Sunday night he had his aides up until three o'clock preparing the necessary documents. His interest in this politically slanted excursion may have been the straw that broke down Garfield's discretion. On July 27, the day that Rousseau and Sanderson left Nashville, Garfield unburdened himself, in a long, confidential letter to Secretary Chase, of his fears for the army and his own good name as a soldier.[33]

"Thus far," he wrote in summing up the trials of the past months, "the General has been singularly disinclined to grasp the situation with a strong hand and make the advantage his own. I write this with more sorrow than I can tell you, for I love every bone in his body, and next to my desire to see the rebellion blasted is my anxiety to see him blessed. But even the breadth of my love is not sufficient to cover this almost fatal delay."[34]

Garfield's words were mild and his provocations great, but this was not a letter that Rosecrans's chief of staff should have written to a member of the government. Had he first asked to be relieved, his report would have been a matter of patriotic duty. But with his time in the service running out, Garfield was reluctant to quit his present post; he was plainly hoping against hope that Rosecrans might swing into another phase of brilliant leadership before it was too late.

The vagaries of Rosecrans's temperament were legion, but early in August Stanton took his turn. Rosecrans received peremptory orders to move forward and to make a daily report of his progress. The orders were issued not only in ignorance of the terrain and the problems of supply but in disregard of the probable reinforcement of Bragg's army. The logical consequence of the fall of Vicksburg was to release troops for Rosecrans as well as Bragg, but Stanton refused to reinforce the Federal commander. Rosecrans's only prospect of help in his campaign was the cooperation of an independent expedition ordered to eastern Tennessee under General Ambrose Burnside, and at the time the Federal advance was dictated, Burnside had not left his headquarters at Cincinnati. Stanton was risking the possibility that, in a critical theater of the war, the Army of the Cumberland might be outnumbered by the enemy.[35]

Rosecrans indignantly told his corps commanders that he would offer his resignation unless given more time to make ready. He told Halleck that the order could not safely be carried out literally in regard to troop movements and asked that it be modified or that he be relieved of command. Halleck responded wearily: "The means you are to employ, and the roads you are to follow, are left to your own discretion. If you wish to promptly carry out the wishes of the Government, you will not stop to discuss mere details." Rosecrans speeded up his preparations and moved a week later.[36]

Garfield's hopes had hung on this advance, but he was far from sympathetic with Stanton's attitude. His letter to Chase had contained a hint that the War Department had not always been just in its dealings and a guarded reference to some influence in Washington that had kept "this army back from the most vigorous activity." In the letter of 1867 (quoted above) Garfield expressed the opinion that Rosecrans's political prominence had created alarm at Washington and that "the political leaders . . . were not unwilling to see evil befall him." He left no doubt of the direction in which he was pointing. "Certain it is," he added, "that the War Department seemed very ready to find fault with him from that time forward." [37]

It is impossible to believe that the dedicated secretary of war consciously desired the defeat of the Army of the Cumberland; but Stanton's hostility to Rosecrans was fast becoming an obsession. The orders to advance, without reinforcements, suggest a blindly vindictive purpose to leave Rosecrans to get out of the scrape in which his delays had involved him. [38]

From Halleck Rosecrans had received the impression that the President was dissatisfied with him, and on August 1 he wrote directly to Lincoln. In his response ten days later Lincoln made it clear that he had seen most if not all of Rosecrans's dispatches to Halleck and that he had indeed had misgivings concerning Rosecrans's reluctance to move. But he ended by assuring the unhappy general that he thought of him "in all kindness and confidence" and that he was not watching him "with an evil-eye." [39]

Garfield had fallen seriously ill after the trip to Nashville. He had nearly been invalided home but, resisting such an action with all his might, traveled to the Tennessee on a cot loaded on a railroad car. His influence over Rosecrans had strongly regained the ascendant. He willed himself to remain and to get better. "There is so much of myself in the plan of this campaign that I must help realize my ideas," Garfield wrote Crete on August 23, shortly after reaching the north bank of the Tennessee. "It is not vanity for me to say that no man in this army can fill my place during this movement," he wrote again a week later. Under the devoted care of Captain Swaim, Garfield gradually recovered. By the time the army had crossed the river, he was able to mount Harry for the advance across the ragged terrain of northwest Georgia. [40]

The plan of campaign was the flanking movement at which Rosecrans excelled, and he executed it with spirit. Burnside was at last in eastern Tennessee and had occupied Knoxville, but he was not within supporting distance of Rosecrans. Lookout Mountain proved to be a formidable barrier, forty miles long and penetrated by widely separated passes. But Rosecrans did not hesitate. He sent Crittenden's corps to the northernmost gap, just below Chattanooga, and ordered

Thomas and McCook to proceed by lower routes and threaten Bragg's communications. The daring maneuver succeeded. Bragg fled from the trap of Chattanooga, and Crittenden pressed forward to occupy the city. Rosecrans followed with his staff and made his headquarters in a house set in a grove of oak trees high above the river. "Chattanooga is ours without a struggle, and East Tennessee is free," he jubilantly telegraphed Halleck on September 9.[41]

Rosecrans had gained a prize of strategic importance second only to Vicksburg in the West. In his exultation he did not stop to secure it, concentrate his army, or find out where Bragg had gone and what he intended. He was sure that the Confederates were again on the run and this time could be caught and whipped. Messengers went to Burnside to urge him to speed on his cavalry. With Garfield at his elbow, Rosecrans issued orders to disperse his force still more widely. Holding a single brigade at Chattanooga, he rushed the rest of Crittenden's corps to the east, beyond Missionary Ridge, to intercept the enemy's retreat. The other two corps were instructed to push on through the distant gaps in Lookout and cut off the westerly avenues of escape. Garfield's part in these impetuous decisions must be assumed—and deplored. Rosecrans, in this crucial hour, was in need not of a spur but a steady hand on the bridle. For the premise on which he scattered his army was totally mistaken; the Confederates were not in retreat. Already reinforced from Knoxville as well as Vicksburg, with troops on the way from Lee's army in Virginia, Bragg was preparing to attack. While his outposts threatened Thomas's front, his army was gathering in the mountains twelve miles southeast of Chattanooga, beyond a sluggish stream called Chickamauga Creek.[42]

September 11 brought Rosecrans the first grim warnings that he might have exposed his army in detail. It also brought a visitor to his headquarters—Assistant Secretary of War Charles A. Dana, a professional journalist who was acting as a "field observer" for the War Department. Dana was apt at touching off the various generals in shrewd and sometimes malicious little character sketches that were highly valued by Stanton and by the President. He was not popular with some of the officers of the Army of the Cumberland nor with the rank and file, who suspected that he was there to unseat "Old Rosy." Soldiers sometimes jeered him as he rode around the camp, pretending that he was a sutler, a breed held in low esteem; Gordon Granger was later to call him *"that loathsome pimp, Dana."* But Rosecrans, after an initial flare-up, welcomed him to his headquarters and his councils.[43]

Rosecrans's intimacy with Dana was a puzzle from the first; the hostile authority that his visitor represented was vividly present in his mind. At this same time, Colonel Sanderson returned to Chattanooga, burning with indignation at the antagonism that he and Rousseau had encountered at the War Department—and especially at the unconcealed enmity with which Stanton had spoken of Rosecrans. Sanderson feared that Stanton was going to have Rosecrans removed, and he spilled out the whole story to the general in a loyal desire to prepare him for his fate. Perhaps, in those days of desperation when the concentration of his army was "a matter of life and death," Rosecrans grasped at the hope of a friend in the War Department. And Dana acted like a friend; he was a good listener and a good observer. After an evening of talk and map study with Rosecrans, he sent to Stanton the next morning a factual statement of what he had learned. On the day following he set out with Rosecrans and his staff on an overnight visit to Thomas's headquarters. He was impressed by the tremendous achievement of the Army of the Cumberland in "crossing the Cumberland Mountains, passing the Tennessee, turning and occupying Chattanooga, traversing the mountain ridges of Northern Georgia, and seizing the passes" leading southward, and he let Stanton know it in a telegram from Stevens Gap. He did perceive one danger: that Rosecrans's "long and precarious line of communication" might be threatened by a sudden movement of Confederates to his right. To avoid this danger he urged that troops be brought from the Mississippi. Halleck, as it happened, was already aware of the problem and had sent orders for the movement of forces from Grant's army to cooperate with Rosecrans.[44]

The visit to Thomas had produced a general feeling of relief. Bragg had muffed his chance to crush the Federal army piece by piece. The concentration of the three columns was proceeding in good order without interference from the enemy. Fears of an impending battle had brushed even Garfield's buoyant mind, but they vanished in a comforting sense of reprieve. On September 16 he wrote Crete that the battle would probably be deferred until the troops arrived from Burnside and Grant, but he looked forward zestfully to "the finishing great blow" to the rebellion. This was the last letter that Garfield would write for a week.[45]

Rosecrans did not return to Chattanooga after the ride down Lookout but set up headquarters on the west bank of Chickamauga Creek, where Crittenden's wandering brigades had been ordered to occupy a defensible position while awaiting the arrival of the rest of the army. The terrain was not one that Rosecrans would have chosen for a battleground. The Federals would be massed in a narrow, thickly wooded strip of valley, with the stream in their front and the massif of Missionary Ridge towering in their rear. Though hemmed in by mountains, the valley itself had no considerable heights for observation, and

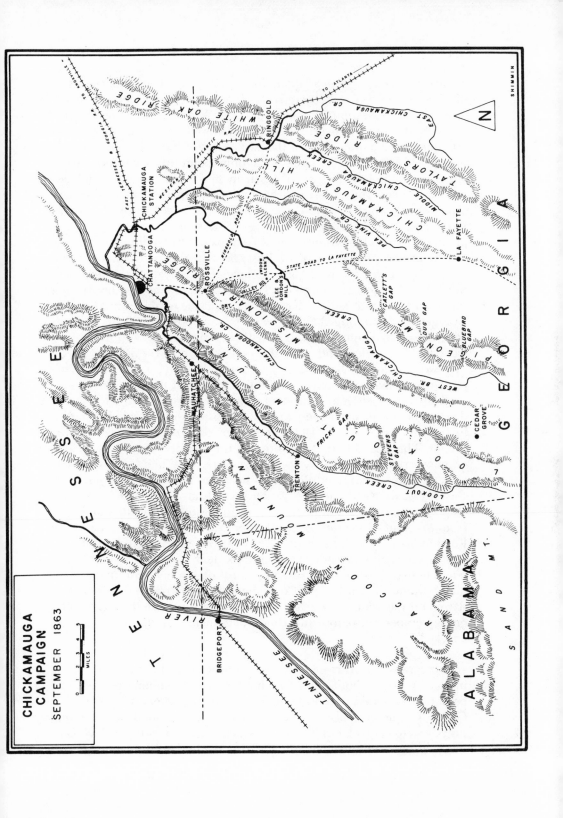

CHICKAMAUGA
CAMPAIGN
SEPTEMBER 1863

0 1 2 3 4 5
MILES

SHIMMIN

its heavy woods were ill-adapted for artillery and communications; a still graver concern to Rosecrans was its relation to the defense of the prize whose possession he had impulsively hazarded. His dream of a Federal offensive was over; his back was, literally, to the mountain wall that guarded Chattanooga on the east. The fortified city was his only base of matériel and supplies, his only point of telegraphic communication, the only refuge for his army in the bitter event of defeat.

Three main routes led to Chattanooga from the valley. The Dry Valley Road, which wound through a gap in the center of Missionary Ridge and passed through the village of Rossville, was a westerly approach of secondary interest in Rosecrans's calculations. His anxiety was to protect the gap east of Rossville and the roads that crossed there, eight miles south of Chattanooga: the Lafayette or State Road, which ran due north through the Federal position, and the intersecting Ringgold Road that led to Chattanooga from the east. General Gordon Granger, commanding the reserve corps, was posted in front of Rossville, but he had come up with only three brigades. Should the enemy flank the Union left and seize the crossroads and the Rossville Gap, they would regain Chattanooga and force the Federals to accept surrender or defeat in the passes and blind valleys of the mountains.

This was a battle, an officer of Crittenden's command later wrote, that ought not to have been fought. Burnside did not send the reinforcements that the War Department had ordered and Rosecrans besought. The troops from Mississippi had not started on their way. The outnumbered Federal army faced desperate odds, and a week of nervous tension had strained Rosecrans nearly to the breaking point.[46]

This was a battle that the Union should not fight—but the knowledge came too late. Before his footsore divisions began to stumble in from Lookout, Rosecrans decided to ensure his hold on the Lafayette Road by moving his line farther north. It was nearly midnight of September 18 when Crittenden's troops took their position at the new center. Thomas pushed his corps forward on an exhausting all-night march to the distant left. McCook showed up at army headquarters at dawn and was ordered to place his oncoming forces on the right. Early on September 19, before the Union alignment was completed, Bragg attacked.[47]

Rosecrans moved close to the field to the rear of the center, setting up headquarters about noon on a hill behind Crittenden's position in a bare little log cabin whose owner survives in history as the Widow Glenn. The fierce collisions in the smoke-shrouded woods were beyond his power to control, but all day he issued a spate of orders which Garfield, sitting at a large table brought from the back of the cabin, embodied in precise language and dispatched. As Thomas's position came under repeated attack, Rosecrans sent brigades and whole divisions to his support. When darkness settled over the shattered trees and the litter of dead and dying, the battered Union lines still held, but the right and center had been badly disorganized and the imbalance was aggravated by orders issued during the night and the next morning.[48]

About two hours after the battle reopened, while Rosecrans's mind was still riveted on Thomas, the Confederates massed for a smashing attack on the battered Federal right. An order from Rosecrans, based on a misapprehension and literally obeyed, precipitated a Federal disaster. An entire division was withdrawn from the line just as Longstreet's famous corps burst from the woods. Eight brigades in battle formation, they crashed through the breach, isolating the Union right and piercing and crumbling the center. Rosecrans and his officers rode into the melee in a valiant effort to halt the rout, but, attacked in flank and rear, the troops stampeded toward the Dry Valley Road. Rebel soldiers overran the Widow Glenn's and scattered staff officers and orderlies. Rosecrans gained the rear with Garfield and a few others; they started on a direct route to Thomas but were blocked by surging enemy columns. Under a shower of musketfire, the little party made for the Dry Valley Road, pressing through and around its heavy traffic of caissons, wagons, ambulances, and fleeing troops. Rosecrans seemed sunk in apathy, all will and purpose broken. He rode in silence toward Rossville, appearing abstracted, as though he neither saw nor heard the jostle and clamor of the retreat.[49]

Thomas's position had now become the front. With the reinforcements that were on their way to join him, he was in command of seven of the ten divisions of the Army of the Cumberland. Garfield's uneasiness mounted as they moved away from the battlefield, the cannonade still roaring at their backs. At Rossville, in the midst of milling fugitives, he and Rosecrans dismounted and spoke apart, knelt and put their ears to the ground, then spoke again. Garfield said that he urged Rosecrans to return to the field and, getting no response, asked permission to go himself. Rosecrans assented "listlessly and mechanically." He took leave of his chief of staff as if never expecting to see him again.[50]

Rosecrans rode on to Chattanooga, so dazed that he needed help to get down from his horse and enter his headquarters. Garfield, accompanied by an aide, an orderly, and one or two officers of Thomas's staff, spurred Billy through the Rossville Gap and down the Lafayette Road to the thunder of guns on the Federal left.[51]

Garfield reached the front unscathed, though the orderly and a horse had been killed and Billy wounded. He made haste to send Rosecrans the glorious news that, after terrible fighting, Thomas still held on. "I think we may in the main retrieve our morning disaster," he wrote. He urged the commanding officer to come back to Rossville that night and bring badly needed ammunition. Before he received this report, Rosecrans had ordered Thomas to assume command of all the forces and retire on the village.[52]

About sunset Garfield received from Rosecrans a similar order to be communicated to Thomas: "Should General Thomas be retiring in order, tell him to resist the enemy's advance, retiring on Rossville." The possibility of making a stand at Rossville had occurred to Garfield, but by the time he had learned of Rosecrans's intention his natural optimism had been stimulated by Gordon Granger, a mettlesome and somewhat showy soldier who was sure that the rebels were "thoroughly whipped." Garfield and Granger "strenuously urged" Thomas that the order was discretionary and should not be obeyed. Thomas, however, was already preparing to retire. There seems to be little basis for Garfield's lifelong conviction that the cautious and strictly subordinate Thomas would have held his ground had Garfield and Granger been present when the first order was received. The last of the Federal forces marched to Rossville under cover of darkness.[53]

Though badly disappointed, Garfield did not relinquish hope that the fighting would continue. He eagerly dispatched Rosecrans from Rossville that the morrow might "crown the whole battle with victory." A later message sounded a less confident note; Garfield had had a chance to observe the disorganization and impaired morale of the routed troops and their disgust with Crittenden and McCook, who had both followed Rosecrans to Chattanooga. A talk with Thomas led Garfield to report the conclusion that the army did not seem to be "in the best trim for an early fight." By morning he had succumbed to abysmal discouragement. Garfield advised the commanding general that perhaps he had better remain at Chattanooga for the present, and he himself rode up to resume his duties at headquarters.[54]

Garfield's last hope had plainly been pinned to Thomas. He had seen that stanch soldier in battle and thrilled to the heroism which he had inspired in his troops. But Thomas would not presume to fill the void of leadership at Chattanooga; his deference to Rosecrans was absolute and uncritical. Garfield accepted the inevitable with a stoicism that hid a rebellious heart. The battle, he bitterly wrote Crete, "was won, and then abandoned."[55]

Rosecrans was intent on pulling in his army and defending Chattanooga. Orders went to Thomas to withdraw all forces at Rossville to a line in front of the city. The Confederates followed to invest it closely on the south and east. Federal troops labored to throw up earthworks and brushwood abatis against the attack that was expected hourly. At the first sign of hostile demonstration toward Lookout Mountain, Rosecrans called in the brigade that occupied its northern slopes, guarding the main route to the Federal supply depot at Bridgeport on the Tennessee. Garfield and Granger protested that the mountain and the road must be held, but Rosecrans brushed aside their objections and left the heights to the Confederates.[56]

The situation at Chattanooga flooded Garfield with alarm for the army and the whole Tennessee campaign, and on September 23 he telegraphed Secretary Chase a warning that help must come within ten days. He specifically advised that 25,000 men be sent to Bridgeport to secure middle Tennessee in case of "disaster" at Chattanooga. Since the War Department had not succeeded in moving reinforcements either from Grant or Burnside, this advice might have seemed fancifully optimistic; but a similar—though less urgent—request from Dana had goaded Stanton into taking drastic action.[57]

No member of the government felt more keenly than Stanton the double calamity of the defeat and its bearing on the impending state elections. He sneered that Rosecrans had failed because he "ran away" from the battle, but a large section of the press blamed the War Department, and Stanton had to support the despised general effectively and at once. His method of dealing with the emergency was to summon a midnight council at the War Department and bully its doubtful members—including the President himself—into approving orders to send two veteran corps of the Army of the Potomac to Bridgeport. By a wartime miracle of slashing red tape and commandeering railroads, the troops began pouring into Bridgeport seven days later.[58]

News that strong reinforcements were on the way put an end to Garfield's fears for the military situation, but his one letter to Crete from Chattanooga following the decision in Washington disclosed little else. For a period of more than three weeks he is a nearly shadowy figure lighted by rare gleams of comment. The pen of Colonel Sanderson, acting aide to Rosecrans at this time, fretfully described a chief of staff of limited ability, disorganized, overconfident in his opinions, and lacking in respect for more mature minds. General James B. Steedman, one of the heroes of Thomas's stand at Chickamauga, recalled a dearly loved friend who talked him out of resigning his commission after a violent quarrel with Rosecrans. Henry Villard's reminiscences suggest a perplexed and uneasy man oppressed by the necessity of masking his thoughts and feelings. Villard gathered that Garfield had lost confidence in Rosecrans and thought it natural that he found his position embarrassing.[59]

The commanding general was much occupied with reorganizing the army, but the problem of supplies was crucial. By early October the consequences of the withdrawal from Lookout were painfully apparent. Having occupied the heights, the Confederates fanned out to invest Chattanooga on the west and all but sever its communications with the supply depot. Rosecrans was working on a plan to transport supplies by boat. It was a good plan, but he made slow progress in carrying it out. The soldiers went on short rations and animals starved and died while the Federal army languished in the trap that Rosecrans had expertly set for Bragg only weeks before.[60]

Rosecrans was nervous and irresolute, oscillating between determination and despondency. Consumed by a rage of self-justification, he lashed out at mistakes made by Stanton and Halleck and some of his general officers and refused to acknowledge fault or failure of his own. In his private mythology, Chickamauga had been a victory because it had saved Chattanooga. His official report affirmed that the battle had been "absolutely necessary to secure our concentration and cover Chattanooga" and, ignoring the reports of his generals, he concluded that his army "really beat the enemy on the field."[61]

Here was a deep, neurotic need for approbation that reason could not reach. Garfield's loss of trust in his commander was swallowed up in pity for his friend. His later letters to Rosecrans supply the key to his attitude; he tried to comfort, calm, and reassure. He counseled Rosecrans to avoid an open breach with the War Department. He spoke of "the almost unparalleled success" with which Rosecrans had planned and executed his "vast campaigns." But Chickamauga in the letters is little more than a name. In passing over the battle, Garfield played a double part; the incident at Rossville lay, like an ambush, in his path.[62]

Rosecrans had explained Garfield's return to the front by saying that he had sent the chief of staff to find Thomas and report, while he himself took charge at the base, as was the duty of the commanding general. According to Dana, Rosecrans privately questioned the validity of his "excuse" on learning that he was censured, along with Crittenden and McCook, for having deserted the battlefield. But his doubts evidently dissolved in the necessity for asserting his competence during the battle. The decision at Rossville, with its implication of steady poise and judgment, became a vitally important article of his vindication of his conduct. He never alluded to his nervous collapse; in time he undoubtedly annulled the humiliating memory, as he annulled so much else.[63]

Rosecrans's account of his conversation with Garfield had been implicitly accepted by his staff. As Garfield entered no demur, his concurrence was taken for granted. He did not recognize that his silence might bear the stamp of duplicity if his own version became known;

and Garfield was not going to remain silent. His ride to Thomas was the shining exploit of his military career, and he took particular pride in having made it on his own initiative. At Chattanooga he confided the story to the trustworthy Villard. Once he was relieved of duty Garfield would tell his story often—and less discreetly.[64]

Garfield was on more cordial terms with Dana than were Rosecrans's other friends, but so was Rosecrans. The informer for the War Department was still an honored guest at headquarters, sitting at Rosecrans's table and drawing him out in private conversation. Since it was Dana's practice to pump any officer who was willing to talk to him, it may be assumed that he tried to pump Garfield; but he elicited very little that was worth reporting to Stanton. He classed Garfield among certain "officers of prominence and worth" who spoke anxiously about the army's loss of confidence in the commanders who had left the battlefield, especially Crittenden and McCook, but also including Rosecrans. Garfield was evidently guarded in his speech, though he does not appear to have shared the prevailing indignation over Dana's presence. Thomas became so incensed that he bluntly warned Rosecrans, but he did not succeed in dislodging Dana.[65]

To exaggerate Rosecrans's diminished popularity—he had in fact kept a remarkably strong hold on the affection of his troops—was one of Dana's favorite devices. Ever since Chickamauga he had been working to discredit the commander by insinuating reports of his military errors and misconduct. When he came out for putting Thomas in command, Stanton was highly gratified. He had sounded Rousseau on the matter a month before the battle, and he now asked Dana to convey to Thomas his effusive compliments and his desire to see him in command of "an independent army." But Thomas had heard from Rousseau what army Stanton had in mind and coldly rebuffed the overture.[66]

A more serious obstacle to Stanton's designs was the President's partiality for Rosecrans. Lincoln placed great reliance on Dana's reports. When Dana urged that Crittenden and McCook be removed, Lincoln signed the order; but he balked at removing Rosecrans. Dana stepped up his campaign. On October 12 he prepared a waspish account of Rosecrans's personal foibles and then moved in for the kill. ". . . With great love of command, he is a feeble commander . . . ," his dispatch read. "Under the present circumstances I consider this army to be very unsafe in his hands, but do know of no man except Thomas who could now be safely put in his place." Stanton surely felt that his object was nearly realized when he handed this message to the President.[67]

The armies of the Union had no finer soldier than Thomas. Stanton and Dana were not ill-advised in their choice, but they were precipitate and vengeful in their zeal to decapitate Rosecrans. There was no necessity for haste. Rosecrans's retirement from the Army of the Cumberland had been virtually assured by the recent decision of the Washington government to unite the western armies under command of Grant. Stanton, however, did not intend to give Rosecrans the dignified choice of resigning. Before leaving to meet Grant at Louisville in the middle of October, he obtained the President's permission to let Grant choose between Rosecrans and Thomas. Grant's dislike of Rosecrans was well known; in consenting to leave the decision to him, Lincoln washed his hands of Rosecrans.[68]

The humiliation of Rosecrans bore an obscure imprint of injustice. He was a good and honorable man, a brilliant, very nearly a great soldier. His personal courage was beyond reproach. He lacked the fighting heart that is strong in adversity. Unable to defy military failure and political subversion, he might have destroyed himself had Stanton not anticipated him. Steedman, in after years, pronounced perhaps the final verdict for the history books: "The times were too broad and red and grand for a man of Rosecrans' caliber."[69]

On October 15 Rosecrans regretfully relieved Garfield from duty and entrusted him with his official report to be delivered to the War Department with a personal explanation of the situation at Chattanooga. In company with Steedman, who had been called to Washington, Garfield made the slow journey to the north, sending back frequent reports to Rosecrans on the way. At Nashville on October 19 he was alerted by rumors that Stanton and Grant were conferring at Louisville. "What does it mean?" he telegraphed Rosecrans. Garfield's final report was a warning that came too late; the axe had fallen on Rosecrans before his message was sent.[70]

While Rosecrans remained at Chattanooga, Stanton's nerves were on edge. Rushing from Washington on a special train, he boarded Grant's train at Indianapolis, and the two men conferred at length en route to Louisville and in the city itself. Grant made the choice between Rosecrans and Thomas, assumed command of the new Military Division of the Mississippi, and forwarded the two generals the War Department's order relieving the one of the command of the Army of the Cumberland and naming the other as his successor. Near midnight on the evening of October 19, Grant, having been summoned by a nervous secretary of war, sent another telegram—an order to Thomas to hold Chattanooga at all costs. Stanton had grown fearful—the result in part at least of Dana's dispatches—that the city might be abandoned.[71]

Grant had left for Chattanooga when Garfield and Steedman reached Louisville. Stanton was waiting to question them on Rosecrans's conduct during the battle. He was an expert courtroom lawyer, skilled in browbeating cross-examination, and Dana's dispatches had told him where to probe. Undoubtedly Garfield would have preferred to dodge the postmortem inquiry. Undoubtedly, too, he was angered by Stanton's insulting remarks—"a damned coward" was one of his comments on Rosecrans. In the heat of the inquisition the two officers admitted enough to "more than confirm the worst" of the reports from Dana.[72]

Garfield went on to spend a few days in Cincinnati and Hiram and did not deliver Rosecrans's report until the next week. He presented letters from the general to Halleck and the President and in several interviews "went over the ground" with them. Stanton had calmed down and treated Garfield cordially. When Garfield approached the President and the secretary of war to ask for a promotion for Dolson Cox, he learned—with surprise, he wrote Captain Swaim—that he had been promoted major general for his services at Chickamauga. On Garfield's first visit to the White House, John Hay heard him describe the colloquy at Rossville and deplore Rosecrans's fixed and frequently unreasonable convictions. But Hay observed that Garfield always referred to his late commander "with kindness, even tenderness."[73]

As an army officer Garfield was required to report to Washington authorities; as a responsible citizen and incoming member of Congress he was morally bound to do so. In writing to Rosecrans, he glossed over these conversations or entirely omitted to mention them. His letters were those of a solicitous friend, shocked by a "great wrong" and a "great mistake," which he was sure the popular verdict would rebuke. "You are a power among the people," Garfield wrote, "which no action of the War Department can destroy." It does not appear that the stunned and broken general looked beyond these comforting assurances or pressed for an account of the interrogations which his chief of staff had inevitably encountered at Washington.[74]

Garfield went back to Ohio in November with a mind ablaze with the memory of the last stand at Chickamauga. Thomas's star had steadily risen to the ascendant. As the events of the battle became known, he was celebrated as the "Rock of Chickamauga," a sobriquet well suited to his solid form and granite features. Garfield's gallant tale found eager listeners—and talk has wings, as he should have learned from his experience of Hiram gossip. Republican circles in Ohio were soon humming with the drama of Garfield's dash to Thomas and the glorious scenes of which he had been a witness.

When Lieutenant Colonel Goddard, lately an assistant adjutant general to Rosecrans, paid a visit to Cleveland in December, he was disagreeably surprised to hear from a number of prominent citizens that

Garfield had gone to join Thomas of his own accord. "He has seen a chance to aggrandize himself," Goddard irately wrote Rosecrans, ". . . and has not been man enough to resist the temptation." He entreated Rosecrans to "tell them" that he had *sent* Garfield. If the letter caused Rosecrans some momentary worry, it passed with Garfield's speech in his defense on the floor of the House on February 17. His belief in Garfield's "loyalty" was firmly established.[75]

The President was evidently uneasy about the decision on Rosecrans which he had evasively countenanced. He found occasion to praise Rosecrans and to disclaim responsibility for his removal by placing the onus on Grant. Shortly after taking his seat, Garfield went to the White House with Senator Ben Wade of Ohio to ask the President to assign Rosecrans to active duty. "I am anxious to do it for several reasons," Lincoln told them in the course of a lengthy commendation of Rosecrans's services to the Union, "and not the least of them is to show General Rosecrans that I am still his friend." Rosecrans was shortly assigned to the command of the Department of Missouri. He discharged his duties ably, but he was subjected to petty harassment by the War Department, and in less than a year was abruptly removed, apparently at the instigation of Grant. He did not receive further orders, and he resigned from the army in 1867.[76]

Until the end of his embittered days, Rosecrans saw himself as a simple, honest, faultless soldier who had been crucified by the War Department for the crime of patriotism. His friendship with Garfield endured for seventeen years after their parting at Chattanooga, but, with Garfield's growing political prominence, stories began to circulate that he had been disloyal to Rosecrans while serving as his chief of staff. The leading instigator of these reports was Charles A. Dana, who, as editor of the *New York Sun,* became hostile to Garfield and attacked him violently on a score of charges. One allegation made by Dana was that Garfield had had Rosecrans ousted from command by writing a detrimental letter to Chase from Chattanooga. Here was a curious displacement of responsibility; Stanton's principal agent in getting rid of Rosecrans had been Dana himself, and Dana once claimed the credit in a conversation with Villard at Washington.[77]

Garfield, though burning with anger, made no public reply to Dana's assaults. Early in 1880, in response to a letter from Rosecrans, he penned an unqualified denial that he had ever been unfaithful to their friendship. "I fearlessly challenge all the rascals in the world to publish any such letters written by me," he wrote of Dana's charge. "They are welcome to all the capital they can make out of them." It seems hardly possible that Garfield had forgotten his letter of July 27 from Nashville or that he did not wonder whether it had fallen into the hands of his political enemies. It had been written weeks before Chickamauga and contained no intimation that Rosecrans should be removed; but it was not, all the same, a letter that Rosecrans would regard as evidence of Garfield's faithful friendship.[78]

The friendship of the two men was a casualty of the political campaign of 1880. Rosecrans, who lived in California, was a Democratic candidate for Congress—a successful one, as it turned out. A vigorous partisan during the contest, he was criticized by a California newspaper for having listened in silence in a public meeting over which he was presiding to a virulent attack on Garfield, whom he himself had praised so highly in 1863. In a widely circulated "card," Rosecrans responded that seventeen years was a long time and that "many a splendid young man, in less time," had "descended from honor to infamy, and mortified admiring and devoted friends, all Christian gentlemen, by being put in the penitentiary." Rosecrans's resentment was fueled by newspapers, letters received by him on the subject of Garfield's "treachery," and by his discovery that Bundy's biography of the Republican presidential candidate extolled Garfield's services as chief of staff and glorified his voluntary ride to Thomas while picturing the commanding general as "easily 'stampeded' when his command seemed broken." Yet it was Rosecrans who, after the campaign was over, sought a return to "the old ground of cordial regard"; for Garfield Rosecrans's "card" was "an insuperable barrier" to the restoration of the old relations.[79]

Some six months after Garfield's death, the *New York Sun* finally obtained and published a letter from Garfield to Chase. It proved to be the anachronistic letter of July 27—an anticlimax to Dana's vivid accusations. Its source was presently identified in the obscure person of Jacob W. Schuckers, who had been one of several part-time secretaries employed by Chase and had published an authorized biography of the statesman following his death in 1873. Schuckers had been a rather sycophantic admirer of Garfield for twenty years. As a newspaper reporter at Columbus, he had attached himself to the rising young member of the legislature and sought his influence in obtaining the Treasury clerkship which led to his confidential connection with Chase. Schuckers was grateful for Garfield's kindness and, during Garfield's service in Congress, sent him a number of letters assuring him of his admiration and personal regard, though opposing with emotional vehemence his advocacy of "honest money." The currency question, in the hard times that followed the panic of 1873, was an inflammatory issue. Schuckers, distracted and possibly deranged by financial worries and losses, eventually forgot his gratitude. In 1882 he furnished the *Sun* not only with Garfield's letters to Chase but with a letter of his own, composed in part of unfavorable references to Garfield's record as chief of staff to Rosecrans. Yet, though Schuckers had free access to Chase's correspondence, he was unable to produce a letter from Garfield at Chattanooga urging that Rosecrans be removed from command of the Army of the Cumberland.[80]

Lacking the evidence of a letter, many of Garfield's enemies blamed his interviews at Louisville and Washington, but their accusations are invalidated by the erroneous assumption that these conversations were held before Rosecrans was removed. The positive and persistent belief that Garfield was responsible has never been adequately explained. After Chickamauga, Chase had shown the President his letter of July 27. Possibly it exerted, as Dana said Stanton had told him, the decisive influence on Lincoln's mind; in view of Dana's dispatches from Chattanooga, this seems a very remote possibility indeed.[81]

Garfield's personal devotion to Rosecrans is established beyond question. Over the years he exerted himself to oblige and favor him. He eloquently lauded Rosecrans's services on the floor of the House. He made the other's wrongs his own, hotly resenting the continued antagonism of the War Department. He imposed a severe restraint on his public utterances, pronounced or signed, scrupulously omitting any word that could be construed as prejudicial to his former commander. His letters to Rosecrans expressed an esteem that came unmistakably from the heart. Yet, when all is said, the tune does not ring quite true. Garfield's friendship for Rosecrans was stained by a deception that no kind acts or words could wash away.[82]

This relationship had touched Garfield at two vulnerable points— his tendency to evade a clean decision and his reluctance to hurt a friend. "It is my greatest weakness," Garfield once wrote to Harry Rhodes, "to feel almost unable to criticize anyone I love." His dilemma at Chattanooga had not been an easy one; a harder man would have shrunk from speaking the brutal truth and rending the veil of delusion in which Rosecrans wrapped his wounds. Garfield had stumbled into a trap of equivocation which he never frankly faced. In effect he chose to regard Rosecrans as two separate men: the friend whom he loved and the commander whom he had come to distrust. Because he was true to the first man and forbore public criticism of the second, he believed his loyalty was complete. He was outraged to learn at last that Rosecrans and his sympathizers construed his steadfast attentions as proof of a guilty conscience.[83]

In some buried recess of his being Garfield may have felt a sting of guilt, a need for atonement. If so, he never permitted the ignoble emotion to enter his thinking mind. His attitude would seem less ambiguous if he had faced the duality of his feelings and let the wartime friendship fade into a nostalgic reminiscence of a once vital relationship. But this, out of his own peculiar amalgam of yielding sentiment and impregnable self-deception, Garfield was unable to do.

# CHAPTER 9

# CONGRESS

DURING HIS STAY in Washington Garfield had made up his mind to take his seat in the new Congress, which would begin in early December. It was not an easy decision. The war was not over, and he was reluctant to abandon the field. Dolson Cox was sure that his friend's health was the decisive factor. There were other considerations. The President, who had just elevated Garfield to major general, urged him to turn law-maker. The House, Lincoln said, needed Republicans and men who understood the needs of the army. That he had promoted Garfield with the understanding that the young officer would resign his com-mission, as Charles Dana is reported to have said, seems doubtful. There was ambition too, and Congress might give him better opportu-nities for distinction than the army. In choosing Congress, Garfield did not give up all thought of the army; there was always the possibility of going back. On the day that he resigned his commission, the secretary of war assured him that he would hold his place open for him. Garfield never liked to close a door completely.[1]

Home again on a visit before the opening of Congress, Garfield ex-perienced the profound sorrow of his life—the death of Trot. The small girl whom he had found an ever-increasing source of delight and who had contributed so much to expanding his power to love died of diphtheria at the beginning of December after a long struggle during which Garfield sat helplessly at her bedside. "We buried her," he wrote to Corydon, "on the third day of December, at the very hour she should have reached the end of her fifth month of her fourth year. . . . It seems as if the fabric of my life were torn to atoms and scattered to the winds." On the day after the funeral Garfield started for Wash-ington, leaving behind a grieving Crete and a seven-week-old son who was still unnamed.[2]

In the capital, although Garfield felt lonely and desolate, he had little time to mourn. On the evening of his arrival he hurried off to a Republican caucus at which Schuyler Colfax was chosen as the party's candidate for Speaker and Garfield made a member of a committee to oversee the organization of the House. The next day he resigned his commission and on the following day was sworn in as a member of the Thirty-eighth Congress. Ahead of him were seven months of grinding labor.[3]

In the new House of Representatives there were 183 members, 103 of whom were Republicans. Sixty percent of the members had not sat in the preceding Congress—a startling percentage in the light of present-day experience. Lawyers predominated; in the Ohio delegation all nineteen members had made at least some study of the law. College graduates were a minority. The House, operating under rules in need of revision, functioned by means of the committee system. The Speaker, chosen by the majority party, was a person of prestige and influence but lacked the power of some later speakers. Members were assigned seats but no offices (the imposing trio of House office buildings located today across Independence Avenue from the Capitol are all twentieth century creations). A member disposed of his correspondence at his desk on the floor of the House, in an available room, or in his living quarters; if he found it impossible to keep up with it without aid—as did Garfield—he made private arrangements. A member received a salary of $3,000 (increased to $5,000 in 1866), an allowance for stationery and travel to and from his district, the franking privilege, and free snuff. As a public man he often enjoyed the privilege of free passes on railroads. As a body the House was less prestigious, less dignified, and rowdier than the Senate, which in 1863 had only fifty-one members. The life expectancy of a gavel in the hands of a determined Speaker was short; gavels sometimes disintegrated in a shower of splinters. The House had many moods. To understand its "temper" was the study of those who aspired to lead it.

There were a number of men in the House during Garfield's first term who remained there or in the Senate throughout all or most of his years in Washington and whose careers were significantly linked with his own. These included Republicans William Boyd Allison of Iowa, James G. Blaine of Maine, Henry L. Dawes of Massachusetts, William D. Kelley of Pennsylvania, and Justin Smith Morrill of Vermont and Democrats Samuel Jackson Randall of Pennsylvania and Fernando Wood of New York.

Of these, the most important for Garfield was Blaine, who was two years older than the Ohioan. Born and educated in Pennsylvania—he was one of the college men—Blaine moved to Maine in 1854 and became a newspaper editor and a prominent figure in state politics. He was an attractive man with "his powerful frame and erect head, and bright black eyes as round as marbles, and ready shake of the hand, and sympathetic response." Much has been made of his "magnetism"—there is no doubt that he had the quality when he wished to exhibit it—but he owed his success to something more than charm. He was an egoist. (Albert Gallatin Riddle thought that Garfield lacked egoism.) He was more aggressive than Garfield, more of a fighter. His interest in the machinery of politics, as Garfield himself once noted, was greater. "I wish Blaine were less of a politician," he wrote (a curious statement for a politician to make and one that might have puzzled Blaine but would not have disturbed him). These traits—egoism, aggressiveness, a flair for political manipulation—help to explain why Blaine, who entered Congress with Garfield, became Speaker in 1869 while Garfield had to be content with the chairmanship that Blaine assigned him and that was not what he wanted. It was not until Blaine left for the Senate in 1876 that Garfield became first among Republicans in the House.[4]

Garfield was fortunate in the district he represented. It was sturdily Republican as it had been sturdily Whig before the birth of the new party. It believed in keeping a good man in office when it found one— had not Joshua Giddings represented it in the House for two decades, and his predecessor for fifteen years? It was made up of five counties in the northeastern corner of the state, a region of farms, villages, and small towns. There were two changes in the composition of the district during Garfield's tenure. For ten years he represented Ashtabula, Geauga, Mahoning, Portage, and Trumbull counties; for the next six years Lake County was in his district and Mahoning was not; during his last term Mahoning replaced Portage. Although Garfield was never without rivals and critics within the party back home, he endured. Other members of the Ohio delegation came and went; twelve who were members at the opening of the Thirty-eighth Congress were not re-elected in 1864. Only once did Garfield's share of the total vote fall below sixty percent—in 1874, when half of Ohio's delegation were not returned. With such a base in the most populous state west of the Appalachians, Garfield could aim at national leadership.

Individuals, newspapers, and political committees in the district provided him with a network of intelligence and support. Foremost among the individuals was Harmon Austin of Warren, who was ever ready throughout Garfield's congressional career to inform, advise, and act; hundreds of letters passed between the two men. Charles Henry, an Eclectic old boy and veteran of the Forty-second Regiment, rendered great service. Garfield secured Henry's appointment as railway mail agent in the Post Office Department in 1869 and, four years later, his promotion to special agent. The appointments made it possible for "Captain" Henry to serve his benefactor—to whom he was personally devoted—by supplying information and advice on matters related to the post offices in the Nineteenth District, by passing on his gleanings in respect to politics, and by undertaking special missions.[5]

Every county in Garfield's district had one or more politically oriented weekly newspapers. Garfield had warm friends and supporters among the Republican editors—Lyman and Halsey Hall of Portage, Julius Converse of Geauga, Jonathan Scofield of Lake, William and Joseph Howells of Ashtabula. For William Cooper Howells and his family Garfield had an affection that went far beyond politics.[6]

Cleveland was outside the Nineteenth District, but its papers circulated there, and items from them were reprinted in the country papers. Garfield's strongest ties among Cleveland editors were with Edwin Cowles, editor and sole proprietor of the *Cleveland Leader*. Although handicapped by deafness and a speech impediment, he had become one of the most influential and best known men in Ohio. A founder of the Republican party, a fiery Unionist, a man of forceful personality and unshakable convictions, Cowles was, for Garfield, a man worth cultivating. One of Cowles's employees, Frank H. Mason, was particularly close to Garfield; like Charles Henry, he had been at the Eclectic and in the Forty-second Regiment. For many years he worked on the *Leader* as reporter, editorial writer, and managing editor. In 1876 he published his history of the Forty-second, which did nothing to diminish the reputation of the man who had led it in the eastern Kentucky campaign.[7]

A Republican committee existed in each of Garfield's five counties, and a district committee brought together representatives from the county committees. The county committees were composed of leading Republicans from a number of towns; the district committee was likely to be made up of the most active and influential county leaders (Harmon Austin, for example, was a leader for many years both in Trumbull County and on the district committee). Thus the committee system gave Congressman Garfield lines to local leaders and provided bases of political support and action.

Garfield sought to serve his district well, but he resented efforts to dictate to him. A crisis came after his first term. Garfield had fallen under the spell of the brilliant Henry Winter Davis of Maryland, a vigorous opponent of Lincoln and his policies. After Lincoln killed the Wade-Davis reconstruction bill by pocket veto, Davis and Benjamin Franklin Wade, Ohio's roughhewn radical senator, published the Wade-Davis Manifesto, a blast at the President. Garfield came under fire in his district, where some believed that the manifesto expressed his views; it was even rumored that he had written it. When the Republican district convention, stanchly pro-Lincoln, met to nominate a candidate for Congress, it expected Garfield to denounce the manifesto as the price of renomination. Garfield faced the convention boldly. Although he denied authorship of the document, he did not condemn it, saying in effect that he only regretted the necessity of its having been written. Furthermore he took a forthright stand for independence: he could not represent the district except as a free man. The convention, having passed a resolution condemning the manifesto, renominated Garfield by acclamation.[8]

Throughout his career in Congress Garfield did not depart from the stand he had taken. He must use his best judgment, he would not take orders; if the district did not want him on these terms, it could find another man. When iron manufacturers of the Mahoning Valley were dissatisfied with his position in respect to duties on iron, he wrote to Harmon Austin: "Whether it costs me my head or not these men shall all know that I am not to be scared or driven in regard to any vote I give in the House. . . . The fact is many of these men want a Representative that they can own and carry around in their pantaloons pocket. They shall certainly know that I am not a piece of merchandise subject to their caprices and wishes."[9]

But, as Garfield well knew, there were limits to his freedom. "He fully realized," Dolson Cox wrote in 1885, "that he could not speak his own thoughts or advocate or support the measures he really believed to be best for the country, but was limited to doing the best he could *consistently* with maintaining his position in his district and in his party."[10]

Committee memberships determined to a large degree the life of a member of the House. On important committees he spent endless hours, and in the process, if he had intelligence and ambition, he became an authority on the legislative areas with which they dealt. Much of his speaking and writing was likely to be on matters related to his committee work. It was natural that Garfield's first assignment was to the Committee on Military Affairs, of which Robert Schenck, another Ohioan and a former major general, became chairman. Schenck, a fiery partisan more than twenty years older than Garfield, had had four terms in the House in the 1840s and 1850s; a useless right hand was the result of a wound at Second Bull Run. He is still remembered as an authority on draw poker, about which he published a book. He and Garfield became close friends as well as colleagues and for a time shared living quarters. Garfield worked hard, gained useful experience, and rendered good service to Lincoln and the Union cause in respect to legislation designed to maintain an adequate army.

Garfield had no intention of making a career of military affairs. When the war was over, the army would shrink to a tiny force and the importance of the military committee would dwindle. Garfield foresaw that financial problems would be as great in peacetime as in war; a monumental debt, fiat money, a chaotic tax structure—these were matters with which Congress would have to struggle. Accordingly, he sought and received assignment to the Committee on Ways and Means, whose purview was the entire economy of the United States in relation to the financial needs of the government. Chairman of the committee was Justin Morrill, who was beginning his sixth and last term in the House. On Morrill's elevation to the Senate in 1867, Garfield expected to succeed him as chairman. Instead Speaker Colfax, for reasons of his own—Garfield thought he acted out of cowardice—made Schenck chairman of Ways and Means and gave Garfield Schenck's old position at the head of Military Affairs.[11]

Blaine became Speaker in 1869, Colfax having become Grant's Vice President. In soliciting Garfield's support, Blaine had suggested that it would be an advantage to Garfield to have someone in the chair on whose friendship he could rely—*"and,"* he added, *"I trust you can rely on mine."* Garfield's spirits were dampened when he learned that Blaine was planning to remove him from his chairmanship and give him a subordinate position on Appropriations. He made known his disappointment, and in the end Blaine made him chairman of the Committee on Banking and Currency. This assignment produced one interesting task that led him to greater prominence—the investigation into and report on the celebrated Gold Panic of 1869, an event brought about by a conspiracy on the part of Jay Gould and others to corner the gold market.

Two years later, Schenck having been defeated for re-election, Garfield confidently looked forward to the coveted assignment, the top chairmanship in the House. Again he had put too much faith in Blaine; the Speaker gave the chairmanship of Ways and Means to Henry Dawes of Massachusetts, who had wanted to retain his chairmanship of Appropriations, and gave the chairmanship of Appropriations to a disgruntled Garfield.[12]

Blaine had not acted out of caprice. A tariff revision was in prospect, and he was trying to set up a Ways and Means committee that would not accomplish too much. Under some pressure from New England wool manufacturers, he gave the chairmanship to Dawes, a strong protectionist, and counteracted Dawes's protectionism by appointing a committee at odds with the chairman's views. It was just as well that Garfield failed to get what he wanted; Dawes, who deserved better, had a miserable session.

The disappointment did not last long. With characteristic energy Garfield threw himself into the work of his committee as whole-heartedly as he had ever undertaken any challenge. During his four years as chairman he achieved mastery of a complex subject. He became acquainted with the activities and needs of every department and bureau of a rapidly expanding government and with leaders in and out of government. In opening the debate on his first great appropriations bill, he delivered an address in which he sought to take a larger view of appropriations than had hitherto been attempted—to discuss the philosophy of appropriations, as he once described his theme. It was an impressive achievement, one that exhibited a command of principle as well as detail, a knowledge of the past as well as the present; he managed somehow to make appropriations an intellectually stimulating subject.[13]

The years from 1871 to 1875 were Garfield's great years as a committeeman. Then Republican good times ended when the Democrats organized the House in 1875 for the first time since 1860. During the rest of his time in Congress, Garfield was a member of the minority; a Democrat presided over the House, and Democrats chaired all the committees.

Not that the Democrats treated him badly; the Speaker acknowledged his position of leadership by appointing him regularly to the Committee on Ways and Means. But the minority had small influence on this committee, and on important issues it could do little more than file minority reports. Samuel Jackson Randall, who became Speaker in 1876, also paid his respects to Garfield by naming him to the Rules Committee, a post he had always had under Blaine. Under Randall, however, he had the opportunity to participate in a general overhaul of House rules—something of a landmark in the history of that body. For one Congress he was also a member of the Committee on the Pacific Railroads.

There were special committees from time to time. Most notable of these in Garfield's experience was that on the census, established in 1869 in anticipation of the census of 1870. Although Garfield was nominally second on the committee, he was in fact the head of it. It was an assignment much to his liking, though he worried about not doing a good job in the time allowed. He did an enormous amount of work, beginning with an investigation of the census in all ages. In late May and during much of June (which saw some very hot weather) he and members of his committee labored in a basement room of the Capitol.

The meetings were in effect a seminar or workshop conducted by Professor Garfield. Eugene V. Smalley, a journalist born in Portage County and a friend of Garfield, wrote that he thought all members of the committee would "agree that the weeks they spent with General Garfield in the census work were among the most valuable and agreeable of their Congressional career." The committee introduced two census reform bills, but both died in the Senate.

The work of Garfield and the committee, however, had positive results. It led to immediate changes in the Census Act of 1850, brought forth a considerable amount of census literature, and prepared the way for the Census Act of 1880. Other consequences were a long historical article, "Census," by Garfield and Hinsdale, for an encyclopedia; an address by Garfield on the census before the Social Science Association; and the appointment, on Garfield's recommendation, of the distinguished economist Francis Walker as superintendent of the census of 1870.[14]

In a letter written shortly before the end of the first session of his first Congress, Garfield said, "I have never been anything else than radical on all these questions of Freedom and Slavery, rebellion and the War."[15] What was the nature of his radicalism? He went to war to aid in the preservation of the Union. In the course of his military experience he became convinced that the institution of slavery must be crushed forever. He believed it inevitable that the revolution begun by war would continue until the supremacy of the Union was everywhere established and acknowledged, the freedom of the black race mandated and protected, and the political, economic, and social system of the South remade. These goals were to be reached within the context of the Constitution; Garfield rejected the theory of state suicide but considered it essential that the seceded states not be fully restored to their position in the federal system until fundamental changes had been effected. Thus one may understand his dissatisfaction with the reconstruction policies of Lincoln and Johnson and his support of the Fourteenth and Fifteenth Amendments to the Constitution, the Freedman's Bureau legislation, the Civil Rights Act, and other reconstruction measures.

One can also see why he was not always happy with developments in Congress. In 1867 he wrote that he was trying to be a radical and not be a fool, "a matter of no small difficulty." In 1871 he took a strong stand against provisions of one reconstruction measure—the Ku Klux Bill—that authorized the suspension, under some circumstances, of the right of habeas corpus and the declaration of martial law. He was aware of "many anomalies" in reconstruction legislation and was not prepared to rationalize them. "There are," he said on one occasion, "no theories for the management of whirlwinds and earthquakes."[16]

Garfield's basic views on the issues stemming from the war remained intact; his inaugural address as President is evidence enough. But as years passed he came to believe that the desired goals with respect to the South could be achieved only with the passage of time and through the instruments of education and business enterprise. A few weeks before his inauguration as President he copied in his diary some lines of Coleridge.

> Habitual evils change not on a sudden,
> But many days will pass and many sorrows.

He added, "This might be applied to the southern question. Time is the only healer, with justice and wisdom at work." It was not the language of the radicals of a decade and a half earlier.[17]

All through his congressional years Garfield had to face the thorny problem of monetary policy. In 1878 he described it as "the issue of all issues." The ability of the government to manage the staggering war debt and to meet its other responsibilities, the growth and prosperity of the economy, and the welfare of all workers demanded an adequate, controlled, and soundly based currency. Garfield's views on the subject were matured by a study of history, wide reading, correspondence and discussions with men concerned with monetary theory and practice, and his own experience in government. He concluded early that the fiat money (greenbacks) issued by the Treasury during the war must be reduced in quantity and tied to gold. Consistency—but not rigidity—characterized his positions over the years. He fought greenbackism and supported wholeheartedly the resumption of specie payments, the issuance of notes by the national banking system, and the payment of the national debt in coin. He opposed the efforts of silverites to add to the currency supply by forcing a bimetallic standard on the United States without giving consideration to the status of silver in other countries; at the same time he was aware of the potential of silver as an element in a stronger monetary base. He made himself a leader on the conservative side in the national debate, not only in Congress but in the press and on the platform. In 1876 the *Atlantic Monthly* published his article, "The Currency Conflict." In 1878 he gave an address in Faneuil Hall on "Honest Money," and early in 1879 he spoke in Chicago on "Suspension and Resumption of Specie Payments" at the invitation of the Honest Money League of the Northwest. His advocacy of "sound" money was an important ingredient in his availability for the Republican presidential nomination in 1880.[18]

On the tariff—another perennial issue—Garfield was in the uncomfortable position of trying to occupy a middle ground. Had he become a professor of political economy, he probably would have come close to the stand taken by his Williams professor Arthur L. Perry, who was a free trader, or that of his friend David A. Wells, who moved from protectionism to free trade. As it was, he must face the fact that he was a member of a party that had taken a stand for a protective tariff in its platform of 1860 and had begun a new era of protectionism in the United States by the passage of the Morrill Tariff in 1861. He must also remember that protectionists were a powerful element in his party.

The problem was brought home to him when the iron manufacturers of the Mahoning Valley criticized him for his failure to support their interests more strongly. He tried to take a position that would reconcile his free trade proclivities with the necessity of being a protectionist. "I am," he proclaimed, "for a protection which leads to ultimate free trade. I am for that free trade which can be only achieved through protection."[19]

Extremists were not impressed. High protectionists could not forget that Garfield had been honored with membership in the Cobden Club, a British society dedicated to free trade. William D. Kelley of Pennsylvania, known as "Pig Iron" Kelley or "Old Pig" because of his devotion to the iron industry, refused to vote for Garfield for Speaker of the House. On the other hand, newspapers criticized him in 1880 for favoring only a fifty percent reduction in the duty on wood pulp.

It was the protectionists that Garfield had to worry about most. During his last day in the House he proofread a minority report he had prepared in opposition to proposals by Democrats on Ways and Means for a sharp downward revision of duties. At his side was the secretary of the National Association of Wool Manufacturers, who had furnished a good deal of the material in the report and who later wrote that Garfield, "not a born protectionist," had become "ultimately never an extreme, but a thoroughly practical, protectionist." The minority report became a campaign document, thereby helping to reassure protectionists. Iron and textile manufacturers and wool growers did not want to be caught supporting a free trader for President. During the Republican national convention of 1880, a member of the Pennsylvania delegation wrote a note to Garfield inquiring whether he was a protectionist; he wanted to show Garfield's response to other members of the delegation.[20]

Garfield had a profound faith in education. Education had emancipated him and made it possible for him to make his way in the world. Within the context of the American system it could do the same for others—the black, the Indian, native whites, and European im-

migrants—for everyone, it would seem, except the Chinese. But education was not merely a means of self-advancement; it would be the
salvation of the Republic. He was bothered by Macaulay's assertion that
such a government must lead to anarchy. There was no answer, Garfield thought, except from the schoolmaster: "If we can fill the minds of
all our children who are to be voters with intelligence which will fit
them wisely to vote, and fill them with the spirit of liberty, then we will
have averted the fatal prophecy. But if, on the other hand, we allow
our youth to grow up in ignorance, this Republic will end in disastrous
failure."[21]

He carried his educational philosophy into government. He was a
strong supporter of the Hampton Normal and Agricultural Institute
established in 1868 by his friend Samuel C. Armstrong for the education of blacks. (After the first decade Indians were also admitted, and
for a time Garfield was a member of its board of trustees.) He urged
the Virginia legislature to make the institution a beneficiary of the Morrill Land Grant College Act. He showed a deep interest in the Washington school that became Gallaudet College, which depended in large
part on federal funds; he was a longtime friend of its head, Edward
Minor Gallaudet. In 1883 a bust of Garfield was unveiled in the college
chapel, a memorial to the man "whose support of the college in
Congress had been so constant and effective." It was Garfield who was
responsible for the passage of the act creating the National Department
of Education, later the Bureau of Education. He favored the allocation
to education of funds derived from the sale of public lands.[22]

In his approach to science and scientists Garfield was a modern
man. As early as 1858 he was persuaded that the men who would
"move the world in its higher circles of thought" would be men of
science. As a general principle he held that the federal government
should keep its hands off, leaving scientific experiment and inquiry
to men whose genius led them into research. But he made three exceptions to this general rule, exceptions that left enormous scope for federal activity in the field of science. The government, he said, "should
aid all sorts of scientific inquiry that are necessary to the intelligent exercise of its own functions." Then, when some great popular interest
affecting whole classes or all classes demanded scientific investigation
that private enterprise could not accomplish, the government should
intervene and help if it had the constitutional power to do so. He instanced the investigation of the origins of yellow fever and methods of
preventing it, a topic much to the fore at that time. Finally, he would
leave to the government scientific inquiries of such size and cost that
private individuals could not make them.[23]

As a congressman Garfield became a link between politics and science. His years as chairman of the Appropriations Committee and a House member of the Board of Regents of the Smithsonian Institution broadened his interest in science and brought him into contact with leading scientists in government and elsewhere. John Wesley Powell, working for the establishment of the United States Geological Survey, sought Garfield's help in getting a bill through Congress. Joseph Henry went to Garfield's home to explain his relation to the development of the telegraph. Garfield invited Simon Newcomb to dinner to discuss the approaching transit of Venus, for the study of which scientists were seeking an appropriation from Congress. Louis Agassiz invited Garfield to Nantucket Island to hear a summer series of lectures on science—an invitation Garfield was unable to accept. (On December 14, 1873, Garfield wrote in his diary, "My dear and admired friend Professor Agassiz died today in Boston. . . . Many memories of pleasant intercourse socially, and at the meeting of the Board of Regents, come back to me, now that he is gone.") Ferdinand V. Hayden named a western mountain for Garfield. After the election of 1880, Asa Gray wrote to the chief executive officer of the Smithsonian: "While one does not like to lose from our Board so old and extremely useful and wise a member as General Garfield, it is a satisfaction to know that one of the ablest and best friends of the Institution will be in the Presidential chair." It was fitting that the first use of the new National Museum of the Smithsonian was for Garfield's inaugural reception.[24]

Although Garfield supported the Fifteenth Amendment to the Constitution, he never gave his support to the woman's rights movement or to its central objective, woman suffrage. His views in 1880 on the place of women in society were essentially those of his young manhood when he disagreed with Crete about the propriety of women speaking in public. In 1868, the year the Fifteenth Amendment became law, he was thinking about woman suffrage. "I can hardly tell you how repulsive to my feelings are the leading features of the Woman's Rights movement," he wrote to his friend Whitelaw Reid, who was on the staff of the *New York Tribune*. But he went on to say that there were pages in John Stuart Mill's chapter on suffrage in his *Representative Government* that staggered him more than anything he had read (Mill set forth cogent reasons why women should have the vote). "I am very anxious," Garfield wrote, "to be right on all these themes, and not to follow the lead of my prejudices." But follow their lead he did for the rest of his life. In 1872 he turned down an invitation from Elizabeth Cady Stanton to speak at a suffrage convention. While he sympathized, he said, with efforts that would elevate women and better their condition, he did not believe that suffrage would accomplish that result. Eight years later, when Susan B. Anthony asked him whether as President he would recommend to Congress the submission of a woman suffrage amendment to the states, he refused to answer on the ground that the Republican convention had not discussed the subject. He indicated, however, that he had not yet reached the conclusion that it would be best for women to have the vote. He might reach it, he said, but that fruit wasn't yet ripe on his tree.[25]

Between 1876 and 1880 Garfield became much better known nationally. He was the leader of the Republicans in the House and the party candidate for Speaker in 1876 and 1878. He was prominent in the activities leading to the inauguration of Rutherford B. Hayes. He campaigned extensively in the Northeast as well as in Ohio. He published articles in national magazines. He accepted invitations to speak in Boston and Chicago on the money question.

During the fall and winter of 1876–77, Garfield was immersed in the electoral struggle—from beginning to end, as Hayes said. When questions arose concerning the outcome of the presidential election in South Carolina, Florida, and Louisiana, President Grant asked him and other leading Republicans to go to New Orleans to look after Republican interests there. After fifteen days in Louisiana Garfield was fully persuaded that Hayes was entitled to the electoral vote of that state.[26]

As the electoral dispute became hotter, Democrats in Congress joined with some Republicans in support of a bill to establish an electoral commission to which disputed returns would be submitted for a decision. Garfield strongly opposed the proposal, both on constitutional grounds and because he thought Republican chances of winning the presidency would be weakened if the bill passed. When the bill became law, he was chosen as one of two House Republicans on the commission, which was made up of five members each from the House, the Senate, and the Supreme Court. On the commission he voted regularly with the seven other Republican members to assign the disputed votes to Hayes.[27]

Some House Democrats, however, were not prepared to surrender; they proposed delaying tactics to block the completion in Congress of the electoral count and thereby prevent the inauguration of Hayes on March 4. Fortunately for the Republicans, southern Democrats were more interested in the future of the South than in the election of the New York Democrat, Samuel J. Tilden. Assurances passed in both directions. Southerners were given to understand by Republicans close to Hayes that, if Hayes became President, the new administration would abandon military support for the last of the reconstruction state governments, support subsidies for the building of the Texas and Pacific Railroad, favor internal improvements in the South, appoint a former Confederate to the Cabinet, and give southerners a voice in the distribution of patronage in their section. In return Republicans were given assurances by southern Democrats that they would not block the completion of the electoral count, that the South would treat blacks fairly, and that they would permit the Republicans to organize the new House. Garfield was well aware of the questions at issue and was present at the celebrated Wormley Hotel Conference where they were discussed. At best the so-called Compromise of 1877 was merely an exchange of views and assurances between some southerners and some Republicans. In the matter of the organization of the House Garfield had a deep personal interest; if enough southern Democrats withheld their votes for their party's candidate, Garfield, not Randall, would be the next Speaker.[28]

The fragile nature of the "compromise" was soon apparent. Hayes went to the White House, appointed a Confederate as Postmaster General, sought to conciliate southern Democrats by his appointments in the South, and allowed the last of the reconstruction governments to disappear. The South also gained something in the way of internal improvements. The other elements of the "compromise" were abandoned; the South did not treat blacks fairly, the administration did not support the Texas and Pacific Railroad project, the Democrats did not let the Republicans organize the House.

Hayes had been quite optimistic about Garfield's chances for the Speakership; Garfield had not expected it, but he had not been without hope. Any disappointment he may have felt is understandable in view of the fact that, at the request of the President, he had refrained from seeking the Senate seat left vacant when John Sherman became Hayes's secretary of the treasury.[29]

Although Garfield was always on cordial personal terms with Hayes, he was sometimes—particularly during the first year or so of the new administration—sharply critical of the President and his policies. Garfield's complaints over policy were those of many Republicans in Congress. He did not approve of the President's efforts to conciliate Democrats by making political appointments in the South at the expense of Republicans. Nor did he approve of the President's efforts to purify the civil service by executive action. "I think his vague notions of Civil Service Reform, and his wretched practice upon it, has wrought the chief mischief with his administration," Garfield wrote in his diary at the end of Hayes's first year in office. He was now persuaded that the President was a man out of place. "I am almost disheartened at the prospect of getting anything done by the President," he wrote to William Cooper Howells at about the same time. "I am forced to the conclusion that he is too small for his place, and has the infirmity that men of that class sometimes suffer from—the fear that he will be influenced by others. Day by day the party is dropping away from him, and the present state of things cannot continue much longer, without a total loss of his influence with the Republicans. The situation is gloomy enough I assure you." [30]

Some of Garfield's discontent might be attributed to the President's failure to seek the advice of the House minority leader. But there was more to it than that; so great was the wrath of many Republican politicians against the President that Garfield had to use his influence to block the holding of party caucuses that he knew would bring forth a torrent of criticism. [31]

Garfield and the President differed in temperament. Hayes was more self-confident, more self-assured, more persuaded of the correctness of his views. He accepted the offices that came his way—Congress, the governorship, the presidency—as his due; he was rarely plagued with self-doubt. Having achieved office, he did his duty as he saw it and evidenced no desire to hold the office long. He prided himself on his ability to face a frowning world.

On a Sunday in May 1879, Garfield, calling at the White House, expressed grave concern over the plight in which the Democrats had got themselves during the extra session then in progress. He saw no way out for them "except perseverance in the direction of revolution, or an ignominious backing down." Hayes said that he did not see why Republicans should be depressed and, laughing, asked Garfield if he didn't think they could stand it if the Democrats could. Garfield foresaw disaster whether the Democrats went ahead or backed down squarely. Hayes answered that a square backing down was their best way out and that for his part he would await the result complacently. Complacency was part of Hayes's personality; it was foreign to Garfield's. [32]

There were, however, strong bonds between the congressman and the President. Their Ohio backgrounds gave them much in common. Both were college men who enjoyed books; both were lawyers. Both had been Union officers and were intensely national in their outlook. They were in agreement on a number of hotly debated major issues: They favored the resumption of specie payments, opposed the Bland-Allison silver purchase bill, and held that legislation against Chinese immigration to the United States should await the negotiation of a new treaty with China.

The Democrats made a great contribution to Republican harmony. In the spring of 1878 they launched in the House an investigation into Hayes's title to the presidency—a move that instantly drew Republicans together. The following year the Democrats, who were in control of both houses as a result of the election of 1878, fought a long battle to repeal or amend laws providing for the use of the army and federal marshals at the polls to safeguard federal elections. This effort was the focus of national attention in the spring and summer of 1879, when a special session of Congress was required to pass appropriations bills that had failed to secure the President's approval during the regular session because of Democratic riders relating to the election laws. On this issue Garfield and other Republican congressmen generally were in full accord with Hayes. On May 10, 1879, when the special session had been in progress for nearly two months, Garfield wrote to Crete, who had gone to Ohio, "I spent an hour with the President today, on the veto for the new bill which the Democrats have passed, restricting the use of the army. I think I have never had so much intellectual and personal influence over him as now. He is fully in line with his party. . . ."[33]

As a legislator Garfield had many strengths. He was well educated and intellectually curious, and he had a large grasp of public affairs. When he entered the White House *The Nation* said there was no executive department in the government of which he was not "fully competent to take charge." He was an almost compulsively hard worker. One journalist wrote that Garfield "was the most indefatigable worker" he had ever known. James G. Blaine also used the word "indefatigable" to describe him as a worker. (It is not the right word; Garfield's labors frequently left him completely exhausted.) He devoted long hours to preparation for debates. He was an outstanding speaker—his major speeches were characterized by sound organization, clarity, and rationality, and they were delivered with force and effect. He sometimes spent the midnight hours revising speeches before they were printed in final form. He handled himself well in the give and take of debate. In 1878 a writer in the *Washington Star* called him "the strongest debater on either side" of the House. He was a skilled parliamentarian. He preferred to keep discussions on a high level, avoiding personalities. What strikes one most about him is that he was a well-rounded man—not great, not brilliant, but possessed of many fine qualities, not the least of which was a strong desire to excel. It was the opinion of Thomas Donaldson, who knew many politicians, that Garfield was "one of the most useful men ever in the lower house." This is not a bad epitaph for the public man.[34]

James G. Blaine, whose assessment of Garfield must be treated with respect, said that the characteristics that marked him as a great debater did not make him a great parliamentary leader. Blaine named Henry Clay, Stephen A. Douglas, and Thaddeus Stevens as the greatest leaders in the history of the House, leaving his audience to supply a fourth name. The great leader, as Blaine saw him, was intensely partisan at all times, knowing when and where to strike, avoiding the strength of the opposition, and conquering "often against the right and the heavy battalions." He instanced the young Charles Fox, who "carried the House of Commons against justice, against its immemorial rights, against his own convictions (if indeed, at that period Fox had any convictions)" to unseat John Wilkes and install another man in his place "in defiance not merely of law but of public decency." For such an achievement Blaine held Garfield "disqualified by the texture of his mind, by the honesty of his heart, by his conscience, and by every instinct and aspiration of his nature."[35]

Others were not so kind as Blaine. Some said that Garfield had no "moral courage," that he entered a fight "with the ferocity of a bull and the skin of a rabbit." Donn Piatt, the irrepressible editor of a Washington weekly newspaper, pictured a man who on the floor of the House hesitated and retreated "in the most exasperating manner" and instead of taking positions and dealing blows tried to consider both sides, acting the judge when Republicans expected the advocate. It was said that when he was their leader, Republicans "could never be sure that he would not go wrong at the last moment, or have some private understanding with the Democrats, and leave his own party in the lurch." John Sherman said that Garfield "easily changed his mind and honestly veered from one impulse to another." Hayes, in retrospect, thought that Garfield "could not face a frowning world."[36]

What some of these critics described as lack of moral courage, George Frisbie Hoar of Massachusetts, a Republican member of the House from 1869 to 1877 and the Senate for many years thereafter, attributed to Garfield's intellectual habits. For six years Hoar sat near Garfield in the House, coming to know him well and favorably. It was Garfield's custom, as Hoar saw it, to get to the bottom of any subject before he made up his mind. Until he had investigated thoroughly he was likely to defer to other men's opinions, thinking himself mistaken. But once he had thought a matter through to a conclusion, "nobody and no consideration of personal interest and advantage," Hoar said, "could stir him an inch."[37]

Some of the criticism of Garfield comes down to the fact that on occasion he took a stand or pursued a course of action contrary to the desires and expectations of other Republicans. Frank Mason, for whom Garfield secured an appointment as United States consul in Basel, made a perceptive comment in 1880 in a campaign biography of the Republican presidential candidate prepared for European consumption: "He is not an intense partisan, and some of the thorniest places in his political path have been where he has taken too broad and impartial a view of pending questions to suit the views and purposes of other party leaders. . . ."[38]

Mason might have illustrated this point with reference to an incident that occurred in the House in March 1880. The Democrats were attempting to attach to an appropriations bill a rider relating to federal marshals, and Garfield as House minority leader offered an amendment that would enable them to retreat from their increasingly difficult position without loss of face. The amendment was one that Garfield himself had no intention of supporting as a rider. After his amendment had been added to the bill and the bill had passed, a journalist reported that Republicans were saying that the Democrats would not have succeeded "had it not been for the excessive non-partisanship and surrender of Garfield, whose amendment was adopted by the Democrats with enthusiasm. The fact is that many Republicans are very much disgusted with Garfield's action, and while they claim that his zeal to assist his political opponents out of the bad scrape did not weaken the law, it certainly cannot be commended by some of his party friends, who will no longer regard him as a safe leader."[39]

Blaine, Sherman, Hoar, and Mason were in reality not far apart in their views of Garfield; all were describing a man who was more intellectual than politician. Garfield would not have quarreled with their judgment.

It was one reporter's opinion that Garfield was "the best stump and platform speaker the Republican party had." Republicans had ample opportunity to judge his quality. Year after year he followed the campaign trail in his district and home state, and in New England, New York, Pennsylvania, and elsewhere. He traveled by rail, boat, and carriage in every kind of weather, slept on trains, in hotels and taverns, and in private homes. He spoke in churches, schoolhouses, Masonic halls, and town halls, in the open air and under tents. Some of his audiences were small, others ran into the thousands. He often made two speeches in a day, and occasionally more. In two days in 1879 he traveled 102 miles in carriages and 35 miles by rail and spoke four times in four towns. He was sometimes hoarse, ill, and exhausted, but he seldom failed an audience.[40]

Republicans who turned out for a campaign rally expected to make a full afternoon or evening of it. They also expected a featured speech to be partisan, stimulating, informative, entertaining—and long.

Garfield did not disappoint them. When he was the sole or main speaker he ordinarily spoke for at least an hour and a half, frequently for two hours or more. His imposing figure, strong voice "pitched in the middle key," and "personal magnetism" commanded attention. "His manner in his speeches," E. V. Smalley wrote, "was first engaging by its frankness and moderation, and afterward impressive by reason of its earnestness and vigor. At the climax of a speech he gathered up all the forces of statement and logic he had been marshaling, and hurled them upon his listeners with tremendous force." At times his left hand moved up and down in a curious chopping motion. He gave his audiences opportunities to laugh but was careful not to overdo the humor. It was a legend in Ohio that Tom Corwin would have been President had he not been so humorous, and Garfield himself was of the opinion that S. S. ("Sunset") Cox lost standing in the House by his "intellectual frivolity." [41]

Garfield also knew when to stop talking. Once, in Nashua, New Hampshire, when he shared the platform with his friend Eugene Hale, a Maine congressman, Hale spoke first—for two and a quarter hours. During the last fifteen minutes of his address there were impatient calls for an embarrassed Garfield. When Garfield began to speak he proposed that the audience remain for exactly thirty minutes. He then delivered a thirty-minute speech that left the audience—or part of it—asking for more. He did not continue. [42]

He never ceased to marvel at the mystery of speech-making. Why did not the same effort produce the same result? Why did some audiences "hook on" and others not? Why didn't audiences recognize a poor speech when they heard one? He once delivered a speech in Maine while suffering from a severe cold in head and throat. "I spoke with great effort," he wrote, "and I think I made the most dismal failure of my life." The next day he was surprised to find the press reporting that he had made "a very able and eloquent speech." His comment was, "I know better." Audience and speaker, however, were more often in accord. "Did well and was pleased to see how much they were delighted," he wrote on the occasion of another speech in Maine. [43]

In the presidential campaign of 1880 Democrats made a savage attack on Garfield's integrity as a public man. Much of the ammunition for the attack came from three happenings of the preceding decade: the Crédit Mobilier scandal, the salary grab, and the DeGolyer pavement affair. All three came to public attention between September 1872 and April 1874, and this period and the ensuing six months were for Garfield (and for Crete) the most distressful times of his congressional career; he was engulfed in gloom and despair, subjected to bitter attacks in his own district, and forced to make endless explanations and denials.

During the 1860s the federal government subsidized the building of the Union Pacific Railroad from Omaha to Utah (the eastern part of the first transcontinental). Leaders of the railroad company, which had been chartered by Congress, organized another company, the Crédit Mobilier of America, to build the railroad and to secure for themselves the profits to be derived from construction. It was a fraudulent enterprise from the beginning. In time Oakes Ames, a wealthy and respected manufacturer of Massachusetts and a member of Congress, became the leading figure in Crédit Mobilier (he was himself investing heavily in the railroad). In the fall of 1867, when it appeared that Congress might investigate procedures in the construction of the road, Ames undertook to interest some of the leading members of the Senate and House in investing in the stock of Crédit Mobilier. He represented the company as one organized to invest in and develop lands along the route of the Union Pacific, and he offered the stock as a very attractive investment—as indeed it was. James A. Garfield, chairman of the House Military Affairs Committee and a rising star among the Republicans, was one of those approached.

The story of Ames's stock-peddling in Washington broke late in the summer of 1872, two weeks before the presidential and congressional elections. It reached the public through Charles A. Dana's *New York Sun,* which had secured letters written by Ames concerning the distribution of stock among members of Congress. Garfield, who was among those named by Ames as having subscribed, learned of the disclosure on his way back from a government mission to Montana Territory. After a day in Hiram he set out for Washington, where he shortly authorized the publication of a statement that he had been asked to subscribe to shares of the stock but had declined to do so.[44]

When Congress met in December, scandal was on its doorstep. The House established two investigating committees; that headed by Luke Poland of Vermont was directed to investigate the alleged bribery of members of the House. Ames testified before the committee on a number of occasions. In December he said that he had agreed to get ten shares of Crédit Mobilier stock for Garfield for $1,000 but that Garfield had neither paid for the shares nor received them. In response to a question he said he thought that Garfield had not received any dividends. "He says he did not. My own recollection is not very clear."

In January he returned with memoranda relating to his transactions with members of Congress. He testified—and his memoranda supported him—that he had obtained ten shares of stock for Garfield but that Garfield had not paid him any money. He explained that he had sold Garfield's share of bonds (given to stockholders as a bonus) for $776 and had received a dividend on Garfield's stock in the amount of

$600. He had then deducted from the $1,376 the $1,000 Garfield owed him for the stock, plus interest of $47; this left a balance of $329, which he had paid to Garfield. "That," he said, "is all the transaction between us."

In February Ames said, with reference to the payment of $329, "Garfield understands this matter as a loan; he says I did not explain it to him." A moment later he added, "I supposed it was like all the rest; but when Mr. Garfield says he mistook it for a loan; that he always understood it to be a loan; that I did not make any explanation to him and did not make any statement to him, I may be mistaken." Ames survived the report of the Poland committee, which recommended his expulsion from the House, by only three months.[45]

Garfield's single appearance before the committee came on January 14, before Ames gave his damaging testimony. The statement he presented to the committee was forthright. "I never owned, received or agreed to receive any stock of the Crédit Mobilier or of the Union Pacific Railroad, nor any dividends or profits arising from either of them." He said that after he had been offered stock, more than a year had passed before Ames spoke of the matter again. Then, after another lapse of time, having heard that Crédit Mobilier was involved in a controversy with Union Pacific, he had told Ames that he had decided not to take the stock. He further said that he had once borrowed from Ames $300, which he had repaid.[46]

Why did the Poland committee not recall Garfield for further testimony after Ames revealed the discrepancy between their positions? A letter written by Calvin C. Chaffee to Senator Henry L. Dawes a few days after Garfield became President suggests a reason for the committee's failure to act—and also provides an insight into Garfield's state of mind while the Crédit Mobilier investigation was in progress. Chaffee, a physician who had been a member of Congress during the late 1850s and who practiced medicine in Washington for many years until 1876, wrote: "Do you remember my going to your room one night and finding Garfield there—during the Crédit Mobilier investigation—how thoroughly demoralized he was—how pitiful his condition was—how glad he was to get aid from any and every one? I do—and I sometimes wonder if he remembers such things—and who it was that induced Judge Poland not to recall him to the stand—I have a good memory for some things."[47]

The Poland committee concluded that Garfield had indeed agreed to take ten shares of stock in Crédit Mobilier and that he had received a balance of $329, as set forth by Ames. It concluded also that after this payment Garfield had had no further dividends and no further communication with Ames until after the investigation had

begun. It reported further that it had been able to find no evidence
that he had any other purpose in taking the stock "than to make a profitable investment" or that his interest in the company had affected his
official conduct.[48]

The committee's conclusions with respect to Garfield are supported
by statements of Jeremiah S. Black, a prominent lawyer and Democrat
with whom Garfield had been associated in law cases. It was Black who
in 1870 opened Garfield's eyes to the fraudulent nature of Crédit Mobilier and warned him that a congressman should not be involved in it.
In a letter to Garfield written soon after the scandal became public,
Black sought to aid his younger friend by summing up what Garfield
had told him about Crédit Mobilier in 1870 and suggesting the use of
that narrative as a line of defense. He made it clear that Garfield had
told him of his innocent acceptance of the stock and the dividend. "I
think I am accurate substantially," Black wrote. "It relieves you entirely
of every imputation which A's statement unexplained might cast upon
you. It shows you were not the instrument of corruption, but the victim
of his deception." In a letter to Speaker Blaine a short time later, Black
absolved Garfield of guilty knowledge but carefully avoided saying that
he had not agreed to take the stock or that he had not taken the dividend. Finally, during the campaign of 1880, Black, a supporter of the
Democratic candidate for President, declared that Garfield had taken
the stock and the dividend.[49]

If the Poland committee and Jeremiah Black were correct, why did
Garfield not admit that he had in all innocence been taken in? Did he
feel that, having issued his denial immediately after the storm broke,
he had to stick to his story? Black offered another explanation. "Your
misfortune," he wrote Garfield in January 1873, "has consisted in making common cause with other persons who are indefensible . . . I have
implicit faith in your integrity." Black put the matter more bluntly
when in 1880 he addressed a letter to a Democratic meeting. He said
that he had written to Garfield begging him to stand fast on the defense Black had made for him, "but the party would not let him take it.
The accusation struck at the highest heads in the House and Senate.
They had but one answer, and that was a positive denial that any stock
had ever been taken by them. General Garfield, for the benefit of
others, united in making this defense."[50]

When Congress adjourned on March 4 after the season of Crédit
Mobilier, there was another eruption. On the day before the session
ended the legislative, executive, and judicial appropriations bill—a document of more than twenty pages in the *Statutes-at-Large*—had passed
both houses and been signed by President Grant. Among the many

items in the new law was an increase in the salaries of members of Congress from $5,000 to $7,500—retroactive to the beginning of the session two years earlier. Public reaction was one of fury, in part perhaps because the "salary grab" followed so closely on the heels of Crédit Mobilier. The last increase in pay had been in 1866; that too had been retroactive, but it did not go down in history as a salary grab.

Garfield, the chairman of the Appropriations Committee, encountered heavy condemnation, particularly in his own district. The criticism was not entirely fair; Garfield had foreseen an unfavorable public response and had opposed the increase up to a point. But he had in the end signed the report of the conference committee of which he was chairman, and he had supported in the House the adoption of the conference bill, which included the salary clause. He had walked up and down in the corridor outside the conference room in doubt as to what he should do (Burke Hinsdale, who was in Washington at the time, bore witness to that). Garfield had concluded that as chairman of the Appropriations Committee he had the responsibility of seeing that the bill was adopted before the impending adjournment. If Congress failed to pass the bill by noon on March 4, a special session would be required.[51]

Congressmen recoiled from the public explosion that followed, and Garfield and others hastened to renounce the retroactive windfall. When the new Congress met in December, members rushed to introduce bills restoring congressional salaries to the old level; before the middle of January the change had been adopted. It was many years before Congress had recovered sufficiently from its fright to give itself another pay raise.[52]

In the spring of 1872 the Board of Public Works of the District of Columbia, of which Alexander Robey ("Boss") Shepherd was chairman, was about to place a large order for street paving materials. The De Golyer-McClellan Company of Chicago, which manufactured a patented wooden paving block, agreed to share profits with George Chittenden if he succeeded in getting a contract for them. Chittenden, who was prepared to use a good deal of the company's money to achieve his goal, secured the services of Richard C. Parsons, a Cleveland lawyer who was marshal of the United States Supreme Court from 1867 to 1872. After appearing before the Board of Public Works in support of the DeGolyer paving block, Parsons, according to his own story, was called home to Cleveland. His work unfinished, he enlisted his old friend Garfield (the two men had been together in the state legislature a dozen years earlier) to carry on in his absence.[53]

Garfield's involvement was brief but profitable. On June 2, a Sunday, he traveled in a hired carriage several miles into the country to the home of Boss Shepherd. When Congress adjourned on June 10, Garfield could take up the project in earnest. On June 13 he noted in his diary that he had been "working up the DeGolyer Patent Pavement and laying its claims before the Board of Public Works." The "Chicago business" detained him longer than he had expected, but on June 19 he made an early evening call on Shepherd "and substantially completed arrangements for Chicago plans." A couple of hours later he and his family were on their way to Ohio. The Board of Public Works acted promptly, awarding the contract to DeGolyer-McClellan early in July. On July 27 Garfield recorded in his little cash book the receipt of a fee of $5,000 in the "Pavement Case." The payment came from Parsons, who thereby shared with Garfield the $15,000 that had been paid to him.[54]

The incident came to light in the spring of 1874 in the course of an investigation by a joint committee of the administration of the District of Columbia, which then had territorial status. The disclosure provided additional ammunition for Garfield's foes at home, who were already armed with Crédit Mobilier and salary grab. On the surface there appeared to be nothing wrong with Garfield's activities on behalf of a paving block; many lawyers continued their practice while they were in Congress, and some of them, Garfield included, appeared before the Supreme Court. But Garfield was chairman of the Appropriations Committee, and it was responsible for appropriations bills relating to the District of Columbia. On May 3, 1872, Garfield had noted in his diary, "Heard the Board of Public Works in the District on their request for appropriations." On June 11, the day after the adjournment of Congress and nine days after Garfield's Sunday visit to Boss Shepherd, Garfield's committee met to take up some unfinished business. "Discussed several deficiencies," Garfield wrote, "and ordered a partial deficiency bill. Listened to the request of the Governor of the District of Columbia and Board of Public Works for a hearing. Set tomorrow for that purpose."[55]

Garfield's critics did not have access to his diary, but they knew that his committee dealt with appropriations for the District of Columbia. Questions were inevitable. Was Garfield, in the DeGolyer case, selling his legal services or his influence? Was Parsons soliciting the aid of a friendly lawyer or a committee chairman? Did Boss Shepherd award the contract to DeGolyer-McClellan because of the superiority of their product or because the chairman of the Appropriations Committee asked him to? One thing eventually became clear: the DeGolyer interests had considered it a great triumph to have secured the services of so eminent a man as General Garfield.

To the people of Garfield's district $5,000 seemed an extravagant sum for such small labor; it was what Garfield earned in a whole year as a congressman. Garfield could only point out that Parsons was paid on a contingency fee basis and that the contract amounted to nearly $750,000.[56]

Garfield's reaction to the criticism was one of indignation. Immediately after his connection with DeGolyer was brought out, although "very tired and nearly sick," he paid an evening call on Parsons—who had become a member of the House—and afterward wrote in his diary, "It is time that we ascertain whether a member of Congress has any rights."[57]

Of the three involvements that besmirched Garfield's reputation and caused him so much anguish, that relating to DeGolyer pavement is the most serious. His connection with Crédit Mobilier would appear to have been wholly innocent, though there seems little doubt that he misrepresented the facts in his testimony concerning it. The uproar over his part in the salary increase was greater than the circumstances seem to warrant. In the pavement case he acted obtusely at the very least; always ready to help a friend, he may well have acceded to Parsons's request out of a desire to oblige. There is no reason to suppose that Parsons told him much or that Garfield had any inkling of the range of Chittenden's activities in his efforts to secure the contract. But it is hard to believe that at some point strong doubt did not arise in Garfield's mind as to the propriety of his having accepted such a commission. It was not an undertaking in which the chairman of the Appropriations Committee—indeed, any congressman—should have been engaged.

Several years after the DeGolyer business, Dr. Robison told Crete that Richard Parsons, who was then editor and part owner of the *Cleveland Herald,* was "very mad" at Garfield, who, according to Parsons, had done himself great harm by appearing at a recent convention. "I told the Doctor," Crete wrote to Garfield, "I thought you would be no more harmed than you were when you made Dick Parsons your friend. Whereupon Doctor said 'Amen.' "[58]

After he had been publicly associated with Crédit Mobilier, Garfield said that "the shadow of the cursed thing" would cling to his name for many years. He was never to be free of it or of the other charges against him. Blaine kept him on tenterhooks for months in 1873 by leaving him in doubt whether he would retain the chairmanship of the Appropriations Committee. He had to fight for his political life in his campaign for re-election in 1874. In 1877 a special committee of the House, investigating a real estate pool in the District of Columbia, dredged up DeGolyer pavement and embarrassed anew the man who was now House minority leader. Late in the same year a new Democratic newspaper, the *Washington Post,* began publication. Within a few months it ran a column on Garfield and DeGolyer pavement and at the same time commented editorially: "The importance of this complete explanation at this time lies in the fact that a new House of Representatives is to be elected in a few months, and as Garfield will undoubtedly be a candidate for re-election it is proper that the people of his district should know exactly whom they are voting for. That they may be mistaken as to the man Mr. Garfield really is may be inferred from a recent editorial eulogy of him in the *Cleveland Leader,* which gives voice to the peculiar Radical sentiment of the Western Reserve of Ohio." "The *Washington Post,*" Garfield remarked in his diary, "has revived the DeGolyer pavement slander upon me, and is doing all it can to injure my reputation." Between June 8, 1880, when Garfield was nominated for President, and November 2, when he was elected, the old charges enjoyed a new lease on life.[59]

The Democrats overdid the business in 1880, and their attacks may have redounded to Garfield's advantage. On August 11 *Puck,* a humorous weekly, carried on its cover a cartoon showing Charles A. Dana as a scientist gesturing toward a microscope through which Garfield's corruptions are being viewed by a man with the ears of a donkey. Dana holds in his hand a chart exhibiting the horrors of Crédit Mobilier, DeGolyer pavement, "perjury," and "contracts" in the guise of fierce and slimy lizardlike creatures. Below the cartoon are these words:

### The Republican Candidate in View
C. A. Dana:
"Come and see! Two cents a sight! Great Sun Microscope!
Magnifies 100,000,000,000 Diameters."

Lacking an allowance for a secretary, Garfield managed to get along with part-time help. Wallace Ford assisted him during some of his first term. In the late 1860s George U. Rose began to give him a considerable amount of time and continued to do so until 1881. Rose was a government employee during his years with Garfield (a clerk in the Treasury Department most of the time). He did not serve Garfield on a regular schedule but came to the congressman's home when he was free and his services were needed—evenings, Sundays, sometimes during workdays. He was a faithful and able worker who took dictation, wrote out vast numbers of letters, copied entries into Garfield's diary, and performed such other tasks as were assigned to him. Garfield made no arrangement for paying him regularly; Rose himself said that the first compensation he received came at the end of several years' service. This curious situation suggests that Garfield was Rose's patron in respect to his continuing employment by the government. Rose also seems to have looked forward to a time when Garfield would deal more generously with him.[60]

Late in 1878 another aide made his appearance. Joseph Stanley Brown, twenty years old, was a native of Washington and a product of its public schools. He had begun to teach himself shorthand when he was twelve and when he finished school at seventeen was "a good average stenographer." In 1878 he was secretary to John Wesley Powell, director of the Survey of the Rocky Mountain Region. Powell was then promoting the consolidation of the various western surveys carried on by the government, and Garfield was willing to assist in getting a bill to provide for the consolidation through Congress. Garfield told Powell that he needed secretarial help, his own secretary having been ill for some time, and at Powell's suggestion Brown called on Garfield and agreed to help him with his correspondence outside his own office hours. The bill establishing the United States Geological Survey was enacted into law just before Congress adjourned in March 1879. The following fall Garfield asked Brown to resume his part-time work for him, and Brown agreed. The bright, efficient, somewhat brash young man hit it off well with Garfield, who tried out parts of speeches on him and consulted him on matters concerning the children. Nothing seems to have been said about compensation until June 1880, after Garfield had been chosen the Republican candidate for President. At that time Garfield arranged with Powell to take Brown with him to Mentor and agreed to pay the young man the amount he had been receiving from Powell, $100 a month.[61]

Garfield early recognized that a politician needed more than politics to keep his mind alive; politics alone could "fossilize" a man. He often used the word "growth" to describe the expansion of one's intellectual horizons, and he counted the day lost that had not contributed to his own growth.

Books offered the best means to that end. "His real pleasure," a reporter once wrote of Garfield, "seems to be when poring over his books." Close at hand was the Library of Congress, then housed back of the rotunda, on the west front of the Capitol. Ainsworth Spofford, its head for more than thirty years and himself possessed of a vast store of information, said that Garfield's use of the library was rivaled only by that of Charles Sumner and Oliver P. Morton. Garfield built a library of his own as well, and in the late 1870s an addition to his house enabled him to have a room of about twenty-five by fourteen feet for his books and a large walnut desk. The books, however, overflowed the library. "And, undoubtedly the overflow has been regular," one visitor wrote, "as you can go nowhere in the general's home without coming face to face with books. They confront you in the hall when you enter, in the parlor and the sitting room, in the dining-room and even in the bath-room, where documents and speeches are corded up like fire-wood."[62]

The master of this library read widely and constantly in history, literature, religion, economics, and government. Shakespeare and Tennyson were his favorite English poets, Horace (whose odes he sometimes translated into English) his favorite Latin author. Dickens, Scott, Austen, and Thackeray were among the novelists he held in high esteem. He read with a delight he had "rarely felt for any book" the *Autobiography* of John Stuart Mill as soon as it appeared, and he was "delighted" with Trevelyan's two-volume biography of Macaulay, whose works he had already read. For a time he read everything by and about Goethe he could lay his hands on; Spofford sent him twenty-six volumes in one batch, and after a few weeks of reading he had fifty or sixty pages of dictated notes to show for it. On a trip west in 1875 he heard of a young Swiss teamster in the American army who claimed that his knowledge of the Romany language enabled him to converse freely with an old Cheyenne woman. On Garfield's return home he was confined to the house for some six weeks with a painful rectal condition that required surgery, and he sent to the Library of Congress for books on gypsies and proceeded to read them. He then wrote to Horace Scudder, a Boston writer and editor, asking him to write Charles G. Leland, whose book *The English Gypsies and Their Language* he had just read, to ascertain the author's thoughts about the young teamster's story.[63]

During the same weeks of confinement his readings embraced the two volumes of the newly published *Memoirs of General William T. Sherman,* Froude's twelve-volume *History of England from the Fall of Wolsey to the Death of Elizabeth,* several of Shakespeare's plays, a new play by Lord Tennyson, and Thackeray's *The Newcomes.* Sometimes during his illness he and Crete read together. On occasion Almon F. ("Jarvis") Rockwell, a Williams College classmate whose acquaintance with Garfield had been renewed during the war when both men were serving under General Buell, and who had entered the regular army after the war, came to read and talk about Shakespeare, to whom he was also devoted. Day after day Garfield commented on his readings in his diary.[64]

When he traveled he took books with him, and he read those he found along the way. Without something to read he would have found travel by train unendurable. Once on a train he opened his carpetbag in anticipation of reading Goethe's *Wilhelm Meister* only to discover that he had packed instead a volume containing two novels of the popular writer Mary J. Holmes. At first he put the volume aside in annoyance, but shortly he took it up, read both novels, and commented on them. The next time he was in the Library of Congress he was disgusted to learn that Mrs. Holmes had written eleven novels and was "still firing away. Spofford tells me that her books are constantly called for. This verifies the soldier's maxim, 'Aim low.'"

After a campaign stop in Van Wert, Ohio, he wrote, "Wretched dinner at a wretched hotel. Read *Chuzzlewit* all the time I could steal away from callers. . . . In the evening addressed a large audience in Melodeon Hall. *Chuzzlewit* and bed." In a hotel in New Britain, Connecticut, he found a copy of a history of the church in that town and read it until long after midnight—and took notes. In a hotel in Maine, after making a two-hour speech in the evening, he read several chapters of a new history of the state. Left alone for three hours in a private residence in Defiance, Ohio, after delivering an afternoon speech, he came upon a biography of John Randolph "and read half of the first volume with much interest." That night, "Got to bed early, and read Randolph until a late hour." The next night he was reading "an abominable book," a youth's history of the Civil War. Garfield appreciated the best in books but preferred a very bad book to no book at all.[65]

He sometimes longed for more time to give to literature, but he reflected that if he had abundant leisure, he might fritter it away. "Perhaps that study of literature is fullest," he wrote, "which we steal from daily duties. In the afternoon went to the Treasury and had a long interview with the Secretary in regard to revenues and expenditures. Played billiards with Rockwell for a couple of hours before dinner. Spent the evening in reading Goethe."[66]

Garfield found in the theater another source of stimulation outside politics. Here, for him, Shakespeare reigned supreme; over the years he saw many of the plays and most of the best known Shakespearean actors in America. Two of them, John McCullough and Lawrence Barrett, became his friends. He once gave a three and a half hour breakfast for McCullough that one regrets having missed (among the handful of guests was General Sherman, a conversationalist of the first order). Garfield's taste was not limited to Shakespeare. He came home from seeing E. A. Sothern in *Garrick* and *A Regular Fix* "with sides sore from laughing." He liked *Pinafore* so much that he saw it three times within six weeks. He thought Joe Jefferson "simply wonderful in his humor." In New York he saw "the new play called *Divorce*" and expressed judgment: "A quiet but terrible criticism on the times. A mild Juvenal." Enjoyable as he found playgoing, it was, unlike his reading, only an occasional pursuit.[67]

The practice of law was another activity that Garfield found challenging and enjoyable. It was also profitable; in some years his practice earned him a thousand dollars or so, in others as much as six or seven thousand. One case concerned with the tangled finances of an ailing railroad brought him $5,000 (he had asked for $20,000—more than his client could pay). A suit growing out of the will of the Disciple leader, Alexander Campbell, yielded him $3,500. In handling his cases he was regularly associated with one or more lawyers. He worked hard and long, enjoyed the association with prominent lawyers, and received commendation for his efforts, ever conscious of his lack of a deep knowledge of the law. As a lawyer he made many appearances before the Supreme Court, which was housed with its library in the Capitol.

Near the end of 1876, when the electoral battle was raging, Garfield confided to his diary, "Spent most of the day on the law case, and enjoyed the work very much. I have always found a keen intellectual pleasure in the law. It reaches out into what is impersonal, it is unpartisan, and may be so studied as to enlarge the spirit. I am conscious of not being fitted for the partisan work of politics, although I believe in partisanship, within reasonable limits."[68]

Most lawyers do not begin their practice by pleading before the United States Supreme Court. Garfield did. In the fall of 1859 (when he was first elected state senator) he entered his name as a law student in the Cleveland office of two lawyers, one of whom was Albert Gallatin Riddle. Having satisfied a requirement of the law by this action, and having talked for a few minutes with Riddle about books, he set out to master the law by himself. By 1861 he had sufficient knowledge to pass an oral examination in Columbus, and he was admitted to practice in the courts of Ohio. Five years passed before he began practice. In 1866 he was invited by Jeremiah S. Black to join with him and other lawyers in a case before the Supreme Court. He accepted the invitation, was at once admitted to the bar of the Court, and aided in the presentation of the case.[69]

The case, ex parte Milligan, is one of the most celebrated in American judicial history. During the war Lambdin P. Milligan, a Confederate sympathizer in Indiana, was tried and convicted by court-martial on charges of having engaged in various disloyal activities. President Lincoln commuted his death sentence to life imprisonment. Black, acting with other eminent lawyers on behalf of Milligan, approached Garfield knowing that he had taken a stand in Congress in favor of restricting the power of military commissions. The Court held for Milligan on the ground that, under the circumstances prevailing in Indiana at the time of his trial, he should have been tried in a civil court.[70]

Although he received no fee for his work (he even paid for the printing of his brief and argument) and was the target of sharp criticism from Radical Republicans for having defended a traitor, Garfield gained by his participation in the case. He had made himself better known, had demonstrated his legal talents, and had begun a close friendship and professional association with Jeremiah Black—who, as it happened, was also a member of the Disciples of Christ.

In the mid-1870s Garfield seriously considered abandoning politics for the law and on one occasion came very close to doing so. Attacks on his character, the winning of control of the House by the Democrats in the election of 1874, and his general discontent with politics were probably considerations. He was thinking, too, of his family and his own future security. The needs of the family were steadily increasing; he now had full responsibility for the support of his wife, his mother, and six children. In the fall of 1875 he agreed informally to enter into a law partnership in Cleveland. A long talk the next day with Dolson Cox was perhaps an important factor in changing his mind. Cox, a man of sound sense, doubted that Garfield would make more money as a full-time lawyer than he was then making by combining politics and law. "I told him frankly," Cox wrote several years after Garfield's death, "that I thought it was too late—that I thought he could hardly recover the habits of . . . private office work, and doubted whether his tastes had not become so formed upon the excitement of politics that he would become melancholy and restless in private business." After his talk with Cox, Garfield never again mentioned the Cleveland partnership in his diary.[71]

Hard worker that he was, and possessed of a delicate nervous system, Garfield needed means of relaxing that would be undemanding and social. He dined out often, perhaps enjoying most the all-male dinners at Welcker's, a fabulous Washington restaurant; to be in good company at Welcker's as the guest of the cultivated and genial lobbyist Sam Ward was a rare delight. Garfield played a variety of card games—casino, euchre, bezique, whist, pedro. After Rockwell came to Washington a game of billiards was a favorite way of passing an hour or so. In Ohio he played croquet. In the Washington home there were games with the children, among them puss-in-the-corner. He enjoyed carriage rides about the town and into the country.

Toward the end of his life he developed a new interest. In 1879 the National Club of Washington joined the National Association of Base Ball Clubs, and teams from Albany, Rochester, Springfield, and elsewhere came to play in the capital. On a May day in that year Garfield left the House early to go with Rockwell and Swaim to see a game between the Springfields and the Nationals—a game, he noted in his diary, "handsomely won by the latter." He added, "The pitching of Lynch of the Nationals was wonderful, not only in the strength with which he pitched the ball, but in the skill with which he deceived the batsmen." He saw a number of games in the spring of 1879 and in 1880, the last one a few days before he left Washington for the Republican national convention in Chicago.[72]

Garfield once advised Harry Rhodes to "polarize" his life by "love and marriage and home." Between 1863 and 1881 his own greatest source of happiness became increasingly his wife, his children, and his home.[73]

His first months in Congress were lonely. He lived in rooms and boarded out—the fate of many congressmen who left their families behind when they came to the capital. There was one bright period; Crete (and Almeda) visited him for a month and they stayed in a hotel. When he returned to Ohio in the summer of 1864, Crete spelled out for him her own dissatisfaction with their way of life by handing him a slip of paper showing that in four and three quarters years of marriage they had lived together only twenty weeks. Then and there he resolved that he would not live in Washington again without her.[74]

He kept his resolution. The following winter he rented a couple of rooms for the three of them—the unnamed baby of 1863 was now Harry Abram—and they boarded out. During the next three winters they lived in furnished rented houses. The winter of 1868–69 saw them living again in rented rooms and boarding.

Meanwhile two more children had been born, James Rudolph in 1865 and Mary, usually called "Mollie," in 1867. Mollie was the first of the children to be born in Washington.

In 1869 Garfield decided to build a house. He was brought to the decision by the cost of renting (about $200 a month) and the offer of his old army friend David Swaim to lend him money for the construction. Shortly after being mustered out of the volunteer army in 1866, Swaim had received a commission in the infantry of the regular army but had been assigned to duty in the South as acting judge advocate (he had been a lawyer in civil life). Without an assignment in the spring of 1869, he was hopeful of securing promotion to major and assignment to the Judge Advocate's Department; with Garfield's support his desire was fulfilled at the end of the year. By then, under Swaim's supervision, a new three-story brick building had been completed at the northeast corner of Thirteenth and I streets, across Thirteenth Street from Franklin Park. Enlarged in 1878, it was the Garfield family's Washington home until 1880.[75]

Three more children were born to James and Crete following the move to the new house. Irvin McDowell was born in Hiram in 1870, Abram in Washington in 1872, and Edward in Washington in 1874. Edward died in 1876.

Eliza joined the Washington household for the first time in the winter of 1867–68, after James had rented a large house only a block from the Capitol. "I think if I keep my health I shall pass the winter and Spring very pleasantly," she wrote to Alpha in January. "I have no charge and care of anything. I can read and write or do whatever I please." A month later she reported to Phebe that she was enjoying herself very well, much better than she had expected. "I have evrything for my comfort that heart can wish. I am waited upon as though I was somebody of note, evry dog must have his day." She took advantage of the nearness to the Capitol and attended many sessions of the House and Senate. Day after day she trudged to the Senate chamber to listen to the impeachment trial of President Johnson. She also rode out to see most of the sights of the city and environs. When spring came she confessed that she had not felt so good for a long time: "this doing nothing agrees with me." (In the winter of 1864 she had bitterly charged Garfield with not caring for her as he once had.)[76]

Eliza stayed in Ohio during the short session of 1868–69, then regularly spent her winters in Washington, returning to Ohio with other members of the family for the summer and fall. She kept the folks back home informed of her continued good fortune. "We have had our House repaired new carpets in three Rooms two Halls and the Stairs. My Room is one of them. . . . I think there is not many Mothers has a better Home than I have. . . . I have a grate in my room and have a fire made every morning before I get up." And, "Now I must tell you what I had for a Christmas present . . . about the Handsomest Stuffed Chair I ever saw . . . it cost 25 Dollars. I can roll it all over the Room."[77]

In 1875 Eliza sat for a portrait by Caroline ("Carrie") Ransom, an Ohio artist who was a close friend of James and Crete and who had studios in Cleveland and Washington. In the spring of 1876 the portrait, "elegantly framed," was hung above the grand piano "in a good light" in the parlor of the Garfield home in Washington. There it remained as long as the family occupied the house. "The face is small and beams benevolently from a snowy cap," one viewer wrote. Opposite Eliza's portrait was one of Trot, also by Carrie Ransom.[78]

Benevolence was not Eliza's only mood. Her continuing presence was something of a strain on the household. Two years after Garfield's death, Mollie, then sixteen, wrote of her grandmother in her diary, "My! I don't wonder she nearly worried the life out of Papa and Mamma—such a woman as she is, I just can't stand." Gossip had it that

Eliza and Crete did not get on together. But no evidence suggests that Crete ever treated her mother-in-law with anything but kindness and affection; Eliza in turn seems to have had a genuine regard for Crete. Eliza was an old country woman set in her ways, and residence in the capital of the United States was not going to change her.[79]

It was a lively household. When the family received a letter from New Orleans in which Garfield referred to "our quiet home," Hal "in a half soliloquy said 'quiet, I wonder if he calls it *quiet* at home.' " Everyone laughed with Hal "at Papa's delusion." After a meal with the Garfields, John Q. Smith wrote his wife that "there was lots of trouble to keep the little shavers straight. Miss Mary and Master Jim had to be sent away from the table for being *bad*." Jim was the most difficult of the children. One summer in Ohio his father took him into the woods and gave him a sound flogging—despite having "some doubt about this business of pounding goodness into a child." When Hal and Jim went away to school, their parents wondered whether they would last a month. Their first reports, in which both boys were rated "perfect in decorum," left Crete and James scarcely knowing "which was uppermost surprise or delight." That same year Crete wrote of Irvin and Abe, "They are passing through that dreaded period of boyhood when the chief joy in living seems to be measured by the discomfort they can occasion to everybody else." All of this suggests that the household was not only lively but normal.[80]

The children sometimes reduced Crete to self-pity. "It is horrible to be a man," she wrote to James in the summer of 1877, "but the grinding misery of being a woman between the upper and nether millstone of household cares and training children is almost as bad. To be half civilized with some aspirations for enlightenment, and obliged to spend the largest part of the time the victim of young barbarians keeps one in a perpetual ferment."[81]

The education of the children was the subject of much thought, discussion, and experimentation. Garfield wanted them to have the best. Hal and Jim started in a public school, but their father was soon dissatisfied with the results, one of which was that both boys hated books. "My faith in our public schools is steadily diminishing," he wrote. "The course of study is unnatural and the children are too overcrowded for solid healthy growth and that ought to be the chief business of children and study must not interfere with it too much." He was better pleased with a private kindergarten that the two older boys and Mollie attended for a season. The next year Hal and Jim entered the Emerson Institute, a reputable private school near the Garfield home. The coming of a governess solved the problem of the education of the younger children for several years.[82]

In the winter of 1876–77, following the death of Edward, all of the children were instructed at home. Crete has left an account of some of the activities.

> Miss Mays, a young English woman whom we all love very much, is with us and is teaching Mollie, Irvin and Abram. . . . Hal and Jim are reading the first book of Caesar's Commentaries. They are shut up for two hours each morning to learn their lesson in Latin Grammar and read a lesson in Caesar. I then spend between two and three hours hearing each one recite alone the whole lesson, spell and read. It is their regular work and my chief purpose is to try to get them into habits of thorough careful study without help. In the evening or at dinner Papa reviews them in their Caesar and each Friday he requires of each one some literary exercise, either a declamation or composition. We are all very happy in our winter's work, and I believe are making more progress than ever before.[83]

The children received instruction from Garfield in many informal ways. He read Charles and Mary Lamb's *Tales from Shakespeare* to them and then introduced them to Shakespeare on the stage. Mollie (eight), Jim (ten), and Hal (twelve) went with their parents to see *Macbeth,* and Garfield thought they got "a pretty fair notion of the play." A couple of years later Hal and Jim "were greatly delighted" with *Henry V,* "especially its scenery and costumes." Irvin was taken to see *Othello* when he was nine. Garfield read aloud on a number of occasions from one of Audubon's works and followed up the reading by taking the family to the Smithsonian to see the birds he had read about. When they failed to find three of the sixteen they sought, Garfield sent for an ornithologist who informed them that two of the birds were there under different names and one, the ibis, was not in the museum. Garfield took the three oldest children to the Centennial Exposition in Philadelphia and during the visit drove with them in a carriage to Fairmount Park and Laurel Hill—to the latter to enable Crete and the children to see the statue of Scott and Old Mortality that he himself had seen years before.

The children were expected to write letters to an absent parent and to each other when apart. When Garfield traveled he often addressed letters to the children, giving details of where he had been and what he had seen. Starting from Toledo in the spring of 1875 for a trip by rail to the Pacific Coast, he wrote them a long letter, beginning, "I am going to write you letters every few days while I am gone, to let you know where I am, and also to help you in your knowledge of the Geography of your own country. I will try to write so plainly that Harry, Jimmie and Mollie can read what I write, themselves, and so can improve in learning to read writing. I want you to take the large atlas, and trace my journey, and then recite to Mamma, so as to be able to tell her the places I pass through and tell her what states they are in and what rivers I cross."

The dinner hour was also a time of learning. A book of words frequently mispronounced was a feature at meals in 1880; a word was spelled, the children pronounced it as they thought it should be, and the correct pronunciation was announced. It was an exercise that all the family enjoyed.[84]

In September 1879 Hal and Jim, nearing sixteen and fourteen respectively, entered St. Paul's School in Concord, New Hamphire, which was conducted by Dr. Henry A. Coit, an Episcopalian clergyman. Garfield had employed a tutor to prepare the boys and had also helped them himself. A few days after Hal and Jim had begun their new life, both Crete and Garfield visited the school. Garfield studied the headmaster "anxiously and carefully" and recorded his disappointment in his diary; Coit's brother Milnor and the other teachers he liked very much. "I shall watch the further development with anxious interest."[85]

The return of the boys for Christmas was the occasion for rejoicing. "The whole household," Garfield noted, "were putting themselves in readiness to meet the dear boys, even the little boys being dressed as for a holiday. Little Mollie had fixed herself up quite elaborately. Grandma dressed herself soon after noon as if for company." The next morning, "A quiet and delightful breakfast with our whole family, and only them, the double pleasure of completeness and exclusiveness."[86]

Religion never ceased to be a part of Garfield's life. He had joined the Disciples of Christ when he was eighteen, and sentiment and a sense of historical continuity kept him a member for the rest of his life. Until 1869 Disciples in Washington held services in private homes; in that year they bought a little chapel on M Street N.W. and later moved it to Vermont Avenue above Thomas Circle, an easy walk from the Garfield home. The Vermont Avenue church is that most closely associated with Garfield. Although the church has disappeared, the bench on which he sat has been preserved—a narrow perch for a broad man! We have no record of his church attendance during his first eight years in Congress. From January 1, 1872, when he began once more to keep a regular diary after the lapse of years, the record is nearly complete. The diary reveals that, whether in Washington or Ohio, he attended church services with considerable regularity, usually accompanied by members of his family and sometimes by friends as well. He once wrote that he thought "that a man should maintain the habit partly for his own sake and partly for the sake of others." Most sermons received no comment in his diary. When he heard one that he thought excellent, powerful, good, solid, or able, he said so. When he disliked a sermon, he condemned it in such terms as "very stupid," "rambling and declamatory," "dreary," "scolding," and "a flat foggy bog." On occasion he enjoyed listening to preachers who were not of his own church. In England in 1867 he was much taken by the preaching of the famed Baptist Charles H. Spurgeon; in 1875 he was impressed by "the wonderful directness and earnestness" of the evangelist Dwight L. Moody.[87]

Fellow Disciples who sat beside Garfield in the Vermont Avenue church or in their churches on the Western Reserve might well have been startled and dismayed had they known how unorthodox he had become. In his own preaching days he had had little interest in theological topics, his sermons being strong, as Burke Hinsdale said, "in the ethical rather than in the distinctly evangelical element." Stricter members of the church then faulted him for not being more denominational and for his lack of "unction." As he progressed through life, reading widely, listening to preachers of many faiths, influenced by science, he moved more and more in the direction of a broad non-denominational religious thought. An entry in his diary following a visit to the Vermont Avenue church with Crete, Mollie, and Irvin on a Sunday in December 1875 reflects Garfield's thinking.

> I have come to wonder at those happy mortals who know the whole counsels of God and have no doubts.
>
> Are all religions, past and present, false, except that of Christ? If so, what shall we think of the Goodness and Mercy of God in leaving mankind so many generations without the truth? It is asking a good deal to require us to believe that this alone is the final and perfect form of religious truth, when men of all past ages have so confidently believed they had it, and it is now universally acknowledged that none was final or true unless it be this. Is it not intolerable egotism in us to suppose that we are so exceptionally precious to God, that while He has never seen enough good in the race to make it worth saving until 1,800 years ago, yet then its superiority of virtue and importance led him to make great exertions to save it? It may not be unreasonable to suppose that each age has had as much light as it could use, and the future may open up religious truth on a plane higher than we now know of. Who shall limit the methods of God?[88]

Summers the Garfield family migrated to Ohio, though rarely as a unit. Garfield's movements were determined by his duties in Washington and by engagements elsewhere. The house in Hiram was retained until 1872, when it was sold to Burke Hinsdale. For a few years the Rudolph home was the family's summer base, but they also spent time at Little Mountain, near Painesville, where Cleveland businessmen had established a colony and club. In 1874 Garfield had a small cabin built there, but the arrangement proved unsatisfactory. In late August 1875, forced out of the Little Mountain Club by its early closing, Garfield made this comment: "I hope never again to have my family dragged around as they have been this season." During the centennial season Eliza was the only member of the family to spend as much time as usual in Ohio.[89]

The problem of an Ohio residence was solved in October 1876 when Garfield bought a farm. It was the "old Dickey place" in Mentor, about twenty miles from Cleveland and a few miles from Painesville (half a mile down the road was the farm of Dr. Robison). It was a run-down property, its buildings "in a sad state of dilapidation." The farmhouse was small and totally inadequate to the needs of the Garfield family. A "shaky" barn surrounded by "rubbish" stood close to the street and the house. The pigsty was too near the parlor window. Other old buildings completed "a characteristic pioneer group." But the land was there, 118 acres (Garfield shortly added nearly 40 more), some of it swampy and all in need of attention. "As a financial investment," Garfield wrote, "I do not think it very wise; but as a means of securing a summer home, and teaching my boys to do farm work, I feel well about it."[90]

Good investment or not, the farm was a happy purchase. It was a source of pleasure for all the family, and for the rest of his life it was never far from Garfield's thoughts. When he was there he threw himself zestfully into its life, working in the fields, supervising workers, buying new stock and machinery, planning for the future. He wanted a real farm of which he could be proud, a farm well stocked and well worked, its lands restored, its harvests bountiful. When he was absent he corresponded with his farmer and with Dr. Robison; the operation could not have been carried on without the presence of the rough, strong-minded doctor who could get things done. Eliza expressed her satisfaction to Alpha, "I tell you it seems good to be on a farm." The boys seem to have had a good time, though it is doubtful that they worked much at farming. The farm continued to be the scene of family gatherings long into the twentieth century.[91]

Visitors to the farm in the summer of 1880 saw a place far different from that of 1876. A comfortable three-story house had grown out of the earlier small, decaying structure; there were new barns and other buildings, the pigsty had been moved, the manure piles had disappeared from the site of the old barn near the street. New fruit trees and evergreens were in place. Crops were growing in a once swampy area. A hydraulic ram supplied spring water in abundance. Modern farm machinery was in evidence. A fine Jersey bull (the gift of Abram Hewitt of New York, a prominent Democratic congressman) and two fine Jersey heifers (the gift of Erastus Tyler, the man who had defeated Garfield for colonel in 1861 and was now postmaster of Baltimore) gave promise of an improved dairy herd. The old Dickey place had become General Garfield's farm; reporters were also beginning to call it Lawnfield.[92]

Garfield's sense of domestic well-being can be glimpsed in his diary entry of November 11, 1875.

> This is the anniversary of our wedding which took place 17 years ago. If I could find the time and had the ability to write out the story of Crete's life and mine, the long and anxious questionings that preceeded and attended the adjustment of our lives to each other, and the beautiful results we long ago reached and are now enjoying, it would be a more wonderful record than any I know in the realm of romance. Perhaps I may some day attempt it. For all these lessons and their results I devoutly thank God.

Crete's view of their marriage was in perfect accord with that of James. It was their firm belief that out of the depths they had ascended to the highest level of earthly love.[93]

The sojourn of James and Crete at Howland Springs in the summer of 1862 had been a turning point in their marriage; the year 1867 seems to have marked another turning point. In that year Crete confessed to James, who was then in the East, that the last trace of bitterness in her heart toward Rebecca had been plucked out and cast away; she wanted James to visit Rebecca and tell her of Crete's love for her. On the very day that Crete's letter was written, James called on a woman in New York City to gain possession of "all the papers" that he had feared might some day cause trouble.[94]

Little is known of the episode in New York—where, James told Crete, he had "come closest" to wronging her. The woman was Mrs. Lucia Gilbert Calhoun, a widow or a divorcee thirteen years younger than Garfield. She was then a writer for the *New York Tribune;* over the years she also contributed to magazines and engaged in other literary activities. When did Garfield first meet her? Under what circumstances did their friendship develop? At what point did Crete become aware of the situation? Answers to these questions have not been found. It is clear that James and Crete had discussed the matter before he left for the East early in July 1867 and that as far as both were concerned James's involvement with Mrs. Calhoun was at an end. Still Crete was uneasy about his calling on the lady again. "Somehow I cannot but feel," she wrote, "that to her at least, you would compromise your love for me were you voluntarily to go into her presence. And for her too I believe it would be better to let the fire of such lawless passion burn itself out unfed and unnoticed. If she is a good but misguided woman you will neither be more harmed than now, and if she is wicked or malicious she has less occasion to harm you now than she would have after another interview." Writing to Crete after he had seen Mrs. Calhoun, James reported that he had "tried to deal kindly, honorably and firmly in all the premises" and added, "You cannot be so much relieved in heart and mind as I am, and I now say with a fuller, broader and deeper meaning than ever before that there is between our hearts and lives neither substance nor shadow of sorrow, except that we are separated even for a day."[95]

Near the close of 1867 Garfield spent a few days in New York City and vicinity and wrote Crete, who was in Ohio, of his activities. He had stayed a couple of days in Lewisboro with Rebecca, who also had relatives visiting her. In the city he had called on Mrs. Calhoun and "was confirmed in the wisdom of the course" he had adopted. "I think," he wrote, "she will marry a N.Y. lawyer before very long who has long befriended her and who is able to support her in her literary life. And now, Darling, let me say that out of the darkness we have made and surely shall make good come. . . . I know more surely than I could have known before how deep and abiding, how pure and neverfailing is that love that binds you to my heart, me to yours. That night showed us that the star of love was fixed in our heaven forever."[96]

In Crete's subconscious mind a trace of uneasiness about Rebecca seems to have lingered. In July 1876, when she was in Ocean Grove, New Jersey, and James was in Washington, she wrote him, "Is Rebecca Selleck in Washington, and has she been at our house? I dreamed about her all last night."[97]

Garfield's response was prompt. "Don't let any dreams trouble you. The only lady staying in your house is your Cousin Em—who came just as I was leaving last night and wanted to take one of the upper rooms for a few days. The one you refer to, I have not seen for nearly two years. You never had so whole and complete a power over all my heart as you have now."[98]

No evidence has been found that, after the Mrs. Calhoun episode, Garfield ever again engaged in extramarital dalliance. There were bits of gossip. There was a rumor that during his stay in New Orleans following the election of 1876 he had visited a brothel. In 1879 Crete was much upset to hear that a story had been told to the effect that James had once gone with a "notorious woman" to New York City and that she—Crete—alerted by a telegram from a friend in New York, had gone to confront the guilty pair. In a letter to the woman who she understood had told the tale, she branded "the whole story" as "nothing more nor less than an infamous lie."

At about the same time Mary Clemmer, who had perhaps heard this story, intimated in her widely read column, "A Woman's Letter from Washington," in the *New York Independent,* that Garfield's "moral purity" was not equal to his "intellectual acumen." Incensed, Garfield made two calls on the journalist. Afterward he answered a letter from a disturbed Republican in Massachusetts who had called his attention to the item in the *Independent.* Garfield said he did not think Clemmer was referring to Crédit Mobilier and, if the reference was to his personal life, it was "cruelly unjust." He had no doubt, he continued, that Clemmer had heard something that had raised a doubt in her mind; he himself had heard such gossip, which followed "almost every public man." He "fearlessly" appealed to his church, to the men who had served with him and under him in the army, to men who had sat in Congress with him for sixteen years, and to all who knew his home life to vindicate him from any charge against his moral purity or any act that would bring shame upon his wife and children.[99]

Years after Garfield's death rumors were still afloat, much to Crete's distress. In 1898 she wrote to Hal, "The calumnies spread abroad both before and since your father's death assailing the integrity of his private life are so preposterous and so base that I can scarcely force my mind to consider them even long enough for denial, and you children know how absolutely impossible it was that they could be true."[100]

In July 1867, a few days after Garfield had recovered the "papers" from Mrs. Calhoun, he and Crete sailed for Europe. Their four-month vacation was the longest period of their married life that they were constantly together.

Both needed a change. Garfield was on the verge of a physical breakdown; he had consulted Washington doctors and was satisfied that his life would be short—or his health "wholly lost"—unless he got away from work for a time. In mid-January Crete had given birth to Mollie; Jimmie was then a little over a year old, Harry a little more than three. Crete had hesitated about making the trip. But Mary had agreed to look after the children, and James had learned that Crete could have free passage to Europe. She arrived in New York a few hours before sailing time. She was pregnant again.

Eliza did not approve of their going abroad. In a letter to James and Crete after she had learned of their arrival in England, she expressed gladness that they had not made food for sharks. "I daily pray for your safety in so hazardous attempt in crossing the broad Atlantic seeking for pleasure instead of profit. . . . I hope you will regain your health and be willing to stay at home a small part of the time." The boys needed James. Harry was headstrong and naughty, and Jimmie acted just like Harry; both were stubborn as mules. "You don't know all and never will by my telling." On another occasion she reported that Harry had come near having congestion of the brain and that little Mollie had been sick more than half the time since they had been gone. James and Crete hadn't said, she complained, when they were coming home or whether they were coming at all. Leaving a family of small children and being gone so long seemed to her "almost without a parallell."[101]

It was a good trip, though James probably enjoyed it somewhat more than Crete, who experienced some "bodily discomfort." James followed the advice of his good friend Francis Lieber, the distinguished political scientist, and kept a diary (otherwise, Lieber said, he would "carry away nothing but a chaos"). The journal has an entry for each day and contains an abundance of detail. The Garfields visited England, Scotland, the Low Countries, Germany, Switzerland, Italy, and France; they ended their European stay with a train ride from Dublin to Cork, whence they sailed.[102]

Soon after they reached their hotel in London, Garfield set off for the House of Commons, accompanied by the secretary of the American legation in Britain and the editor of the *New York Times*. That evening he visited the House of Lords, then debating the Reform Bill of 1867. One day he listened for many hours to the debate in the Commons, sitting, through the courtesy of John Bright (to whom Garfield had carried a letter from Chief Justice Chase), "back of the Peers' seat under the Speaker's Gallery," where he had an excellent view. On that day he heard Gladstone, Disraeli, and Bright and saw, among others, John Stuart Mill, whose *Representative Government* he had read. "I left the Commons a little before midnight," he noted, "having witnessed the practical consummation of the greatest advance towards political liberty made in England in a century."[103]

It was Rome that moved Garfield most deeply, though he had less than a week to spend there. Sitting on the train in Florence, he was stirred by the sight of his ticket. *"To Rome*—the home and centre of so many years of my life and thought!" The day after their arrival, one "never to be forgotten," was devoted entirely to antiquities. The last day—"a day to be marked with a white stone"—began with a visit to the Borghese Palace and ended with a stroll through the Forum. "Felt more regret than at any parting since I left home. Rome is indeed 'my country'—dead, but alive forever more."[104]

The months together, away from the family and daily chores, had bound James and Crete more closely. They had, Crete told him, "deepened and perfected the earnestness" of her love for him. James rejoiced also; he had done better than the alchemist had sought to do. "I have been able to transmute gold into esthetic joys, intellectual growth, heart life—and, better than all, have been permitted to see it transformed into sweet and beautiful decorations of the noblest and truest woman I ever saw, and she as glad to be mine as I to be hers. This surpasses alchemy. It is divine."[105]

There was a sad aftermath to their long journey. The baby that Crete had carried all over Europe and whose arrival she had dreaded was stillborn in February, nearly a month before its time.[106]

During the summer and fall of 1879 Garfield threw all of his strength into the political campaign in Ohio. He spoke in many parts of the state, in places as far apart as Cleveland and Cincinnati, and before huge crowds. "On the whole," he decided at the end of the campaign, "I think I have done better work on the stump than ever before."[107]

On October 14 Republicans elected as governor Charles Foster ("Calico Charlie"), a wealthy dry goods merchant, and regained control of the legislature, which they had lost in 1877. Garfield promptly let it be known that he was a candidate for the United States Senate to succeed Allan G. Thurman, a Democrat whose term would expire on March 4, 1881. In January 1880 the legislature would choose the new senator.

Garfield reached the decision with some reluctance. He said that if he were to follow his own preference he would remain in the House and run for Speaker when the Republicans once more controlled it. He gave three reasons for not doing so. First, he thought that the hard work associated with his leadership in the House and the necessity of campaigning for election every two years would damage his health. "A seat in the Senate will delay the catastrophe." Second, it would be unfair to friends in his district who aspired to his seat in the House "not to get out of their way" when he had a chance for promotion. Third, some people had charged him with cowardice when he had refused to be a senatorial candidate in 1877, and to refuse again would seriously injure him "in the public estimation." He concluded, "I shall therefore be a candidate, preferring to be defeated, rather than not make the race. But I do not think I shall be defeated."[108]

He had always shunned the governorship, though he had been urged on a number of occasions to become a candidate. President Hayes expressed the opinion that Garfield's refusal of the governorship in 1867 had been his chief political mistake. "He intimated," Garfield wrote, "that it was the surest road to the Presidency." (It was the road Hayes had taken.) Garfield's lack of interest and his efforts to discourage activity on the part of his friends resulted from the nature of the

office and the low salary attached to it. When Ohioans drew up their
first constitution, they reacted to the vigorous leadership for fifteen
years of Arthur St. Clair as territorial governor by making provision
for a governor with little power; during the three quarters of a century
since then, they had not overcome their hostility to concentrating authority in the chief executive, who still lacked the veto power. Dolson
Cox told Garfield that during his two years as governor he had had
more leisure time than in any other two years since manhood. Any justice of the peace in Cleveland, Garfield thought, had more to do than
the governor. "The mere upholstery of office, I never cared for," he
told Eugene Cowles of the *Cleveland Leader*. "A place to work and
achieve something intellectually has always been more attractive to me."
As for the pay, "I am too poor to be governor of Ohio."[109]

At the outset Garfield's success was by no means assured. Three
other nationally known Republicans had their eyes on the Senate seat:
former governor William Dennison, former senator Stanley Matthews,
and Alphonso Taft, a leading Cincinnati lawyer who had been in President Grant's cabinet. Although John Sherman, who was preoccupied
with presidential ambitions, had told Garfield in July that he was not a
candidate for the Senate, he did not publicly remove himself from consideration until several months later. Even as a noncandidate, however,
Sherman was in a position to help or hinder the fortunes of the candidates. When Garfield was asked late in the year to take a public stand
in favor of Sherman for President, he let it be known that what he did
in the matter would be determined by what Sherman did with reference to the senatorship.[110]

Garfield refused to go to Columbus to promote his candidacy.
There was no need; he sent his friends. In the course of his travels during 1879 as special agent for the Post Office Department, Charles
Henry had worked for him in every part of the state. As the day of
decision drew near, Henry went to Columbus to manage his friend's interests, and other friends of Garfield were also there, alert and active.
On January 6, the day the Republican legislative caucus met to nominate a candidate for senator, Dennison, Matthews, and Taft withdrew
from the race, as Henry expected they would. Garfield was nominated
by acclamation. Friends of Sherman had helped to bring about this
result. "The manner of it," Garfield wrote, "is more gratifying than the
nomination itself." A week later the legislature elected him senator.[111]

A jubilant Garfield, accompanied by Hal, arrived in Columbus the
day after the election. When the faithful Captain Henry came to call,
Garfield threw both arms around him in glee, lifted him from the
floor, and swung him around "with his old time boyish way." After supper with Governor Foster and his family, Garfield was escorted to the

senate chamber, where a grand reception was held, attended by more than a thousand people. Most of the legislature, Democrats and Republicans alike, were there; among them was Garfield's proud cousin, William Letcher of Bryan. Garfield made a short address that included a graceful tribute to Senator Thurman, the Democrat whom he was succeeding. One exuberant remark came to be often quoted: "I say, moreover, that the flowers that bloom over the garden wall of party politics are the sweetest and most fragrant that bloom in the gardens of this world." At one o'clock in the morning the senator-elect and his son took the train for Cleveland.[112]

In Washington, too, it was a time for congratulations and rejoicing. Cousin Orrin Ballou came for a week's visit. Congressmen Amos Townsend of Cleveland and Anson McCook of New York gave Garfield a dinner at Wormley's that was attended by about twenty persons, including the Speaker of the House, the Sherman brothers, and Congressman Randolph Tucker, a Democratic friend of Garfield's from Virginia. Two thousand people under the leadership of the Ohio Republican Association serenaded him at his home. Congressman Simeon Chittenden, a wealthy New Yorker, gave him a card reception; the large number of guests included President Hayes and justices of the Supreme Court. About ninety people turned out for a meeting of the Literary Society (of which Garfield was then president) in the Garfield home. Letters poured in; answering them was a formidable task for the senator-elect and his helpers.[113]

After the Republican caucus had nominated Garfield for senator, a reporter asked politicians in Columbus whether the action meant "Ohio for Sherman for President." One member of the legislature responded, "No, it is a Garfield boom, and it means that James A. Garfield will be the next Republican candidate for President."[114]

*The Bride (Garfield): "But it was such a little one!"*

"Forbidding the Banns" (*Puck,* 25 August 1880). W. H. Barnum, chairman of the Democratic National Committee, seeks to stop the wedding of Garfield and Uncle Sam by bringing forward an illegitimate baby labled "$329," the sum Garfield was alleged to have received from Oakes Ames as return on an investment in Crédit Mobilier stock. The bridesmaids are Carl Schurz, left, and Whitelaw Reid, editor of the *New York Tribune*. Behind them is Marshall Jewell, chairman of the Republican National Committee. In the upper right, from the left: James Donald Cameron, Simon Cameron, John A. Logan, and Roscoe Conkling.

At the polls in Mentor, 2 November 1880. Garfield's carriage with aged voters; escorts are wearing campaign regalia.

A smiling Garfield. Date uncertain; Garfield sat for Mathew Brady on a number of occasions, and as late as 23 April 1881.

Man with hat, 1880.

Lucretia Garfield.

Eliza Garfield,
1881.

James R. Garfield, c. 1881.

Harry A. Garfield, 1881.

Mollie Garfield, c. 1881.

Irvin McD. Garfield, c. 1881.

Abram Garfield, c. 1881.

Giles B. Harber, friend of the family. Congressman Garfield's first appointee (1865) to the U.S. Naval Academy; he achieved the rank of rear admiral.

President Garfield delivering his inaugural address, 4 March 1881.

Reviewing the inaugural parade, 4 March 1881. Seated next to the President on the right are Mr. and Mrs. Hayes; seated next to him on the left is Mrs. Garfield.

"Inaugural Reception and Promenade Concert" at the new National Museum, 4 March 1881.

The White House or Executive Mansion.

Roscoe Conkling.

President Garfield and his cabinet. Around the table from the President's right: James G. Blaine, State; Robert Todd Lincoln, War; Thomas L. James, Post Office; Samuel Kirkwood, Interior; Wayne MacVeagh, Justice; William H. Hunt, Navy; William Windom, Treasury.

"A Harmless Explosion" (*Puck*, 25 May 1881). Depicts the end of Conkling's struggle to prevent the confirmation of W. H. Robertson as collector of customs of the port of New York. Senator T. C. Platt is shown as a deflating balloon attached to Senator Conkling's coattails. Vice President Arthur, presiding, holds the resignations of the New York senators in his hand as he looks on in consternation. Administration senators are dancing with joy.

Carriage bought by President Hayes in March 1877 for $1,150, lent by him to President Garfield, and now on display in the Hayes Museum.

Charles Julius Guiteau.

Scene in the depot of the Baltimore and Potomac Railroad, Washington, D.C., 9:20 A.M., 2 July 1881. A contemporary print. Secretary of State Blaine is in front of the President.

Waiting for news at the White House gates.

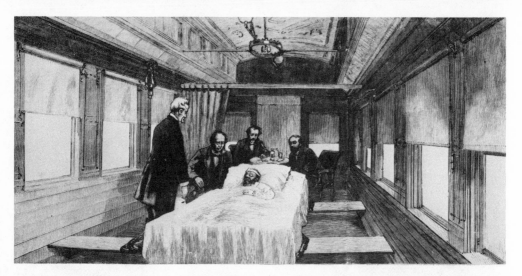

On the train, Elberon, and the arrival at Francklyn Cottage, 6 September 1881.

Remains of the President lying in state in the Rotunda of the Capitol, 22 and 23 September 1881.

# CHAPTER 10

# THE PRESIDENCY

WHEN GARFIELD was elected senator in January 1880 the Republican presidential pot was already boiling in anticipation of the national convention that would open in Chicago on June 2. Hayes was out of the picture. He had announced in 1876 that he would not seek a second term, and the politicians were taking him at his word. Three men, all more prominent than Garfield, occupied center stage.

John Sherman was making it clear that he wanted the nomination and that he thought it was his due. He had been a leading figure in national politics for a quarter of a century—a member of the House of Representatives for six years and the Senate for sixteen years and Hayes's secretary of the treasury since 1877. His years in the Treasury, where he pursued a conservative monetary policy, had enhanced his reputation and enabled him to build support for his presidential ambitions. Although he had the reputation of being a cold man and could never hope for the popularity of a Blaine, most Republicans would have agreed that his years of service and his solid if not spectacular achievements placed him in the top rank of his party.

James G. Blaine was expected to be a candidate again. He had lost to Hayes in 1876, but his quest for the nomination had enhanced his prestige. Robert G. Ingersoll's celebrated nominating speech, in which he pictured Blaine as a "plumed knight" marching "down the halls of the American Congress" to throw "his shining lance full and fair against the brazen forehead of every traitor to his country and every maligner of his fair reputation," lingered in the American mind and on the lips of elocutionists, making the man from Maine a romantic figure. He had been in the Senate since 1876 and had maintained his preeminent position in the party.[1]

[ 201 ]

The third name was one to frighten all other candidates; a movement to nominate Ulysses S. Grant for a third term was under way. Grant would have been willing to stand again in 1876, but he was not strongly supported. The traditional opposition to a third term was strong, a great depression hung over the land, Grant had been ill-fitted for the presidency, and his popularity with politicians, if not with the people, had eroded. Soon after he left office, he had embarked on a trip around the world that had lasted for about two and a half years. Tumultuously welcomed on his return to the United States in September 1879, he was soon on everybody's list of potential nominees for the presidency.

A few leading Republican politicians set out to exploit Grant. Three of the most populous states were involved: New York, Pennsylvania, and Illinois. The political bosses in these states were threatened by factionalism in the party; they needed Grant in the White House to bolster their own positions. In New York there was Senator Roscoe Conkling, who had got along very well indeed with Grant but not at all with President Hayes, whom he despised. Conkling and Blaine had been bitter enemies for more than a decade. In Pennsylvania there were the Camerons—old Simon, who had helped put Lincoln and Grant into the White House, and his son James Donald ("Don"), who had been secretary of war during the closing months of the Grant administration. When Hayes refused to reappoint Don to the cabinet, Simon resigned his seat in the Senate and saw to it that his son was elected to fill the vacancy. In Illinois there was John A. Logan, who had achieved the rank of major general in the army (he had resigned from the House to enter the service) and after the war had become a leading figure in the Grand Army of the Republic. He had been a member of the Senate during the last six of the Grant years, and in 1879, after a lapse of two years, was back again.[2]

Once Garfield had been elected to the Senate he could not long postpone a public endorsement of John Sherman for President—an endorsement that Sherman had been "exceedingly anxious" to have in December. Sherman had kept his word with respect to the Senate seat, and now Garfield had no other choice than to support him. Even were he not morally bound to do so, political expediency required the act; next to President Hayes, Sherman was the most prominent political figure in Ohio and the only Ohio resident who was an active Republican candidate for President. Senator-elect Garfield's refusal to endorse him would result in a political explosion in the state. Accordingly, ten days after his return from Columbus, Garfield wrote to a member of the Ohio legislature who had supported him for senator and who had written asking him for a "public expression" on the "Presidential question."

"I expressed the opinion that the State of Ohio ought to support Sherman," Garfield noted in his diary.[3]

Garfield's "magnificent success at Columbus," as one newspaper called it, could not fail to be widely noted. Very quickly his name began to be linked with the presidency. Within three days of the senatorial election, an editor of a small Nebraska newspaper (who hailed from Ohio's Nineteenth District) said that it would be his greatest pleasure to vote for Garfield for President in November, and a Duluth paper announced that the newest boom it had noticed was a Garfield boom. A few weeks later the Reno (Nevada) *Evening Gazette* described Garfield as "the finest steed in the stable of dark horses by all odds" and added, "He would sweep the Pacific coast like a broom."

Letters to Garfield also introduced the presidential theme. Some letter writers suggested that he was now thane of Cawdor and might be king thereafter—an allusion that must have given pause to a Shakespearean like Garfield. A resident of Marion, Ohio, wrote that a Garfield Club was being formed in that city. Harry Rhodes told his friend that he had found "lots of people" in California who would be glad to see him nominated. Wharton Barker, of Philadelphia, wrote early in February that many leading Republicans in his state who were opposed to the other candidates were looking to Garfield "as the man who must come to the front" at the convention.[4]

Barker was to play a significant role in the Garfield movement. Still in his early thirties, he had intelligence, wealth, energy, and social standing. He was a member of a Philadelphia banking firm and a financial adviser and agent of the Russian government. An independent Republican, he was a foe of the Cameron machine and a strong opponent of a third term for Grant. As he read the signs, the candidates most often discussed would nullify each other, leaving the way open for a dark horse. He had made up his mind that Garfield should be the winner. In February he called on his candidate in Washington and outlined his views. Garfield told him that he would not be a candidate and would be available only if none of the leaders was nominated. Wharton's interest in Garfield was in no way diminished. He was back again in April to explain how the independent Republicans of Pennsylvania would block the nomination of Grant, following which New York and most of New England would "break" Blaine. He also reported that President Hayes had told him that Sherman was in the field to prevent the nomination of Blaine or Grant and that if his rivals were broken, he would give way to Garfield, who could have the solid support of Ohio's delegates to the convention. "In short," Garfield wrote in his diary following the visit, "Barker thinks this is likely to be the outcome. I do not. I should be greatly distressed if I thought otherwise. There is too much

possible work in me to set so near an end to it all, as that would do."
Garfield was only forty-eight years of age.[5]

Another February visitor to Garfield was Thaddeus C. Pound of
Wisconsin, a member of Congress and a former lieutenant governor.
His call is of interest in view of his state's part in the nomination of
Garfield four months later. Like Wharton Barker, he had concluded
that the convention would have to turn to someone other than Grant,
Sherman, or Blaine and that the someone would be Garfield. Garfield
professed disbelief in such a development and said that he would act in
good faith toward Sherman and do nothing to interfere with his
chances. He added that he would consider suggestions Pound might
make —"always within the limitations just mentioned."[6]

Garfield read the newspaper comments about him (and had some
of them pasted in his scrapbook), read his letters , and listened to those
who speculated about his future—and undoubtedly took satisfaction in
doing so. But he was realist enough to know that the chances of his
being the victor at Chicago were remote. He wanted to be President
some day, but he did not expect 1880 to be his year; he was looking
forward to being a member of the Senate.

Of concern to both Sherman and Garfield was the strong antagonism to Sherman on the Western Reserve—antagonism attributable to
his prominence in an administration that was unpopular there and to
the intense personal dislike that some people had for him. Garfield's
friend Lionel Sheldon was virulently anti-Sherman. If Sherman could
not command the support of all the Ohio delegates to the convention,
his chances of success in Chicago would be minimal. For Garfield the
situation was an embarrassment; there was not much he could do about
it, yet Sherman and his followers were likely to blame him if defections
in his own territory reduced Sherman's strength.[7]

In late February Garfield paid a visit to Ohio; it was said that Sherman had urged him to do so. Before he returned to Washington he
had a conference in Cleveland with some of the leading Republicans in
the Reserve, including the mayor of the city. He explained to those
present why Grant should not be nominated and expressed the opinion
that Ohio should support Sherman to give him and Blaine enough
strength to prevent the nomination of Grant. "It is evident, however,"
Garfield wrote after the meeting, "that it will be very difficult to carry
this part of Ohio for Sherman." A newsman gave additional information: Garfield had been given to understand that if he himself did not
wish to receive the votes of some of Ohio's delegates, his friends would
support Blaine.[8]

Should Garfield be a delegate to the Chicago convention? He was
not eager to go, especially as a delegate from his own district. The

Shermanites there wanted to send him to Chicago, but with the help of friends Garfield managed to avoid being chosen. Being a delegate at large was another matter; he told Burke Hinsdale that he preferred not to go at all but that if chosen delegate at large he supposed he had better go. Honest, blunt Burke, who on occasion could talk quite plainly to his friend, reprimanded him, saying that Garfield's published letter in support of Sherman "logically" involved his going to the convention. "If such letters as yours are but parts of a 'job'—if men are to propose candidates publicly that they are opposed to privately—if politics consist largely of 'throwing dust'—then you can decline to be a delegate. But if politics be a sincere affair, I do not see how you can refuse." Years later Sherman said that Garfield had told him he wanted to go to Chicago to work for him. In any event, Sherman saw to it that Garfield went. On April 28 the Ohio Republican state convention, dominated by Sherman supporters, chose four delegates at large who had been picked by Sherman himself: Garfield, Governor Foster, William Dennison, and Warner Bateman, a Cincinnati lawyer who was an intimate friend of Sherman. The responsibility for Sherman's campaign in Chicago would rest largely on these men.[9]

The tension under which Garfield had been living brought on, as it usually did, a disturbance of his digestive system. He started taking medicine for his stomach and went on a diet of "toast and milk and steak cooked without grease." His life story could be written in terms of his physical reaction to stress.[10]

Soon after the state convention it became known that Garfield would place Sherman's name in nomination at Chicago. It was a wise choice; Garfield was the best man for the job, and his acceptance of it bound him more strongly to the secretary's bandwagon.[11]

Although Garfield did not expect Sherman to win the nomination, his support of the treasury secretary was genuine. But his continuing commitment did not arise from any belief that Sherman was the best man to be President; had he been completely free to choose, he would have been with Blaine, to whom he was much closer. His support resulted, rather, from a conviction that strong Sherman and Blaine forces at Chicago were the only hope of preventing the nomination of Grant—a possibility that Garfield could not contemplate with equanimity. (Garfield had wished in 1872 that Grant would refuse a second term.) If Sherman could not muster a respectable number of votes, Grant's early nomination seemed certain. To persuade the convention that he was a viable candidate, Sherman needed the wholehearted support of the Ohio delegation.[12]

In supporting Sherman, Garfield was also helping himself. If Grant, Blaine, and Sherman should fight each other to a standstill, as Barker

and others were predicting, and the convention were forced to look for
a compromise candidate, Sherman would prefer to have his votes go to
Garfield. Sherman himself had told Garfield so.[13]

Garfield arrived in Chicago on May 29, four days before the opening of the convention. He had gone reluctantly, disliking, as he said,
"the antagonisms and controversies" likely "to blaze out" there.[14]
Antagonisms and controversies were already in evidence. Chicago
was "full of Republicans" gathered into "hostile camps" teeming with activity. When he reached the Grand Pacific Hotel, Garfield put himself
in touch with fellow delegates at large, and he was soon in the midst of
a discussion of what was sure to be the most important and mostly hotly
debated procedural question to come before the convention.[15]
The question was simple enough: Should votes for President and
Vice President be recorded under the district rule or the unit rule?
Under the district rule, which the Republicans had hitherto followed,
the vote of each delegate was recorded as cast, regardless of how other
members of his delegation might vote. Under the unit rule all the votes
of a state would be recorded for the candidate receiving the majority of
the votes of the delegation.
The implications of the question were great; the method of voting
was likely to have a decisive influence on the selection of the presidential candidate. The adoption of the unit rule would go far toward assuring a Grant victory. Although Conkling, Don Cameron, and Logan
had failed to secure delegations wholly committed to Grant, the former
president had the backing of the majority in each. Under the unit rule
the three states would cast 170 votes for Grant; under the district rule
they would cast about 110 votes for him. Many other delegations were
divided also; the unit rule would not always favor Grant, but on balance it would.
From the beginning Garfield was alert to the necessity of preventing
the adoption of the unit rule. Before his first day in Chicago was over
he had urged Foster, Dennison, and Bateman "to take a bold and
aggressive stand in favor of District representation" and proposed cooperation with the friends of candidates taking the same view. Two
days later the Ohio delegation agreed on resistance to the unit rule. It
was clear, however, that Sherman would have the support of not more
than thirty-five of the forty-four delegates, with Blaine receiving the
votes of all or most of the remainder.[16]
The excitement and frenetic activity increased in the course of the
convention, which was in session for six days (no session was held on
the Sunday that fell between the fourth and fifth days). Circumstances

brought Garfield to the fore and placed him in opposition to Roscoe Conkling, leader of the Grant forces. When Conkling tried to bring about the expulsion of three West Virginia delegates who had voted against his resolution that it was the sense of the convention that all delegates were honor bound to support its nominee, Garfield came to their defense. His action forced the senator to back down and won for himself the cheers of delegates.

As chairman of the Rules Committee, Garfield presided over a three-hour meeting in which the question of the unit rule was debated; he then presented to the convention the majority report of his committee, which included a rule that the vote of each delegate should be counted as cast. A New York follower of Conkling presented a minority report containing a rule that left it to the chairman of a delegation to invoke the unit rule if he chose. The convention adopted the majority report.

On the fourth day Conkling stood on a table to nominate the man who hailed from Appomattox in an eloquent speech that offended the friends of other candidates. After the Grant demonstration had quieted, Garfield stood on the same table to nominate Sherman in a speech that emphasized the need for Republican unity—an idea that had come to him as he listened to Conkling. The New York senator walked out on Garfield. To the galleries and to the delegates, these two men, the haughty New Yorker (who was visiting the West for the first time) and the more genial Ohioan, were the commanding figures of the convention. "Garfield," one newspaper correspondent wrote, "is the member of the convention who divides with Conkling the popular welcome at every opening."[17]

Conkling took Garfield more seriously than he did Sherman. On the first day of the convention he had passed a note to him that read "New York requests that Ohio's real candidate and dark horse come forward. We want him in our seats while we prepare our ballots."[18]

Balloting for presidential candidates began on the fifth day. Six names were before the convention: Grant, Blaine, Sherman, George F. Edmunds of Vermont, William Windom of Minnesota, and Elihu Washburne of Illinois. The results of the first ballot were: Grant, 304, Blaine 284, Sherman 93, with 74 votes divided among the other three candidates. To win the nomination, a candidate required at least 378 votes. Twenty-eight ballots were taken that day; on the twenty-eighth Grant had 307 votes, Blaine 276, and Sherman 93.

For a time Conkling announced the New York vote in this fashion (or a variation of it): "Two of the New York delegates, Mr. Chairman, are said to be for Mr. Sherman, 17 for Mr. Blaine, 51 are for Grant"—

with heavy emphasis on "are." He abandoned this formula after the chairman of the West Virginia delegation had imitated him a number of times.[19]

On the third ballot Garfield—though his name had not been placed in nomination—received one vote. During the rest of the day he had one or two votes on all but five ballots. For the most part the votes were furnished by two members of the Pennsylvania delegation, at least one of whom had been asked by Wharton Barker to keep Garfield's name before the convention. According to Barker, another of his arrangements was a Garfield claque in the galleries. He had come to Chicago several days before the convention began, and he had been hard at work to make his prophecy come true.[20]

Balloting resumed on the morning of June 8. Five ballots were taken without significant change from the results of the previous day. On the thirty-third ballot Grant had 309 votes, Blaine 276, Sherman 110, and Garfield 1. There was still a scattering of votes among other candidates.

The break began on the thirty-fourth ballot when Wisconsin cast for Garfield 16 votes that had previously gone to Blaine, Washburne, and Sherman. Garfield, red-faced, jumped to his feet to challenge the votes cast for him. George F. Hoar, who was in the chair, told him he was out of order and ordered him to resume his seat. On the next ballot Indiana joined Wisconsin, giving Garfield 27 votes that, for the most part, had been going to Blaine. A few other votes brought Garfield's total to 50. Excited but weary delegates responded to the signal. On the thirty-sixth ballot Garfield went over the top with 399 votes; he had received the support of most of the Blaine, Sherman, and Washburne delegates. The New Yorkers who, under the lead of William H. Robertson, had defied Roscoe Conkling switched to Garfield on this ballot (most of them had been voting for Blaine). Grant received 306 votes. Conkling made the motion to make the vote for Garfield unanimous. But the Grant men did not forget; Grant medals were struck to commemorate their stand.[21]

As cannons were fired outside the hall and excited delegations with their banners gathered around him, Garfield sat as if stunned, his face pale. He had gone to Chicago aware of the interest in him as a possible dark horse, he had known that the interest increased as the convention wore on and that there was a great deal of activity on his behalf, but the knowledge that he was the second choice of many delegates had not prepared him for the reality of the thirty-sixth ballot. Later in the day William Walter Phelps and Whitelaw Reid found him in his room "recovering from the blow, and in a dazed-way thinking aloud, 'I don't know whether I am glad or not!' " Captain Henry, who was in Chicago, said years afterward that "Garfield never seemed the same man after he was nominated for President."[22]

Several wildly excited members of the class of 1856 of Williams College, one of whom was at the convention as a delegate from New York, sent a telegram to Mark Hopkins: "Glory to God, glory to Williams, glory to Garfield."[23]

A candidate for Vice President was still to be chosen. Our national political conventions have rarely acted with intelligence or deliberation in making the choice of a man for the second place on the ticket; in 1880 the important thing seemed to be to placate Roscoe Conkling—or so it appeared to the Ohio delegation. The delegation authorized Dennison to commit its votes as New York or the friends of Grant might direct. Dennison so informed the New York delegation. When the convention assembled after a recess, Stewart Woodford of New York nominated Chester A. Arthur, a Grant supporter in the New York delegation and an associate of Conkling. William Dennison seconded the nomination. Only one ballot was required.[24]

Conkling was not placated. One story has it that he told Arthur that if he wished his favor and respect, he would "contemptuously decline" the nomination.[25]

Many Republicans were horrified by the selection of Arthur. They knew that he was a member of the Conkling organization, that he had been collector of customs of the port of New York, and that President Hayes had suspended him from office and appointed a new collector. John Sherman thought that his nomination was "a ridiculous burlesque . . . inspired by a desire to defeat the ticket."[26]

Two weeks after the Republicans left Chicago, the Democrats convened in Cincinnati. Although a number of prominent politicians (including House Speaker Randall) received support, the winner of the presidential nomination was Winfield Scott Hancock, a Pennsylvanian who had been in the army since his graduation from West Point in 1844. For his running mate the convention turned to Indiana, a doubtful state, in choosing William H. English, a wealthy businessman who had been in Congress before the war.

After a few days in Cleveland, Hiram (where he attended Commencement), and Mentor, the Republican candidate set out for Washington. During a brief stay he attended to personal affairs, gathering up papers and arranging for the packing of households goods to be taken or sent to Mentor. He talked with Hayes, Sherman, and Blaine, dined at the White House, and attended a banquet given in his honor by veterans of the Army of the Cumberland, a reception by the Literary Society (members wore Garfield badges), and a wedding.[27]

He did not confer with Roscoe Conkling. He said later that he had called on the New York senator, but it is probable that he simply left his card at Wormley's, where the senator was staying. When Garfield returned to the Riggs House one afternoon, he found Conkling's card. He promptly sent off a note asking him to name a time the next day when Garfield could call; he wanted to see him, he said, away from a crowd of visitors. Conkling did not respond. He may have been miffed (it has been suggested) on learning that when he was at Garfield's door, Garfield was riding with Secretary of the Interior Carl Schurz, a civil service reformer who did not count Conkling among his friends and admirers. Conkling's nephew, in his biography of the senator, offered another explanation: "Mr. Conkling's reason for avoiding a personal conference with the candidate was that he was unwilling to trust to Mr. Garfield's imperfect memory of a private conversation, however unimportant." The trivial incident was an ill omen.[28]

Roscoe Conkling is one of the most interesting and perplexing figures in American political history. He was an impressive-looking man, over six feet tall, with a fine physique in which he took great pride. A Hyperion curl of his sandy blond hair adorned the middle of his forehead; his carefully tended beard contributed a note of elegance. Flamboyant dress completed the appearance of the character that he was portraying. Everyone acknowledged that he was a man of ability; in his own state he dominated his party for years, and in the Senate, where he sat from 1867 to 1881, he was one of the strong men.[29]

He was a hard man to get along with or to like. He and his wife, the sister of Horatio Seymour, usually went their separate ways; Mrs. Conkling rarely went to Washington. He had followers rather than friends. He was a good hater who never forgot an insult or an injury. His personality was unpleasant and at times repulsive. The word "sneer" is often used to describe his remarks; one of his sneers concerned "the smell of the cowyard brought into the White House by Ohio men." Descriptions of him are full of pejorative terms: he was vain, haughty, condescending, vindictive, overbearing. The most popular of his nicknames was "Lord Roscoe." After his death one writer offered an assessment of the man: "He had all the qualifications of a great leader of men and director of their opinions, except the art of conciliation."[30]

An episode in 1879 must have caused him extreme anguish because it made people laugh at him. For several years Conkling—who, according to report, had had many extramarital liaisons—had been closely associated with Kate Chase, who was unhappily married to William Sprague, governor of Rhode Island from 1859 to 1863 and a member of the United States Senate for a dozen years thereafter. The friendship was no secret; Kate came to the Senate chamber to see her hero in action, and the two were frequently seen together elsewhere. In August 1879 Kate's husband left their eighty-room mansion on Narragansett Bay for a visit to Maine, and Conkling arrived before the day was out. Sprague returned home unexpectedly the next night. When he went into town the following morning he learned that the New York senator was at his home. Rushing to the house, he got a shotgun and gave the visitor five minutes to make his departure. Conkling left. Sprague, shotgun in hand, pursued him to Narragansett Pier where, outside a restaurant, a "noisy confrontation" occurred between the two middle-aged men, much to the astonishment of bystanders and passersby. The publicity surrounding the incident was not likely to enhance the senator's prestige in his own state or cause him to take a kindlier view of his fellow men. Only six weeks earlier Mary Clemmer had written of him, "It must be terrible to despise and hate people as much as he looks as if he did."[31]

Garfield, who was in New York City shortly after the incident, wrote to Crete. "I send you some New York papers in the Sprague-Conkling affair which explain themselves. You will remember my prediction in reference to the outcome of this infatuated pair. This Narragansett Pier outburst may save a more fatal tragedy—but everybody will read between the lines more than is printed."[32]

Kate was at the Republican national convention in Chicago in June 1880—"strictly incognita," she told Chester A. Arthur. She wanted the New York delegate to get better seats for her and a woman companion; where they were they could neither see nor hear. One hopes that Arthur obliged; it would have been a pity for Kate to have missed Conkling's oration on behalf of Grant—or that of her old friend Garfield on behalf of Sherman.[33]

Garfield labored over his formal letter of acceptance of the nomination for President. He asked for advice and received many suggestions as to its content. The final version touched on a number of topics: the supremacy of the Constitution and laws made in pursuance of it, the rights of citizens, education, protection of home industries, restriction of Chinese immigration to the United States, finance, and the civil service. Grant was amused when he heard of the number of letters of advice Garfield had received. "He said," a correspondent reported, "he was elected president twice and no one ever offered him a suggestion about his letter of acceptance, and he never thought any more of it than of any other letter he had to answer."[34]

Many of Garfield's friends, among them President Hayes, Carl Schurz, and George William Curtis, editor of *Harper's Weekly*, were disappointed by his failure to take a stronger stand for civil service reform. He had written the paragraph dealing with the subject with great care, knowing that the men he had to worry about were not the reformers but the politicians like Conkling, whose political organizations were oiled by patronage. Speaking of the civil service, he declared that "without invading the authority or necessary discretion of the Executive, Congress should devise a method that will determine the tenure of office, and greatly reduce the uncertainty which makes that service so unsatisfactory. Without depriving any officer of his rights as a citizen, the government should require him to discharge all his official duties with intelligence, efficiency and faithfulness." Having tossed this modest offering to Curtis and his kind, he went on to say that the wise selection of men best fitted for office required "an acquaintance far beyond the range of any one man" and concluded, "The Executive should, therefore, seek and receive the information and assistance of those whose knowledge of the communities in which the duties are to be performed best qualifies them to aid in making the wisest choice." To the reformers it appeared that Garfield was sending a message to the spoilsmen, too.[35]

Although it was considered unseemly for a presidential candidate to take to the stump in his own behalf, Garfield was not silent. A man who had been speaking for so many years, he remarked, could not at that late date play dummy. In his own state he attended three soldiers' reunions, a fair, and two unveilings of soldiers' monuments—and had something to say on each occasion. In early August he went to New York City to confer with Republican leaders, and his journey to and from the city was marked by many platform appearances and many brief talks. In New York he spoke for fifteen minutes one evening from the balcony of a building on Fifth Avenue. On the way home he stayed over Sunday at Chautauqua, New York. Although he refrained from speaking in public on the Sabbath, he addressed a crowd of about 5,000 on Monday.

During September and October numerous groups journeyed by rail to Mentor to pay their respects to the Republican candidate: 500 members of the Lincoln Club of Indianapolis, seven carloads of Germans, 900 ladies from Cleveland and vicinity, 200 people from Portage County. On a rainy day in late October the groups converging on Lawnfield numbered over 5,000 people. A typical group arrived by special train from Cleveland, marched down the farm lane leading from the rail stop to the Garfield house, and assembled near the house to greet their host through a spokesman, to hear his response, and to shake his hand. Garfield's responses were small masterpieces, each appropriate to the occasion that called it forth. No other Republican candidate had ever made so many public appearances.[36]

Constantly interrupted by delegations and other visitors, Garfield tried to keep abreast of the campaign and handle the daily flood of mail. A one-room building behind the house became a campaign office; a telegraph line was run to it and Otis L. ("Ollie") Judd installed as operator. Joe Brown struggled endlessly with correspondence. (He always looked back on that summer, fall, and winter at Lawnfield as "an unceasing period of drudgery, made endurable only by the charming home life and the fascinating and lightning-like changes that were always occurring in the political sky.") George Rose came from Washington to help out for a time. A young man read newspapers and clipped them for future reference. Major Swaim, on leave from the army to aid Garfield, sometimes left Lawnfield on confidential missions. Thomas Nichol, a resident of Racine who had been the mainspring of the Honest Money League of the Northwest and at the convention a liaison between the Ohio and Wisconsin delegations, rendered much assistance in Mentor and elsewhere.[37]

The work of the farm went on amidst the hurly-burly of politics. Garfield's diary of the period contains observations any farmer might have made, but they are interspersed with references to activities having nothing to do with agriculture. September 10: "Over 60 letters came today. Most of them were answered. Commenced getting in wheat on the upland north of the young apple orchard, and sowing 'blue stem' and putting with it 250 pounds of Detroit Phosphate to the acre." September 19: "Did not attend church, but made a tour over the farm, inspecting the cattle and crops. Also cleared up the accumulation of mail which had gained on us during the week. In the afternoon George A. Baker called and gave his views of the situation from the intelligence he has gathered from Democrats." September 25: "Green hauling in potatoes, after he finished housing coal. Large mail—showing much anxiety about Ohio." October 7: "A large mail came today. Many answers from my letters of inquiries to the different counties. About 25 or 30 visitors came in the afternoon. The boys got off a large number of documents and I ran through the mail . . . Old Father Barnes has been closing up the wood house opening to keep out the cold when winter comes. Green has finished hauling in the clover."[38]

Garfield's visit to New York City in early August was made reluctantly. The demand for his presence originated with the thirty-eight-year-old Stephen W. Dorsey, the energetic and unprincipled secretary of the National Republican Committee. Garfield received many letters relating to Dorsey's proposal and was slow in making up his mind. In

the end he yielded to the pressure; even Marshall Jewell of Connecticut, the chairman of the committee, who had not favored Dorsey's proposal at the outset, concluded that the candidate had better come.[39]

The problem was Conkling and his followers. To Dorsey and others
it appeared that little would be done to carry Garfield to victory in New
York State until the Conklingites had been satisfied that the Garfield
administration would not be a repetition of Hayes's as far as patronage
was concerned; they wanted to come in out of the cold. Burke Hinsdale
wrote Garfield from New York. "Secretary Dorsey tells Phillips that
what Mr. Conkling wants to know is, *whether,* in case you are elected,
you will give the country a Republican or Democratic administration!
My advice to you is this—if you can make up your own mind which it
will be, you had better tell him when you see him. If Conkling can be
assured that your administration will be Republican and not Democratic, he is inclined to take hold, and so is Governor Cornell with his
25,000 canallers." (The New York State Republican machine controlled
thousands of jobs on the Erie Canal.)[40]

A visit of the candidate to New York was fraught with some peril.
Garfield's standing would not be enhanced if the public concluded that
his trip to the city was for the purpose of making a deal with New
York's Republican boss. To protect the candidate, the original plan for
a small meeting was scuttled in favor of a large assembly of leading
Republicans to confer on various matters related to the campaign.

The conference occupied only an afternoon and was mainly window dressing: speeches by Blaine, Sherman, Logan, the venerable
Thurlow Weed, and others. Conkling, to the embarrassment of his
friends—and perhaps to Garfield's relief—did not appear. During that
day and the next Garfield talked with a great many people. He asked
Levi P. Morton, a leading New York banker, to be chairman of the finance committee, and Morton, who was aligned with Conkling, acqui-
esced. Thomas C. Platt, another Conkling man, said in his
autobiography published thirty years after the event that Garfield had
promised Morton the choice of several positions, including that of secretary of the treasury.[41]

On the morning after the general conference the candidate was
driven to the home of Whitelaw Reid, editor of the *New York Tribune*
and Garfield's chief campaign adviser on New York politics—and a foe
of the Conkling machine. There Garfield conferred with Jay Gould,
whose support was not yet assured. Although there is no record of
their conversation, it is probable that one of the topics touched upon
was Garfield's attitude toward railroads. Gould and other railroad fi-
nanciers were aware that he had once discussed in an address the
dangers inherent in the modern corporation, particularly the railroad

corporation, and the need for social control. The railroad men were also unhappy about the Supreme Court, which in 1877 had upheld the right of a state to regulate railroads; they hoped that the next President would make appointments to the Court that would meet with their approval. Garfield came away from the talk, which had probably been quite general, with the belief that Gould would aid in the campaign.[42]

In the afternoon of the same day Garfield had a long conference with Chester A. Arthur, Levi P. Morton, Richard Crowley, and Thomas C. Platt; their leader, Senator Conkling, did not attend, although Garfield had probably expected him. How unfortunate that no shorthand reporter was present! In his diary entry for the day Garfield simply recorded the fact of the meeting and on his return home commented about his trip in general. "Very weary but feel that no serious mistake had been made and probably much good had been done. No trades, no shackles, and as well fitted for defeat or victory as ever." An unnamed "gentleman who was present" at the meeting reported that Garfield said that it was his intention to appoint one member of his cabinet from New York "and that in making federal appointments in New York which extended beyond a Congressional district, he would consult the party organization as represented by the Senators in Congress, the Vice President, the Governor of the State and the State Committee, and that he would be guided by such organization, provided the persons recommended were fit and proper for appointment." Platt, whose autobiography was published in 1910 (the year of the author's death at seventy-six), claimed that Garfield told them that if they took hold "with zeal and energy" and insured his election, the wishes of the element of the party they represented would be paramount with him in matters of patronage. He also claimed that Garfield promised that, in dealing with the "rebellious element" in the New York delegation at Chicago, he would consult with the Conklingites and "do only what was approved by them."[43]

The statement by the unnamed gentleman—published in 1889—is probably a reasonably accurate representation of what Garfield said; the views attributed to him do not conflict with those on appointments set forth in his letter of acceptance. Platt's reminiscences are not to be taken too seriously; it was not in character for Garfield to promise that he would do for the Robertson element only what their enemies approved or to promise Morton the office of secretary of the treasury if he wanted it.

All parties at the meeting would have agreed that there was a good deal of talk. Garfield was there to persuade the Conkling forces that he proposed to deal fairly with them. He was doubtless full of assurances of goodwill and good Republicanism in his administration. The four men from the Conkling camp perhaps read into his words meanings that he did not intend to convey; his promise to consult may have meant more to them than to him. This was Garfield's only experience in dealing on its own grounds with the Conkling machine; the easterners did not speak the same language as the man from the West.[44]

That Conkling joined the campaign in support of the party's national ticket cannot be taken as evidence that he was fully satisfied with Garfield's assurances. The truth is that he had little choice but to support the nominee of his party if he wished to continue in politics. If the Republicans lost New York and the result could be laid at Conkling's door, his future as party chieftain was likely to be of short duration. Whitelaw Reid wrote Garfield that Platt and other close friends had talked with Conkling "with great plainness, not to say severity," and that Conkling had answered that he was in the hands of his friends and would do whatever they asked.[45]

Conkling entered the campaign on September 17 when he addressed a huge throng in New York's Academy of Music for three hours and forty minutes. He discussed Garfield only once, just before the close of his speech. This was the last of the four sentences he devoted to the party's standard-bearer: "That he is competent to the duties before him, there seems to me no reason to doubt."[46]

In late September and early October the New York senator made a number of speeches in Ohio and Indiana, states in which he had never before spoken. In Ohio he first appeared in Warren, in Garfield's own district, where a wigwam had been built for the occasion (Arthur having informed Garfield that Conkling's health would not permit him to speak in the open air). General Grant, who had urged Conkling to get into the campaign, presided and even made a short speech. When Conkling had left Ohio, having spoken in Cleveland and Cincinnati, Garfield wrote to Harmon Austin. "Conkling is a singular compound of a very brilliant man and an exceedingly petulant spoiled child. For myself, I do not care to be praised, but it was a narrow and unmanly thing on his part to make such a manifest effort as he has done in Ohio to avoid mentioning the head of the ticket in any generous way."[47]

Although Garfield had refused to go to Warren for the meeting (Harmon Austin and other advisers had urged him to attend), he entertained the Conkling party at Lawnfield after the meeting was over. A special train on the way to Cleveland from Warren stopped at the Mentor station. Grant, Conkling, Logan, Morton, and about fifteen Clevelanders were driven to Lawnfield in a dismal autumn rain. Joe Brown, who sat beside the driver in the carriage bearing the four distinguished visitors, heard General Grant say, "Well, I never like to give a man the benefit of the knowledge that I dislike him," and Conkling "in a round, sonorous and pompous voice" respond, "I do."[48]

Dr. Robison met the carriages and led the guests to the house, where Garfield gave them a warm greeting. They were introduced to Crete, Mrs. Rockwell, Eliza, and others who were on the scene. After a short period of conversation Crete served lunch. Garfield introduced Grant and other guests to a couple of hundred townsmen who had gathered outside the house. A heavy downpour having begun as they were preparing to enter the carriages, the party went back into the house, where they sat for a while, smoking cigars and talking, in an upstairs room. When it was all over Garfield wrote, "I had no private conversation with the party, but the call was a pleasant and cordial one all around." The visit had lasted about an hour.[49]

Some people could not accept the brief call for what it was. Stories were soon being circulated of a deal between Garfield and Conkling, and references made to the "treaty of Mentor." Tom Platt claimed in his old age that Conkling had told him that at the meeting he had exacted a pledge from Garfield in regard to New York patronage. When he came to this portion of his reminiscences, Platt had apparently forgotten his own account of how completely Garfield had committed himself in New York.[50]

The campaign was bitter and hard-fought, its outcome never a foregone conclusion. The Republicans neglected the South, concentrating their money and their energies elsewhere, particularly in four important and doubtful states, Connecticut, New Jersey, New York, and Indiana. Any early confidence that they may have felt was dissipated in mid-September when they failed to gain the governorship and lost seats in the national House of Representatives in the state election in Maine.

Indiana, whose state election (along with Ohio's) was on October 12, was a battleground from the beginning of the campaign. The state had gone to Tilden in 1876, and Garfield, Jewell, and Dorsey were all fully cognizant of its importance for Republicans in 1880. In a long letter to Swaim at the beginning of September, Dorsey spoke bluntly about the campaign there: *"There is only one question about carrying Indiana, and that is the question of money, and the majority we get will keep pace with the amount we expend."* He himself went to Indiana to organize for victory. A few days before the state election, Thaddeus Pound had praise for Dorsey and his cohorts. "Dorsey, Gorham and Filley are a *Trinity,* and well up in organizing *such* a campaign." Burke Hinsdale spent fifteen days in the state, working among Disciples of Christ. He came away convinced

that Indiana politics was "deplorably degenerate and corrupt" and that
the corruption was not all on one side. After the October election, in
which the Republicans won a narrow victory, Jewell told Garfield, "The
Indiana victory was a great thing; but it left us strapped,—flat broke."
And November 2 was just around the corner.[51]

The Democratic attack on Garfield's character assumed a curious
form in the latter part of September when the "$329 mania" reached
epidemic proportions. The figures—harking back to Crédit Mobilier—
appeared all over the country, on sidewalks, fences, doorsteps, streets
and roads, and posts. The secretary to the President was reported to
have found them on the horseblock in front of his house, the secretary
of state on the headboard of his bed and on his hat, the secretary of the
treasury on an envelope in his mail, the secretary of war on his napkin
at breakfast, the commissioner of agriculture on a beet left on his desk.
According to a news dispatch from New Haven, the sum had been
chalked on every pavement and at thousands of doorsteps in the city.[52]

On October 20, two weeks before the election, a letter appeared in
*Truth*, a New York City labor paper, that dismayed Republicans and
caused Democrats to rejoice. The letter purported to be one written by
Garfield on January 23, 1880, to H. L. Morey of the Employers' Union
of Lynn, Massachusetts, on "the Chinese problem." The writer expressed the view that individuals and companies had the right to buy
labor where they could get it cheapest and indicated that he was not
prepared to say that our treaty with the Chinese government should be
abrogated until manufacturing and corporate interests were "con-
served in the matter of labor."[53] The sentiments expressed in the letter
were contrary to those set forth by Garfield in his letter of acceptance
(he favored restrictions on Chinese immigration after the Sino-
American treaty had been modified), but it was feared the letter might
do great harm to his candidacy in the Far West and in some parts of
the East, where anti-Chinese sentiment was strong.

The Associated Press sent Garfield a copy of the letter by wire, and
he informed them that the letter was a forgery. He was confirmed in
this view when a copy of *Truth* arrived the next day. But he was shaken
soon after midnight when a telegram from New York informed him
that Abram Hewitt—the Democratic congressman who had given Garfield the Jersey bull—had said that he had seen the original and believed that the letter was genuine. Garfield's uneasiness arose from the
date of the letter; it was in the period after his election to the Senate,
when he was deluged with letters and had help in answering them. He
wondered whether Tom Nichol might have sent it out on his own. He
sent George Rose to search the files in Washington, but Rose found

nothing. The next day Garfield breathed a sigh of relief when a lithographic facsimile of the letter arrived. "It is not," he wrote, "in the hand writing of any person whom I know, but is a manifestly bungling attempt to copy my hand and signature." He immediately wired Jewell, authorizing him to release the telegram he had sent to New York the night before denouncing the letter as a forgery.[54] Meanwhile some damage had been done. Democrats were busy distributing thousands of copies of the letter in facsimile, and many of the copies went to the Pacific Coast.

Garfield had a good many things going for him in the campaign. One was the story of his life, epitomized after the election in the titles of two biographies, William M. Thayer's *From Log Cabin to the White House* and Horatio Alger's *From Canal Boy to President*. President Hayes had been quick to seize upon the appeal of the candidate's origins and upward struggle. A few days after the nomination, he jotted down some thoughts.

> We must neglect no element of success. There is a great deal of strength in Garfield's life and struggles as a self made man. Let it be thoroughly presented. In facts and incidents, in poetry and tales—in pictures—on banners, in representations, in processions, in watchwords and nicknames.
>
> How from poverty and obscurity—by labor at all avocations he became a great scholar, a Statesman, a Major General, a Senator, a Presidential Candidate. Give the amplest details—a school teacher—a laborer on the Canal—the name of his boat. The truth is no man ever started so low that accomplished so much in all our history. Not Franklin or Lincoln even.

In the ensuing campaign Republicans made the most of their opportunity; no element in the Garfield story as outlined by the President was neglected.[55]

Other factors favored the Republican candidate. Garfield had been elected to Congress nine times and had a thorough knowledge of the federal government; Hancock had spent his life in military service. Garfield had taken a stand in favor of protection for home industries; Hancock dismissed the tariff as "a local issue," opening himself to the charge of ignorance. Garfield was a Civil War hero leading the party of Abraham Lincoln and the Union; Hancock, though a war hero and a devoted Unionist, headed a party that to many northern minds was tainted with treason. One of the Republican campaign songs included this stanza:[56]

> A Union General leads, my boys,
>     Secession on the field,
> We'll meet it with brave deeds, my boys:
>     Once more foredoomed to yield!
> He waves our flag in vain, my boys!
>     His stars go down in night!
> Secession dies again, my boys,
>     Though HANCOCK for it fight!

More than nine million votes were cast on election day. Garfield's plurality was less than 10,000 (the Greenback candidate garnered enough votes to keep either major candidate from getting a majority). Garfield won 215 electoral votes, Hancock 189. Garfield carried New York by a slim 21,000; the state's 35 electoral votes were indispensable. The Republican investment in Indiana yielded a small plurality. The plurality in Connecticut was even smaller. Hancock carried all the former states of the Confederacy (this feat marked the emergence of the Solid South), Maryland, Delaware, West Virginia, Kentucky, Missouri, California (five of six electoral votes), Nevada, and New Jersey. To what extent the Morey letter affected the results in the latter three states is not clear; Garfield believed that it was decisive in California and New Jersey and perhaps so in Nevada.

Although winter provided Lawnfield some protection from the outside world, Garfield had little time to relax during the four months between the election and his inauguration. Friends and relatives came to visit, politicians came to ask favors and to advise. Mail continued to pour in. In late November both James and Crete spent a busy week in Washington, he conferring with politicians, she packing in the house they were leaving forever. Back again in Lawnfield, Garfield struggled with his inaugural address and confronted the thorny task of cabinet-making.[57]

There were seven top cabinet posts to be filled and a large number of deserving Republicans from whom to choose. Some attention must be given to sectional representation; New York, Pennsylvania, and Illinois, by reason of their importance in the nation and in the party, each expected an appointment. The wishes of party chieftains—Grant, Blaine, Conkling, Logan, the Camerons, Sherman—must be taken into consideration. Factions within the party must be appeased. Whatever the decisions, there were bound to be disappointments, criticisms, antagonisms. It was not the kind of assignment that Garfield relished; Blaine would have enjoyed it thoroughly.

Blaine, inevitably, was under consideration from the beginning.

Garfield knew him well, liked him, respected his ability, recognized his preeminent position in the party, and owed much to him and his followers for their support in Chicago. It might be salutary for the party in Maine to have Blaine out of the Senate for a time, and his appointment to a cabinet position would be adequate recognition of New England. Garfield was a little worried that the irrepressible politician might use a cabinet post to further a campaign for the presidency in 1884. In Washington in November, he expressed his concern to Blaine, who assured him that he would not again seek the presidential nomination. A few days before Christmas Blaine accepted Garfield's invitation to become secretary of state.[58]

Conkling posed the most difficult problem; he was determined that Levi P. Morton should have the Treasury. Governor Alonzo Cornell of New York and two other emissaries went to Lawnfield in December to press for Morton's appointment, saying that the banker had understood that the position of secretary of the treasury was one of several places he might choose. Garfield denied that he had given Morton the option or that he had offered him the Treasury by implication. He pointed out that a banker was not eligible to hold the office and expressed the opinion that giving the place to New York City "would be most unwise in a party sense." After three hours the men left, "evidently disappointed."

Cornell returned in January accompanied by Thomas C. Platt, who had just been elected to the United States Senate. They stayed for three hours, "urging Morton for the Treasury." Faced with an impasse, Garfield considered naming Conkling himself to the post. At the end of January the perplexed president-elect invited Conkling to come to see him; it was more than ten days before he received a reply, but the senator did come, and he remained for eight and a half hours. The meeting went well enough, but no progress was made on the central question. Conkling thought Morton "would do well in the Treasury"; Garfield told him he "thought the objections insuperable." Ten days after Conkling's visit, Garfield took the bull by the horns and offered the post of secretary of the navy to Morton; the New Yorker accepted. At least one New York problem seemed resolved.[59]

No other offers of cabinet positions were made before Garfield left Mentor for Washington. He had decided, however, on three appointments: Senator William Windom of Minnesota for the Treasury (Sherman preferred Windom as his successor), Robert Todd Lincoln for the War Department (he had been suggested by Don Cameron and enthusiastically supported by Illinoisans), and Wayne MacVeagh of Pennsylvania as attorney general (MacVeagh was the son-in-law of Simon Cameron but was not part of the political machine run by his in-laws).

For the Interior Department Garfield narrowed his choices to the senators from Iowa, William Boyd Allison and Samuel J. Kirkwood; it had become traditional to have a westerner at the head of that department. For postmaster general Garfield was considering two southerners, his old army friend Don Pardee, who had long been a judge in Louisiana, and William H. Hunt of the same state, who was a member of the United States Court of Claims.[60]

The inaugural address gave Garfield a good deal of trouble. A few days before Christmas he began reading the inaugural addresses of his predecessors, beginning with George Washington. The address of John Adams, he wrote, was "far more vigorous in ideas than Washington's. His next to the last sentence contains more than 700 words. Strong but too cumbrous." Jefferson's he characterized as "stronger than Washington's, more ornate than Adams'." He noted a "tone of self-depreciation" in the addresses of Jefferson, Madison, and Monroe. In January Tom Nichol summarized some of the documents. At the end of the first week in February Garfield found himself "strangely disinclined to work on the inaugural." His inclination was not to give one—but he supposed he must. Another week passed before he could report that he had got his first satisfactory start. When he left for Washington, the address was still unfinished.[61]

In 1881 Sigmund Freud received his M.D. degree at the University of Vienna. On January 20, 1881, Garfield and Swaim went to Cleveland, where they spent the night at the home of Lionel Sheldon. The next day the president-elect made a careful record of a dream he had had during the night.

Last night I dreamed that General Arthur, Major Swaim and I were on an excursion to attend some great ceremonial. We were on a canal packet during the night. A heavy rain came on, and in the gray of the morning Swaim and I awoke just as the packet was passing a point to enter a deep broad basin. We leaped ashore, and in looking back saw that the packet was sinking. Just as it was sinking I noticed General Arthur lying on a couch very pale, and apparently very ill. In an instant more, the packet sank with all on board. I started to plunge into the water to save Arthur, but Swaim held me, and said he cannot be saved, and you will perish if you attempt it. It appeared that we were naked and alone in the wild storm, and that the country was hostile. I felt that nakedness was a disguise which would avoid identification. In this dream, for the first time in a dream, I knew I was President-elect. After a long journey, we somehow found a few yards of calico each for partial coverings. After a long and tangled journey we entered a house, and an old negro woman took me into her arms and nursed me as though I were a sick child. At this point I awoke.[62]

It was with sadness, even foreboding, that Garfield looked forward to life on "the bleak mountain" he called the presidency. He dreaded the loss of freedom and the isolation that his new position would entail. He knew, too, that he would miss old friends and that some of them would be disappointed in him and some alienated. In Hiram, where he had gone to attend a funeral, he spoke of his feelings to faculty and students. "To-day is a sort of burial-day in many ways. I have often been in Hiram, and have often left it; but, with the exception of when I went to the war, I have never felt that I was leaving it in quite so definite a way as I do to-day."[63]

At nine o'clock on the morning of Tuesday, March 1, a special train arrived at the Washington depot of the Baltimore and Potomac Railroad. From it descended the president-elect and Mrs. Garfield, Eliza, Mollie, Irvin, and Abe, Mary McGrath, Swaim, Joe Brown, Ollie Judd, Lionel and Mrs. Sheldon, and Captain Henry. A welcoming committee quickly whisked them through the large crowd that had assembled. The President's son Webb drove Eliza, Abe, and Mary McGrath directly to the White House; the rest of the party started for the Riggs House. Crete began to keep a diary that day after the lapse of a quarter of a century. "It was a strange coming back to Washington—so many years our home; and as we drove through Pennsylvania Avenue—the sun shining a warm welcome, banners and flags fluttering out a 'Hail to the Chief' from every street corner and almost from every house top—the tears would tell of the strange excitement that had touched my heart."[64]

From the time of his arrival at the hotel, there was no respite for Garfield. "The rush and swirl of callers," he wrote, "was too much to be remembered without discomfort. Interviews with Blaine and several leading men. Slate generally approved, but Allison pressed instead of Windom. Morton pleased with his new place but his N.Y. friends not." Late at night he took up his inaugural, was dissatisfied with it, and began to rewrite it. Although it was two o'clock when he went to bed, he was in good spirits; the tonic of Washington life, as he said, was good for his mind.[65]

After four hours of sleep he faced another trying day. Morton, who had been routed out of bed at four o'clock by fellow New Yorkers and pressured by them to give up the Navy post, came to ask for his release. "The N.Y. delegation," Garfield wrote, "are in a great row because I do not give the Treasury to that state." Still determined to have a New Yorker in his cabinet, he sent for Thomas L. James, the able post-

master of New York City, "to measure him for Postmaster General."
He then drove to Judge William H. Hunt's and invited him to become
secretary of the navy. That night Garfield had only three hours of
sleep.[66]

The day before the inauguration brought some progress and some
pleasure. Postmaster James came for an interview and satisfied Garfield
that if he entered the cabinet his first loyalty would be to the administration and not to Conkling. Afterward Conkling, Arthur, and Platt arrived, "the former full of apprehension that he had been or was to be
cheated." They asked Garfield to appoint former senator Timothy
Howe of Wisconsin to the Treasury. That evening Senator Allison accepted the office that Conkling wanted for Howe. After dinner at the
White House with the President and his cabinet, Garfield went to
Wormley's, where sixteen of his Williams classmates were assembled in
his honor. He told them that he had no elation in view of the position
he was about to fill. "I would thank God," he added, "were I to-day a
free lance in the House or Senate." At 2:30 A.M. he wrote the last sentence of his inaugural. Joe Brown spent the rest of the night making
the copy that Garfield would read from and two other copies for the
press.[67]

Inauguration day began inauspiciously with rain and sleet and, inside the hotel, another problem for Garfield. He had risen early and
was busily preparing for the long day when Senator Allison arrived and
"absolutely declined the Treasury," pleading family reasons and the
opposition he was likely to encounter.[68]

The rest of the day went well. Even the weather improved; the sky
cleared before noon and there was some bright sunshine. At midmorn-
ing President Hayes, who had been delighted by Garfield's nomination
and election, came to the hotel to drive his successor to the executive
mansion. From there, accompanied by a senatorial committee, they
went to the Capitol, where, after witnessing in the Senate chamber the
inauguration of Chester A. Arthur as Vice President, they were escorted to the east front for the presidential inauguration. Crete and
Eliza and all the family were there. Eliza, in her new finery, was "happy
and proud," the first mother in American history to see her son inaugurated President of the United States. To Crete it seemed that all eyes
in the vast concourse were centered on James, "the one majestic figure." Soon he "stood out before the people and with the inspiration of
the time and the occasion lifting him up into his fullest grandeur he became in the magnificence with which he pronounced his Inaugural almost superhuman."[69]

The address shows few traces of midnight oil. It will stand comparison with the inaugurals of Garfield's predecessors. It is a clear, forceful,

sometimes eloquent statement grounded in idealism and optimism, concerned with the realities of the present. The opening paragraph set the theme and tone.

> We stand to-day upon an eminence which overlooks a hundred years of national life—a century crowded with perils, but crowned with the triumphs of liberty and law. Before continuing the onward march, let us pause on our height, for a moment, to strengthen our faith and to renew our hope by a glance at the pathway along which our people have traveled.

For today's reader the living part of the address is that dealing with our constitutional heritage, the trial and triumph of the Constitution in the Civil War, and the black race in American society. He described the elevation of the blacks from slavery to citizenship as "the most important political change . . . since the adoption of the Constitution" and declared that no thoughtful man could fail to appreciate "its beneficent effects upon our institutions and people." After paying tribute to the progress already made by the emancipated race, he made a ringing declaration. "So far as my authority lawfully extends, they shall enjoy the full and equal protection of the Constitution and the laws." He faced the black suffrage issue squarely and declared that the question would "never give safety or repose to the State or to the nation until each within its own jurisdiction" made and kept the ballot free and pure by legal sanctions. Acknowledging the danger arising from the ignorance of voters, he offered his remedy: "the saving influence of universal education." [70]

After the ceremonies at the Capitol, the Garfields went to a lunch with the Hayeses, a grand parade past a reviewing stand in front of the White House, and an evening reception and promenade in the new National Museum. Eliza, in her eightieth year, missed none of these activities. It was eleven o'clock when James and Crete returned to the house that they expected to be their home for the next four years. The Hayeses had gone to spend the night with John Sherman before heading for Ohio and freedom. (Sherman had been elected to the Senate to fill the vacancy created by the resignation of Garfield.) For Garfield the day was not yet ended. William Windom came to confer, and after about an hour the President asked him to be secretary of the treasury. Windom went home to think it over. [71]

The cabinet was completed the day after the inauguration. Windom accepted the Treasury in the morning, and a few hours later Garfield decided to appoint Kirkwood secretary of the interior. The nominations were hurried to the Senate, which had been called into special session to confirm appointments and to consider treaties with China and

Japan. By dinner time the President had been notified that all the men had been unanimously confirmed. He thought that, though it was not an ideal cabinet, it was a good combination of substance and appearance. *The Nation* was not concerned whether the cabinet was filled with first-rate men; there was no department, it said, of which the President himself could not take charge. "He would have nothing to learn from any man in public life whom he could possibly put at the head of any of them." [72]

Settling in at the White House was made easier for the Garfields than it might have been by a number of circumstances. They had discussed some matters with Hayes and his wife, and they had inherited William T. Crump, the White House steward, a most important functionary. Other members of the staff also remained. Two of their own servants, Daniel Sprigg and Mary McGrath, would be there to help. President Hayes had graciously offered to leave his carriage and horses for their use until they acquired their own.

The White House family was complete. Hal and Jim and their friend Don Rockwell had persuaded their parents to let them study in Washington under a tutor instead of returning to St. Paul's School after Christmas. Dr. William H. Hawkes, who was recommended by a college classmate of Garfield and Rockwell, was brought from Montana Territory to instruct the boys. The thirty-five-year-old Hawkes, who arrived in January, taught the boys in the home of the Rockwells, where Hal and Jim were living under the strict supervision of the head of the house. After the inauguration the boys came home and a schoolroom was established in the White House. Dr. Hawkes received an additional assignment; he was asked to cope with Irvin and Abe also. (Mollie was enrolled in Madame Burr's School on New York Avenue.) [73]

When the new administration began, the President had not yet selected a private secretary. The lack was not the result of indifference or oversight; Garfield had given a good deal of thought to the matter. Hayes had named to the post a personal friend who, it turned out, was not especially well qualified. Garfield hoped to upgrade the office by persuading Congress to provide a more attractive salary. He was more interested in having that position well filled than he was some of the cabinet positions; he was persuaded that it was as important a job. He decided early that he wanted the forty-two-year-old John Hay, who had been Abraham Lincoln's secretary, a member of the foreign service, a writer, and, since 1878, assistant secretary of state. Hay was married to the daughter of Amasa Stone, a wealthy Clevelander who was a friend and supporter of Garfield. In spite of considerable pressure, Hay declined. He found the prospect of intimate relations with the Garfields, he said, a temptation almost more than he could resist;

"the other half of the work, the contact with the greed and selfishness of office seekers and bull-dozing Congressmen" was "unspeakably repulsive" to him. Lionel Sheldon was also considered, but he seems to have looked upon the post as beneath his dignity. Blaine thought that he was the worst man that Garfield could choose—there was tar sticking to him that would not out (a reference to Sheldon's postwar years as a carpetbagger in Louisiana).[74]

In Mentor Garfield had once said jokingly to Joe Brown that he might have to take him for a secretary. When Joe called on Colonel Rogers, the secretary of Hayes, on March 4, a White House attendant addressed him as "Mr. Secretary." The news spread rapidly that the new secretary had arrived, and employees found excuses to pass the office to get a look at him. The next morning President Garfield directed Joe to take charge of the office until he had time to give the matter further attention. After two weeks the President, who had been observing the young man's work with interest, said that he was satisfied if Joe was and that he could have the position if he wanted it. The twenty-two-year-old graduate of a public high school seems to have performed his duties to everybody's satisfaction, including those who worked under him.[75]

Joe may have already fallen in love with Mollie, who was just fourteen when she moved into the White House. It was not until 1888, after Mrs. Garfield had sent Joe to college and he had altered his name to Joseph Stanley-Brown, that the wedding took place at Lawnfield.[76]

What of George Rose, the faithful helper for a dozen years? Garfield seems to have concluded that he was not qualified for the position. He was willing to give him a lesser place in the White House office, but Rose was not to be appeased. Garfield was "greatly distressed" to receive from him a bitter letter. Relations between the two men came to an end. After the President's death Rose asked for a settlement for past services, contending that he had not been adequately paid. He and Mrs. Garfield finally turned the problem over to Burke Hinsdale, who came up with a formula that would yield Rose less than he had sought. Eighty years later, Rose's daughter Lucretia ("Crete"), who was born in the Garfield house in Washington in 1881, said that her mother had hated Garfield. She didn't know why.[77]

Garfield had always been happiest when he had old friends about him. Now, more than ever, he needed the companionship of men to whom he could turn for an hour of relaxation, men with whom he did not have to maintain an official reserve. He saw to it that some of his best friends were given offices that would keep them close to him. They were his insulation against a cold and demanding world. Hayes, as a courtesy to Garfield, had appointed Swaim judge advocate general of

the United States Army; he would not have to return to Fort Leavenworth. Rockwell was already on duty in Washington, but Garfield
wanted him in a more intimate relation and made him superintendent
of buildings and grounds; the White House and its grounds were part
of his domain. (Like his predecessor in the office, Rockwell introduced
the guests at receptions of the first lady.) In May Captain Henry was relieved of his post as itinerant special agent for the Post Office Department and made marshal of the District of Columbia; before he could
receive the appointment it was necessary for the President to find another office for the incumbent, black leader Frederick Douglass. No
suitable post was found in Washington for Sheldon; he left shortly to
become governor of the Territory of New Mexico. The *New York
Herald,* in a series of sketches, satirized the intimate group around the
President as "the Chums" and the "Chum cabinet."[78]

From the first day the new President encountered a mad scramble
for office, a torrent of greedy and ruthless men. He was face to face
with the spoils system in all its ugly reality, and he did not like it at all.
He spoke of "the indurated office seeker who pursues his prey with the
grip of death," of "disciplined office hunters" who drew papers on him
"as highway men draw pistols." He would have to struggle "to keep
from despising the office seeker." After two weeks in office he was
"vexed with the thought that I am wholly unfitted for this sort of
work." He resented the fact that he had little time to deal with ideas, to
do what he thought a President ought to be doing. He had said in his
inaugural that he would recommend civil service legislation to Congress. His statement would have been more heartfelt and forceful had
it been made at the end of March instead of at the beginning.[79]

On Sunday afternoon, March 20, Senator Conkling spent two and a
half hours at the White House with the President, "reviewing the New
York situation." Senator Platt was out of town. Garfield was cordial,
agreeing to many of the suggestions of the senator with respect to appointments, all of which concerned the visitor's friends. When Garfield
told him that he must recognize some of the men who had supported
him at Chicago, Conkling proposed that they be given foreign assignments. Garfield was unwilling to exile them. "I will go as far as I can to
keep the peace," the President wrote in his diary, "but I will not abandon the N.Y. protestants." In his diary the President did not mention
the office of collector of customs of the port of New York, the most important federal position in the senator's state. Conkling himself said
that he had raised the question of the collectorship as he was departing
and that Garfield had replied that they would leave it for another
day.[80]

The next day Conkling sent a note to the President, indicating that it would not be necessary to delay the New York appointments because of Platt's absence. In a brief response, Garfield referred to Conkling's message and added, "But I would be glad to know what can be done for Jacobins. If you have found anything in that direction, please drop me a note." The senator never dropped a note.[81]

On the Tuesday following his conference with Conkling, Garfield sent to the Senate a large number of nominations, including "most of the N.Y. vacancies." Conkling and his friends had every reason to be gratified. The New Yorkers named to the more important posts were all readily identifiable as Conkling people; the independents had received no recognition. Many drew the obvious conclusion: the President had turned over the federal patronage in the state of New York to its senior senator.[82]

Blaine was crushed by the news. That evening Garfield was called from the dinner table by his unexpected appearance. The meeting with the secretary of state lasted through two or three courses. When the President returned, he was "looking very pale, but composed." No one dared to ask what had happened, and the head of the household offered no explanation. Later, in the privacy of their room, he unburdened himself to Crete. "I have broken Blaine's heart with the appointments I have made today. He regards me as having surrendered to Conkling. I have not, but I don't know but I have acted too hastily. Perhaps I ought to have consulted Blaine before sending in some of those New York appointments."[83]

The President, "in real distress," could not sleep. He decided, according to Crete's account, that because of Blaine's anxiety he would on the morrow send to the Senate "another batch of appointments" that would "thoroughly antidote the first." He had not expected to send them so soon but, "urged by Mr. Blaine," had concluded that now was the time.[84]

The shock the next day was almost more than the Senate could stand. William H. Robertson, the symbol of open rebellion against the Conkling machine, was nominated collector of customs of the port of New York.

The nomination of Robertson necessitated some changes. Edwin A. Merritt, the collector appointed by Hayes in 1878 as successor to the ousted Chester A. Arthur, was named consul general in London. Adam Badeau, who held that post, was nominated minister to Denmark. The incumbent in Denmark, Michael Cramer, was transferred to Switzerland.

The reception of the second batch of nominations was mixed. Robertson was delighted, and other New York Jacobins were happy to know that they were not forgotten. Hayes and civil service reformers were dismayed by the transfer of Merritt; in the normal course he would have remained in the customhouse for four years. Adam Badeau was not pleased with his new assignment, nor was his friend General Grant. The former president was also outraged at the treatment of his New York friends. Postmaster General James was alarmed lest Senator Conkling think that he had something to do with Robertson's appointment. (Cramer was glad; he had wanted to get out of Denmark.) The New York legislature, to the surprise of almost everyone, passed resolutions endorsing the nomination of state senator Robertson.

"The new list was sent in," Mrs. Garfield wrote, "and the two New York factions stood looking into each others eyes astonished and enraged, but feeling themselves thoroughly fettered and outwitted. The Conkling faction may make a struggle yet, but before the country they are powerless."[85]

No appointment that Garfield could have made would have been so hard a blow to Conkling as that of Robertson to the New York customhouse. Although the senator had fought the confirmation of Merritt in 1878, he now much preferred the continuance of the status quo to the taking over of the customhouse by his archenemy. For a party machine the customhouse in the great metropolis had enormous potential. It was a vast operation with hundreds of employees; a large percentage of the imports of the United States passed through it. If a political machine controlled the collector, the customhouse itself became in effect a part of that machine. The appointment of Robertson struck at the foundation of Conkling's political power. Sherman had told Garfield in January that Conkling could not rise above a post office or customhouse. When the customhouse was in the greatest port in the nation, a state political boss could not afford to rise above it.[86]

After the Robertson nomination had reached the Senate, Conkling lost little time in going to the Post Office Department to confer with its head. He asked James to call on the President and see what could be done, and he suggested that James talk the matter over with Attorney General MacVeagh before going to the White House. James found MacVeagh ready to leave for Philadelphia, and the two men agreed to postpone their call on the President until his return. The attorney general had his own reason for being disgruntled: the President, at Blaine's request and without MacVeagh's approval, had appointed William E. Chandler of New Hampshire solicitor general in the Justice Department.[87]

On MacVeagh's return the two cabinet members called on the President and told him they felt compelled to resign. Garfield in "his hearty and affectionate manner laid his arm around the shoulder of each" and told them that he needed them too much. He also told them to have Conkling come over in the evening; the cabinet would be there, and it would go hard if they didn't get the matter settled before they separated.[88]

The emissaries found Conkling in his room with Platt. James, Mac-Veagh, and Platt all urged Conkling to see the President. According to James, Conkling was about to yield when a telegram arrived from Governor Cornell of New York; the governor advised the senator to abandon his antagonism in the matter of Robertson on the ground that there was not enough support at home for his stand. Angry, Conkling threw down the telegram and refused to budge, saying that he was no place hunter. Garfield's diary entry for March 25 noted, "An appointment for Vice President, Conkling and Platt but they failed to come."[89]

The President's nominations piled up in the Senate, which was deadlocked over the question of organization because neither party had a majority. Between March 23 and May 4 no executive sessions were held, hence no nominations were confirmed.

During the days following Conkling's failure to keep his appointment at the White House, Garfield fortified his position. He asked Merritt to write a letter "expressing his willingness" to leave the customhouse for the consulate. He gave the cabinet a report on the "condition of the N.Y. fight" and received their support for his position. He let a number of senators "know that the vote on Robertson's confirmation was a test of friendship or hostility to the administration." He reviewed the situation fully with Senator Sherman during a long ride; Sherman, who had at first objected to the transfer of Merritt, agreed to lead the fight in the Senate for Robertson.[90]

Two days after Garfield's ride with Sherman he had a call from Senator Platt, who suggested that the President withdraw all of the New York nominations and then appoint Robertson United States attorney for the southern district of New York. The President refused to take the initiative or to suggest any change to Robertson.[91]

As time passed, Garfield urged Republican senators to break the deadlock in the Senate in order to enable that body to go into executive session to act on his nominations.

Conkling and Platt were not the only Republican senators disturbed by the furor. It was unseemly for a Republican President to force his friends in the Senate to choose between him and two fellow senators of the same party. The custom known as the courtesy of the Senate—a custom Garfield had criticized when he was in Congress—dictated that senators should not under ordinary circumstances vote for the confirmation of a presidential appointee if objections were made by one or both senators of the state concerned (provided that the objecting senator was of the President's party). The instinct of Republican senators, therefore, was to support Conkling and Platt.

An alternative was to reach an understanding with the President. The Republican caucus in the Senate established a five-member committee of conciliation headed by Henry L. Dawes. The committee's first step was to let Conkling present his side of the controversy. The New York senator talked for two and a half hours, making what Dawes considered his greatest speech. At the close of the speech Conkling announced that he had in his pocket a letter written by Garfield that, if published, would cause the President to "bite the dust."[92]

The letter was one that Garfield had written during the presidential campaign to Jay Hubbell, chairman of the Republican Congressional Committee. The Republican nominee asked Hubbell to tell Thomas Brady, an assistant postmaster general, that he hoped that he would give all the assistance he could—and inquired how the departments generally were doing. The references were to the practice of bringing pressure on the executive departments for contributions for campaign purposes. A few weeks before Conkling made his threat, Brady had been forced to resign because of his connection with the star route frauds. When Garfield learned of Conkling's remarks, he was willing to publish the letter immediately but was held back by Blaine.[93]

After hearing Conkling, the committee of conciliation called on the President to discuss three matters. One had to do with Republican relations with Senator Mahone of Virginia, whose support was needed for the organization of the Senate. The other topics were the importance to the administration of executive sessions and the possibility of harmony in the Senate over the New York nominations. Garfield made it clear that executive sessions were urgently required; he needed 300 vacancies filled. As for the nominations, they were his best judgment and would not be withdrawn. "The Committee," the President noted in his diary, "had been bulldozed by Senator Conkling."[94]

The next evening Dawes was back for two hours, working for a compromise. "I told him," Garfield wrote, "there could be no peace by evading the N.Y. contest. I wanted it known soon, whether I was the registering Clerk of the Senate or the Executive of the government."[95]

On May 4, as a result of a Republican arrangement with Senator Mahone, the deadlock was broken and the Senate could proceed to the consideration of nominations. The first day's activity was not reassuring to the President; one of the original New York nominees was confirmed, but Robertson's nomination was not taken up. This caused Garfield to fear that all of Conkling's men would be confirmed and Robertson's "contested" nomination postponed.[96] To prevent such a development, Garfield took a step that Blaine had urged on him a month earlier. He withdrew the nominations of the five principal men recommended to him by Conkling. "This," he said, "will bring the Robertson nomination to an issue." A number of senators called on him that evening to "deplore the contest" and suggest that he do something to avoid it. Garfield urged them to act on Robertson.[97]

A few days later a motion was made in the Republican caucus to postpone action on Robertson until fall. Conkling supported the motion in a long speech. The next day the motion was withdrawn to prevent its defeat and another adopted that would delay action for the time being in the hopes of a settlement.[98]

On May 15 Dr. Silas Boynton, who had come to Washington to help look after Crete, mentioned the situation in a letter to his mother. "James is having quite a time with Conkling and other Senators but he will not back down and Senator Conkling will have to come down from his High Horse." The following day both New York senators came down from their high horses: they resigned their seats in the Senate. Two days later Robertson was confirmed. Conkling and Platt were soon in Albany, trying desperately to win re-election and vindication. At the beginning of July it seemed certain that they would fail.[99]

After his victory Garfield resisted the temptation to send to the Senate an entirely new slate of nominees for the positions he had assigned to Conkling men. Three of the names on the new list were the same as before, but the President had replaced two of the Conkling men because he had heard enough about them to be convinced that they should not have been nominated in the first place.[100]

Was Garfield wise in precipitating the contest between himself and the Republican boss of New York? Did the contest have any meaning other than as a brawl over offices? The questions could be debated at length; historians and biographers have given varying interpretations of the famous confrontation. Conkling's personality, character, and history being what they were, a clash between him and the new President could not have been long deferred. Conkling would have expected nothing short of capitulation by the executive in matters of appointments to office within his state. Garfield, to be sure, could have gone into the fray a bit more courteously; he could, at the outset, have told Conkling what he proposed to do and why. As for the meaning of the struggle, one may look at it as an incident in the perennial tug of war between Congress and the executive. In this instance the appointment power of the executive, which had been eroded by the courtesy of the Senate, was proclaimed and maintained, if only for a brief period. Garfield thought that he was standing for a principle; it remains an open question whether he chose the best means of making his point. All will agree on one thing: In view of the effect of the prolonged struggle on the unbalanced mind of Charles Guiteau, the victory was not worth the price.

Those close to Garfield rejoiced that the nation now knew what they had always known. "He has risen immensely in popular estimation, and got credit for a backbone he was never thought by the masses to possess," Garfield's old friend Harry Rhodes said. "I guess they have found that he has got some Back bone yet," Eliza wrote.[101]

As the Conkling drama neared its denouement at the Capitol, Garfield received a letter from Grant (who was in Mexico) that ended the cordial relations that had existed between them during and after the campaign. The former president spelled out over several pages his dissatisfaction with Garfield's New York appointments. He had given Garfield, he said, strong and hearty support from the time of his nomination until election eve. He was claiming no credit for this; he had been honored by the party and by the nation as no other man had been, and it was his duty to serve both. "But," he went on, "I do claim that I ought not to be humiliated by seeing my personal friends punished for no other offense than their friendship and support." He hoped Garfield would see the matter in the same light he did and, if not, believe that he had no other object in writing than to serve him, the party, and the nation.[102]

Garfield's response was respectful, dignified, and forthright. He set the general straight on a couple of matters of fact, and he defended at length his appointment of Robertson. There was no apology, no retreat.[103]

At the seaside at Elberon with Crete in June, Garfield saw Grant on two occasions. One late afternoon, when the President's carriage passed the cottage of Jesse Grant, the general was standing outside. Grant bowed and lifted his hat. The next day the President held a reception in the parlor of the hotel where he was staying. The former president made an appearance, remaining only two or three minutes.[104]

A storm that had long been brewing burst forth in the early days of the Garfield administration. Numerous people had known that something was wrong in the Post Office Department. Congress had investigated and newspapers had called attention to abuses, but nothing had been done to correct the situation. Hayes had had intimations of trouble but had seen no reason for demanding a full investigation. The general public was unaware that there was gigantic fraud involved in the swift completion of their appointed rounds by contractors for the delivery of mail in isolated regions.

In 1881 most mail was carried to its destination in the United States on trains and steamships. But there were large numbers of out of the way places, especially in the vast and changing West, that had to be served by other means. The solution was found in the creation of star routes, over which the United States mails were carried under private contract, on horseback and in wagons. Inhabitants of an isolated area without mail service would petition the Post Office Department to establish such a route; if the department consented, it would let a contract for the regular delivery of mail over a designated route. The contract specified the length of the route, the number of trips to be made each week, the amount of time allowed for the making of a trip, and the annual sum to be paid for the fulfillment of the contract.[105]

No one could object to this practice. The people of the remote regions needed and deserved the service, and national unity required it. But the operations of contractors and the department itself were open to the most serious objections. Thomas Brady, who was in charge of star routes, became the center of a network of intrigue, deception, and corruption. By 1881 the service was costing the government about six million dollars a year—and it was not getting its money's worth.

The scenario went something like this: Someone desiring a contract for mail delivery would make a reasonable bid for a route and be awarded a contract. Soon petitions would be flowing to Washington from citizens in the area being served, asking for more frequent and faster service. Services were then improved—and costs went up dramatically. The cost of delivering the mail over the route from The Dalles to Baker City, Oregon, increased from about $8,000 to more than $60,000 within one year. A contract for carrying the mail between Phoenix and Prescott in Arizona Territory (a distance of 140 miles) was let for just under $700; additional service soon brought the cost to over $32,000. Over one route that was costing the government $50,000 a year, no letter or newspaper was carried during a period of 39 days. Such a system could not have developed or survived without the cooperation of officials within the Post Office Department.[106]

Among those interested in star route contracts was Stephen W. Dorsey, a carpetbag senator from Arkansas from 1873 to 1879 and secretary of the National Republican Committee in 1880. Two weeks before the inauguration, William E. Chandler, who had no use for Dorsey, remarked of the secretary and his crowd, "The 'Star Service' is the grand prize which is to nourish them and to furnish the scandal of the next presidential fight."[107]

James G. Blaine was alert to the dangers in the Post Office Department. In January 1881 he wrote Garfield, "The P.O. Dept in some of its most important bureaux has been a nest of unclean birds under

Hayes. Another flock of like color is preparing to take the same roost under Garfield. Your Administration must be as *actually* and *veritably* clean as that of Hayes is *pretentiously* and *ostentatiously* so."[108]

Garfield was determined that something be done quickly. When Thomas James came for an interview prior to his appointment as postmaster general, he told Garfield that, if appointed, he would like to investigate the city free delivery service in London. Garfield said that could be arranged. "He then said," according to James, "that from what he kept hearing he was afraid that there was something very wrong in the Department itself; that if so, he expected me to find it out, and then put the plow into the beam, and after that, to subsoil it. He asked what I knew of the frauds." James had read the newspapers, followed the investigations, and heard talk.[109]

When James had first been considered, early in the year, for the Post Office, Dorsey strongly opposed him—perhaps because he knew too much. At the same time Dorsey assured Garfield that he did not have and never had had the slightest interest in any contract or business with the Post Office Department.[110]

Soon after James was installed as postmaster general, the President sent for him and brought up the subject of the star route service and the proposed investigation of it. When asked how he intended to proceed, James sketched his plans. The investigation began, disclosures were made, and Brady's resignation demanded (Garfield wanted to fire him but was prevailed upon to allow him to resign). The bitter animosity of the *National Republican* (Washington) to Garfield may be attributed in part to the fact that at the end of 1880 Brady had become a large stockholder in the newspaper company.[111]

The star route frauds were to make the headlines long after Garfield's death. There were indictments, trials, charges of jury tampering, acquittals—another scandal for the history books.

As July began Garfield was nearing the end of his fourth month in office. The period since the inauguration had been a time of severe trial for the President. The crush of office seekers had distressed and almost overwhelmed him. The illness of Crete had shaken him to the core. The fight with Conkling had threatened his standing in the party and in the nation. The star route investigation had been an unsavory and disturbing affair. But the baptism by fire had left him a wiser, stronger, more confident man; the time seemed at hand when he could be the kind of President he wanted to be, a real leader. He looked forward to a vacation in his beloved New England, a long relaxing summer with the dear one, the planning of four major speeches to be delivered in the South during the fall. The dangers seemed past, the future bright.

One sad note marked his last active day. News came of the death of Cousin Cordelia Boynton. A week earlier the buggy in which she and Uncle Thomas Garfield were riding had been struck by a train. Uncle Thomas had died almost immediately; now Cordelia. What a wealth of memories surrounded Uncle Thomas and the Boyntons! But this was no time to mourn.[112]

The cabinet had never seen the President so lighthearted as he appeared that afternoon during its long session. He was, the secretary of the interior said, "the life of the meeting," interspersing "the proceedings with anecdotes and jokes." He spoke, too, of Mrs. Garfield's convalescence and the pleasure with which he was looking forward to the trip he would begin in the morning.[113]

It was midnight when the President opened his diary and made his last entry. The day, which marked the beginning of the new fiscal year, had been full of work. He had appointed nearly twenty-five ministers and consuls, dismissed a minor official for insubordination, called for the resignation of another. He had appointed Walker Blaine third assistant secretary of state, wishing to compliment "the bright and able young man" as well as his father. Joe Brown was back from his trip to London, "greatly refreshed." Last, there was the news of Cordelia.[114]

# EPILOGUE II

# A HOT SATURDAY MORNING
# IN WASHINGTON

IT WAS WELL AFTER eight o'clock when the President sat down to break-fast with Hal and Jim, Joe Brown, Dr. Hawkes, and Ollie Judd. He was still at table when Crump announced the arrival of Blaine, who had come in a State Department carriage to accompany the chief executive to the Baltimore and Potomac Railroad depot at Sixth and B streets, where the National Gallery now stands. Garfield went upstairs with Crump to get $500 from the safe. He and Blaine talked for several minutes in the cabinet room before going into Joe's office to say good-bye, the President in his familiar way placing his hand on the young man's shoulder. Forty years later Joe still remembered that both men appeared "at their very best," debonair in their new spring suits and boutonnieres.

Garfield and Blaine came outside as Colonel Rockwell and Don arrived in the White House carriage to pick up Hal, Jim, and Ollie Judd. The baggage cart was just starting for the depot. Farewells to the staff were quickly made, the State Department carriage—a small coupe with seats for two passengers sitting across from each other—drew up, and the President and the secretary of state were driven off. Rockwell and his companions followed, stopping for a moment to pick up Dr. Hawkes at his rooming house. At Seventh Street, Rockwell's party passed the presidential carriage. It was about 9:15 A.M.[1]

Charles Guiteau was already at the depot. He had risen at five o'clock at the Riggs House at Fifteenth and I streets, where he had been stopping for a couple of days. He had walked for a while and sat in Lafayette Park, across from the White House, reading a newspaper, resting, and enjoying "the beautiful morning air." Returning to the

hotel, he had breakfasted and then taken from his room a loaded revolver that he had bought three weeks earlier. Shortly before nine
o'clock, after spending another half hour in the park, he had boarded a
horse car for the Baltimore and Potomac depot, aware that the President's train was scheduled to depart at 9:30. The short, slightly built
man with a small moustache and a thin, dark beard, dressed in a dark
business suit and wearing a slouch hat pulled down over his forehead a
little more than was his usual habit, was not likely to attract much attention.[2]

The thirty-nine-year-old Guiteau had not had much success in life.
Born in Chicago, he had moved around a good deal. As a young man
he stayed in Ann Arbor for a time, expecting to enter the University of
Michigan. Instead he joined the Oneida Community of John
Humphrey Noyes near Utica, New York, where he remained for five
years. He went to New York City, thinking of founding a religious
paper; he returned to Oneida, then left for the city again after a few
months. In New York he read theology and tried to collect from Noyes
for his years of work for the community. Having acquired some small
knowledge of the law, he was admitted to the bar in Chicago after a
perfunctory examination. He married the librarian of a YMCA that he
frequented.

Incapable of practicing law, Guiteau made a living of sorts by taking
bad debts for collection—something he could do well. When he had
money, he paid his bills; when he lacked funds, he ran out on his debts.
His wife led a miserable existence, and after five years of marriage she
divorced him in New York City, where they had gone after the Chicago
fire; Guiteau obligingly slept with a prostitute to give her grounds for
divorce. His sister's husband, a Chicago lawyer, got him out of trouble
in New York and took him back to Chicago. There he attended meetings of the evangelists Moody and Sankey, frequently acting as usher.
Having read further in theology, he set out on a lecture tour. Arrested
in Detroit for nonpayment of bills, he escaped from custody and continued his tour in Ohio, Pennsylvania, and New York. He failed everywhere.

"I had ideas but no reputation," he later remarked. He could make
himself pleasant and agreeable; he prided himself on his neat appearance. (At his trial he insisted that he had been well dressed, with a clean
shirt, on the morning of the assassination.) He did not smoke, drink, or
use tobacco. Merchants readily turned over their bad debts to him,
train conductors sometimes let him ride without a ticket. "I dead-
headed from Toledo, Ohio, to Washington," he boasted, "on the
strength of my appearance with the conductors." He began to describe
himself as "lawyer and theologian." He had some of his lectures

printed, and in 1879 he brought out a little book, *Truth, A Companion to the Bible* (although the book was privately printed for him in Boston, it bore the name of a commercial publisher).[3]

Guiteau was also interested in politics. In 1872 he supported Horace Greeley, whom he had long admired. He wrote campaign speeches (which were not delivered) and went to political meetings. He was confident that political office would come to him. In 1876 he was for Hayes; in 1880 he expected that Grant would be nominated but accepted Garfield cheerfully. A few days after Garfield's nomination he went to New York from Boston (where he had been living), intending, he said, to go into politics. He settled down to convert a Grant speech he had written into a Garfield speech—"had to work it all over to fit General Garfield," he said. He spent several weeks in Saratoga and Poughkeepsie in unsuccessful efforts to deliver his speech. He was back in New York in time to greet Garfield during his visit to the city in early August for the Republican conference. The day after the conference Guiteau had his speech printed; thereafter he hung around the rooms of the national and state Republican committees, seeking speaking assignments and handing out copies of his speech. His one speaking assignment, at a rally in Harlem, was not a success. No one took him seriously, though he sometimes got a word or a nod from a leading politician such as Chester A. Arthur.[4]

The election having been won by the Republicans, Guiteau looked forward to an appointment. Indeed, he had written to Garfield two weeks before the election to indicate his desire for the Austro-Hungarian mission. "Next spring," he said, "I expect to marry the daughter of a deceased New York republican millionaire and I think we can represent the United States Government at the Court of Vienna with dignity and grace." On the last day of December he wrote again to say that he would present an application in March (among the signers he hoped for were Grant, Dwight L. Moody, and Henry Ward Beecher); in closing he wished the president-elect a happy new year.[5]

Garfield was inaugurated on Friday, March 4; Guiteau arrived in Washington the following Sunday morning. A few days later he was among the throng at the White House desirous of seeing the President, and, according to his own story, he actually pushed into the room where Garfield was conferring with Levi Morton and a number of other men. He left a copy of his speech. During the weeks that followed, Guiteau, always short of money and frequently unable to pay his bills, boarded at a number of places while he sought the attention of the President and the secretary of state. Although he was frequently at the White House, he was never able to talk with Garfield. Sometimes he went into Joe's office; at other times he sat for an hour or two in a room opposite. He left a number of notes—neat, mild, courteous. Having concluded that the Viennese mission would not be vacated, he asked in a note to Garfield on March 8, "What do you think of me for Consul General at Paris?" On three occasions Brown told him to apply to the head of the State Department. About the middle of May, White House ushers were instructed that Guiteau "should be quietly kept away."[6]

At the State Department Guiteau was more fortunate in that he managed on a number of occasions to talk with Blaine, although he never received encouragement. At length the secretary's patience was exhausted; on May 14 he told Guiteau that there was "no prospect whatever" for him and asked him never to mention the matter again.[7]

"Charles Guiteau, Chicago" appears on the White House steward's list of those who called socially on April 26. Guiteau testified that he attended one of Mrs. Garfield's receptions and told her that he was one of the men who had elected her husband; he found her, he said, "quite chatty and companionable."[8]

An assiduous reader of newspapers, including such anti-Garfield papers as the *New York Herald* and the *National Republican* (Washington), Guiteau was dismayed as the drama of the Conkling-Garfield struggle unfolded within his party. On April 29 he wrote to Garfield "in the spirit of a peacemaker," asking whether it would not be well to withdraw Robertson's nomination, Conkling having "worked himself into a white heat of opposition." In his mind Guiteau was persuaded that the Republican party was the only bulwark against the renewal of civil war. The President (or "our President czar," as the *National Republican* called Garfield on May 9), whose policies seemed to be leading to the ruin of the party, was a danger to the united nation.[9]

At his trial Guiteau told how the idea of "removing" the President first came to his mind a few days after the resignation of Conkling and Platt on May 16. He had gone to bed one night "greatly depressed in mind and spirit" by the turn of events; soon an impression came to his mind "like a flash" that if the President were out of the way all would be well. The impression was still with him the next morning, and it stayed with him, working on him, grinding, pressing, for about two weeks. By the beginning of June he was convinced that the removal of the President was the will of God and that he was God's chosen instrument. He had made his last appeal to Garfield on May 23. "I have been trying to be your friend," he wrote. In this letter he attacked Blaine ("a wicked man") and declared that Garfield ought to demand his immediate resignation—otherwise the party and the President would come to grief. God's pressure, however, was already at work.

Perhaps the letter was Guiteau's last anguished effort to avert the awful responsibility that was being thrust upon him.[10]

On about June 6 Guiteau entered a store at the corner of Fifteenth and F streets—across from the Treasury—kept by John O'Meara, a dealer in guns, sporting goods, and cutlery. Pointing to the largest calibre revolver on display, he asked to examine it and did so carefully, inquiring about its accuracy. On June 8 he returned with money borrowed from an old acquaintance; for ten dollars he obtained a pen-knife, a revolver, and a box of cartridges. The revolver, known as the British Bull Dog, was a .44 calibre five-shooter; bone on the handle gave it a touch of elegance that pleased Guiteau—the gun would look well, he thought, when it was placed on display after the "removal" had been accomplished. The dealer loaded the pistol and told the new owner where he could practice firing it. Twice Guiteau went down Seventeenth Street to the Potomac flats to practice, discharging four rounds in all. On the first occasion a solitary black man, on the second two or three idlers, witnessed the grim rehearsal.[11]

Guiteau was now obsessed with his mission. He made a trip to the District jail, where he expected to be taken after the "removal," and, though it was not a visiting day, managed to slip into the warden's office for a quick look around. "I thought it was a very excellent jail," he commented later. "It is the best jail in America, I understand." The days passed as he read, revised his book on religion (a new edition would be in order after its author had achieved fame), and watched and waited for the right moment.

On Sunday, June 12, he went to the little Disciple church on Vermont Avenue, where the President had gone with the Boyntons. After the service was over and Garfield had left in his carriage, Guiteau went around the outside of the church to a window close to the Garfield pew to determine whether a shot through it would be possible. Although he insisted that he had not gone to the church to shoot the President, he admitted that it might have been a good opportunity. "I could not think of a more sacred place for removing him than while he was at his devotions."

On June 18, when President and Mrs. Garfield and their party arrived at the railroad depot to board a special train for Long Branch, Guiteau was there with his loaded revolver. Two days earlier he had prepared an Address to the American People in which he charged the President with "the basest ingratitude towards the Stalwarts" and with having wrecked, in his madness, "the once grand old Republican party." As for the President's death, he wrote, "This is not murder. It is a political necessity." Any plan Guiteau may have had of carrying out his mission in the depot that morning was abandoned when he saw

Mrs. Garfield on her husband's arm, "a thin, delicate, sickly lady."[12]

After ten days had passed during which he could only wait in the summer heat, Guiteau was once more a man on the edge of action. At four o'clock in the afternoon of Monday, June 27, Garfield returned to Washington, having left Crete to continue her convalescence at Long Branch. Guiteau was at the depot to watch the arrival of the special train bearing the President, the secretary of the navy and his family, the postmaster general, and Colonel Rockwell. He soon learned that the President expected to leave for an extended trip on Saturday. On Wednesday, as he sat in Lafayette Park in the early evening, revolver ready, he saw a carriage leave the White House with the President, Captain Henry, and Harry. It was "very warm," and when the carriage had not returned in half an hour, Guiteau "let the matter drop for that night."

On Friday afternoon he sat again in the park until he saw the President leave the White House and walk in the direction of Blaine's house on Fifteenth Street. Guiteau followed at a short distance on the opposite side of the street. Garfield entered the Blaine house, presented Mrs. Blaine with a bound copy of his inaugural address, and sat chatting with her for some time as he waited for her husband's return. Guiteau watched from the Wormley Hotel half a block away. Blaine arrived, and the President and the secretary soon emerged, arm in arm, "in the most delightful and cozy fellowship possible; just as hilarious as two young girls." Guiteau stood on the steps of the hotel until they had passed, then followed them through the park. He did not shoot; it was very hot and sultry, Guiteau was weary, and the President was not alone.[13]

On the morning of July 2 he was again at the depot. This time he must act or face a long wait for another occasion. He spoke to a cabman about driving him in the direction of the Congressional Cemetery (which was near the District jail), had his boots blacked, and entered the depot. He went into the water closet and inspected his revolver, then left a number of papers at the newsstand. Going outside, he walked around the depot for a few minutes. He noted the time—9:20—and entered the ladies' waiting room.[14]

The Rockwell carriage had reached the depot, and Rockwell had gone to the baggage stand. The boys were still outside; the cabinet officers and other members of the party had boarded the train or were on the platform. The President's carriage drove up at the B Street entrance. The President inquired of Police Officer Patrick Kearney, who was leaning against a lamppost, how much time they had. Kearney held out his watch: about ten minutes. The men in the carriage continued their conversation briefly, then descended, the President taking Blaine's arm as they started up the steps. Officer Kearney raised his hat and saluted them. Blaine moved slightly ahead as the President turned back, smiling, lifted his hat to Kearney, and passed into the ladies' waiting room.[15]

The President and the secretary moved across the room toward the door of the main waiting room. They had gone about two-thirds of the way when there was a loud report a few feet behind them, quickly followed by another. Blaine touched Garfield, as though to hurry him out of trouble that he did not relate to them. Almost at the same time Garfield threw up his hands, crying, "My God! What is that?" Guiteau, pistol in hand, passed Blaine on the right, heading toward the B Street exit. Blaine instinctively followed him a few feet, then quickly turned back. The President had sunk to the floor. Soon all was confusion. Sarah White, matron of the ladies' waiting room, cradled the President's head in her lap. Rockwell, still at the baggage stand, heard the "sharp explosions" and, immediately after, Blaine calling his name. Tossing his handbag and coat to Daniel Sprigg, he hastened to the Sixth Street entrance, toward which bystanders were pointing. Finding that Guiteau was already in custody, he went into the station through the B Street entrance and found the President lying on his back. Hal and Jim were there, Jim crying and Hal trying to be brave and helpful. Cabinet officials and others had rushed to the scene. Rockwell sent for doctors. The President began to vomit. A mattress was brought from a sleeping car and the wounded man carried up winding stairs to a large empty room.[16]

Guiteau had been seized just inside the depot by Officer Kearney, who had rushed to the B Street entrance when he heard the shots. Kearney took his prisoner in the direction of the Sixth Street door. The ticket agent made a dash at Guiteau, grabbing his neck and knocking his hat off. Another police officer came to Kearney's assistance, and the two officers succeeded in getting Guiteau outside, where he said, "I did it, and will go to jail for it. Arthur is President and I am a Stalwart." The officers walked Guiteau to the police headquarters on Four and a Half Street, where Kearney's statement that their prisoner had shot the President met with derision. It was only then that Kearney took the revolver out of Guiteau's pocket. In Guiteau's possession was a letter addressed "To the White House," dated July 2. "The President's death," it read in part, "was a sad necessity, but it will unite the Republican party and save the Republic. Life is a fleeting dream, and it matters little when one goes. A human life is of small value." Guiteau had also written a letter to be handed to General Sherman, notifying him of the shooting and asking him to call out the troops and take possession of the jail.[17]

In the depot there was excited activity. Dr. Smith Townshend, District health officer, was the first medical man to arrive. The President's coat and waistcoat were removed, stimulants given, and the patient examined. Dr. Willard Bliss, whom Garfield had known in rural Ohio, took command when he arrived at the depot fifteen or twenty minutes after the shooting. Other physicians gathered around the stricken man. The first bullet had grazed the right arm, the second had entered the body three and a half inches to the right of the spinal column, between the tenth and eleventh ribs. Dr. Bliss made two or three probes with instruments (one of them was Nélaton's probe, invented in France for the detection of bullets); he also probed with his finger. (The doctors never learned the location of the bullet until they made the postmortem examination.) Rockwell sent a guarded telegram to Swaim, who was with Mrs. Garfield in Long Branch. Garfield beckoned to Rockwell. "Jarvis, I think you had better telegraph to Crete." He then dictated a "very pathetic dispatch" that Rockwell signed and sent off. A little later the President made another suggestion. "I think you had better get me to the White House as soon as you can." Rockwell had already sent for the police ambulance.[18]

Down the winding stairs and through the depot, passing over the very spot where he had fallen, the President was carried to the waiting ambulance. Colonel Rockwell sat beside him, taking his hand and supporting his head. The vehicle clattered over the rough cobblestones near the depot, then reached the asphalt pavement of Pennsylvania Avenue. The galloping horses were followed by an excited crowd all the way to the White House.[19]

Joe Brown had risen to the emergency. When the first news came over the White House telegraph, he had refused to believe it; when the report was speedily confirmed, he ordered the gates closed, instructed Crump to have the President's bedroom made ready, asked the secretary of war for military aid, alerted the chief of police to the need for patrols, and handed out passes to reporters to assure a full and authentic report to the public.[20]

Soon the ambulance arrived at the rear door of the White House, "and this splendid man," Joe wrote years later, "abounding in health and the joy of living . . . was laid on a bed from which he was never to rise again." Mrs. Blaine and Mrs. MacVeagh were standing in the hall as a dozen men carried the President to his room. When he saw the ladies, he kissed his hand to them. A little later, in the bedroom, he begged Mrs. Blaine to stay with him until Crete came. "I took my old bonnet off and just stayed," she wrote the next day. "I never left him a moment. Whatever happened in that room, I never blenched, and the day will never pass from my memory."[21]

Brought to the city by special train, Crete arrived in the early evening, "frail, fatigued, desperate, but firm and quiet and full of purpose to save." Garfield, who had inquired about her frequently, asked that they be left alone for their meeting.[22]

The President lived for eighty days. Until the morning of September 6 he lay in the White House under the care of a number of doctors, not all of whom served throughout the period. Doctor Bliss remained in charge—ruining his own practice, he later claimed. Two eminent surgeons were brought in: David Hayes Agnew of Philadelphia and Frank Hastings Hamilton of New York City. The doctors whom Garfield knew best, Silas Boynton and Susan Edson, were relegated to the status of nurses, both of them being homeopathic physicians; Silas never ceased to be indignant at the treatment he received from his fellow doctors. Few besides the doctors and nurses, the family, Daniel Sprigg, Rockwell, and Swaim got into the sickroom; Rockwell and Swaim saw to that. The doctors issued regular bulletins, and the secretary of state kept the world informed.

As usual, Washington's summer was hot and long. Suggestions for the comfort of the patient poured in, and some success in reducing the temperature in the bedroom was achieved. While the doctors inside the White House debated, probed, and made incisions, prominent doctors outside studied the medical reports and took public issue with those in attendance on the President. Alexander Graham Bell was brought in to hunt for the bullet with electrical devices. At his trial Guiteau, while admitting that he had shot the President, held that his death had been caused by the newspapers and doctors. An Irish servant in the White House took matters into her own hands when she sprinkled holy water in the President's milk.[23]

The object of all the attention slowly and painfully wasted away, never lifting his head from his pillow. Rockwell could not "remember that he ever but once attempted to smile." He lay silently for the most part, though his mind was usually clear. Early in his ordeal he asked what people were saying about the shooting. Crete sometimes read to him from the messages that were pouring in and from the newspapers. He was pleased when he learned that Conkling had lost his bid for reelection to the Senate but said he was sorry for him. Sometimes he spoke of Ohio and of friends and relatives there; once he asked whether there had been rain recently in Mentor and about the prospect for crops. Toward the middle of August he wrote a brief letter to his mother and signed an official document. Day after weary day passed. "He was," Dr. Edson, who was with him more than anyone else, said, "a wonderfully patient sufferer." Like Guiteau, the President was a believer in the will of God.[24]

The summer of 1881 was above all else the summer of the President. The Fourth of July that year was unlike other Fourths; it was not a day of national celebration but one of sorrow and apprehension. It was said that the shooting down of Garfield had aroused deeper and more universal feeling than the assassination of Lincoln. Lincoln was a war casualty; his death came at the end of four years during which the people had grown accustomed to endless lists of the killed and wounded; the madness of Booth was part of the madness of war. The murder of Garfield came after fifteen years of peace, and the reasons for it were difficult to comprehend. The daily bulletins concerning the President's condition were read in every hamlet in America. Special days of prayer were proclaimed, and on Sundays prayers for his recovery were a matter of course in all churches. Queen Victoria achieved new stature in the United States by her continued solicitude. A few days after the shooting, Cyrus W. Field (at whose home Garfield had expected to spend the night of July 2), mindful of the shabby treatment accorded by Congress to Mrs. Lincoln, started a subscription for Mrs. Garfield and her children. More than $150,000 had been contributed before the President's death. Criticisms of Garfield as a political leader were stilled. Vice President Arthur called on Mrs. Garfield the day after the tragedy and came away from the meeting showing deep feeling, seemingly "overcome with the calamity." Roscoe Conkling called at the White House and sent messages of sympathy. In the eyes of the people the President was ennobled by his suffering; he had taken on the dimensions of an ideal man.[25]

After two months the doctors decided to move the President to the New Jersey shore, away from the terrible heat of the capital; the President himself longed for a change of scene. On September 5, 300 men worked through the night to lay more than a half mile of track from the Pennsylvania Railroad's line to Francklyn Cottage on the shore at Elberon, near Long Branch. At six o'clock in the morning Garfield was carried from the White House to an express wagon that conveyed him to a special train waiting at the Baltimore and Potomac depot. Early as it was, there were many people at the White House and along the way to the station. During the seven-hour trip of more than 200 miles, the train passed through many towns and villages; in all of them the people were waiting by the tracks. They stood silent, their hats off, some with bowed heads, some weeping, as the train pursued its course.[26]

For a few days after the arrival at Elberon the doctors were somewhat optimistic. Then there was a turn for the worse in their patient's condition. On September 16 the State Department's cable to James Russell Lowell, United States Minister to England, spoke of "a sensible increase of anxiety" concerning the President. The next day the minister learned that the situation was "probably more grave and critical" than it had ever been. On September 18 he was told of the "gravest apprehensions" excited by the President's condition.[27]

On September 19, the anniversary of the battle of Chickamauga, the wasted body surrendered. Swaim and Daniel Sprigg were alone with the President when he cried out in pain to the major and fell unconscious. Crete and others were quickly summoned. In a few minutes, at 10:35 P.M. death came.

It was after midnight when the cabinet officers who were in Elberon telegraphed Chester A. Arthur in New York, advising him to take without delay the oath of office as President of the United States.[28]

It was nearly a week before the funeral ceremonies were concluded. Crowds filed past the coffin in the rotunda of the Capitol, and services were held there, with the new President and former presidents Grant and Hayes in attendance. At the foot of the coffin was a large wreath from Queen Victoria. From the Capitol the coffin was borne by members of the Vermont Avenue Disciple church to the funeral train for the trip to Ohio. Multitudes lined the route on the long journey. In Cleveland the body lay in state in a grand pavilion built for the occasion in Monument Square. On Monday last rites were held. Dr. Robison presided, Isaac Errett preached the sermon. Then came the procession, four miles in length, to Lakeview Cemetery, where the body was placed in a vault. Captain Henry and Harry Rhodes were among the bearers. Vocal societies sang the Horatian ode, *Integer Vitae,* and Garfield's favorite hymn, *Ho, Reapers of Life's Harvest.* Harry Jones gave an address, and Burke Hinsdale offered a prayer. After the ceremonies had ended, Hal and Jim entered the vault with Colonel Rockwell and Colonel Corbin. Eliza and Crete waited in the carriage.[29]

A

SELECTION

OF LETTERS

OF

JAMES A. GARFIELD

The text of forty-four of the forty-five letters here presented is that of recipients' or letterpress copies. The text of the letter to Ulysses S. Grant is that of a careful, handwritten copy.

Forty-two of the letters are from manuscripts in the James A. Garfield Papers, Library of Congress. The two letters to Rutherford B. Hayes are from the recipient's copies in the Rutherford B. Hayes Library. The letter of 9 December 1869 to Whitelaw Reid is from the recipient's copy in the Whitelaw Reid Papers, Library of Congress.

In editing the letters some minor liberties have been taken in the interest of the reader. The form of the information as to date and place of writing has been standardized and the information itself expanded on occasion to include the name of a town, state, or district. Names and addresses of persons to whom the letters were written have been omitted, the relevant information appearing in the introductions. Some punctuation has been supplied, some superfluous commas and dashes omitted, and some dashes replaced by commas. Misspellings of all proper names and of a few other words occasioned by a slip of the pen have been corrected. Some abbreviations have been expanded.

*On March 6, 1849, Garfield (age 17), his cousin William Boynton, and his friend Orrin Judd made the short trip from Orange to Chester to enter Geauga Seminary, an academy maintained by Free Will Baptists. It was Garfield's first school away from home. After more than three weeks in Chester he made this report to his mother and brother Thomas. At the top of the letter he wrote "First Epistle of James." "Phonography" was a system of phonetic writing in shorthand introduced by an Englishman, Isaac Pitman, in 1837.*

[ 251 ]

Chester, Ohio
March 31, 1849

Dear Mother and Brother,

I improve the present opportunity to write you a few lines to inform you of my health etc. My health is first rate for me and I think it is improving rapidly. I like the school better every day and I think I am learning very fast and if nothing prevents I shall get a good insight into Philosophy and Algebra. I am studying Phonography—we have a school once a week. It is a great improvement in spelling and writing. Our studies and evening schools keep us very busy but we chop wood enough to exercise us sufficiently. I think that we are as well situated as we can wish to be. Nothing hinders us from learning if we wish to. Last night we were aroused by the shrill cry of fire, fire. We rushed down stairs and William seized a pail full of milk (not knowing that there was milk in it) and dipped it into the rain trough to get water to put out the fire, but it proved to be a false alarm. Some persons had seen a large smoke coming out of the little shop (where a couple of girls from Bainbridge live) and thought it was on fire. Our provisions holds out very well. We have got pork enough to last the whole term and flour enough to last a month longer. I have got $1.48 left and do not have to pay out much now. My bed broke down last week and I bought 75 feet of flax cord (for 3 p) and I guess it will hold me now. We chop wood Saturday afternoons for Prof. Branch and through the week chop our own and Mrs. Reeds. There are upwards of 100 students here from all parts of the country and all appear very friendly. I want you to send my Kirkham's Grammar, and if you can get those Phonographic books I wish you would. Send out my Cashmere pants some neck handkerchiefs and so forth and so forth. I remain yours

J. A. Garfield

P.S. Please send me an epistle.

*By the winter of 1852–53 Garfield had been romantically involved with Mary Hubbell for more than a year, and their friends (and her parents) expected them to marry. But Garfield decided that their romance must come to an end, and in this letter, with great care, he broke the news to Mary.*

Hiram, Ohio
February 27, 1853

Dear Mary:

Not having a convenient opportunity of conversing with you as I would like to have, I will write to you upon a subject which has long occupied my mind and upon which justice demands that I should speak frankly and fully. The relation which has subsisted between us has been, to me, of the most pleasing character. I have ever found in you the affectionate sister and faithful friend, both in sickness and health, joy and sorrow; and further, as you are aware, my intentions have been of a still more serious character; in short, though there has been no plighted faith, or verbal engagement between us, we have known the minds of each other as far as intimacy can reveal the feelings of another. You are the first and only woman to whom I ever sustained *such* a relation, and, as I told you about one year ago this time, I determined never to hold out any false hopes or assurances, or deceive by making any promises which coming years might not fulfill. I then spoke to you of my previous boyish affection, which had been fickle and ever-changing, and that I did not then dare to trust it upon a question of such momentous importance, for I did not know my own heart. With these considerations before me permit me to speak plainly and freely. In this matter I have not been guided entirely by fancy or *blinded* by affection. In the fear of God and with an eye to our future destiny and happiness, I have studied both our natures, dispositions and tastes. For this work it has needed not merely a casual glance—the acquaintance of a day—but earnest and careful observation. I have also reflected that my path has ever been, is now, and, perhaps, ever *will* be a rugged one, of poverty and toil. The result of all these reflections, over which I have spent many wakeful and prayerful hours, is that such a relation would not be conducive to our mutual welfare and happiness, and with this conclusion in my mind I should do you great injustice not frankly to tell you. I have confidence in you, that you will not regard me as having attempted to win, and then trifle with the affections of your heart; for, think not Mary, that it has been without a struggle that I have come to this conclusion; or that I have withdrawn my affections from you and placed them upon another, for such is not the case, for I can never cherish other than feelings of affection for you, and shall always be happy to enjoy your society, if agreeable to you, and be regarded as a friend and brother. Now Mary do not think that I have faults to find or charges to make, for I have not; and though that "unfortunate note" may have had some influence upon my mind, yet I do not cherish one unkind feeling toward you. I hope to have your mind upon this subject, as fully and plainly as I have given you mine. With the kindest regards I am ever your friend and brother,

J. A. Garfield

*In November 1853 Garfield made a brief holiday trip via Lake Erie to Buffalo and Niagara Falls. At Niagara Falls on November 16 he wrote his*

*first letter to Lucretia Rudolph. Lucretia responded on November 30, a few*
*days after she had received his letter, and enclosed her translation of an ode*
*of Anacreon that she had promised him. On December 8 Garfield wrote in*
*his diary, "I am writing a letter to one of my lady friends. I very seldom do*
*so. I know not the upshot of it. But I will venture at this place to write the*
*word Epoch."*

Hiram, Ohio
December 8, 1853

Much respected sister:

Many thanks to you for your kind and very welcome letter, which
was received last Monday morning. I well understand your feelings in
reference to your school, that your whole being is absorbed in the work
of moulding and giving direction to the plastic minds of the youth
placed under your care. To know that we are handling the delicate machinery of mind, and impressing thoughts and principles that shall
remain forever, must necessarily impress us with a sense of great responsibility. I think every person should teach, at least one school, to
obtain true views of humanity and human life.

I have never read Carlyle's work, but have heard it spoken well of,
and very much desire to read it. I am fully satisfied that text books
alone will not make the mind rich and over-flowing with that fulness of
thought that every one desires, and I know that for my part I am very
deficient in general knowledge. I am however trying to do something
this winter. I am now reading Macaulay's *History of England* and some
miscellanies. I have a book called *The Heroines of History,* which I like
very much, so far as I have read it. Also a book called *Hurry Graphs* by
N. P. Willis, in which there are some fine things. Have you ever read
them? There is great beauty in his writings, but it is said that his personal character is rather exceptionable. Should we allow that consideration to influence us in reading an author?

I spent the forenoon of the day after I wrote you in wandering
through the beautiful islands above the falls, writing, pondering and
admiring. I have no words to describe the emotions inspired by that
awfully sublime scene. To see the majestic Niagara, two miles in width,
with its surface placid and smooth as polished silver, first become
gently ruffled, and then the sloping channel stirs its crystal depths, and
maddens all its waters. An embattled host of billows come leaping down
the opposing rocks of the rapids until they reach the awful brink where
all surcharged with frantic fury, leap bellowing down the rocky steeps
which thunder back the sullen echoes of their roar, and shout God's
praises above the cloudy skies. O that the assembled millions of the
earth could once behold that scene sublime and awful, and learn to

adore the Everlasting God, whose finger piled those giant cliffs, and sent his sounding seas to thunder down, and shout in deafening tones; We come from out the hollow of His hand, and haste to do his bidding. I loved to be alone, but still I wished all my friends were by my side to gaze with me upon that scene. I must sometime see it again—if I live.

That afternoon I took the cars for Buffalo, and at 4 o'clock P.M. was seated in the splendid cabin of the Steamer *Ohio,* bound for Cleveland. A cloudy night succeded, and I contented myself with visiting the boat and its inmates. I went into the hold, where were 40 or 50 Irish and German emigrants. I made some of their acquaintances, listened to the songs and stories of their dear *"Father Land,"* then viewed the complicated machinery of the powerful engine, and then walked talked and discussed with the passengers in the cabin. Among these were a Canadian editor, and a young Catholic who is educating himself for a priest. With these I spent much time in discussing the comparative merits of England and America, and of Protestantism and Catholicism. We were, on account of head winds etc., all that night, the next day, and next night till nearly midnight upon the lake.

The last evening just as we were leaving Fairport, and as Virgil says *"urbesque terraeque recedebunt,"* the virgin moon rose in a clear sky. I stood upon the hurricane deck alone. Her blush paved the lake with silver, and she looked down upon her own bright face mirrored in its crystal depths. Then I gazed far back towards the receding city, and beheld the swirling waves of the steamer's wake, sparkling in the moonbeams like diamond gems, and then a slight breeze arose, which rippled gently the bosom of the Lake that glittered then with drops of gold and pearl. You ask me "if any of my youthful conceptions of a home on the billows were realized?" I will not trouble you with that long, strange story of my early youth, but only say, for years my soul longed for a home upon the deep blue sea, and even yet, when higher aims and objects fill my heart, I love the ocean with its foaming waves; and let me often from the cares of life retire, and listen to its deep-toned music, and gaze upon its crested waters.

The latter part of that night I spent at the Forest City House, where lingered the recollections of a former visit—and the next evening I was in Hiram.

The school is going on quite pleasantly, though among the 240 that are here we have some unruly ones. Today the Virgil class finished the third book and are going about 50 lines per day. Are you ahead? I presume so. Won't you come into both Greek and Latin in the spring? We miss you very much in those two classes. What are your views now with regards to studying the classics? Have you reconciled yourself to giving a few years more to them? I would like to hear your reasonings on the subject. I would much rather converse *"ore quam calamo"* but it seems that our leisure hours do not synchronize, and will you therefore excuse me for inflicting so long a letter upon you?

I should be much pleased to receive another bundle of thoughts from you, if you deem it worth your time to send them. I thank you for redeeming your Anacreontic pledge which I had by no means forgotten.

Have you concluded to keep closed doors, or to admit spectators to your schools, your winter's empire? I have some interest in the decision.

Hoping that you will overlook these many imperfections, and pardon them, I am

> Truly and sincerely
> Your Brother
> James

*At the end of his first year (his junior year) at Williams College Garfield looked forward to his first trip back to Ohio. He had been elected to the editorial board of the* Williams Quarterly *in the spring.*

> Williams College, Massachusetts
> July 22, 1855

My Dear Mother,

I have not heard a word from you for a long time and I will sit down and write a little though I can hardly sit up. I have been afflicted for several weeks with boils and now I have one on the back of my neck on the large cord. When it throbs it makes me so dizzy I can hardly see. But I think it will be better by tomorrow morning. I am coming home soon to have you cure me up and cleanse my blood which I suppose is out of order. I have not yet had time to get that dock that you spoke of so I guess I will wait till I see you and then I will have you go out with me when I dig it.

Bro. Wilber starts for home tomorrow morning, but I have the first number of the *Williams Quarterly* to publish and cannot leave until after Commencement. Charles is about tired out and thinks he must go now. Perhaps you will see him before I come. I will try to have him visit you shortly after he returns home. I expect to see you four weeks from tomorrow.

Is Thomas coming home then? I haven't heard from him for nearly two months. I shall write again and see what he is calculating to do about coming home. I want him to come very much. I have a great deal to do this term besides my regular College studies. I have had to prepare for an exhibition which came off last Wednesday evening. (I send you a card and programme.) I have the principal labor of the *Quarterly* and in Bro. Streator's absence go to Poestenkill once in two weeks. Next Lord's day I go there again. I received an invitation from a Baptist church (Close Communion) to preach to them next Sunday afternoon and I am going to do so. They have never heard a Disciple, and though their preacher has an appointment at that time they said he would give way if I would come. Their church is on a mountain about five miles from Poestenkill. I hope to break the ice among them so that our brethren may get a foothold among them. They are very kind to me at Poestenkill and there are many noble hearts among them. Sister Learned was very thankful to you for that poem you sent. Where did you find it? It is very beautiful. I have had it published.

Give my love to Mary and Hitty and all our folks. I have at last received a letter from Harriet for which I was very thankful.

Now mother write to me soon and tell me how you are in health and spirits.

As ever your
Son Jag

*As a result of the efforts of Ohio friends Garfield was promoted to brigadier general; the commission, dated February 20, 1862, was retroactive to January 10, the date of the battle of Middle Creek. The great battle referred to in this letter was Shiloh, fought on April 6–7. The number killed, wounded, and missing on both sides was more than 24,000.*

Headquarters, 20th Brigade
Army of the Ohio
Battlefield 25 miles from
Corinth, Mississippi
April 11, 1862

My Dear Sister Mary,

I should have answered your good letter a long time ago, but I was so much hurried about the time it was received that I could not write. On Sunday the 16th of March I fought the Battle at Pound Gap, and on my return to Piketon found an order commanding me to go with some of my regiments to Louisville, Ky. I left as soon as I could, passed through Cincinnati on the second day of April, reached Louisville the same night, where I found an order to leave my regiments there and go immediately to Nashville to join Gen. Buell. I started next morning, reached Nashville that night, but found that Gen. Buell had gone on toward the enemy with a large army. I hurried on, rode one whole night on horseback, and reached him on Thursday the 4th. He at once put me in command of 4,000 men and we hurried on. After marching all day Sunday, we got orders to leave behind all our baggage and hurry through as rapidly as possible. We marched all night Sunday night. All day and night we could hear the cannon roaring ahead. Monday noon we reached the river and went directly on board steamers which took us up to the battle which had been raging with great fury for two days. I marched my men to the front, just in time to see the close of the greatest battle ever fought on this continent. The battlefield is six miles long and six miles wide. I can never begin to describe the horrors I have witnessed. Hun[dreds] and even thousands of dead were lying around, and a great many thousands were wounded. The cannon balls fell thick around me, but I was mercifully spared. The next day I chased the enemy five miles. Our force engaged their cavalry, the Texan Rangers, and finally drove them, but even in that little fight we lost 20 killed and 40 wounded. I have slept on the ground, in the rain without tents, for nearly a week, but my health is very good. We shall have a great deal more fighting here yet for there is a large army yet before us. Give my love to Mother and all our folks. Write to me soon and often. In order to insure that the letters shall reach [me] they must be directed to "Brig. Gen. J. A. Garfield, 6th Division, Army of the Ohio, near Savannah, Tenn."

Ever your brother<br>James

*This letter was addressed to Mark Hopkins (1802–1887), a Congregational clergyman associated with Williams College for more than a half a century and its president from 1836 to 1872. Garfield was strongly attracted to Hopkins as man and teacher and remained a devoted friend. At an alumni banquet in 1871, Garfield made the remark that in time became the familiar quotation, "The ideal college is Mark Hopkins on one end of a log and a student on the other." The book by Hopkins referred to in the letter is Lectures on Moral Science (1862).*

Washington, D.C.<br>December 12, 1863

My Dear Sir,

On my return to this place one week ago, I found your very kind letter of Nov. 8th awaiting me. I am sure you do not know how great a gratification it is to me to know that I am kindly remembered by you, whom I so much reverence, and to whom I am under so many obligations. It heightens my regard to know that what you did for me you are daily doing for others. I know of no prouder place in the world of work and duty than that which is worthily filled in leading young men to a higher and truer life. I bought your work on moral philosophy last winter and read it in camp. Added to its truths were the happy memories of college life, and your discussions of the same themes. I am anxious to know how it has been received by the theologians and scholars of the day.

God has been very merciful to me in the strange, sad work of the last two years and a half, and I have many times been made to feel, when others have fallen beside me, and I was spared, that His claims to my love and service grew stronger than ever before. He has also laid his chastening hand upon me. Ten days ago I buried my only daughter, a sweet little girl of three and a half. It has made the world look very desolate to me. I pray that it may draw me nearer to our Father.

I have resigned my place in the army, and have taken the seat in Congress. I did this with regret, for I had hoped not to leave the field till every insurgent state had returned to its allegiance. But the President told me he dared not risk a single vote in the House, and he needed some men in the Congress who were practically acquainted with the wants of the army. I did not feel it right to consult my own preference in such a case. Should the war continue I may return to the field in the spring. The late successes at Chattanooga and Knoxville give solid promise for our future. I have met your sons Harry and Archie. They are spoken of here and in the army as you would wish them to be. I hope you will ask them for me to visit me whenever they can.

Will you please send me the last Triennial Catalogue? I remember Lawrence well. Present me kindly to him, and to the rest of your family. You have certainly furnished your quota to the army. With the most cordial regards I am

Very Truly Yours<br>J. A. Garfield

*William Cooper Howells (1807–1894), to whom this letter is addressed, was proprietor and editor of the* Ashtabula Sentinel *in Jefferson, Ashtabula County (in Garfield's congressional district). Howells and his wife, Mary Dean Howells, were the parents of eight children, one of whom was William Dean Howells (1837–1920). Garfield was on friendly terms with the family; there are several hundred letters in the Garfield Papers written by Garfield to members of the Howells family or by members of the family to him. When this letter was written Garfield was a member of the House Committee on Military Affairs. The so-called Fort Pillow Massacre was an engagement at*

*Fort Pillow, Tennessee, on April 12, 1864, in which Confederate cavalry almost wiped out the Union garrison, which had included black soldiers.*

Washington, D.C.
June 18, 1864

Dear Sir,

I was greatly surprised this morning on receiving the *Sentinel* of June 8th to see in it an editorial note stating that my course in reference to the pay of Negro troops was not approved by the people of the District.

I regret that you did not write to me in regard to the matter. I shall always with pleasure receive any suggestions or criticisms you may make in reference to my action as a public officer, and I feel quite sure that you would not have published the note referred to, if you had known what my course was in the case.

Allow me to state the case. We have been very much troubled in the Military Committee (which is composed of five Union men and four Democrats) from the fact that Frank Blair—nominally a Union man—was opposed to equalizing the pay of colored and white soldiers. This made a majority against us, and the Committee was not able to report such a bill as we who were the more radical men desired, till Blair left, which was about the close of April.

A majority of the Committee was in favor of a sliding scale paying the Negro soldiers $10 for the first six months, $12 for the next six, and equal pay with the white soldiers after one year's service. I was in favor of placing them on an equality at once. The Fort Pillow massacre created a strong feeling in favor of immediate equality, and on the 2d of May the Committee reported back a Senate bill to that effect.

In the mean time however the Senate had appended the main provisions of its original bill for pay of Negro troops as an amendment to the Army Appropriation Bill, which the House had passed several weeks before. The House discussed the Senate amendments, and amended them so as to make them still more favorable to the Negro. I voted for all these favorable changes, as you can see by examining the several lists of ayes and noes recorded in the *Globe* of May 3d. The bill was then submitted to a Committee of Conference of the Senate and House, and on the 25th of May that Committee reported the result of its labor, which was that the pay and emoluments of all soldiers should be the same without regard to color after the 1st day of Jan. 1864, and those colored regiments in the North enlisted prior to the 1st of Jan. who had been promised equal pay by the War Department should have it also. I was satisfied with the report as the best we could get, and in view of the great embarrassments of the Treasury, I thought probably as far as we ought to go, though I had in the first place voted to extend the increase of pay back to the date of enlistment in every case, without regard to existing law. Twenty-five of our best and most radical men voted with me to agree to the report. Every Copperhead in the House voted against it, in hopes thereby to embarrass and defeat the bill. A large number of our good men also voted against it, in hopes of reaching further back than Jan. 1st. I told them all the time we should never get it in so good a shape again, and the event has proved I was right. Five days ago (June 13th) another Conference report was made, and finally adopted, leaving the whole question of increase of pay of the negro, prior to Jan 1st 1864, to the decision of the Attorney General, who may be changed any day. The radical men—of whom I have always been counted one—do not feel as well satisfied with the law as it now stands, as they did with the shape it was in when I voted to agree. That was the only vote on the subject in which I am recorded against the majority of our party. If I have not been prominent in the discussion of that question, it has been for the twofold reason that we did not need discussion on so plain a proposition—but votes rather—and that I was completely overwhelmed with my work on the Military and Treasury investigating Committee. Such are the facts in the case. In addition to this history, let me say, I have never been anything else than radical on all these questions of Freedom and Slavery, rebellion and the War. I have had neither inclination or motive to be otherwise. I only desire to use a wide discretion and not lose a practical good for a remote possibility of something better. I feel very sure that our people would not disapprove my course in this matter if they knew what it had been. Indeed I have gone much further than most of our party in voting to give the rights of suffrage to colored people in the Territory of Montana.

I should have answered your letter in reference to Gen. Buckland before now, but I have waited to hear from the War Department as to the action it will take in the case. The papers were forwarded to the Secretary of War.

With kindest regards I am

Very truly yours
J. A. Garfield

*The amendment to which Garfield refers in this letter to Burke Hinsdale is the Fourteenth (the civil rights amendment). Proposed by Congress in June 1866, it had not yet been ratified by three-fourths of the states; nonratifiers included ten former Confederate states. In March 1867 Congress made ratification by these southern states a condition for the readmission of their representatives to Congress. The decision of the Supreme Court is that in the celebrated case,* ex parte Milligan. *It was Garfield's first law case; the Court's decision was much criticized in the North, and Garfield himself did not escape criticism for representing a Confederate sympathizer. Mrs. Garfield was known among a small group of friends as the Lady Kensington.*

Washington, D.C.
January 1, 1867

Dear Burke,

For the purpose of acknowledging yours of the 21st inst., but still more for the purpose of keeping up our old custom of remembering each other on each New Year's day, I write now. I am now nearly recovered from the very serious attack of influenza, which kept me confined to the house ten days, and to the bed three. I am less satisfied with the present aspect of public affairs than I have been for a long time. I find that many of the points and doctrines, both in general politics and finance, which I believe in, and desire to see prevail, are meeting with more opposition than heretofore, and are in imminent danger of being overborne by public clamor and political passion.

In reference to reconstruction, I feel that if the southern states should adopt the Constitutional Amendment within a reasonable time, we are morally bound to admit them to representation. If they reject it then I am in favor of striking for impartial suffrage, though I see that such a course is beset with grave dangers. Now Congress seems determined to rush forward without waiting even for the action of the northern states—thus giving the south the impression, and our political enemies at home a pretext for saying that we were not in good faith when we offered the Constitutional Amendment. If we could succeed in an impeachment of the President it would be a blessing—probably—but it is perfectly evident that with the Senate constituted as it is we cannot effect an impeachment. Still Ashley and such like impracticable men are determined to push the insane scheme of making the attempt, and setting the country in a ferment. Generally there seems to be a fear on the part of many of our friends that they must do some absurdly extravagant thing to prove their radicalism. I am trying to do two things, viz. be a radical and not a fool, which if I am to judge by the exhibitions around me is a matter of no small difficulty. I wish the south would adopt the Constitutional Amendment soon, and in good temper. Perhaps they will.

Next, the Supreme Court has decided the case I argued last winter, and the papers [are] insanely calling for the abolition of the court. In reference to finance—I believe that the great remedy for our ills is an early return to specie payments, which can only be effected by contraction of our paper currency. There is a huge clamor from all quarters, against both, and in favor of expansion. You know my views on the Tariff. I am equally assailed by the Free Traders and the extreme tariff men. There is passion enough in the country to run a steam engine in every village, and a spirit of proscription which keeps pace with the passion. My own course is chosen, and it is quite probable it will throw me out of public life. Now on rereading what I have written, I fear I have exhibited more atrabiliousness than you suggest you did. I find, however, underlying all my apprehension, a stratum of faith, which makes me hope we shall come out right. I am a careful reader of the *Christian Standard*, and am ready to say that if our people [Disciples] don't want it, [it] is because they are unworthy of a great paper. I still think however—If the general news Department was enlarged it would make the paper more popular.

My love for Latin and Greek, and the history of antiquity, is growing every day. I have stolen many hours since I have been here and given them to Cicero and Horace. I am also trying to study French— but I presume I shall be cut short when Congress gets to work. I am reading up the history of the rise and fall of the United States Bank— in order to meet and resist a strong purpose among many members of Congress to abolish the National Bank System, and have the Government issue Greenbacks instead. I wish I could see you. It was a very great disappointment to me not to have seen you more before I left home. Kensington and the little ones are well. She desires to be kindly remembered to Mary and husband. Let me hear from you as often as the spirit moves, and tell me what you read.

Ever yours
J. A. Garfield

*Lyman W. Hall and his son Halsey R. W. Hall, of Ravenna, who owned and edited the* Portage County Democrat *(a Republican paper whose name was later changed), were friends and supporters of Garfield. This letter was addressed to Lyman.*

*On February 22, 1868, the House of Representatives, controlled by the Radical Republicans, voted to impeach President Andrew Johnson, with whom the Radicals had long been at loggerheads. Early in March the House adopted eleven articles of impeachment. The trial began in the Senate on March 13 with Chief Justice Salmon P. Chase presiding. On May 16 a vote was taken on the eleventh article, the "omnibus article." Thirty-five senators voted against Johnson and nineteen voted for him; the President's foes were*

*one vote short of the two-thirds necessary for conviction. It was nearly two*
*weeks before votes were taken on two other articles, with the same results.*
*The trial then ended.*

*Benjamin F. Wade, a powerful senator from Ohio, was president of the*
*Senate. Had President Johnson been removed from office, Wade would have*
*succeeded him. Garfield intimates that the prospect of Ben Wade's becoming*
*President of the United States influenced some senators to support Johnson.*

Washington, D.C.
May 20, 1868

My Dear Friend,

I have been so stunned by the events of the past few days, that I
have not felt like writing to any one. By unparalle[le]d treachery, we
have lost the 11th Article of Impeachment and probably all the others
will fail; still I do not abandon all hope that the 2nd may yet carry. I
have never felt like suspecting my fellow men of venality, but I hardly
see how the conviction can be resisted that some corruption has attended this result. Of course I do not believe that any pecuniary consideration could have influenced such men as Fessenden or Trumbull.
But I have no doubt that personal dislike of Mr. Wade had more power
over them than they are aware of. I presume you have seen in me a
great unwillingness to take out of my heart any man who has ever
found a warm place in it. It is like shedding my blood, to pull down
from his place any old friend. You know how I have defended and
maintained my friendship for Mr. Chase, even to my own hurt, so
many years. Now, I am compelled to the conclusion that Impeachment
has failed more by his work than that of any other living man. He has
taken doubtful senators to his home and thrown upon them the whole
weight of his official and personal influence, against the conviction of
Johnson. For my own part, I have never felt at liberty, even in the
privacy of strict confidence, to urge any senator one way or the other. I
have never spoken to any senator on the question how he ought to or
should vote. If it was improper for me to do so, much more was it improper for him, who had no vote, and in that sense was not a member
of the court, to take any part in determining the action of senators. Mr.
Chase is desperately determined to be somebody's candidate for President, and I have no doubt he is now working for the nomination by the
Democracy in July next—or if that should fail, I think he will try to organize a third party. Such conduct from the Chief Justice of the U.S.
needs no comment from me. It requires some effort to preserve from
destruction one's faith in human nature.

I am glad to tell you, that the speech I made on the 15th inst. was
received here with more attention, and seems to have made a deeper

impression than any other I have made in Congress. I do not expect the District papers can publish more than the leading points of it; but I will be glad if they will copy some of the notices of it which are appearing in the leading papers. I am aware that the positions I have taken will meet with much opposition in some parts of the West, but I am glad to see that there is a strong reaction setting in against inflation and I have no doubt that in the long run, the views which I hold will ultimately prevail. It will be observed that I do not advocate any contraction of the present volume of the currency—but only that Congress adopt a settled policy and give the business of the country a settled and fixed basis.

In reference to the nomination, I hear good reports from all parts of the District. Howells writes me that his paper will be on my side whenever it is necessary to speak, and he thinks Cadwell cannot get a majority of his own county. In Warren, I have more enemies than in any other town in the District. They are bitter and active, but my friends there think the town will be carried for me. I rely upon the judgment of yourself and Halsey more than upon all others, as to the prospect in the northern half of the District. Remember me kindly to him and be sure that your letters and his are always welcome. My family are with me and send kind regards.

Very Truly Your Friend<br>J. A. Garfield

*Whitelaw Reid (1837–1912) of Ohio, an experienced journalist, joined the staff of Horace Greeley's* New York Tribune *and during the Civil War worked in Washington as a reporter and as librarian of the House of Representatives. After Greeley's death in 1872, Reid won the struggle for succession and remained in control of the paper until his death. Under his editorship the* Tribune *was a powerful aid to Garfield in the election of 1880 and during the months of his presidency, and Reid became a confidential adviser of Garfield on New York politics.*

Washington, D.C.<br>December 9, 1868

My Dear Reid,

I express to you my regret last evening that a previous engagement would prevent me from hearing Mr. Greeley on the woman question, and from what I have heard today of the lecture itself I am led to regret it still more. I intended to call on him today; but have just learned that he left for N.Y. this morning.

I am surprised in the first place that he has awakened so much en-

thusiasm on a subject so nearly hackneyed, and I am specially delighted
to hear that he fully exposed the absurdity of the claim set up by Mrs.
Stanton and her followers, that woman should have all the rights of
man, and still enjoy all the exemptions which a chivalric regard for her
physical inferiority has so long conceded to her. I can hardly tell you
how repulsive to my feelings are the leading features of the Woman's
Rights movement; but there are two pages and a half of the chapter on
Suffrage in John Stuart Mill's book on *Representative Government* which
stagger me more than any thing else I have read. The substance of the
argument is that the ballot is given to a human being, not so much that
he may govern others, as that he may not be misgoverned by others;
that it is a great help to a person to possess what other people very
much want, but what he can give or not as he pleases, and that the
ballot is such a possession; that it is a weapon of defense, and that
women being physically weaker than men, need it even more than they,
and finally that women's influence on politics is now powerful but irre-
sponsible, and of the worst character, and that the ballot would make it
open, direct and responsible. Were I intimate with Mr. Greeley I
should ask him to tell me what he thinks of that chapter of Mill. If you
have an opportunity please draw him out on these points, and tell me
what he says. I am very anxious to be right on all these themes, and not
to follow the lead of my prejudices. I regret that I could not see more
of you while you were here. Don't let the *Tribune* deprive me of a
delightful correspondent. I hope to hear from you often.

As ever your friend
J. A. Garfield

*In 1868, through the efforts of Samuel Chapman Armstrong, who had com-
manded a black regiment during the Civil War and afterward been associated with the Freedmen's Bureau, a school for the training of blacks was
opened in Hampton, Virginia, that in 1870 was chartered as the Hampton
Normal and Agricultural Institute. Chapman was the guiding force in the
institution for nearly a quarter of a century. Garfield was a member of the
school's board of trustees from 1870 to 1875.*

Hiram, Ohio
September 27, 1870

My Dear General,

I have just reached home for a few hours after an absence on the
stump of nearly two weeks, and find yours of the 13th inst. awaiting
me. I am sorry not to have seen it sooner. I have read your paper with
great pleasure. It is good, strong and sensible. I have only two sugges-

tions to make for your consideration and I presume we do not greatly differ on them, if we do at all:

1st.   I would not, were I in your place, commit myself absolutely to the policy of manual labor schools as a principle of general application, for the reason that hitherto all such experiments have finally failed—and for the stronger reason that very much manual labor is inconsistent with a very high degree of mental culture. If you have not already seen it please read Eliot's paper in the *Atlantic Monthly* for February 1869, particularly the first half of page 217—where he discusses this topic. This and one other article on the same subject made him President of Harvard. While I endorse this view as a general principle, I fully and cordially support the labor feature of your school as the proper course at least for the present. I defend it on the ground of the peculiar and exceptional situation in which we now find the colored race of the South. The question is how best to lead them up from the plane of mere drudgery to one of some culture and finally of high culture. We must take them where they are and the labor system is a most excellent bridge to carry them over the intermediate or transition period. Again their pecuniary necessities require it. But I apprehend that you will find that the labor feature [will] be less and less needed as the race rises in the scale of culture, and that by and by they will require a course much nearer the ordinary college than they now do. I suggest then that in your address you throw an anchor to windward, and plant your defense of the labor feature more on the special situation of the race than on general principles, and that we do not so commit ourselves to the doctrine that we may hereafter be required to retract and apologize.

2nd.  Your views of the classics as part of the Hampton course are sound and wise, and it occurs to me that it might be added that where a student was found to possess special aptitude for the high culture of the classics, it might be well to hold out to him the prospect of admission to the Howard University, rather than to incur the expense of providing at Hampton for so small a number as would be likely to want that course. If all the normal schools of the south would thus become feeders of the University, it would be more economical and probably result in a higher culture to those who are really fit for it.

To secure both the objects we suggested would need but a few paragraphs added to your admirable address. But I beg you not to

allow yourself to be annoyed by these suggestions. I only make them to
let your own mind do with them what it pleases.

. . . I hope nothing will prevent my being present at the meeting of
the Board on the 10th October. How long will we be kept?

Mrs. G. joins me in kindest regards to you and yours.

Very Truly Yours
J. A. Garfield

*This letter was written in response to a letter from James Harrison
("Harry") Rhodes, Garfield's old Eclectic friend, now thirty-four, married,
and living in Cleveland. Rhodes had written: "You have outgrown the
necessity of such love of mine as once seemed so necessary to you. This is all
natural and healthy and I do not speak of it in any complaining spirit. I
know that you are stronger for having risen from the life of feeling and sentiment to the life of manly thinking over the great problems of the state. It
would have been very pleasant for me to have been more fully your companion du voyage of your later years in your intellectual advances." Rhodes
said he often felt that the place he had once held in Garfield's thoughts had
been usurped.*

Washington, D.C.
January 5, 1871

My Dear Harry,

I have been in bed most of the time for three days and have had the
Doctor three times. I have been seriously threatened with some sort of
fever; but I am better now, and shall try to go to the capitol at noon,
though I feel weak and miserable. Before I start however, I must answer your most welcome letter of New Year's eve. I therefore devote to
you the first fruit of my pen for 1871. Your letter had led me back
through our past and has made me feel like a delighted child revisiting
the home of his love and early life. All your views of our long life
together, that leads you to love and cherish it, find the strongest and
most loving response in my heart. And here let me declare it, and put it
on record to remain while I shall live, that I no longer look to the future for a life of love, or of loving friendships. The conditions of my
present life are so mingled with temporalities and matters of policy and
prudence that I cannot put new acquaintances even in the old niches
made vacant by the death of some friend of other days. For the highest
and purest friendship I do not look nearer to this time than the 42nd
regiment. That file of soldiers stands guard on the frontier limits of my
enchanted land. From their picket line the camp of my love extends
back to Orange, and my earliest childhood, and the Head Quarters of

it all is the Hiram of the past. Within that camp no party rancor, no dangerous knowledge of the baseness of mankind, no commercial motives, not even the struggle for bread entered as a controlling motive, or threw the shadow of doubt over the sincerity of any friendship, or the purity of any love. I tell you with all the emphasis I can use, that it is only within the above limits that I feel safe and perfectly happy in my friendships. I have never been deceived by one of the dwellers in that camp who had ever exchanged confidences with me. The rank that you hold on the roster of that old army, you know well, and there has never been a moment when you were either displaced, or when any other of woman born had the least chance of taking your place. I should be most false to my own heart, to my intellectual life and to the whole order and harmony of the world to which you and I belong were I to tolerate or desire any change. What book did I ever read during nearly ten years whose pages are not filled with memories of that sacred few who shared all such joys in common? A hundred passages throng my mind as I write, among others this:

> The tide flows down, the wave again
> Is vocal in its wooded walls;
> My deeper sorrow also falls,
> And I can speak a little then.

Don't you remember that when you and I were taking in the fresh beauties of *In Memoriam,* and commiting to memory the stanzas in which the above passage occurs, that we stopped our horse and buggy on the old bridge across the dam above the Cuyahoga Rapids, and looked up the stream and saw from the tall trees on either side, what Tennyson meant by "wooded walls"? And can it be that more than ten years have laid their weight upon us since then? When I shut my eyes and think, I can feel no consciousness of having grown older. It is only when I look about me, when I see the romping children that call me father, and strangers who call me names alien to our world of which I have written, it is only then that I feel and in grief realize that I am no longer a boy. You speak kindly of my successes, and it would [be] pretense in me not to confess that they are gratifying to my own feelings. But I speak with deliberation, when I say that I care more for causes than for results. In public life, results are mingled with so many strange and accidental elements that we seldom know whether success springs from worthy causes or from base ones. The life that you and I lived in Hiram was full of causes of the roots of things, of the forces out of which results are made, and I look upon those days of causes, those primal blows which we struck in the quarry, as revealing more truely the quality of our minds and hearts than the successes of later life.

I lament that so much of my present life must be given up to the gross questions of office and the endless wants of a great grasping crowd—but it seems to be the inevitable condition of things. Yet as you say of the law, there are resulting compensations. When the day (and here a large part of the night) is done, it is every year more sweet to lose myself in the sweet circle which has gathered round my hearthstone. All the other successes of my life, united, are not equal to that one, which gave me such peace after long years of groping in the darkness, and after the agonies which seem now only the vague memories of some horrible dream. The triumph of love could not be more complete. There is not a day when I do [not] inly fear such completeness will not be allowed to last long on this earth. Of all this, the world in which I now live knows nothing. It is all of that golden past, golden I say, though it was like the *ramus aureus* of Virgil, plucked from the confines of hell. I am rejoiced that you are finding the peace and joy that home gives, and that the centrifugal forces of your life are checked and orbed into the sphere of domestic love. There is safety—there is rest—as well as inspiration. We both know it with rejoicing—"Deep answereth unto deep." All our hearts in this circle respond to all in yours, and wish you the happiest of all the new years—and whenever business and the husks of things fill my letters remember that they do not fill my heart.

Ever as Ever Yours<br>
J. A. Garfield

*In 1872 many Republicans, thoroughly disenchanted with the Grant administration, joined in a movement to prevent the re-election of the President. Early in May dissidents met in Cincinnati to draw up a platform for the Liberal Republican party and to nominate candidates. To the consternation of many of the liberal Republicans the convention nominated Horace Greeley for President. The Democrats reluctantly endorsed the Liberal Republican candidates. This letter was addressed to Lyman Hall, editor of a Portage County newspaper.*

Washington, D.C.<br>
April 6, 1872

My Dear Friend,

Your kind favor of the 4th inst. came to hand yesterday. The subject which you discuss is the very essence of our future politics, and has deeply engaged my interest for several months past. Personally I have kept aloof from all combinations, and have devoted myself unreservedly to the work of legislation.

A more than usual responsibility has been placed upon me, and I have tried to do the work faithfully and well and let others attend to intrigues and machinations. But I am made deeply solicitous for the future by the manifest tendency throughout the party to make our issues personal.

It seems to me we are rapidly reaching that period when the two great political parties must dissolve their present organization; must die from exactly opposite causes. The Democratic Party, because every substantial idea it has advanced for the last twelve years is now utterly and hopelessly dead. The Republican Party, because every substantial idea it has advanced has been completely realized. The career of one is likely to end by failure, the other by having finished its work. Both parties have still a great compact organization, but out of which the informing life has nearly departed.

I fear it is true that no party ever rises to any moral height above that which it had at its creation; but that, on the contrary, its tendency is downward; though I hope each new party, at its birth, rises a little above its predecessors, and thus I think there is a general tendency upward.

That which distresses me most in the present attitude of our party is the tendency to make everything about it personal; to make allegiance to a few individuals a proof of party fealty. If I were free to follow my own judgment, I should say that every consideration of national good requires a new candidate for the presidency.

I should be glad to be able once more to throw whatever strength I have in the canvass in support of some man before whose personal character, intellect and morality, I could unsandal my feet in real manly reverence. There is little prospect I can do so in the coming canvass. The thing that troubles me most is this; whether a break in our columns may not result in putting a man into the presidency chiefly by the aid of the Democratic Party with all its ugly traditions of hatred to the war and its results. Such a thing I cannot contemplate without the profoundest feelings of alarm. But I will not be a party to the raid which is now being made on every Republican who sees fit to attend the Cincinnati Convention, and do what he may to bring about a better state of things.

If the Democratic Party would in fact dissolve its organization, I should see hope in that movement at Cincinnati. But thus far, they hold the shell of their party intact. And though it is like a hollow dead tree, I fear there is enough strength in it to stand through the coming campaign and perhaps control the candidate of the Cincinnati Convention, should he be elected.

Your words of encouragement about my course and conduct are

always a help to me. I have been doing the best I could, but I fear I am overworking myself, and this last day of the week finds me exceedingly weary.

When I see the attempts being made to cut me off from the old district, and also the entanglements which surround the future, I feel very much like withdrawing from public life and entering upon my profession to see if I can not acquire a competency for myself and family. I am seriously discussing that question now, but as yet have reached no conclusion.

With kindest regards to Halsey and all your family and thanking you again for your kind letter, I am

As ever your Friend
J. A. Garfield


*The Williams College Commencement of 1872 was, as this letter to Burke Hinsdale indicates, of more than ordinary interest to Garfield.*

Washington, D.C.
June 30, 1872

Dear Burke,

I arrived here this morning and found yours of the 26th awaiting me.

After spending all day Monday on the law case in Cleveland, I took the train for Williamstown, which I reached in the evening. Staid through the examination and until Friday morning. The exercises were very solemn and impressive. The resignation of Dr. Hopkins was a noble act, and the final speech in which he delivered up the keys to his successor was one of the rarest grandeur and simplicity. His first paragraph was this:

> Why do I resign? *First.* That it may not be asked why I do not resign.
> *Second.* Because I believe in the law of averages and the average man of seventy is not able to bear the burdens of this Presidency, and though I can now bear it, and many of my friends think I should continue to bear it, I think it safer to test the law of averages.

Does not that strike you as very novel and sensible?

I spoke for the Alumni on the occasion of the inauguration. I hope you will see my speech which will appear in the pamphlet record of the transactions.

I have many things to tell you about the exercises.

I staid with Dr. Hopkins as guest and it was very touching when the old President bade me good-bye, saying: "You will observe that I reserved for the concluding and final act of my official life, before laying down the office, the conferring upon you the Degree LL.D.; I was glad to have my work thus associated with your name."

Of course I have learned nothing since my arrival in Washington concerning the Montana trip, but shall do so at the earliest opportunity. I think from something I have heard that the Indian work will not be ready for me before the beginning of August.

I have hopes of getting through my work here so as to leave for home by Wednesday evening.

Since leaving home I have finished Bulwer's two novels [volumes] on the last days of Pompeii. It is a very able and striking work and sets forth in scholarly terms the struggles of the early Christians with mythological religion.

As Ever Yours,
J. A. Garfield

*In November 1871 President Grant, acting in accordance with a provision of a treaty with Montana Indians of 1855, ordered the removal of the Flathead Indians living in the Bitter Root Valley to the Flathead Reservation north of Missoula. In June 1872 Congress passed a removal act that modified and supplemented the President's order. Secretary of the Interior Columbus Delano, an Ohio man, appointed Garfield commissioner to arrange with the Flatheads for their removal. Garfield was accompanied from Fort Leavenworth by an old army friend, Major David Swaim. The two men traveled by rail as far as Corinne, Utah, and thereafter in horsedrawn conveyances. When away from home Garfield usually wrote often and at length to his family; this letter was addressed to Mrs. Garfield, who, with Mollie, Irvin, and a girl to look after the children, was staying at Fort Leavenworth with Mrs. Swaim (Jennie) during Garfield's absence.*

Black Rock, Idaho
107 miles north of Corinne
Midnight, end of August 13, 1872

My Darling,

We have reached the end of the second driver's run, and the supper is being got ready. We have had a beautiful night thus far, clear and cool but not uncomfortable. Just before sundown, we passed the divide and came down into the Marsh Valley, which is tributary to the Snake river. At 9 o'clock we entered Port Neuf Cañon, and have rapidly descended toward the valley of the Snake. We are still in the Cañon, but in two or three miles more, we shall reach the broad valley. I have caught a few snatches of sleep and so has Swaim, but sleeping is no easy matter with nine in a small box. It may amuse you and Jennie to know the *personel* of our inside company. The back seat is occupied by a very gossipy Englishman and his fidgety, gabby wife and a dunce of an impertinent boy. They are now sitting across the table, backbiting all their neighbors—and especially the passengers who are now asleep in the coach. On the front seat sit three people facing to the rear. One is a Salt Lake banker, and a fine fellow of middle size. Next to him sits a good looking portly doctor, who is returning to Montana after three years absence, sick of civilization and the dulness of N.Y. City. Next him sits a jolly, burly German woman weighing 200, who left Hamburg July 15 and has since then made 6,500 miles of her way back to Montana, which she left last October not intending to return. In the middle seat, which is six inches wide and 18 inches distant from the front seat, sits a lank Methodist preacher, with a big basket full of chickens and apples, and who shuts down his window to keep from catching cold and thus suffocates the rest of us. By his side sits Swaim and by him I sit. The six pairs of legs interlock in the closest possible fit. The lean Methodist and slim banker making one set, Swaim and the plump doctor another, and the fat German woman and I are the third. If you can imagine a more united party than that telegraph the result at my expense. But supper is nearly ready, and this is a region of mountain trout, and their savory odor already greets our nostrils from the next room. Wishing you and Jennie were eating them with us, I am as ever and forever

Your James

*In this letter to Secretary of the Interior Delano, written the day following his arrival in Virginia City, Garfield summed up what he had learned about the Indian situation. Benjamin F. Potts of Ohio was governor of Montana Territory; William H. Clagett was territorial delegate to Congress; Jasper A. Viall was superintendent of Indian affairs for Montana Territory.*

Virginia City, Montana
August 17, 1872

Dear Sir,

In pursuance of the authority and instructions of your letter of June 15th in relation to the removal of the Flathead Indians to the Jocko Reservation, I left Ohio, July 31st and proceeded to Fort Leavenworth, Kansas—and at my request, Gen. Pope detailed Major D. G. Swaim, Judge Advocate, to accompany me to Montana.

We left Leavenworth on the 8th inst. and on the 12th reached

Corinne where we took the stage for Helena. When we reached Gaffney's Junction, we were met by Gov. Potts, who wished us to accompany him to Virginia City to consult with him on the condition of Indian affairs in the Bitter Root Valley as they had been represented by parties who had lately called upon [him] for assistance.

We reached here last evening, and since then I have learned what I could of the situation as understood here by the governor and leading citizens of the place. The situation, as alleged and understood here, is substantially as follows:

1. It appears that since the notice required by the statute was served upon the Flatheads, they have manifested great opposition to the removal, and that the opposition has become nearly unanimous.
2. Within the past two weeks, a considerable number of the Nez Percés and Spokanes have come to the Bitter Root Valley, and though on their way to the waters of the Missouri to hunt Buffalo, they have espoused the cause of the Flatheads, and declare that they will stay and aid them in resisting removal. These visiting Indians are said to number fifty or sixty lodges.
3. The white settlers in [the] Valley appear to be a good deal alarmed, and are apprehensive of hostilities from these associated Indians, and are already taking steps to protect themselves. At three places in the Valley (Missoula, Aetna and Corvallis) they have already organized home guards and the whole number enrolled amounts to about 300. At each place of enrollment a messenger was sent to this place to procure arms from the Governor to arm their companies. At these meetings it was resolved to furnish sufficient bonds for the value and safe keeping of the arms should [they] be given. The Governor has granted their wishes and the arms and ammunition are about to be forwarded. At these meetings resolutions were also passed, asking the Governor to aid them in securing a detachment of two or three companies of U.S. cavalry to be posted in the valley for the better protection of the inhabitants.
4. It appears that citizens of Missoula have been, for some time, selling whiskey to the Indians, in violation of law, and that this has had much to do with the state of feeling among them. The same meeting of citizens at Missoula, that asked the Governor for arms, also asked for a force of deputy-marshals to aid in enforcing the laws against selling liquor to the Indians.
5. It is also alleged here that the missionaries among the Flatheads

have advised the Indians to stay in the valley, and insist upon their right to do so. Of this I have no other word than the general rumors that have come from the valley.

I enclose an editorial article from *The Montanian* of the 15th inst., a weekly paper published here, which Governor Potts thinks fairly represents the feeling of the citizens of the Bitter Root Valley.

Of course I am not yet able to reach any satisfactory conclusion in regard to the real state of affairs, but I write what appears on the surface from this stand-point. It is manifest that there is a good deal of apprehension of trouble. But I am inclined to believe that much of it is groundless, and perhaps it is partly the result of a desire to secure a military post in the Valley. It would be inconsistent with the whole history and character of the Flatheads if they should resort to violence in a case like this.

Governor Potts has concluded to accompany us to the valley, and we leave here this evening for Helena. I have telegraphed Mr. Viall requesting him to accompany us, and I now expect to start from Helena on Monday morning for the valley. I shall also see Mr. Clagett on the way, and get all the information I can before meeting the Indians themselves.

I hope to find things in a much more favorable situation than they appear here—and of course I shall do all I can to quiet the apprehension of the people in reference to hostilities.

Very Respectfully
Your Obedient Servant
J. A. Garfield
Special Commissioner etc.

*The attacks on Garfield relative to the salary grab of March 1873 and the Crédit Mobilier scandal made him more distrustful of the press—particularly the urban press. In this letter to William Cooper Howells, editor of the* Ashtabula Sentinel, *he distinguished between metropolitan and country newspapers. "Will" was William Dean Howells, then editor of the* Atlantic Monthly. *Annie was his sister. "Professor Longfellow" was the poet and Harvard professor Henry Wadsworth Longfellow. The new Congress that met in December 1873 devoted a considerable amount of time to proposals to repeal some or all of the increases in salary provided for in March. About two weeks after this letter was written, salaries of members of Congress were restored to their former level.*

Washington, D.C.
December 29, 1873

Dear Friend,

I reached home this morning after an absence of a week in Boston, where I went with a portion of the Committee on Appropriations to take testimony concerning the value of land adjoining the Post Office Building in that city. I worked very hard and had but little leizure; still I got time to go out to Cambridge on Friday and spend a delightful evening with Will and his family. Professor Longfellow was there and altogether it was one of the most pleasant visits I have ever had. I know of no man so peculiarly blessed in his family relationships as you. It is clear that Will is the centre of all that is best and brightest of the thought of Cambridge and Boston. Annie is looking exceedingly well and I tried to persuade her to come on with me and spend some weeks with us, but she could not leave.

I find this morning awaiting me your note of the 26th, and the package of *Sentinels*. I will see that your article on "Exchanges" is put in the hands of those who will appreciate it. I have come to the conclusion that I shall advocate the free circulation of weekly newspapers within the counties where they are published. This is one of my reasons which I would like to have you consider and tell me what you think of it.

I believe the Metropolitan Press, particularly the great daily press, has become so utterly reckless of the truth and has fallen into the hands of a few men who are disconnected and unacquainted with the real aspirations of the American people, and that they are false leaders and are doing their utmost to break down not only the present administration and the Republican Party, but all the people who do not follow their wishes. I believe that the real genuine press of the country is the local country press and to that we must look for the greatest and best influence of the press upon the people. The country press is a better exponent of public sentiment, for the reason that its editors are brought in daily contact with the people themselves. What young man that conducts some of our great daily journals knows anything of the real sentiment of the people in Ohio, for example. Rising from champagne suppers and entering their offices to run over the telegraphic dispatches from Washington and pronounce upon the virtue or vice, the wisdom or folly, of public men at the first glance.

What think you; would it be prudent to say these things in Congress and assign them as a reason for making free postage on county newspapers?

I should be glad to know what the people of Ashtabula County think of my speech in reply to Stephens.

I greatly regret that we could not have finished the salary business before adjournment. But 153 new men cannot easily and gracefully glide into working shape. There was just about so much talk had to be got off. The bill as it passed the House was not satisfactory and as you have seen intimated in the papers, I shall try to ingraft a simple and sweeping repeal upon my first appropriate bill.

My wife joins me in kindest regards to all your household.

As ever yours
J. A. Garfield

*In this letter to Victoria Howells, daughter of William Cooper Howells and sister of William Dean, Garfield reported on his efforts in behalf of an old friend. It is interesting to note the speed with which the secretary of state acted on a request by the chairman of the House Appropriations Committee. Howells passed his examination late in May and was confirmed by the Senate shortly thereafter.*

Washington, D.C.
May 10 [9], 1874

Dear Friend Victoria,

Your letter came duly to hand, and I feel almost like blaming you and your father for not writing me long ago in reference to your desires in connection with the Consulship at Quebec. When your father wrote me a few weeks ago, he did not then say that it was for himself. If I had known it I should have made more particular inquiry in reference to the subject.

This morning, before going to the House, I went to the State Department and called the attention of Secretary Fish to his letter, in which he stated there was no prospect of a vacancy in the Consulship at Quebec. He then explained the facts to me which you will notice are curious enough. Shortly after he had written me that note, which I sent to your father, there came a request from two consuls, one at Leghorn, Italy, and the other at Quebec, to exchange places, each wanting the place of the other. The Secretary saw no objection to the arrangement as it would oblige them both, and he therefore sent in their names to the Senate. The man who held the Consulship at Quebec was confirmed by the Senate to the Consulship at Leghorn, but strange enough for some reason not known to me nor to the Secretary the Senate has just rejected the nomination of the Leghorn man for the Quebec Consulship. This has left an unexpected vacancy.

So soon as the Secretary gave me this information, I asked him if it would not be possible to appoint your father to the vacancy at Quebec. He said that he would be glad to do so, provided the President had not promised the place to anybody else. He took your father's name and said he would see the President during the day. I then went immediately to the President, and asked him to appoint your father if possible. He took the name and said he would see the Secretary, who was to call on him during the day. I then went immediately to the Capitol, where I have been at work all day in the House on my appropriation bill. On my return home this evening I find a letter from the Secretary of State, which I copy entire:

Department of State
Washington, May 9, 1874

*Personal*
Dear General:
   'Tis done! A notification to Mr. Howells to appear for examination for the Consulship at Quebec goes to him by mail this day.

Faithfully Yours
Hamilton Fish

I am delighted to have been able to gratify your desires in this matter and make this slight return to your father and his family for the many good things they deserve from all their friends and especially from me.

That clause in the letter concerning examination for the Consulship, I do not understand. I will ascertain what it means and write you by the next mail after this. There has been a new report sent to Congress, within the last week or two, from the Civil Service Commission, and it may be that some regulation has been adopted there that I am not familiar with. Whatever it is, I am sure it will not stand in your father's way; and if his letter of instructions from the Secretary requires him to come here, I hope he will bring you with him to make us a visit.

I appreciate all you say in your letter concerning the pleasure it will give you all to reside for a while in Quebec. But, while feeling this, I am conscious of a little feeling of selfishness at the thought of losing you from Jefferson. How can I go there and not find you in your pleasant home among the maples? Perhaps I will make up for it by visiting you on the banks of the St. Lawrence.

With love to all the family in which Mrs. Garfield joins, I am,

As ever your Friend
J. A. Garfield

P.S.

Perhaps it is best that nothing should be said about the appointment until I hear more from the Secretary.

J.A.G.

*The Republican party was dealt severe blows in the elections of 1874; as a result, a decade and a half of Republican control of the House came to an end. This letter was addressed to Harmon Austin.*

Washington, D.C.
March 14, 1875

Dear Harmon:

Yours of the 11th inst. came duly to hand. I wrote to Mr. Morgan and to Mr. Wise, two days ago, in reference to the reappointment of Wise as postmaster at Warren; and I hope that before this reaches you, the matter will be concluded. As I explained to them, the President put off most of the appointments until after the close of the session; and for this reason, the letter which I sent to the department, asking Wise's reappointment, was not acted on until last week. I have no fear of anything my enemies can do to prevent favorable action in his case. I have accepted an urgent invitation of the Republicans of Connecticut to aid them in their campaign; and I shall go there before I go home to Ohio. The partial success which our friends have achieved in New Hampshire has made Connecticut an important battle-ground, and the contest there will have an important bearing on our Ohio campaign next fall. As I look at the political situation, the disasters our party suffered last fall, did not indicate any new love of the people for the Democracy, but rather a dissatisfaction with the Republican party. Now, after they have thus expressed their feelings, they are likely to turn upon the Democracy, and give them a similar declaration. I should say that the two prevailing sentiments of the people are: disgust with the administration, and *distrust of the Democracy.*

This invitation of the leading Republicans of Connecticut is another of the many indications that the public mind is recovering from the feeling of doubt and distrust which the attacks of the last two years have raised against me. I believe I have never held a position of such recognized power as I now hold here. How it is in the country generally, I do not know; but I presume there is still much of the old leaven of distrust. Soon after the Connecticut election is over, I shall go to Ohio, and then I want to see you and have a long visit. I shall probably leave my family here until warm weather, and let the children get through their spring term of school. I hope you will find time to write to me occasionally before we meet.

I have printed this letter on a machine called the "type-writer," which an agent has left here for me to try. It is about the size of an ordinary sewing-machine, and is arranged with keys like a piano. By placing the paper in proper position, and striking the keys, the printing is done as you see it in this specimen. I have not used it long, and cannot operate it very fast; but I have printed this letter in about twice the time it would have taken me to write it with a pen. The agent who brought the machine here can print nearly twice as fast as I can write. I thought you would be interested in seeing its work. I sent a letter to Hinsdale, printed in this way, and suggested to him that such a machine would considerably improve his hand-writing. All the family send kind regards. We are all in good health except me; and I am recovering from a very bad cold. I enclose a letter, which please read and return.

As Ever, Your Friend<br>James A. Garfield

*On April 19, 1875, Garfield left Cleveland on a vacation trip to California. Westward from Chicago he traveled in the private car of the directors of the Union Pacific Railroad, which had been put at the disposal of the wife of William C. Ralston, president of the Bank of California. The invitation came from Ralston (through Garfield's friend Henry R. Linderman, director of the mint) and from Jay Gould, a director of the Union Pacific Railroad.*

*Politicians and journalists were looking ahead to the presidential election of 1876. In Chicago Garfield heard gossip that raised a question about James G. Blaine's availability as a candidate. Mrs. Garfield discounted the effect of the story on the voters even if it was true and added, "My opinion of Mr. Blaine would be rather heightened than otherwise by the truth of such a story; for it would show him not entirely selfish and heartless." She could "scarcely understand how such a strong positive, self-asserting intellectual nature as Mrs. Blaine's" could have been so tempted, and she preferred to believe the story she had heard that the Blaines had been secretly married.*

Chicago, Illinois<br>April 21, 1875

My Darling,

How very trying it is to stay here, perhaps five days, when I might have remained with you, and still have reached San Francisco as soon as by waiting here. The time is too long to spend here, and too short to go back to you, and return. Yesterday afternoon the superintendent of the road telegraphed that our train had not better leave here before Saturday morning unless we had different orders sooner. If I knew we should not leave before Saturday, I would go to Cleveland and spend a day, or would go to Michigan and see brother Thomas. But the break in the Union Pacific Road may be repaired sooner than is now expected, and so I must stay here and lament that I cannot be with you, or on my westward way. I telegraphed you last evening, so that I might hear from you once, at least, before I leave here. Today I have had a long visit with Frank Palmer, late a member of my Committee, but now the editor of the *Inter-Ocean,* and a still longer one with Joseph Medill, the editor of the *Chicago Tribune,* with whom I discussed the question of the next Presidency—and especially Blaine's chances. He told me a curious thing which I never heard of before. He says that Halstead of the *Cincinnati Commercial,* and Watterson of the *Louisville Journal,* are strongly inclined to support Blaine, but that a circumstance occurred in his early life which is likely to be brought out against him, in case he is a candidate— to this effect. It is alleged that when he was school-master, in Kentucky, many years ago, he met a Yankee school-mam, and their warm blood led them to anticipate the nuptial ceremony, that thereupon he took her to Pennsylvania, his home, and married her, that they went thence to Maine to begin life in a new place, and that there their first child was born about five or six months after their marriage. It is said that the editor of the *Cincinnati Enquirer* has quietly been procuring affidavits of these facts, and will publish them in case Blaine is nominated. How does this story strike you? If it is true, should it have weight with the people in the Presidential Campaign? Please give me your thoughts on the subject. I think I ought to write to Blaine on the subject; and yet I hesitate to do so; there may be nothing in it—and it is not a pleasant thing to write about if there is.

Last evening I met Mrs. Ralston and her party, which consists of an old lady named Mrs. Petty, a young Miss Leland, daughter of Warren Leland, late of the Metropolitan Hotel, and two other young misses, who go with her. The invitation is so very cordial, both from her and her husband, who has telegraphed on the subject, and also from the manager of the road that I think I will accept their offer. If we were to go at once, I should be glad, for I am in danger of getting homesick by this delay.

I enclose a few pages of my Journal for Mr. Rose to enter in the Diary—I may conclude to keep [it] in a book as I go, but for the present I will send it back in installments.

Now, Darling, please remember our talk about writing me the little and great particulars of your daily life. Take enough time from your daily duties to tell me what you are doing and thinking. Tell me of what you read, and let our minds and hearts keep track of each other. Life will be too short to tell all our love, so let us seize the hours as they fly and make them yield the sweets of love and life.

As ever your own
James

*Garfield arrived in San Francisco on Friday, April 30, and the next day went to Belmont, the country estate of William C. Ralston. This letter to Mrs. Garfield gives an account of the visit. The following weekend Garfield made another overnight visit to Belmont. Ralston's death by drowning in August 1875 filled Garfield "with deep grief." Whether Ralston committed suicide is still a matter of speculation; the Bank of California was in deep financial trouble, and Ralston's resignation as president had been called for the day of his death. On August 28 Garfield wrote of Ralston in his diary, "I earnestly plead with him, when we parted, to draw in from his greatly expanded business, and warned him of his dangers."*

*When the Garfields were in England in 1867, they visited Chatsworth, the huge Derbyshire estate of the Duke of Devonshire. Aaron A. Sargent was a Republican member of the U.S. House of Representatives, 1861–1863, and of the U.S. Senate, 1873–1879. Henry Hart, an agent of the Pacific Mail Steamship Company, looked after the Ralston party on the trip from Chicago.*

San Francisco, California
May 6, 1875

My Darling,

Since my arrival, I have been whirled away through so many scenes that I have fallen behind in my account of them; and I will now try to bring up part of the arrears. In my last, or perhaps, next the last, I stated that I went to Belmont. If you look at a recent map of California, you will see a railroad running south from San Francisco along the shore of the bay. A ridge of high hills—a part of the Coast Range—hides the ocean and the road winds along among beautiful slopes that touch the hills on the west and the bay on the east. Belmont is a little station twenty miles from the city, and half a mile back from it, nestled among the hills, is [the] country residence of Mr. Ralston. He has there about 400 acres of hill, valley and ravine, decorated with every variety of fruit and ornamental tree, and in the midst of it, excepting Chatsworth, the finest country house I ever saw. He frequently entertains fifty guests, with the most familiar and open handed generosity. In his stable I counted 25 magnificent horses—and his grounds are a marvel of beauty. He is not yet 50 years old, was born near Mansfield, Ohio, and came here, a poor boy in 1850. He has the reputation, and I should say justly, of being the most powerful business intellect on this coast. The amount of work he performs daily is something enormous. He rises at six; works incessantly, and with the utmost rapidity, is the President and soul of the Bank of California, an institution whose operations are larger than all others in this city combined. He is the chief mover in several of the great railroads here, is the owner and manager of a very large real estate, and is personally superintending the building of the Palace Hotel, which is much the largest Hotel in the world. His wealth is away up in the millions, and he manages the whole with such keen, prompt, decisive effectiveness, that I look upon him as one of the very most remarkable men I have ever met. His only recreation is at Belmont. He leaves the city at 2 P.M. each Saturday, spends the night at home, drives or rides on Sunday, and in the evening, returns to the city to resume his week's work. He received me with the greatest kindness, and treated me as though we were old acquaintances. He has one iron habit, which probably makes his career possible. He goes to bed not later than 9.30 P.M. no matter how many guests may be visiting him. His wife is a woman of strong sense, and fine qualities, and between them, they have the faculty of making their friends feel the utmost freedom at their home. Everything is rich, generous, and what is more striking, in severe good taste. The kitchen is in keeping with the rest of the house, and is kept in the most perfect order by their Chinese servants. Billiards, games, music, pictures and statuary make the house brilliant with attraction. As Mr. Ralston bade us good night, at half-past nine, he said there would be a cup of coffee ready at seven in the morning, and at half-past seven, carriages would start for a drive. At that hour he took the reins, and with 13 people in his four horse carriage, we drove 12 miles and back, after visiting some places of rare beauty. All doors were open to us, and we came back laden with the richest flowers that bloom in these semi-tropical gardens. We returned at 11 A.M. and at 11½ sat down to breakfast with 25 at the table. I led Mrs. R. to breakfast, and read her that beautiful first page of your letter of the 19th April, and told her, that she and her husband had fulfilled the prophecy of the text you quoted. At 2 P.M. we drove ten miles more, towards the city, stopping at several beautiful places and at 4.30 took the cars for the city. Among the guests at Ralston's was John W. Young (and wife) a son of Brigham Young. I had a long talk with her in reference to the Mormon faith, and especially in reference to polygamy—which I will tell you of when we meet.

You will understand better the nature of this society when I tell you that the energy of its people and the wonderful resources of this country have made an unusual number of rich men here. It is said that there are more than 200 millionaires in this city, and there are perhaps a dozen or twenty men who are worth from 10 to 40 millions each. They did not make their money slowly, by those small methods which make men narrow and penurious; but they did it partly by great boldness in enterprise and partly by the lucky accidents which attend a mining country. Hence they are generous and broadminded. I find it necessary to brace myself against the inclination to rebel against the fate that place[d] me in such a narrow grove in reference to business and property. But after all, I come joyfully back to this solid fact, that with your love I am richer than they all are. Bless you darling.

On Monday, Sargent went with me to the Mint, and we spent nearly four hours in going through that great building, and examining the processes by which the silver and gold of this state are turned into the coin of commerce.

On Tuesday, Mr. Hart took me through the great Steam Ship, *The City of Peking*—the second largest steamer in the world—and at 2 P.M. we started on a four hours trip through the Chinese quarters—which I must spare you until another letter. In that I will try to write something that will be of interest to our dear little ones. I am very well, except that the hemorrhoids have visited me again, with savage fury—notwithstanding my buckeye. I have however gained one pound in weight since I left Chicago. If you knew how I longed for your letters you would not hesitate to make your letters long and frequent.

Ever and ever your own
James

*On the visit to the Consolidated Virginia and the California mines in Nevada, described in this letter to Mrs. Garfield, Garfield was accompanied by John W. Mackay and James G. Fair, associates in the exploitation of the Comstock lode. Persuaded that these mines were of great value, Garfield wrote to Fair in the fall of 1875 (after a great fire in Virginia City had depressed their stocks), asking him to buy shares for him and draw on him for the margin. Garfield's diary entry for December 4 reports: "He [Fair] bought 200 shares of stock of California for me, Nov. 15, at $55 the share, and I have today paid $5,000 in gold on the account. The stock has already risen to about $70, and I hope to realize well on it." James W. Nye, William M. Stewart, John P. Jones, and William Sharon, all members of the U.S. Senate from Nevada while Garfield was in the House, found success and wealth in Nevada.*

Carson City, Nevada
June 1, 1875

My Darling,

After leaving Sacramento, where I finished my last letter, No. 20, and put it on the train, I started eastward at 3 P.M. It was the hottest day I have seen on this coast. The sun beat down fiercely, and the sea gave no relief, as it does at San Francisco every afternoon. I put on a linen coat and then sweltered for two hours. But the locomotive was bringing relief, for we were very rapidly climbing the mountains into the cooler air. All the way from Sacramento, we saw in the deep blue distance the serrated peaks of snow; and by 6 P.M. we needed overcoats. The snow water was tearing down the sides of the road, clear and cold as the glacier streams on the Alps. I went to sleep near the western summit of the Sierra Nevadas, and when I awoke, our sleeping car had turned off from the Pacific Road at Reno, and we we[re] near Carson City. There we changed to the day car, and went in by the wildest and most crooked R.R. I ever saw, to Virginia City, the seat of the great silver mines. In a straight line Virginia City is not more than 20 miles from Reno. By the wagon road it is not much more. By the R.R. it is nearly 60, and we climb 2,000 feet in going over the line. I stopped at the hotel—built on the steep slope of Mt. Davidson—and from its balcony look out upon a wild, treeless country of mountains and valley. Around me, was a city of 20,000 inhabitants—half the population of the whole state—and probably not one person in the place who intends to remain here. In fact, it is a mining camp—and yet in sight, indeed under my feet, lay the richest body of silver and gold yet known in the whole world. The energy, the great ability which are in active exhibition there every day, is one of the marvels of our American life. This is the country made famous by Mark Twain in his *Roughing It*. Just across from my hotel was the newspaper office where he began his career as a writer. Out of this state, with less than one quarter of the population of my Congressional District, have gone out Nye, Stewart, Jones and Sharon, and, what has been of vastly more consequence to the country, there go out annually not less than 40 millions of gold and silver bullion. Just now, twice that amount is going out.

The tales of Aladdin are here more than realized. I came on the cars from Sacramento with an Irishman, who was poor two years ago, but a man told me yesterday that now his wealth would exceed 60 millions before the end of this year. If it be only a tenth of that sum, it is wonderful enough. To give you an adequate idea of the richness of that place, let me say that running north and south through Mount Davidson is a vein of quartz from one hundred to 500 feet thick and averaging from $50 to $5,000 per ton. It takes a cube only 3 ft. on a side to make a ton [of] it. They have explored the vein to the depth of 2,000 feet, and as yet find no bottom.

I wrote the foregoing in my room, before the people were stirring. I am writing this at the office, where I can put it in ink.

I left off with some general reflections on the character of Nevada and its enterprise. After I had taken breakfast yesterday morning, I went to the mills and the mines. The superintendent took me with him through two of the best mines—the Consolidated Virginia, and the California. We stripped off all our clothing, and put on a flannel shirt, woolen pants and socks, heavy shoes and coat and a slouch hat, and then were let down 1,500 feet perpendicular into the mine. It grows very hot as we descend, and but for ventillation a man could not live ten minutes in the lower reaches of the mine. On reaching the bottom, we laid off our coats, and entered the drifts which extend hundreds of feet in exact right angles north, south, east and west from the shaft. After the shaft enters the quartz vein, they make lateral drifts at each 100 feet; so that the mine is a vast series of stories, one above the other, and each of 100 feet in height. A lateral drift is run out one hundred feet east, another 100 feet north, and from the two ends of these, drifts are again run at right angles, so as to meet and form an exact square of 100 feet on a side. The same thing having been done on the level 100 feet above, they thus surround a cubicle mass of ore 100 feet on a side, and then blast and pick it out. They are taking out 600 tons per day, and from it, are milling and shipping over 1,000,000 dollars gold and silver per month—I mean from this one mine, the Consolidated Virginia, whose property is but 600 feet long in the vein. The miners work naked, except that they wear hats, pants and shoes. The thermometer stands at 100° to 130°, and the perspiration poured from us all in streams. I picked out some pieces of ore that are said to be worth $10,000 per ton. From this hurried and imperfect sketch, you can form some idea of the stupendous fortunes that lie in the "Comstock lode" as it is called. I remained in the mine an hour and a half. It was the best sweat bath I ever took. I went through the great quartz mill, where the ore is crushed, and then through the assay and refining offices where it is put into bars of bullion. When I get home I shall be glad to tell the children all about it. The story is too long for a letter. At four o'clock I came here, and in the evening visited the mint in this place, dined with an old Washingtonian, and took a good night's rest from the activities of a very busy, but a deeply interesting day. I believe my nature was made for mountain life. The blues which infected my last letter have all dissipated in this wonderful air, and the wheels of my intellect sing as they roll. If you were with me, I would stay here a week. But soon after breakfast I shall take a ride of 16 miles to Lake Tahoe, whence I will write you again. With a heart full of love, and delighted with the hope of seeing you before many weeks, I am all and always your

James

*The presidential election of 1876 was held on November 7. The next morning it appeared that Samuel J. Tilden, the Democratic candidate, had been the victor over Hayes. But Republicans saw some hope in the elections in Louisiana, South Carolina, and Florida. In Louisiana the Returning Board was required to canvass the election returns from the various parishes of the state and announce the results. On November 10 President Grant asked Garfield and a number of other prominent Republicans to go to New Orleans and remain until the Louisiana vote had been counted. The Democratic party also sent representatives to Louisiana to protect its interests there. The Returning Board requested and invited five members of each group of northern visitors to witness its proceedings. Garfield arrived in New Orleans on November 14 and left for Washington on December 2; this letter was the fifth that he wrote to Mrs. Garfield from New Orleans.*

New Orleans, Louisiana
November 20, 1876

My Darling:

Soon after I mailed my letter yesterday, yours of the 16th came, with its birthday benediction, and kept my heart warm till I slept. The day was quite cold, as is this. I am sitting in the hall of the Board of Canvassers, the State Senate House, with my overcoat on, and occasionally go to the stove to keep warm. Strange, that in the land of flowers so cold a day should look down upon roses and orange groves. The weather seems to have imparted its fickleness to the people, who smile in the morning and murder at night. My old opinion of the Latin races is confirmed, that they have not the genius for self government. I am sitting here as one of the five Republican witnesses to the count of the returns. To avoid a crowd, and the turbulence and delay it would occasion, the Board have excluded all but those legally authorized to be present, and the five "distinguished northern visitors" from each political party. Every hour, I am learning most curious things about this curious people, and am getting a clearer view of the strange muddle into which the war, and the partisan struggles which followed it, have involved this state. The value of our visit here may be twofold; first to aid in reassuring and calming the public mind which is in a state of dangerous inflammation; and second, to be prepared for the great discussion which is almost certain to follow in the House, if Hayes is declared elected, as I am now almost sure he will be. The Board are now counting the vote of those parishes (counties) concerning which there is no contest. When these are counted, they will take up the contested parishes, and hear testimony upon the charge of intimidation and fraud. It is impossible to tell how long it will take to complete the count; but the eyes of the whole nation are upon the work now going on in this room; and the election of our President probably depends upon what is done here. When you reflect that the interest and passion of 45,000,000 of people are concentrated upon the work going on in this room, you can imagine the stress and strain of the hour—and how much steadiness of mind and nerve are needed to bear one's self through it, and keep his head level. I shall have another man in my place tomorrow, to enable me to accept the invitation of Captain Eads, to go down to the mouth of the Mississippi to see the great work going on there to deepen the channel of the river by means of jetties—one of the greatest works of its kind ever attempted. The boat leaves this evening and will not return until tomorrow night, so that I may not be able to send you a letter during the day tomorrow. How much I want you with me, to see this remarkable country! Besides needing you every hour, for my own sake, I want you here for your sake, that you may see all that I see; for I want you to share all my experiences that are instructive and pleasant.

This morning, a delegation from Mississippi called on me, and made a remarkable statement of the outrages and intimidation practiced in that state by the rebel Democracy. If half they tell is correct, the election in that state was an outrage on good government beyond endurance. And yet, as that state is wholly in the hands of the Democracy, and as they have carried all their electors and Congressmen, there seems to be no means of correcting the wrong; and so that state must be counted for Tilden, and its congressional vote must give the House to the Democracy. I hope the discolsure of the facts will result in awakening our people to the necessity of putting national elections under the control of national officers, and bringing the result under national supervision.

I have a new occasion to thank Mollie for the good letter in which she has, a second time, remembered her absent papa. I wrote her and Harry a long letter which I hope they will have received before this reaches you. I am well, and I want you to dismiss all anxiety about my personal safety. These people are on their good behavior, and no harm will happen to any of us who are visiting them.

Ever and all your own
James

*On December 6 two sets of electoral returns for President and Vice President were submitted to the President of the United States Senate from Louisiana, South Carolina, Florida, and Oregon; all 19 of the electoral votes of the three southern states were in dispute, while only one of Oregon's votes was disputed. If Hayes could secure all 20 of the contested votes, he would have a 185 to 184 victory over Tilden. Many Democrats hoped to throw the election into the House by preventing either candidate from receiving a majority of electoral votes; they proposed to act under a joint rule of the Senate and House adopted in 1865 that enabled either house to prevent the counting of the electoral vote of any state. Republicans argued that this rule was no longer valid. In this letter to Hayes, Garfield took up a vital question— whether the Republican party could come to an understanding with Southern Democrats (particularly those who had once been Whigs) that would result in the counting of a majority of the electoral votes for Hayes.*

*The following members of the House of Representatives are mentioned in the letter: Speaker Samuel J. Randall, Democrat from Pennsylvania; Fernando Wood, Democrat from New York; Benjamin H. Hill, Democrat from Georgia; Hiram Casey Young, Democrat from Tennessee; and William B. Williams, Republican from Michigan. Young was believed to be in favor of a coalition of Republicans and southern Democrats to settle the dispute in favor of Hayes.*

Washington, D.C.
December 12, 1876

My Dear Governor,

I did not intend to vex your silence so soon; but there are some elements here, which seem to be moving now in a hopeful way; and if any good can be accomplished with them, it should be undertaken soon. You have seen that the more violent Democratic leaders are trying to create as much sensation and popular clamor as possible. Randall and Wood and their special followers, are seeking to impeach the President; to assert their right to review the action of Returning Boards; to insist on the validity of the 22nd Joint Rule, and the right of the House to act under it, and reject the vote of any state it pleases etc., etc. They are ugly; and partly mean mischief, but are partly bluffing, in order to keep up the popular excitement until their committees get back from the South, when they hope to make such a case as to aid them in breaking down the count in February, and thus throw the election into the House. In the meantime, two forces are at work. The Democratic business men of the country are more anxious for quiet than for Tilden; and the leading southern Democrats in Congress, especially those who were old Whigs, are saying that they have seen war enough, and don't care to follow the lead of their northern associates who, as Ben Hill says, were "invincible in peace and invisible in war." After my speech today, on the point of order as to the validity of the Joint Rule, Hill came to me and said: "You are clearly right, and I don't intend to follow our people in this sort of reckless warfare."

Several of our most thoughtful Republicans here, have said to me, during the last three days, that they believed it possible to make an inroad into the Democratic camp—which would, at least, result in dividing them on their policy of violence and resistance; and that, if anything is to be attempted in that direction, it should be done during the lull, before the southern committees return. This morning I received a letter from Judge Williams, of Michigan, one of our good, sensible members of the House, which I enclose to you. The gentleman to whom he refers, I find, is Gen. Casey Young, of Memphis, who stands well with southern members. I don't quite believe that there are so many southern men as he supposes, who would follow in the direction he indicates; but if a third of that number, would come out for peace, and acquiescence in your election, it would do much to prevent immediate trouble, and to make your future work easier. Just what sort of assurances the south wants, is not quite so clear, for they are a little vague in their expressions; but I have no doubt it would be possible to adopt a line of conduct which would be a great help to them, and at the same time be consistent with the best interests of the country, and just to our party.

Let me say, that I don't think any body should be the custodian of your policy and purposes, at present, or have any power to commit or embarrass you, in any way; but it would be a great help, if in some discreet way, these southern men, who are dissatisfied with Tilden and his violent followers, could know that the South is going to be treated with kind consideration by you. Several southern men have said, within a week, that in matters of internal improvements, they had been much better treated by Republicans than they were likely to be by the Democrats—and they talk a good deal about the old Whigs having been forced, unwillingly, into the Democratic party. I think one of the worst things in all our past management of the South, has been the fact that we have not taken into our confidence, and invited to our support, a class of men, whose interests are identified with the South, and who will help to divide the white people politically. It has occurred to me that I might, by and by, make a speech and say something like this.

1. Insist firmly upon the fact that you have been fairly and legally elected; and that the only safe and peaceable solution of the difficulty in which the nation is now involved, is to acknowledge that fact. In this connection, I would give a brief summary of the

grounds on which we base the claim that you are elected, handling the Louisiana and Oregon cases with sufficient fulness
to make them clear to fair minded men.

2. Insist that the Republican party proposes to pursue a broad national policy—to preserve the public faith, and the national
credit, to build up the industrial interests of every section of
the country, and to invite the cooperation of all men north
and south who believe in the new birth of the nation.

3. That so far as the South is concerned, they can not ask a more
liberal and generous policy than is set forth in your letter of
acceptance and that all who know your character and spirit will
feel assured that you will carry out the programme, set forth in
your letter, faithfully and fearlessly. That I hope the day will
soon come, when parties in the South shall not be divided on the
color line; but when the constitutional rights of the Negro may
be as safe in the hands of one party as the other, and that thus,
in the South as in the North, men may seek their party associations on the great commercial and industrial questions, rather
than questions of race and color. If you feel at liberty to say
anything to me in the way of suggestions, I shall be glad to have
you do so, and will treat it as wholly confidential, if you desire it.

Very Truly Yours

J. A. Garfield

*In December 1876 the Senate and the House of Representatives each ap-*
*pointed a committee with authority to confer and act with its counterpart to*
*propose a plan for dealing with the electoral crisis. As a result a bill was re-*
*ported to the Senate on January 13. The bill provided for the counting of the*
*electoral votes in joint sessions of the two houses. When a state was reached*
*from which more than one return had been made, the case would be turned*
*over to an electoral commission made up of five senators, five represen-*
*tatives, and five associate justices of the Supreme Court. A decision of the*
*commission would be final unless both houses agreed to reject it. Although*
*Garfield and a large majority of Republicans in the House voted against the*
*bill, it became law on January 29. Four associate justices were designated by*
*the bill; the fifth was to be chosen by the other four. Of the fourteen members*
*already selected, seven were Republicans and seven Democrats; thus the*
*choice of the fifth justice was crucial. It had been expected that he would be*
*David Davis of Illinois, who was considered to be something of a political in-*
*dependent. On January 25, however, Davis was elected senator from Illi-*
*nois. The four associates already designated thereupon chose Joseph P.*
*Bradley as the fifth justice.*

*Garfield was chosen by the House as a member of the commission. In this letter to Hayes, written a week before the electoral commission bill passed the House, Garfield expressed his great dissatisfaction with the plan for a commission and asked for advice. There had been fears that Senator Roscoe Conkling of New York would desert the Republican party "on the Presidential question." Senator Thomas W. Ferry of Michigan was President of the Senate; it would be his constitutional duty to open the electoral certificates in the presence of both houses.*

Washington, D.C.
January 19, 1877

My Dear Governor,

I have no words strong enough to describe my indignation at the fact and manner of the surrender which the Senate has made of our position. The danger of violent resistance to your inauguration had absolutely passed away with the failure of the 8th January conventions. Nothing in the world was necessary, but for the Senate to support its presiding officer in following the early precedents, which were made under the fresh impulses of the constitution then recently adopted. A little bluster, a new burst of newspaper wrath, and all would have been over. I don't believe one half of one per cent of our party had any doubt of the justice, and essential fairness of your election, and of the right of the President of the Senate to declare it. And now those Republicans who have borne the brunt of the campaign, and of the struggle against fraud and violence since the election, see the certainty of an assumed result, traded off for the uncertain chances of what a committee of one majority will do; and the senators who have made this surrender, are those who did the least toward securing our victory. Our friends on the House side of the committee would never have agreed to the bill, but from the conviction that enough Republican senators would follow Conkling, to leave Ferry without support. Probably the mischief is irreparable. A compromise like this is singularly attractive to that class of men who think that the truth is always half way between God and the Devil, and that not to split the difference would be partisanship. Pardon my scolding; for I sat down to ask your opinion. While the bill surrenders a great advantage, it does not necessarily defeat us. Probably it leaves us an even chance—possibly more than even. The Republican members of the committee are confident that you will be declared elected under the bill. The worst that the four judges can do is to choose Davis as the fifth wheel to this compromise coach. If they fail to agree upon a choice, they must cast lots, and that would give us three chances out of four—with Davis as the fourth. My present inclination is to fight the bill from beginning to end, and wash my hands of all responsibility for its result. I shall certainly do so, if I find any hope of defeating it. But the present outlook is that it will pass by a very large majority. Those of our friends who favor the bill are anxious to have me on the commission, and for that reason, are urging me not to oppose it. I understand that the Democrats and Republicans on the committee have personally pledged each other that each party may name its own committee [commission] men. I wish you would write me at once, what seems best to be done under the circumstances. Do you see any changes that ought to be attempted in the bill before it comes to a final vote?

As Ever Yours
J. A. Garfield

*Early in May 1879 Garfield escorted Mrs. Garfield, his three youngest children, and Martha Mays from Washington to the Mentor farm. He soon returned to Washington, where a special session of Congress called by President Hayes for March 14 was still in progress. Hal and Jimmie stayed with their father, studying under his direction. The Forty-fifth Congress had expired on March 4 without having made the necessary appropriations for the next fiscal year for the army and for the three branches of the government. Garfield's suggestion of "Veto" as a name for the new dog was related to the political situation. President Hayes had already vetoed one bill since the special session began and was preparing to veto another as Garfield wrote. Both vetoes were the result of efforts of the Democrats to force the acceptance, as the price of passing the appropriations bills, of legislation aimed at preventing the use of the army or federal marshals at places where elections were being held. Garfield was in the midst of the struggle against the Democrats and strongly favored both vetoes.*

Washington, D.C.
May 11, 1879

Dear Little Abe,

Your very good little letter made me very glad. It was written much better than Papa could have written at your age, and the map of South America was exceedingly nice for a six year old boy. If you keep on, I shall surely call you my *"Great Abe"* as I have sometimes done at the table. We let the little dog come up stairs to see us this afternoon, and he had a great time with us. How would you like to have him named "Veto"? We will send him soon. I hope in a few days you will be able to write me again that you "have had good lessons all the week." I haven't heard of any boys fighting with "Marvin," since you and Irvin left. What is the reason? Hal and Jim send love, and so do I. Your loving

Papa

*Garfield's suggestion of "Veto" as a name for the new dog did not win in-*
*stant acceptance from all the family; Irvin, age eight, had his own ideas*
*about choosing a dog's name.*

Washington, D.C.
May 17, 1879

My Dear Irvin,

I have read your letter to Hal, and think you are quite right in your
view of the way to name the dog. The whole family ought to be heard
on the subject; and you may call him "pup", or any other name you
please until we get home. Then we will hold a meeting of the Garfield
family and have the name voted on—each man, woman and child to
have a vote. I am pleased with the report of your lessons and hope you
will keep them as good all the time. We want to hear whether the dog
got home safely, and how he acts, and what "Tip" does to him.

I hope [you] will write to us often. It improves you and does us a
great deal of good. Give my love to Abe and Molly and Martha—and to
the girls and men at the farm.

Affectionately Your Papa
J. A. Garfield

*The letter of Irvin ("Burton") to his father on June 18 began, "Do come*
*home soon and bring the lads, the strawberries are going but the cherries are*
*coming." In a letter to Garfield on June 17 Mrs. Garfield gave a humorous*
*account of a fishing expedition that day by Irvin, Abe, and Eddy Green. Abe*
*and Irvin lost their lines, Irvin lost his suspenders (having taken off his*
*clothes "only to sit down in the water"), and Abe got a fishhook in his toe and*
*finger. They caught no fish. Eddy gave Irvin his line to tie on his pants. "I*
*put the two adventurers down by a warm fire where they talked over their*
*exploits until bedtime and no doubt now they are dreaming them over*
*again."*

Washington, D.C.
June 21, 1879

Dear Irvin:

Your terse letter of the 19th inst. came duly to hand this morning.

I have delivered your message to the "lads." They will be likely to
go for you when they get home for calling them such a small name, but
I tell them that the venerable Burton is right to speak of young people
as "lads," for he was once "a lad and served a term" himself.

The farm news you send me is very gratifying and I hope that the
"lads" and I will be able to visit the farm before long.

Push the fishery question, my son, until you make a success of it. I will pay for all the necessary wear and tear, and loss of suspenders, but I hope that you will be as saving of that kind of dry goods as you can.

Affectionately Your Papa
J. A. Garfield

*In July 1879 John Sherman had indicated to Garfield that he would not be a candidate for the U.S. Senate when the Ohio state legislature met in January 1880, but he made it clear that he was desirous of the presidential nomination. As time went on it appeared that the Ohio delegation to the Republican national convention in June 1880 might not be solidly for Sherman. Garfield's position in relation to Sherman's candidacy was a delicate one since he himself was being seriously discussed as a possible presidential candidate. As usual when Garfield faced a political problem in his own district, he turned to his old friend and adviser, Harmon Austin, who was at this time chairman of the Republican Central Committee of the district. Henry B. Perkins, a well-to-do resident of Warren, was also a member of the committee.*

Washington, D.C.
February 14, 1880

Dear Harmon:

John Sherman sent for me last evening and said that he had heard that a strong movement was being made in Trumbull and Mahoning counties in favor of Blaine and wanted my assistance to prevent a division of the Ohio delegation on the Presidential question. I write now to say that in view of the talk from various quarters of the country favoring me for the Presidency it will be very embarrassing should there appear a division in my Congressional district. It would almost certainly be said that I had gotten up a division so as to break Sherman's strength and pave the way for a movement in my own favor. This I am anxious to prevent. I hope our Trumbull friends will see the propriety of giving Sherman their support. They can send men who are friendly to Blaine or any one else they please as second choice so as to be ready to act in case they find Sherman cannot be nominated.

After quiet and judicious inquiry such as you always make please write me what the prospects are whom you think will likely be chosen as delegates from Trumbull to the state convention. Do you know how Henry B. Perkins stands on a Presidential candidate?

As Ever Yours
J. A. Garfield

*In this letter Garfield gave Harmon Austin another task.*

Washington, D.C.
April 16, 1880

Dear Harmon:

I am between two fires. One set of people, Sherman's supporters, insist that I shall go as a Delegate to the Chicago Convention, from the Nineteenth District. This they said nothing of until about two weeks ago, by which time I had already answered a number of gentlemen from the District, who wished to be candidates if I was not, that I would not be in their way.

This, I think is the attitude I should take: I will not offer myself as a candidate nor decline if it is tendered me. On many accounts I would be embarrassed to go to Chicago, while on the other hand I do not wish to shirk the responsibility, nor appear to be negligent of Sherman's interests. While I do not think he has much of a chance, if any, of the nomination, I still think, if we want to prevent Grant's nomination, we ought to give Ohio to Sherman.

I write this that you may keep an eye on the doings of the convention that meets in Warren on the 19th and not allow me to be put into a false position.

I will answer your letter on agricultural topics very soon.

As Ever Yours
J. A. Garfield


*Garfield reached Chicago on May 29. The convention was to begin on June 2. William Dennison was elected chairman of the Ohio delegation. A pre-convention poll of the delegation showed 34 for Sherman, 9 for Blaine, 1 for Senator George F. Edmunds of Vermont. Close friends of Garfield present for the convention included Major David G. Swaim and Charles E. Henry. Thomas M. Nichol of Wisconsin, an alternate delegate, was secretary of the Honest Money League of the Northwest. Garfield's oldest sons— Hal and Jim—were attending St. Paul's School in Concord, New Hampshire. Despite Garfield's frenetic pace at the convention, he wrote seven letters to Mrs. Garfield from Chicago.*


Chicago, Illinois
May 31, 1880

My Darling,

Another day nearly over, full of the extraordinary passion, suspicion and excitement of this convention. I have tried to keep my head

cool; and have sailed rather steadily over its rough seas—yet all the
while longing for land—especially the little farm where my hopes and
loves are centered.

I begin to feel quite confident that neither Grant nor Blaine can get
the nomination and I fear that the bitterness already engendered—and
yet to be—will make it impossible for the convention to restore harmony to the party.

You can hardly imagine the embarrassment I have been in, from
the moment of my arrival here, by the number of delegates from all
quarters who are openly expressing the wish that I was the Ohio candidate. So much of this is said as to put me in constant danger of being
suspected of ambitious designs; but I think I have been so prudent as
thus far to disarm most of the suspicious ones. I shall do no act that will
in the smallest degree be untrue to myself or my associates—and I do
not [think that] any thing will come out of the deeps to me. But I am
greatly surprised at the number of prominent delegates who want to
bring out my name. Many are firmly of the belief that all the candidates
will be dropped and that I will be taken up. I hope you do not think I
am disturbed by this—or in the slightest degree elated. I shall do
nothing—and ask nothing—far better please[d] to have nothing but the
knowledge that many desire me. I————June 1, 7 A.M. I could not
finish this last evening—and I now close it by saying that the meeting of
the National Committee of last night indicates a most serious row in the
convention. Swaim, Henry, Nichol, and a host of good fellows are
here—too many to make it possible to write a connected letter.

> As Ever and
> Forever Your Own
> James

P.S. Please send my love to the boys at St. Paul's.

*This was Garfield's last letter to Mrs. Garfield from Chicago. On June 5
Roscoe Conkling nominated Grant in an eloquent speech that did nothing to
placate the anti-Grant forces. Garfield's speech, nominating Sherman, followed; Garfield stressed the need of Republican unity. On June 4 Mrs. Garfield had written, "I begin to be half afraid that the convention will give you
the nomination, and the place would be most unenviable with so many disappointed candidates. I don't want you to have the nomination merely because
no one else can get it, I want you to have it when the whole country calls for
you as the State of Ohio did last Fall. My ambition does not fall short of
that."*

Chicago, Illinois
June 6, 1880
7.30 A.M.

My Darling,

The mental and physical strain of the week ending with two days and nights of Chickamauga were hardly less [more] than that which Chicago has brought upon the men of this convention. You have doubtless followed the course of events and will see, before this reaches you, the steps of progress. For any man to have kept his head upon his shoulders is no small matter. If I have succeed[ed] better than most, it is largely due to the fact that I see always before me your calm sweet face, counseling wisdom, prudence, and truth. On the work of last night, as on all since I came, I hope I have your approval. There have been times in the convention when it seemed that it could not be in America, but in the sections of Paris in the ec[s]tasy of the Revolution, and again, it was old Ephesus, where the claquers of the silver smiths cast dust in the air, and by the space of two hours, cried "Great is Diana of the Ephesians." I shall never be able to give you any adequate idea of the scene which preceeded the vote [on] the Illinois contested seats and the similar scenes of last [evening wh]en the different [names of] candidates were put in [nomination]—I will not try now. I persevered to the end in not writing a speech; I marshalled a few ideas in line, and left room in their ranks for any things that might come from the suggestions of the hour, and in this I think I was fortunate, for Conkling's extraordinary speech gave me the idea of carrying the mind of the convention in a different direction. In that I think I had some success. At least it was success of a better kind than his. Of all these things we will talk soon. I think the good opinion of the convention towards me is not lessening.

Your suggestion of a mahogany set for Mother's room is so good of itself that were I less able than I am to bear the expense I should approve. Do it. Esthetics join with filial duty in its favor. It is needless to tell you [how] anxious I am to be with you and I shall be happy if I am let alone by this convention. Your sentence on that subject is a very crystal of wisdom and pride. Loving you with all my power to love, I send kisses to all the dear circle, and am always your

James

*Hal and Jimmie Garfield, to whom Garfield wrote about a week after his nomination, were students at St. Paul's School, Concord, New Hampshire, from September 1879 to December 1880. Colonel Almon F. Rockwell, with Garfield's help, secured a transfer from the West to Washington, D.C., in*

*1874. From that time the two men were together frequently. Rockwell's son
Don attended St. Paul's with the Garfield boys; Hal was at one time in love
with Rockwell's daughter Lulu. The signature has been cut from this letter.*

Washington, D.C.

June 16, 1880

My Dear Boys:

I know you will pardon me for having neglected you of late, for
you have never known me to be so overwhelmed with work as I have
been within the last eight days. I came here yesterday to settle up my
business preparatory to my return to Ohio.

Congress adjourns today and I shall go back home not later than
Friday of this week.

I hope you are holding on steadily to your work and not allowing
your heads to be turned by any of the events that are passing around
you.

From all I have heard you are behaving very manfully and sensibly
and I have the fullest confidence in your discretion and good judgment.

Don't say any thing about my nomination that indicates any feeling
of exultation or pride. It is a very serious business and it is particularly
important that all my children behave prudently in regard to it. I do
not say this because I doubt you, but only to express my approval of
your course thus far.

I enclose ten dollars for your allowance and such little expenses as
are necessary for yourselves.

I have arranged with Colonel Rockwell to send money to bring you
and Don home to Mentor. I will send full directions about coming and
he and Mrs. Rockwell and Lulu will meet you on your arrival.

If Mr. Hargate has any bills against me, have them sent to me at the
end of the Term. With a heart full of love I am

As Ever Your Papa

*In an interview with Garfield at Mentor after his nomination, Susan B.
Anthony, vice president at large of the National Woman Suffrage Association, failed to get from him a commitment to her cause. She had particularly
wanted a promise that as President he would recommend to Congress the
submission of a woman suffrage amendment to the states. On August 16 she
wrote him a long letter on the subject of woman suffrage, enclosing a short
official letter asking him whether as President he would recommend to
Congress the submission to the states of the desired amendment. This letter
was Garfield's response.*

Mentor, Ohio
August 24, 1880

Dear Miss Anthony,

Your letter of the 17th inst. came duly to hand. I take the liberty of asking your personal advice before I answer your official letter.

I assume that all the traditions and impulses of your life lead you to believe that the Republican party has been and is more nearly in the line of liberty than its antagonist, the Democratic party, and I know you desire to advance the cause of women.

Now in view of the fact that the Chicago convention has not discussed your question, do you not think it would be a violation of the trust they have imposed in me to speak of as their nominee and add to the present contest an issue that they have not raised?

Again, if I answered your questions on the ground of my own private opinion I shall be compelled to say that while I am open to the freest discussion and fairest consideration of your question, I have not yet reached the conclusion that it would be best for the women of the country that she should have the suffrage; I may reach it but whatever time may do to me, that fruit is not yet ripe on my tree. I ask you therefore for the sake of your own questions—do you think it wise to pick my apples now.

Please answer me in the frankness of personal friendship. With kindest regards I am

Very Truly Yours
J. A. Garfield

*Maine held its state elections in September, Ohio and Indiana in October. In presidential election years politicians anxiously awaited returns from these states as indicators of what might be expected in the presidential election in November. In 1876 both Maine and Ohio had elected Republican state tickets in early fall and electors for Hayes in November; in Indiana the Democrats had triumphed in both elections. For Garfield, Indiana, with its fifteen electoral votes, was of paramount importance in 1880. Garfield wrote this letter to Chester A. Arthur of New York, the Republican candidate for Vice President. Stephen W. Dorsey, a Republican member of the U.S. Senate from Arkansas, 1873–1879, was secretary of the Republican National Committee in 1880 and largely in charge of the campaign. Levi P. Morton, a wealthy New York banker and member of the U.S. House of Representatives, was chairman of the Republican finance committee in 1880.*

*The other men mentioned by Garfield were all Indianans. Thomas A. Hendricks, the Democratic candidate for Vice President in 1876, had been a*

*candidate for the presidential nomination at his party's convention in June
1880. Joseph E. McDonald was a Democratic member of the U.S. Senate,
1875–1881. William H. English was the Democratic candidate for Vice
President in 1880. Franklin Landers was the Democratic candidate for governor in 1880. Gilbert De La Matyr was a member of the U.S. House of
Representatives, 1879–1881; he had won with the support of both Greenbackers and Democrats. John C. New was chairman of the Republican State
Committee of Indiana in 1880.*

Mentor, Ohio
August 30, 1880

Dear General,

It is clear to me that we are now at the most critical point of the
campaign—and the victory will be made certainly possible or seriously
imperilled, by our management of Indiana during the next fortnight.
In what I now write, I assume that we shall carry Maine in September.

If we carry Indiana in October, the rest is comparatively easy. We
shall make a very serious, perhaps a fatal mistake, if we do not throw
all our available strength into that state. I have taken great pains to ascertain the situation of the parties there, not from extensive correspondence alone, but I have sent intelligent and trustworthy observers
to various parts of the state, to make special inquiries on various aspects
of the contest. Let me summarize the situation as it now appears:

1. There is much internal disagreement among the Democratic
   leaders—the bitterness of Hendricks over his defeat, his jealousy
   of McDonald, the general unpopularity of English, the soft-
   money record of Landers, in collision with their national platform and the hard money views of English and McDonald, and
   finally the anger of the Greenbackers at the Democracy for
   dropping De La Matyr, and going back [on] the Greenback party
   generally.
2. There is almost perfect harmony in our ranks—and much more
   enthusiasm than we have seen in that state at any time since
   1872.
3. The hard times of recent years was felt with exceptional severity
   in that state, and the reaction which prosperity brings has been
   correspondingly great. Many business Democrats in various
   parts of the state have openly joined us, on the ground that they
   fear the prosperity will be imperilled by the success of the Democracy.
4. From 25,000 to 30,000 voters of Indiana are members of the de-
   nomination of Disciples and at least half of them are Democrats.

A quiet but very earnest movement wholly outside the State Committee has been organized, and is being vigorously and judiciously pushed, with the strongest probability that at least 2,500 changes of vote in our favor will result.

I conclude this summary by saying that from the hundreds of reports and interviews I have had, hardly one admits a doubt that we can carry the state.

To do this, we must overcome a Democratic majority of 6,000. Our danger arises from two sources.

1. From the unusually large number of doubtful voters disclosed by the canvass which is now nearly completed for the whole state. While that canvass is strongly in our favor, it shows the field in which the Democracy will use their peculiar influences, and in which we must confront them.
2. From importations from neighboring states where no elections are held in October. The recent successes of the Democracy in Indiana have been gained mainly by this means and their money has been largely expended for this purpose.

Our friends have the full census reports to aid them in checking importations. They say they will be able to secure the friendly cooperation of nearly all the Rail Roads running into the state. They will have U.S. Supervisors appointed for the first time. They propose to station active and trustworthy Republicans in all the border counties to watch the importing movements of the Democrats. All these plans require the employment of a large number of men and much money.

And this brings me to the chief point. It is indispensably necessary that the means for putting these plans into vigorous execution be furnished at once. The work has been started and must be supported promptly to insure success. I have written thus fully, because I understand that our friends in New York are in doubt about the wisdom of making much effort for Indiana. I am certain this is erroneous. Success in Indiana will be an immense help to N.Y. and all other close states. Please read this letter to Morton, and if you concur in the views I have taken, urge him to act as promptly and vigorously as possible. I went over the whole ground with Senator Dorsey when he was here, en route for Chicago, and his letters since his arrival there, strongly confirm my opinions.

Another thing: He told me that Senator Conkling would make his opening speech in the West at such time and place as you and I thought best. Dorsey and New write me that a great convention of Republican clubs is to be held at Indianapolis on the 15th September—

which will bring together a great assembly of the most active Republicans of at least a dozen states—and they are very anxious to have the Senator address that meeting. In view of the nature of the meeting, and its importance to Indiana, I am sure he could do great good by accepting their invitation. If you concur, please present the request to him for us both.

Please let me hear the result of your conference with Morton as soon as possible.

Very Truly Yours
J. A. Garfield

*After a long silence following the Chicago convention—a silence that aroused fears among Garfield Republicans that he would not participate in the campaign—Roscoe Conkling made a campaign speech of three and a half hours before a large audience in New York City, referring briefly to Garfield at the close of the speech. Conkling then agreed to give three speeches in Ohio, one of them in Warren in Garfield's own congressional district. Whether Garfield should be in Warren on the occasion of Conkling's visit was a question anxiously debated by Garfield and his friends; Garfield remained firm in his determination not to go. The final paragraph in this letter to Harmon Austin refers to four of Austin's workmen (Austin Flagstone Company) who had been laying flagstones at Lawnfield.*

Mentor, Ohio
September 23, 1880

Dear Harmon:

Yours of the 19th inst. is received. I should be deeply grieved if I thought General Grant or Mr. Conkling would think me lacking in courtesy to them by not attending the Warren meeting but it seems to me that in the public estimation my presence at that meeting would be equivalent to taking the stump. I admit that I do not consider it certain but that I ought to take the stump, but whatever I shall finally conclude on that subject, I ought not to take the stump on that day which is devoted to Mr. Conkling, and who should be the chief speaker. All other speeches ought to be subordinated to his. It is his first visit to Ohio and everything ought to be done to give him the most generous welcome and make it understood that it is his meeting. Furthermore I think it would be embarrassing to the speakers who are advocating my election to have me present at their addresses. I have invited General Grant to come here and spend the night of the 27th but have received a letter from him stating that he cannot reach Cleveland until the morning of the 28th, and hence must go direct to Warren. I shall now try and have him and Mr. Conkling come from Warren here by way of the Ashtabula Road and spend the night of the 28th with me. In this way I think I can show my appreciation of their services to the cause.

I am almost inclined to doubt my own judgement when I find myself differing from such men as Mr. Perkins and yourself, but it seems to me that I am right in this view.

I want you to let your 4 men know that I think they did better work and more of it while they were here than any other 4 men I have ever seen. They did the steps and walk exceedingly well.

Very Truly Yours
J. A. Garfield

Mentor, Ohio
October 6, 1880

My Dear Harmon:

Yours of the 3d instant came duly to hand. I am glad that our friends agree that it is [was] well for me not to be at Warren. You had a great meeting and I hope and believe it has done much good.

Conkling is a singular compound of a very brilliant man and an exceedingly petulant spoiled child. For myself, I do not care to be praised, but it was a narrow and unmanly thing on his part to make such a manifest effort as he has done in Ohio to avoid mentioning the head of the ticket in any generous way. It has become pretty apparent that he and some of the men who are working with him are more concerned in running Grant in 1884, than they are for carrying the Republicans safely through the contest of 1880.

The scare the Ohio Republicans have had during the last two weeks has done them good and they are better organized and harder at work than they would have been if we had carried Maine. What is needed most is thorough personal work among the Republicans.

In several towns in the state, Republican business men have agreed to close their stores and shops on election day and devote their entire time to the election. I think that would be a good thing for the citizens of Warren to do, and especially to take action in advance so that other towns may follow the example at Warren.

With kindest regards, in which all the family join, I am

Very Truly Yours
J. A. Garfield

*Garfield wrote to Hal and Jimmie the Sunday before the presidential election. The* New York Tribune, *edited by Garfield's friend and adviser Whitelaw Reid, was a source of great strength for Garfield in 1880. O. L.*

*Judd was brought to Lawnfield to work as telegraph operator during the campaign. Joseph Stanley Brown was serving there as Garfield's secretary.*

*The "Morey letter," first published in facsimile in a New York paper,* Truth, *on October 22, aroused a good deal of excitement during the last days of the campaign. The handwritten letter, bearing Garfield's name, made it appear that Garfield favored the continued importation of Chinese labor. Although Garfield denounced the letter as a forgery (as it was), the Democrats used the letter against him in the Far West and elsewhere.*

Mentor, Ohio
October 31, 1880

My Dear Boys,

This is the first time for many weeks when we have no visitors; and I take a few moments to write. I suppose mamma and Mollie have kept you informed of the course of affairs here, during the last fortnight. You have also seen from the Daily *Tribune* something of what I have been saying. I take this occasion, just on the eve of the election to call your attention to some of the peculiar phases of the contest. During the months of June and July, the *leaders* of the Democratic party discussed questions of public policy; and none but the lowest class of orators and editors descended to personal abuse. But when they saw that the people were afraid to trust the financial and business interests in the hands of the "Solid South," and that the fair discussion of the merits of the two parties was hurting their chances, they began a personal warfare upon me that has hardly been equalled for violence and malignity in our history. Among other things they insisted, and published everywhere, that I did not enjoy the confidence and support of my friends and neighbors. This was handsomely answered by the fact that the 19th District gave a Republican majority of more than 12,600—being an increase of 1,606 above the majority which Gov. Foster received last year.

The failure of the Democrats to capture Ohio, and their loss of Indiana, made them unusually desperate—and hence to their other attacks they have added the forgery of a letter on the Chinese question, which they still insist is genuine. I think that many intelligent and honest Democrats will hesitate to support a party which uses such means to secure a victory. As the case now stands, I think the Republican chances of success are good. There would be no doubt of it, were it not for the very large foreign vote of New York City. But our friends there are quite confident of success. So far as I am concerned, I have not allowed myself to become so absorbed in the contest, as to lose sight of the great array of forces against us. Nor have I at all set my heart upon success as necessary to my usefulness and happiness. I want you to know that I neither sought nor wished the nomination. On many accounts, I would have preferred to go into the Senate, and enjoy the freedom of study and debate. But now that I am nominated and have borne in silence the abuse and falsehoods of the campaign I shall be glad to be successful. I have replied to no slander except the Morey forgery. In the nature of the case, no one else could reply but me; and you have seen my letter. When this reaches you the election will be in progress; and a few hours later, the result will be known. I know that you will both feel a deep interest in the outcome, but I have learned to trust your discretion, and so have no fears that you will be unduly cast down if I am defeated, nor that you will do or say any thing unseemly if I am elected. You have by inheritance and education so much of the equipo[i]se and prudence of your mother, that I have long ago, ceased to have much anxiety about you—so far as discretion of speech and action about family affairs are concerned. Above all, Dear Boys, whatever shall happen, I beg you to keep on the even tenor of your way, holding up, with even a little more than usual vigor and steadiness to your work. It would make me very proud to know that during the first week of November 1880, my boys marked a little higher in studies, decorum, punctuality and industry than in any previous week of the term—and that they were in no wise thrown off their balance by the Presidential Election. The family are all well, although a little tired out by the crowds of visitors. "Veto" is growing in size, experience and discretion. Hal's colt is doing well, having nearly recovered from a few scratchets received by running into the wire fence. The Alderney calf has been sold for $100, and taken to Illinois, but two younger ones, of purer breed, have come from Baltimore. The back yard, side yards, and part of the front yard have been turfed. The entrance to the woodshed has been enclosed for winter. The new steam engine has come, and is soon to be in its place under a lean-to soon to be erected on the east end of the old engine house. The huskers are busy in the corn. The buckwheat will be threshed before the week ends, and we will greet you with Indian pudding and buckwheat cakes when you come home for the holidays. Five loads of apples have gone to the cider mill, and twelve barrells of cider are fermenting on the north side of the office. Judd has gone home to Michigan to vote; and if our two pilgrims were here there would be no absentees, and none present but the family and Mr. Brown. This, in brief is the situation on the eve of the battle.

The whole house-hold join me in tenderest love to you both. And now, my brave lads, Good night.

As Ever Your Papa
J. A. Garfield

*Burke Hinsdale's services to Garfield during the campaign included the writing of a biography of his friend and the delivery of many speeches in Ohio and Indiana; the check enclosed in this letter was to cover some of Hinsdale's expenses during the campaign. Garfield was the first member of the Disciples of Christ to be elected President of the United States.*

Mentor, Ohio
November 17, 1880

My Dear Burke:

Yours of the 6th instant came duly to hand.

I enclose my check on the Second National Bank for $48, amount to cover additional bills.

I read with great pleasure the *Herald* extract from your speech in Hiram. It is surprising that, with no consultation or comparison of views, you should have so perfectly expressed my own attitude on questions of the future.

I insist that I have a right to be silent for the next two or three months and take observations. Lincoln said in his homely way, that he wanted "to take a bath in public opinion." I think I have a right to take a bath before I do much talking.

I note what you say in regard to the expectations of our brethren and I want your help in that direction. This is about the sum of my reflections.

First. Our people must not use me as the promoter of the views of our brethren. While I shall cheerfully maintain my old relations to them, I want it understood that it is the broad general views and not the special particularities of our faith that I desire to promote.

Second. Our people must not make too much fuss about it. For example: they must not undertake to build a showy house in Washington. They do need a new church building. It should be neat, and elegant, but modest, as I have written to the Pastor there in answer to inquiries.

Third. Our people must remember that they are not a very large percent of the whole Republican party, and a still smaller percent of the whole American people, and it would not be difficult for me to injure the administration, by giving undue prominence to the Disciples in matters of appointment.

Let us not flaunt ourselves in the face of the American people, as though we had made a special conquest, but, by modesty and moderation, bear our part worthily and take whatever resulting advantages may come.

In the hurry of my last letter, I do not think I said much, if anything, concerning your work in the campaign. Few men in the country have made more solid contributions to our success than you have and our long and intimate acquaintance and friendship made your work exceptionally valuable.

You will know without my enlarging upon it, how deeply grateful I am.

I go in the morning to Solon, to attend the funeral of sister's daughter, Hattie Palmer.

I hope we shall meet before long.

Very Truly Yours

J. A. Garfield

*Garfield and Mrs. Garfield were in Washington from November 23 to November 29. George Rose, Garfield's longtime secretary, and his family were occupying the Garfield house. When Hal first proposed that he, Jimmie, and Don Rockwell study in Washington under a private tutor rather than return to St. Paul's after Christmas, his parents were not inclined to approve. As this letter indicates, they had changed their mind. St. Paul's School was founded by Episcopalians; its rector from its beginning until 1895 was Henry A. Coit, an Episcopal clergyman. Early in October Dr. Coit invited Hal to join his next confirmation class (after consultation with his parents) and to become an Episcopalian if he chose. Hal's parents were reluctant to have him act hastily, knowing that he would soon be at Williams College, where Congregationalism was the dominant religious influence.*

1227 I St.

Washington, D.C.

November 26, 1880

My Dear Boys:

I have tried all day to find a moment to write to you; but the rush of callers and business have not allowed me to do so until now. We came to close up our house affairs here, and ship to Mentor what things we shall need for the farm home. I have not yet determined whether I will sell the house or rent it. I think we will let Mr. Rose and his family occupy it a while longer, until I can get a good price or a fair rental. You can hardly imagine how much I dislike to leave the little nest which has been our happy home so many years. But of course we must bow to the inevitable, and as we are not able to keep it, and may never again need it, I must realize its value as nearly as I can and let it go into other hands. I have carefully read your letters which came this afternoon, and have gone over the question with Col. Rockwell, which you raise in reference to studying under a tutor during the last half of the school year, rather than to stay at St. Paul's. In discussing the case we have taken into account first your best interests, and second your wishes. On the latter point we know you can work more cheerfully and happily when your wishes are gratified. But we also know that you are not sufficiently drilled in some of the primary branches, and the next half year at St. Paul's will not give you that drill. We have therefore agreed to accept your plan. Col. Rockwell will at once set about finding a suitable tutor, and when your holiday vacation in Mentor is over, you are to come here, board at Rockwells until we come and then live at home but all three study under the tutor, until you have brought up back studies and are thoroughly fitted for College. This will require, on your part a resolute and persistent determination to push your studies, and not be drawn off by the excitement of Washington. And we will trust you to be faithful and diligent. Of course we are greatly pleased with the prospect of having you at home, but we want to avoid making the home life a damage to you. Now, Hal, on the subject of your confirmation, I say again you must be perfectly free to decide for yourself in all matters relating to religion. Neither Mamma nor I desire to control your choice. And certainly no body else should. Do not permit yourself to be persuaded or influenced to act hastily. I greatly prefer that you take no preliminary step, or binding obligation, until after the holidays, for I have some suggestions to make which I think will aid you.

Remember that all the influences now around you are in one direction, and you may be a broader man, for having looked on all sides before acting. Please do not forget that the ministers of almost every church are drumming up recruits for their own sect. I do not mean this in a bad sense; but I do mean, that it often amounts to undue influence. I have never asked you to join my church, and I don't want any other man to take away your liberty. You are still very young. Your heart is fresh and pure, and I think the long experience of Mamma and Papa, who love you as no stranger can, may be of service to you, and I think it would do you good—and you would feel better about it after you have decided—to have had a full talk with us before your decision.

And now dear boys, hoping to hear from you at Mentor, on Tuesday next, I am as ever

Your affectionate papa
J. A. Garfield

*On November 19, 1880, Garfield asked Albion W. Tourgée for his opinion of the effect of the election on the solid South. Tourgée, the author of the novels* A Fool's Errand by One of the Fools *(1879) and* Bricks Without Straw *(1880), both of which dealt with Reconstruction, responded with a*

*letter of fourteen pages in which he discussed the political situation in the South and expressed his views as to the policy that Garfield should pursue in relation to the South. Garfield gave Tourgée's letter to Burke Hinsdale to read. In this letter to Hinsdale Garfield indicated his own views in relation to the South; they were views with which Tourgée could have found little to quarrel.*

Mentor, Ohio
December 30, 1880

Dear Burke:

Yours of the 21st inst. came duly to hand and was read with interest.

Some of the points you made on Judge Tourgée's letter I had observed as I read it. I have no doubt that the final cure for the "Solid South" will be found in the education of its youth, and in the development of its business interests, but both these things require time. We are likely therefore to have a southern question for many years to come. I do not believe a speedy cure is possible. Patronage to Democrats has been tried and has proved a dreary failure. Rebel Democrats appointed to office by Republicans take one of two courses—either they suffer complete ostracism by their neighbors, or they become more fierce assailants of the Republican party to keep themselves in good standing at home. In fact the "Solid South" accepts all patronage at the hands of the Republican Administration as a confession of our weakness and their superiority.

I am not sure that the appointment of southern Republicans, however worthy, to prominent places is treated by the Solid South as any favor to that section. In my opinion the real trouble can be summed up in this: our government is a modern Republic; the South was rooted and grounded in feudalism based on slavery; and the destruction of slavery has not yet destroyed the feudalism which it caused. Nothing but time can complete its dissolution. I do not know a better way to treat that people than to let them know that this is a modern free government, and only men who believe in it, and not in feudalism, can be invited to aid in administering it; then give the South, as rapidly as possible, the blessings of general education and business enterprise; and trust to time and these forces to work out the problem.

I shall look anxiously for your article. If I do not see you sooner I shall hope to visit Hiram not long after the holiday recess of Congress is over.

As Ever Yours
J. A. Garfield

*During the months following his election Garfield spent considerable time as-*
*sembling a cabinet and conferring with Republican politicians at Mentor*
*concerning appointments. Garfield had to reward those who had supported*
*him at Chicago while placating the Grant faction, which, under the leader-*
*ship of Conkling, Cameron, and Logan, had supported him during the cam-*
*paign. Conkling wanted a New Yorker under his influence to be secretary of*
*the treasury—an appointment Garfield was determined to avoid. Cameron*
*had been to Mentor to talk with Garfield since the election; Conkling and*
*Logan had not. In December Blaine accepted Garfield's offer of the State*
*Department, but Garfield withheld public notice of this appointment lest it*
*complicate his dealings with Conkling and other stalwarts. Thomas L.*
*James, a friend and supporter of Conkling, was postmaster of New York*
*City; Garfield was hopeful that Conkling would be satisfied by the appoint-*
*ment of James as postmaster general, but he wanted to be sure that James*
*would be loyal to the President. Another problem for Garfield was finding a*
*suitable southerner for the cabinet.*

Mentor, Ohio
January 24, 1881

My Dear Blaine,

I have yours of the 20th. I can see some advantages of a visit to
Washington—and would be glad to relieve my friends of embarrassment. But I think a trip there, and back here again, would make more
trouble than it would cure. The Conkling men want me *to go to them.*
They hear rumors which disquiet them—that they are to be ignored
etc. The road to Mentor is open, and they shall be welcomed and
treated fairly. Cameron came, and I do not hear that he complains of
his treatment. One senator writes me that Conkling has heard that I in-
terfered against him in the N.Y. Senatorial election (which is not true)
and the writer thinks that I ought to go to Washington and disabuse his
mind on that question. I am not a suitor for favors at the hand of any
who do not care to open correspondence with me—and to appear to be
so, would create a world of misunderstandings. If, in the end, they are
treated fairly, it will cure the apprehension of evil they now feel. In
making the visit, I should necessarily be compelled to decline interviews
with so many people, that the wounded birds would be a majority. Besides, I know it will not be possible to gratify the wishes, and even ap-
proximately meet the expectations of most of those I should consult.
Two courses are open to me, as a substitute for the proposed visit—1st.
To go to Washington a week or ten days before the inauguration, having the full cast of the Cabinet open until then, 2nd. To invite Conkling
and Logan and such others, as may be thought best, to visit me here
soon. What do you think of these propositions?

I understand your embarrassment in coming. It is enhanced by the
talk of a class of people that you are to dominate the administration to
the exclusion of other elements. You can do a great deal to allay that
fear. If those I have named should come, or even be invited, it would
relieve your visit of embarrassment. I have only cared to keep your des-
ignation to the State Department a secret, until well into February.
Then, I prefer it should be known. The public has already passed
judgment upon the wisdom of the choice; and the only motive I have
had for secrecy was to prevent the jealousy of rival forces. I must see
you by or before the middle of February. You speak of James of N.Y.
Has he the necessary independence and will to stand by his chief in a
fight, against all opposers? If I were perfectly sure of that, I would
think the suggestion a good one. I mean to make an appointment for
N.Y. which shall give Conkling no just ground of complaint, and no
undue advantage if he means fight.

The southern member still eludes me—as Creusa's image eluded
Aeneas. One by one the southern roses fade. Do you know of a magno-
lia blossom, that will stand our northern climate?

As Ever Yours
J. A. Garfield

*Sunday, March 13, 1881, was a crowded day for the President. Charles
Foster and Carl Schurz were guests at breakfast, and with the latter Garfield
had a long talk. Accompanied by his wife and mother, the President went to
church, where they found "another crowd outside and in." On the way home
he stopped to call on a sick friend. After lunch he learned of the assassination of Alexander II of Russia and ordered the dispatch of a message of
condolence. He took a long ride with Secretary of State Blaine. In the evening, among many callers, William M. Evarts came to discuss the upcoming
international monetary conference. Somehow the President found time to
write his brother-in-law, Joseph Rudolph, who was in charge of the Mentor
farm during his absence. Thomas Northcott had performed the same service
earlier.*

Washington, D.C.
March 13, 1881

Dear Brother:

Yours of the 11th inst. is received, and proposed changes in management of the farm are noted and approved.

I had hoped that lot No. 1 would prove to be in condition to raise a
fair crop of hay, or make a tolerable night pasture. But since you find

this is not so, it is best to put nearly all the manure you have and add what can reasonably be bought to bring the field into good shape.

Green is mistaken about lot 6. In 1879 it was good meadow; but in 1880 it was not so good and showed some wild grass. Perhaps bone dust will hold it up for another season—but by next year (1882) it must be plowed.

Please tell me, when you next write, what you can get for the surplus potatoes. Perhaps it may be worth while to ship them to me here. If they are in good condition it will save so much purchase.

I regret that Northcott bought 2 years olds—yearlings would have been better.

All the family are well and send their love to the Mentor household.

We envy you the restful quiet which does not yet live in this house.

Please have Peter take the black mare down to the scales and weigh her, and when you next write tell me her weight and height. I am trying to find a match for her.

As ever yours
J. A. Garfield

*When Garfield nominated William H. Robertson to be collector of customs of the port of New York, he had to find a place for the incumbent, Edwin A. Merritt. He nominated Merritt consul general in London to replace General Adam Badeau, whom he proposed to send to Copenhagen. Badeau was a close friend of General Grant; he had been on Grant's staff from 1864 to 1869 and had accompanied the former President on his trip around the world, 1877–1879. Garfield's appointment of Robertson and treatment of Badeau incensed Grant, who wrote angrily to Garfield from Mexico on April 24, entrusting the delivery of the letter to Senator John P. Jones of Nevada. The letter presented here was Garfield's response to Grant. In his diary entry for May 17 Garfield wrote, "I have answered a very remarkable letter from Gen. Grant. Rumors are in the paper that his will be published. If so, my reply shall appear. He seems to have forgotten that he is only one citizen—and hence is unconsciously insolent. I have not answered him sharply, but plainly, and I think conclusively."*

Executive Mansion
Washington, D.C.
May 15, 1881

My Dear General,

Yours of the 24th April was handed to me by Senator Jones the night before last. I was, and always will be, glad to hear your suggestions on any subject connected with the public welfare. I am in hearty accord with every expression in your letter touching the welfare of the country, and the success of the Republican party. You are, however, under serious misapprehension in reference to my motives and purposes concerning the New York appointments, and I beg to refer, in detail, to the points in your letter omitting, for the present, that which is personal to me.

You say that success cannot be achieved by "giving the administration over to the settlement of other people's private grievances." You do me great injustice to suppose that I am capable of permitting such use of the power entrusted to me. It has not been done nor will it be. I have no thought of making any appointment to injure you.

While I heartily agree with you when you say that you "ought not to be humiliated by seeing my (your) personal friends punished for no other offence than their friendship and support," I am sure you will agree with me that worthy and competent men should not be excluded from recognition because they opposed your nomination at Chicago.

That I had no purpose to proscribe your friends in N.Y. but every disposition to deal justly and at the same time cultivate their friendly feelings toward my administration, appears from the fact that I selected for a very important cabinet position one of your warm supporters, and gave ten other important positions to your friends in N.Y. most of whom had been strongly recommended by one or both of the Senators and by other friends of yours. In making a selection of a Collector of the Port of N.Y., an office more national than local, I sought to secure the services of a gentleman of eminent ability, and at the same time, to give just recognition to that large and intelligent element of N.Y. Republicans who were in accord with the majority of the Chicago Convention. For this I am assailed by some of your indiscreet friends. As I said in the Chicago convention, it needed all grades and shades of Republicans to carry the election. So it needs the support of all good Republicans to make the administration successful.

In this connection, let me correct two errors of fact into which you have inadvertently fallen. Judge Robertson did not, as you suppose, oppose your election in 1872, nor did he declare in the Chicago convention that he would not support you if nominated. He was elected State Senator in 1872, running on the same ticket with you. At Chicago, on the roll-call, before any nominations had been made, he voted to support the nominee of the convention whoever he might be.

Now while I agree substantially with you that "it is always the fair thing to recognize the representatives chosen by the people," I am not willing to allow the power of the Executive in selecting persons for nomination to be restricted to the consideration of those only who may be suggested by the Senators from the State from which the selection is to be made. I feel bound, as you did when President, to see to it that local quarrels for leadership shall not exclude from recognition men who represent any valuable element in the Republican party. It is my purpose to be just to all; and while I am incapable of discriminating against any Republican because he supported you, I am sure you will agree with me that I ought not to permit any one to be proscribed because he did not support you.

Before Judge Robertson's nomination I had reason to know that it was the wish of both N.Y. Senators that the Collector should be changed. I knew that in Senator Platt's recent election, he had received the support of Judge Robertson both in the caucus and in the Senate, and I had reason to believe, and did believe that the nomination would be satisfactory to him, and to the Governor of the State, (both of whom were your warm supporters) and that it would be eminently satisfactory to a large body of N.Y. Republicans. I had no reason to suppose that Mr. Robertson was regarded as a personal enemy by Senator Conkling—Judge Robertson had twice voted for Mr. Conkling for U.S. Senator, and had supported him for the Presidency at Cincinnati, so long as the N.Y. delegation presented his name. He occupied a leading and distinguished position in his state and party. His fitness for the collectorship had not been, and is not questioned. Notwithstanding all this when, on the day after the nomination, I heard that it was objected to by Senator Conkling, I made an appointment for a conference with him, Senator Platt and the Vice President, on the subject, and waited an hour and a half beyond the time they had fixed. They did not call— nor has Senator Conkling called to see me since. The course of subsequent events has placed the question far beyond the personal fate of Judge Robertson as a nominee. The issue now is, whether the President, in making nominations to office shall act in obedience to the dictation of the Senators from the State where the office is to be exercised. I regard this assumption as at war with the Constitution, and destructive of the true principles of administration.

To submit to this view would be to renounce the trust I have undertaken.

My dear General, I can never forget your great services during the late campaign. They were given ungrudgingly, and as whole heartedly as I always gave you mine, when our positions were reversed before the people. You supported me without condition or attempted stipulation; and my heart warms generously in response to any request or desire of yours. In this connection, I may say that I shall be glad if I find myself able to carry out your wish in reference to Gen. Badeau.

Be assured that whatever concerns your happiness and prosperity, will always be a matter of sincere interest to me.

With kind regards, I am

Very truly yours
J. A. Garfield

*This is the only letter written by Garfield during the eighty days from the time he was shot until the day he died. Facsimiles of the letter have been widely circulated; a facsimile has sometimes been mistaken for the original, which is in the Manuscript Division of the Library of Congress.*

Washington, D.C.
August 11, 1881

Dear Mother,

Don't be disturbed by conflicting reports about my condition. It is true I am still weak, and on my back; but I am gaining every day, and need only time and patience to bring me through.

Give my love to all the relatives & friends & especially to sisters Hitty and Mary. Your loving son,

James A. Garfield

# ACKNOWLEDGMENTS

Miss Leech had the help of many people and institutions. Mrs. Tamis Erdmann rendered secretarial and research assistance over a long period. Miss Y. B. Garden, Miss Leech's secretary, was of great service. Miss Kate Stewart contributed far beyond the requirements of her position in the Manuscript Division of the Library of Congress. Mrs. Barbara Cooper, librarian of the Lake County (Ohio) Historical Society, gave much aid. Mrs. Margaret Collacott (now deceased) of Mentor, Ohio, was a source of much information and other assistance. Mrs. Ruth Feis, daughter of Mollie Garfield and a friend of Miss Leech for many years, was very generous with her help. Thanks are also due to Mrs. Lucretia Comer (now deceased), daughter of Harry A. Garfield; Edward Garfield, son of Abram Garfield; Mrs. John C. Robbins and her daughter Mrs. John Zimmerman, great granddaughter of Phebe Boynton Clapp; and Dr. and Mrs. William C. Weir. Thanks are owed to Miss Mary S. Romer for information about Rebecca Selleck and for the photograph of Rebecca used in this book. Frederick D. Williams of Michigan State University was helpful on many occasions. The many persons who answered inquiries concerning the Hubbell and Selleck families are also deserving of thanks.

Foremost among institutions whose staffs contributed to Miss Leech's work is the Library of Congress, where David C. Mearns, chief of the Manuscript Division, Dr. Percy Powell, superintendent of the Manuscript Division Reading Room, and other members of the staff of that division contributed greatly to making research there both satisfying and pleasant. Legare O'Bear, chief of the Loan Division, was also helpful. The Lake County Historical Society made a large contribution. Many members of the staff of the Western Reserve Historical Society, whose director is Dr. Meredith B. Colket, were most helpful on many occasions. Thanks are also due members of the staff of the National Archives (particularly H. B. Fant), Williams College Library (Wylis E. Wright, Lawrence W. Wikander, and William J. Cartwright), Teachout-Price Memorial Library, Hiram College (Miss Thelma R. Bumbaugh), Library of the University of California at Los Angeles (James V. Mink), Ashtabula County (Ohio) Historical Society, Geauga County (Ohio) Historical Society, Cleveland Public Library, Ohio Historical Society, New York Society Library, New York Public Library, Westchester (New York) Historical Society, and the Division of Archives, State of New York. I extend my apologies to those persons and institutions whose aid to Miss Leech has not been acknowledged.

My own indebtedness to many of the institutions and individuals mentioned above is very great, and I extend my thanks to them. I am also grateful to many others for their help. Professor Sydney J. Freedberg of Harvard University, son-in-law of Margaret Leech and executor of her estate, sent to me all her voluminous Garfield files. Mrs. Helen Elkiss rendered indispensable service for a year as typist, proofreader, and filer. George Bennett and Susan McMahon also aided with the typing. Several professors at Michigan State University (in addition to Frederick D. Williams, mentioned above) came to my assistance: Eleanor Huzar helped me with proofreading and made many valuable suggestions; Harold B. Fields showed me how to construct the genealogical chart and gave me in other ways the benefit of his long experience as a genealogist; Joseph Druse also rendered genealogical help. Some of the genealogical information used was contributed by Mrs. Margaret Coppess, who has long been interested in the Garfield and Boynton families. John Shimmin prepared the maps and the genealogical chart. John M. Hoffmann, assistant editor of *The Papers of Ulysses S. Grant,* supplied information. I owe a large debt to the Michigan State University Library and its staff, and I am indebted to the Michigan State Library. Portions of chapters 9 and 10 appeared in different form in the Introduction to *The Diary of James A. Garfield,* published by Michigan State University Press. I owe much to Dr. Watt P. Marchman, director of the Rutherford B. Hayes Library, and to his staff. Mrs. Frances Slack and Mrs. Laine Mull of the Lake County Historical Society have been very helpful. I am grateful to Dr. Russell Smith, director of the project for microfilming the presidential papers in the Library of Congress; without the microfilm of the Garfield Papers and the accompanying index I could not have completed this work. I wish to thank Michigan State University for granting me a leave that enabled me to work more steadily on the book than I could have otherwise done.

—HARRY J. BROWN

# NOTES AND REFERENCES

ABBREVIATIONS USED IN THE NOTES

JAG            James A. Garfield
LR             Lucretia Rudolph
LRG            Lucretia Rudolph Garfield
EBG            Eliza Ballou Garfield
L.C.           Library of Congress
JAG Papers     The Papers of James A. Garfield in the Manuscript Division of
               the Library of Congress
LRG Papers     The Papers of Lucretia Rudolph Garfield in the Manuscript
               Division of the Library of Congress
JAG Diary      The Diary of James A. Garfield for the years 1878–1881, in
               the JAG Papers
Diary of JAG   Harry James Brown and Frederick D. Williams, eds., The Diary
               of James A. Garfield, 3 vols. (East Lansing: Michigan State Uni-
               versity Press, 1967–1973). These volumes include all of Gar-
               field's diary through the year 1877.

All letters cited in the notes for which the source is not given are in the James
A. Garfield Papers, Library of Congress.

### Epilogue I. A Hot Saturday Morning in Washington

1. Harry and James were studying under a private tutor preparatory to entering Williams College in the fall. Mrs. Garfield used the expression "bachelors' hall" in a letter to Harry, 11 May 1879, when she and the younger children were in Ohio and
   Harry and James were with their father in Washington.
2. For Mrs. Garfield's illness see JAG Diary, 3 May to 18 June 1881. Her illness may
   also be followed in the New York Tribune, 11 May to 16 June 1881, passim.
3. Murat Halstead, "The Tragedy of Garfield's Administration: Personal Reminiscences
   and Records of Conversations," McClure's Magazine, VI:277 (Feb. 1896). Halstead,

one of the best known correspondents of the day (he was long associated with the *Cincinnati Commercial*), was present at Mrs. Garfield's informal reception on the night of 3 May.

4. JAG Diary, 4–9 May 1881. Dr. Jedediah H. Baxter, chief medical purveyor of the U.S. Army, and Dr. Gustavus W. Pope, a physician who lived near the Garfield house at Thirteenth and I streets, confirmed Dr. Edson's diagnosis. When Baxter sought appointment as surgeon general of the army one criticism of him was that he had consulted with homeopathic physicians during the illness of Mrs. Garfield.

5. JAG to LRG, 29 May 1874.

6. JAG Diary, 8–10 May 1881. Dr. Boynton arrived on the night of 12 May, when Mrs. Garfield had been ill for ten days.

7. Ibid., 10 and 11 May 1881.

8. Ibid., 26–28 May 1881.

9. Ibid., 3 June 1881.

10. Ibid., 31 May 1881.

11. Ibid., 11 June 1881.

12. Ibid., 12 June 1881.

13. Garfield was at Elberon with Mrs. Garfield from 18 June to 27 June 1881. See JAG Diary for the period.

14. Garfield expected to be away from Washington from 2 July to about 17 July. His plans included an overnight stay at Cyrus W. Field's home on the Hudson, a trip to the White Mountains, a stop at the home of Secretary of State Blaine in Augusta, Maine, a cruise along the Maine coast in a revenue cutter, and an appearance before the New Hampshire legislature.

15. Principal sources for Garfield's early morning meeting with Harry and James are Harry A. Garfield's "Life Book," 24 October 1883, and a copy of a letter of Harry to Frances Garfield, 13 March 1939, both of which are in the Harry A. Garfield Papers, L.C. The diary of James R. Garfield in the James R. Garfield Papers, L.C., has only this reference to a pre-breakfast meeting with the President: "Rose at 7, went into Papa's room and talked till 8. . . ."

16. See the first two sources in the preceding note. The quotation is from the letter.

17. Halstead, "The Tragedy of Garfield's Administration," p. 278. "I am in better health—indeed, quite well," Halstead quotes Garfield as saying. "It is curious, isn't it? My wife's sickness cured me. I got so anxious about her I ceased to think about myself." A similar sentiment is expressed in a letter of Garfield to Jacob D. Cox, 22 May 1881, letterpress copy.

18. *Diary of JAG*, II, 24 March 1873; Benson John Lossing, *A Biography of James A. Garfield* (New York, 1882), p. 749. Six weeks before he became President, Garfield recorded a dream that he had had the night before.

19. Garfield's new spring suit is mentioned in "Memorandum concerning Joseph Stanley-Brown's Relations with General Garfield. New York, June 24, 1924," in the Joseph Stanley-Brown Papers, L.C., hereafter referred to as Stanley-Brown, "Memorandum."

### Chapter 1. Eliza

1. JAG Diary, 17 Jan. 1881.

2. Stephen Trowbridge to EBG and family, 1871, LRG Papers.

3. EBG to JAG and LRG, 28 Feb. 1869.

4. Ibid.; EBG to JAG, 14 June 1868; EBG memorandum, 14 Feb. 1869 ("red Irishman").

5. EBG to Alpha Boynton, 19 May 1873.
6. Adin Ballou, *An Elaborate History and Genealogy of the Ballous in America* (Providence, 1888); EBG memorandum, 31 March 1870 (small notebook).
7. EBG to JAG, 1 April 1870.
8. Ibid.
9. EBG memorandum, 31 March 1870 (description of Abram); EBG to JAG, 1 April 1870.
10. EBG memorandum, 31 March 1870. In a memorandum of 7 Feb. 1869, Eliza spoke of their having "sunk a good deal of money on the Canal."
11. EBG memorandum, 31 March 1870.
12. Statement of J. P. Robison to Joseph Stanley-Brown, 10 Sept. 1887, JAG Papers.
13. Alvin F. Harlow, *Old Towpaths: the Story of the American Canal Era* (New York, 1926), p. 248 (EBG on the canal); EBG memorandum, 31 March 1870.
14. EBG memorandum, 31 March 1870.
15. Ibid.
16. A. S. Hayden, *Early History of the Disciples in the Western Reserve, Ohio; with Biographical Sketches of the Principal Agents in their Religious Movement* (Cincinnati, 1875); EBG memorandum, 31 March 1870.
17. EBG to JAG, 19 Nov. 1871.
18. EBG memorandum, 31 March 1870; Jonas M. Bundy, *The Life of James A. Garfield* (New York, 1880), p. 9. Bundy, editor of the *New York Evening Mail*, spent some time with the Garfields at Mentor before writing his biography of Garfield, which was published on 3 Aug.; no doubt he heard from Eliza herself stories of her early life. William M. Thayer, *From Log-Cabin to the White House: Life of James A. Garfield* (Boston, 1881), pp. 30–32.
19. *History of Ottawa County, Michigan, with Illustrations and Biographical Sketches of Some of its Prominent Men and Pioneers* (Chicago, 1882), p. 95; JAG to EBG, 3 Feb. 1857.
20. Bundy, *Garfield*, pp. 9–10. A number of years ago I saw the conveyance of the fifty acres of land, dated 8 Sept. 1834, at the Stratford, Connecticut, home of Carle Robbins (now deceased), the great grandson of Amos Boynton (*HB*).
21. LRG. "Rough Sketch of an Introduction to a Life of General Garfield," Mentor, 1887, JAG Papers; Burke Hinsdale, "Amos Boynton," in Crisfield Johnson, comp., *History of Cuyahoga County, Ohio, with Portraits and Biographical Sketches of its Prominent Men and Pioneers* (Philadelphia, 1879), pp. 495–496; JAG to EBG, 16 April 1853; JAG to Phebe Boynton Clapp, 23 Dec. 1866.
22. EBG to JAG, 10 Dec. 1854; Henry Boynton to JAG, 7 Jan. 1855; EBG to JAG, 5 Nov. 1855.
23. Bundy, *Garfield*, does not mention either Amos Boynton or Thomas Garfield as helpers of the Widow Garfield and her family. "So," Bundy remarks, p. 10, "in all sorts of ways the busy household managed not only to exist, but to live well, as they thought."
24. EBG to JAG, 10 Dec. 1854.
25. Eliza's diaries and letters are sprinkled with references to illness, death, and the grave. For "mouldering" see EBG to JAG, 14 June 1868. In her diary entry for 23 Feb. 1861 she writes, "This day we are nearer to the grave let us be prepared to meet Death." After attending the burial of a granddaughter Eliza remarks that "she has paid the debt to nature that we all owe." EBG diary, 17 Nov. 1880. Her concern when her children are ill is shown in EBG to JAG, 2 Jan. 1854, when he was having trouble with his throat.
26. For Eliza's singing: Bundy, *Garfield*, p. 13; the biblical phrases and her account of her father are in her memorandum of 31 March 1870. It is not certain when Eliza's

frame house was built. John Clark Ridpath, *The Life and Work of James A. Garfield* (Cincinnati, 1882), pp. 28–30, states that it was built in the autumn of 1843 (when James was twelve). "Thomas, who had just attained his majority, had returned from a trip to Michigan with a sum of ready money, and wanted to build his mother a new house. Some of the materials for a frame building were already accumulated, and under the directions of a carpenter the work was begun and rapidly pushed to conclusion. In all these proceedings James took an intense interest." Other early biographers of Garfield tell a similar story.

27. Eliza called herself "your small mammy" in EBG to JAG, 29 March 1860; Mary Larabee to JAG, 22 Nov. 1854, with EBG to JAG, 21 Nov. 1854; EBG to JAG, 2 Jan. 1854 (for tears of Thomas); JAG to Phebe Boynton, 22 Jan. 1853; JAG to Phebe Boynton Clapp, 28 Feb. 1863; JAG to LR, 2 March 1854.

28. EBG memorandum, 14 Feb. 1869.

29. LRG, "Rough Sketch."

30. EBG to JAG, 19 Nov. 1871.

31. *Diary of JAG*, I, 9 Oct. 1853.

32. Married at sixteen to Stephen Trowbridge, school teacher, small farmer, and land speculator, Hitty's life was one of toil and privation. Her old house in Solon was a perpetual grievance to her family until 1877 when Garfield had a small house built for her (see *Diary of JAG*, III, 3 Sept. to 6 Nov. 1877, passim). In 1865 she sued Stephen for divorce but soon asked for a dismissal. Execution Docket, Vol. 32, p. 57, Cuyahoga Co. Common Pleas Court, and Civil Journal, Vol. 41, p. 31, no. 405, Cuyahoga Co. Common Pleas Court, Cuyahoga Co. Court House, Cleveland. Garfield once described Stephen as "a composition of goodness and meanness." *Diary of JAG*, I, 7 Oct. 1850. In 1879 Stephen was living alone in a wretched cabin in Midland Co., Michigan, where he had gone to keep from losing some land there. He was still there in 1880; after the election he wrote Garfield to ask for a job. Perry J. Cleveland to JAG, 18 Aug. 1880; Stephen Trowbridge to JAG, 21 Nov. 1880.

33. Mary Larabee to JAG, 22 Nov. 1854, with EBG to JAG, 21 Nov. 1854 (Mary's companionship), LR to JAG, 8 June 1855 (behavior as boy), JAG to LR, 18 June 1855 (resentment of authority), JAG to Phebe Boynton, 22 Jan. 1853, and *Diary of JAG*, III, 29 March 1877 (respect for teachers), Thomas Garfield to JAG, 15 April 1854 ("sporting"), JAG to EBG and Thomas, 16 April 1853 (JAG and Amos Boynton).

34. JAG to LRG, 15 Feb. 1862.

35. JAG to Harry Rhodes, 19 Nov. 1862.

36. Ibid. Speaking of his children, Garfield wrote, "Their advantages are far greater than mine were at their time of life." *Diary of JAG*, II, 1 June 1874. "When I was ten years of age I had never travelled fifteen miles from home. Such a trip as Hal is now taking would have been a great thing to me." Ibid., II, 11 June 1874.

37. *Diary of JAG*, I 23 June 1854; JAG to Mary Hubbell, 9 April 1852.

38. A seventh child, Bentley, born to Amos and Alpha Boynton, died in infancy. William died in 1857, age twenty-nine. Cordelia died the day before Garfield was shot, as the result of an accident at a railroad crossing in Ohio. Garfield's feelings about Amos are shown in his letters to Eliza and Thomas, 16 April 1853, and to Phebe Boynton Clapp, 23 Dec. 1866.

39. *Diary of JAG*, I, 4 June 1851.

40. Ibid., 18 July 1852.

41. Ibid., 20 Sept. 1871. JAG memorandum, 23 Jan. 1872; A. B. Newburgh to JAG, 16 Oct. 1871; Abram Garfield's canal agreement.

42. *Diary of JAG*, I, 23 Jan. 1853; EBG to JAG, 2 Jan. 1854 ("early grave"). Garfield's diary has a very large number of references to his health.

43. EBG to JAG, 6 Sept. 1854 and 15 June 1855; JAG to EBG, 22 July 1855 and 19 Nov. 1855.
44. JAG to LR, 2 March 1854.
45. *Diary of JAG*, I, 29 July 1854 ("framing . . ."); Phebe Boynton to JAG, 30 April 1853.
46. *Diary of JAG*, I, 9 Oct. 1853.
47. Marriage: Cuyahoga Co. marriage records, Vol. 4, p. 142. Divorce: Cuyahoga Co., Common Pleas Court, Execution Docket No. 18, p. 387, and Cuyahoga Co. Common Pleas Journal, S, p. 238. These documents are in the Cuyahoga Co. Court House, Cleveland. The spelling "Guiffeld" is of no consequence; early settlers made many variations on proper names, including their own. In early New England the name was sometimes spelled Gearfield or Gearfeild. The name was usually pronounced "Gaffield" or "Gaffil" in rural Ohio; this was possibly a persistence of New England speech. In the divorce records the name is spelled correctly.
48. Belding's death: *Grand Rapids Daily Morning Democrat,* 16 Jan. 1881; *Grand Rapids Evening Leader,* 15 Jan. 1881; *Grand Rapids Daily Eagle,* 15 and 18 Jan. 1881. On 18 Jan. the *Daily Eagle* corrected the name of William Belden to Alfred Belding. The census records for 1880 for Byron township, Kent Co., Michigan, include an Alfred Belding, the eighty-year-old grandfather in the household of Nicholas Barnes.
49. JAG Diary, 17 Jan. 1881. Thomas Garfield lived in Byron, Michigan, from 1853 to 1856. He then returned to Cuyahoga Co., where he lived until 1867, when he once more settled in Michigan, this time in Jamestown, Ottawa Co., where he lived until his death in 1910. Joseph and Calista Boynton Skinner moved to Byron in 1854.
50. JAG to EBG, 19 Nov. 1855 (accidents and homesickness); LRG, "Rough Sketch" ("almost a score").
51. EBG to JAG, 25 May 1856 ("the iron horse"). The railroad had reached Cleveland in 1851.
52. *Diary of JAG*, I, Jan.–Aug. 1848 (pp. 5–12).
53. JAG's reminiscences, 1877. On 25 Aug. 1877 Garfield was one of the speakers at a Republican rally in Athens, Ohio. That evening he talked about his early life for about two hours in the presence of two persons. Not long after the event one of those present made a record of Garfield's talk. This record was made available at Mentor to biographers of Garfield during the campaign of 1880; it consists of twenty-seven handwritten pages.
54. Ibid. ("a real sailor"); *Diary of JAG*, I, 22 May 1853 ("rushing . . . to destruction") and 30 Aug. 1848. Between Aug. 1848 and 6 March 1849 Garfield did not write in his diary. He repaired the omission by a brief summary under the date 30 Aug. 1848 of his experience on the canal and his subsequent illness.
55. JAG's reminiscences, 1877; account of JAG's canal experience as given by Amos Letcher to James R. Gilmore, in Edmund Kirke (pseudonym of Gilmore), *The Life of James A. Garfield, Republican Candidate for the Presidency* (New York, 1880), chapter 1; *Diary of JAG*, I, 16, 17, 27, 28, 29, and 30 Aug. 1848.
56. *Diary of JAG*, 30 Aug. 1848 (illness, return with Charles), 1 Oct. 1850 (wages), 22 May 1853 ("degraded young men"); JAG's reminiscences, 1877; JAG to EBG, 19 Nov. 1855.
57. *Diary of JAG*, I, 30 Aug. 1848 (summary); JAG's reminiscences, 1877 (intention of returning to canal).
58. *Diary of JAG*, I, 30 Aug. 1848 and 19 Nov. 1855; JAG's reminiscences, 1877; JAG to EBG, 19 Nov. 1877.
59. JAG's reminiscences, 1877; *Diary of JAG*, I, 6 March 1849.
60. JAG to Harry Rhodes, 19 Nov. 1862.
61. *Catalogue of the Officers and Students of the Geauga Seminary . . . for the Year Ending July*

*4, 1849* (Cleveland, 1849), copy in JAG Papers; *Diary of JAG*, I, March 1849; B. A. Hinsdale, *President Garfield and Education* (Boston, 1882), pp. 31–32, quoting letter from Harvey W. Everest (no date given).

62. *Catalogue of Geauga Seminary*, 1848–49; *Diary of JAG*, I, 6 March to 4 July 1849, passim.

63. JAG to EBG and Thomas, 31 March 1849.

64. JAG to Harry Rhodes, 19 Nov. 1862; LR to JAG, 18 Feb. 1856.

65. *Diary of JAG*, I, 28 March, 13, 16, 27, and 30 June, and 1 Oct. 1849. In 1840 Orson Squire Fowler and his brother Lorenzo founded a publishing house in New York City which in 1842 took over the editing and publication of *The American Phrenological Review and Miscellany*. Fowlers and Wells, as the firm soon became, published a large number of other items, including the pamphlets read by JAG, "both of which had reached forty editions by 1844." *Dictionary of American Biography*, vol. 6 (New York, 1931), pp. 565–566.

66. Hinsdale, *President Garfield and Education*, pp. 48–49 (statement by JAG). Garfield's entire lack of initiative in the account given by Hinsdale is not borne out by his diary at the time: *Diary of JAG*, I, 20–22 Oct. 1849.

67. *Diary of JAG*, I, 19 Nov. 1849 (birthday), 13 and 24 Nov., 24 Dec. 1849, and 4 Jan. 1850 (corporal punishment of pupils), 2 March 1850 (close of school).

68. *Diary of JAG*, I, 24 and 31 March, 31 May, 16 Aug., 22 Sept., and 11 Oct. 1850 (Free Will Baptists), 4 March to 6 Oct. 1850, passim (attendance at Disciple meetings in Orange and elsewhere).

69. *Diary of JAG*, I, 3–4 March 1850 (conversion), 29 Sept. 1850 (slavery), 6 Sept. 1850 and 2 Nov. 1852 (participation in government). Garfield's censorious prudery was unattractively demonstrated in the spring of 1853 when, as a student and teacher at the Eclectic Institute, he devoted parts of a number of evenings to spying out misbehaving students around the school. He seemed to take satisfaction in the expulsion of four students. *Diary of JAG*, I, 25–27 April, 2 May, and 7 June 1853. LR to JAG, 18 Feb. 1856 ("Remember Lot's wife").

70. JAG to EBG and Thomas, 22 Aug. 1850.

71. *Diary of JAG*, I, 28 March 1850.

72. JAG's reminiscences, 1877 (empty pockets); *Diary of JAG*, I, 17 Aug. 1850 (dress), 27 Aug. 1850 ("dry knocks").

73. JAG to Corydon Fuller, 28 Jan. 1854.

74. *Diary of JAG*, I, 15 May, 14, 19, 24, and 25 June (JAG's composition), and 1–2 July 1850 (rehearsal and Commencement).

75. Ibid., 23 and 24 Aug. 1850 (arithmetic class), 11, 13, and 15 Oct. 1850 (Fowler).

76. *Pioneer and General History of Geauga County* (1880), p. 100; *Diary of JAG*, I, 25 June 1854; JAG to LR, 3 July 1854.

77. *Diary of JAG*, I, 2 July 1850 (Commencement oration).

78. JAG to LR, 25 May 1856; JAG to Mary Hubbell, 29 May 1852 (quotations).

79. *Diary of JAG*, I, 1 Oct. 1850 ("ripe for ruin"), 22 May 1853 ("ripe for ruin" and "servant of sin"), 1 Oct. 1850 ("ready to drink").

80. Ibid., 24 June 1853 ("checkered life"), 23 June 1854 ("strange . . . history").

81. Ibid., 19 Nov. 1855.

82. JAG to LR, 13 Nov. 1856 ("insipid . . . talk"); *Diary of JAG*, I, 25 June 1853 (boredom with family).

### Chapter 2. The Eclectic Institute

1. Ballou, *History and Genealogy of Ballous*.

2. *Diary of JAG*, I, 27 Feb. to 4 June 1851; JAG to LR, 2 March 1854. Ellis Ballou, who

was three years older than Garfield, attended Ohio University and the Western Reserve Eclectic Institute and married Laura Clark, who had been a student at the Eclectic. He was the author of a treatise, *The Patent Hat* (New York, 1855), in verse and prose (at times satirical), on Christian duty. During the later 1850s he was editor and publisher of the *Western News Boy*, to which Garfield contributed. After the Civil War, during which he had served in the army, he moved with his family to Montana. In March 1881 Garfield nominated him receiver of moneys for the district of land subject to sale at Helena.

3. JAG to Harriet, Phebe, and Cordelia Boynton, 30 March 1851.
4. *Diary of JAG*, I, 19 March to 20 May 1851, passim (school), 16 April 1851 (little children).
5. Ibid., 10 June to 20 Aug. 1851, passim (work).
6. Hinsdale, *President Garfield and Education*, pp. 15–16, 18–22; Corydon E. Fuller, *Reminiscences of James A. Garfield with Notes Preliminary and Collateral* (Cincinnati, 1887), pp. 26–27, 50; F. M. Green, *Hiram College and Western Reserve Eclectic Institute: Fifty Years of History, 1850–1900* (Cleveland, 1901), pp. 47–49; Mary Bosworth Treudley, *Prelude to the Future: the First Hundred Years of Hiram College* (New York, 1950), chapter 2.
7. *Announcement and Catalogue of the First Session of the Western Reserve Eclectic Institute, Hiram, Portage County, Ohio* (Cleveland, 1850). Several new rooming houses for students were erected in 1852.
8. Ibid.; Treudley, *Prelude to the Future*, pp. 53–54 (teachers), 60–62 (finances); Hinsdale, *President Garfield and Education*, pp. 18–20—speech of Garfield at Hiram reunion in 1880.
9. *Announcement and Catalogue of First Session of the Eclectic;* Treudley, *Prelude to the Future*, pp. 66–67; A. S. Hayden to JAG, 10 Aug. 1854, and LR to JAG, 24 Aug. 1854 (Eclectic's boycott of one merchant whose offense seems to have been the sale of liquor to students).
10. F. M. Green, *Hiram College*, pp. 59–72; Treudley, *Prelude to the Future*, pp. 73–75; *Diary of JAG*, I, 24 May 1852. At this time women students at Oberlin were not permitted to deliver orations at Commencement.
11. Treudley, *Prelude to the Future*, pp. 76–77 (colloquies). Colloquies (for which Almeda Booth was largely responsible) appeared regularly on Commencement programs— see *Diary of JAG*, I, 25 June 1852, 24 June 1853, 23 June 1854. Some handwritten colloquies are in the Garfield Papers.
12. *Diary of JAG*, I, 21 Aug. to 15 Nov. 1851; Fuller, *Reminiscences of Garfield*, pp. 31 (appearance of Garfield), 36–38 (Garfield's valedictory).
13. *Diary of JAG*, I, 20 and 24 May 1852; Fuller, *Reminiscences of Garfield*, pp. 52–54. These meetings were held in the Methodist church in Hiram. There was considerable pro-spiritualist feeling in the region. Fuller makes it appear that Garfield's confrontation of Treat was confined to one night; *Diary of JAG* makes it clear that there were two separate occasions.
14. See Garfield's last address in Hiram, 4 Feb. 1881, in Hinsdale, *President Garfield and Education*, pp. 106–108. Garfield was a trustee of the school from 1864 to his death.
15. *Diary of JAG*, I, 23 Aug. 1851 to 23 June 1854, has a vast amount of detail concerning Garfield's Hiram period. See 1 Dec. 1851 to 21 Feb. 1852, passim (teaching at Warrensville), 24 Feb. to 20 March 1852, passim (study of penmanship, drawing, and mezzotint painting), 28 June to 19 Aug. 1852, passim (house building). Hinsdale, *President Garfield and Education*, pp. 26–27 (janitorial work).
16. JAG to Corydon Fuller, 1 April 1855 (soul communion).
17. Garfield's interest in phrenology over a number of years is indicated in *Diary of JAG*, I, 15 Feb. 1848, 2 July 1850, and 9 Dec. 1853 (attendance at lectures on the subject),

18 Jan. 1851 and 6 Nov. 1852 (attendance at meetings of the Lyceum at which the subject was discussed—in the latter meeting Garfield took the affirmative in a debate on a resolution "that Phrenology is a Science"), 10 July 1854 and 28 July 1857 (examination of his head in New York City by L. N. Fowler). See *Diary of JAG*, I, 30 Nov. and 31 Dec. 1853, for Garfield's use of the word "adhesive" in the phrenological sense.

18. The words quoted are written on the back of a sheet containing the words and music of *The Student's Adieu*, undated, apparently dedicated to Garfield, JAG Papers.

19. LRG to JAG, 8 Jan. 1860, EBG to JAG, 29 March 1860, note added by Nellie Larabee, and JAG to LRG, 31 Aug. 1861 (scratching); J. D. Cox, "The Youth and Early Manhood of James Abram Garfield," in *Society of the Army of the Cumberland, Fourteenth Reunion, Milwaukee, Wisconsin, 1882* (Cincinnati, 1883), p. 96 (hugs); *Diary of JAG*, I, 22 Jan. 1853 (quotation).

20. Fuller, *Reminiscences of Garfield*, p. 57, a letter of Fuller to his parents ("a perfect giant"); JAG to Fuller, 31 May 1856 ("twin brother of my heart"). Fuller's book is very valuable for information about Garfield and the early days of the Eclectic; it includes many otherwise unpublished letters of Garfield to Fuller, 1851–1881. About forty of Garfield's letters to Fuller are in the JAG Papers; these include only one written before the end of June 1854, whereas the book contains more than a dozen such letters. Fuller's home was then in Grand Rapids, Michigan, where his father, a carpenter with a large family, had moved some years before, but he had been born in Chardon, Ohio, and reared there in a strict Disciple atmosphere.

21. Wilber to JAG, 10 Jan. 1854.

22. Ibid.

23. *Diary of JAG*, I, 26 Oct. 1852; Fuller, *Reminiscences of Garfield*, pp. 61–62.

24. *Diary of JAG*, I, 26 Oct. 1852 (Hayden).

25. Garfield probably wrote more letters to Hinsdale than to any other person; about 900 exchanges between the two men are in the JAG Papers. Mary L. Hinsdale, ed., *Garfield–Hinsdale Letters: Correspondence between James Abram Garfield and Burke Aaron Hinsdale* (Ann Arbor, 1949), is a well-edited collection of 300 letters. Hinsdale (1837–1900) had a distinguished career as educator and author; he was professor of the science and art of teaching at the University of Michigan, 1888–1900. Garfield planned to appoint him minister to Hawaii. James Harrison Rhodes (1836–1890) settled in Cleveland where, after a period as a journalist, he practiced law. His friendship with Garfield endured until the end of Garfield's life. The JAG Papers include a large number of their letters, 1854–1881.

26. Johnson, *History of Cuyahoga County*, p. 78; *Diary of JAG*, I, 4 June 1852.

27. Statement of J. P. Robison to Joseph Stanley-Brown, 10 Sept. 1887, JAG Papers. It does not appear that James knew Dr. Robison at all before he went to him in 1852. Robison, however, had in earlier years been acquainted with the Garfields and had seen James as a child. Robison was seventy-six when he talked to Stanley-Brown, and his reminiscences were of an interview that occurred thirty-five years earlier. His recollection was undoubtedly also marred by his habit of boasting. But even in old age he remained a vigorous man in full possession of his faculties, and it cannot be supposed that the entire story was pure invention. The gossip at the school was attested by Fuller, *Reminiscences of Garfield*, pp. 65–66.

28. *Diary of JAG*, I, 15 July 1852.

29. Ibid., 24 June 1854.

30. Fuller, *Reminiscences of Garfield*, p. 56 (appearance of Almeda Booth).

31. *Diary of JAG*, I, 24 June 1854.

32. Garfield, "Almeda A. Booth," in Hinsdale, *President Garfield and Education*, pp.

400–403; *Diary of JAG*, I, 9 Nov. 1852, 15 and 21 Feb., 5 March, 26 April, 8 May, 9 July, and 1 Oct. 1853, 25 March and 25 June 1854; JAG to Fuller, 16 May 1853, in Fuller, *Reminiscences of Garfield*, pp. 79–80.

33. *Diary of JAG*, I, 5 March 1853.

34. Ibid., 24 June 1854.

35. Fuller, *Reminiscences of Garfield*, pp. 71–72; *Diary of JAG*, I, 11 Feb. 1851; JAG to Mary Hubbell, 25 April 1852. Solyman and Lucinda Hubbell, parents of Mary, were prominent Disciples. At one time Abram and Eliza Garfield had worked a farm belonging to "Uncle" Jedediah Hubbell, father of Solyman. His younger son Jedediah was a partner in the firm of Woodward and Hubbell of Chagrin Falls, for which Garfield worked as a carpenter in the summer of 1851.

36. The "basement chapel" was not, as the name suggests, in the partly underground basement of the school but on the first floor, directly behind the entrance hall. As a chapel it had been superseded by a large room on the second floor. *Diary of JAG*, I, 20 and 28 Oct and 8 Nov. 1851.

37. Ibid., 24–28 Dec. 1851.

38. Ibid., 28 Dec. 1851 (Thomas), 5–6 Feb. 1852 (Eliza).

39. JAG to Mary Hubbell, 27 Feb. 1853.

40. *Diary of JAG*, I, 10 April 1852; JAG to Mary Hubbell, 25 April 1852.

41. JAG to Mary Hubbell, 9 April 1852.

42. *Diary of JAG*, I, 25–29 June 1852; Henry Boynton, with postscript by Susan, to JAG, 7 Jan. 1855 (reports to Warrensville).

43. *Diary of JAG*, I, 17 July 1852; JAG to Mary Hubbell, 24 July 1852.

44. *Diary of JAG*, I, 29 Aug. 1852; JAG to Fuller, 17 Dec. 1852, in Fuller, *Reminiscences of Garfield*, p. 71; ibid., p. 72 ("in no sense suitable").

45. *Diary of JAG*, I, 22 and 27 Jan. 1853; JAG to Fuller, 17 Dec. 1852, in Fuller, *Reminiscences of Garfield*, p. 71.

46. JAG to Fuller, 19 Jan. 1853, in Fuller, *Reminiscences of Garfield*, pp. 72–73; JAG to Phebe Boynton, 22 Jan. 1853; *Diary of JAG*, I, 3 and 22 Jan. 1853.

47. Ibid., 22 Jan. and 27 Feb. 1853 ("rake"); JAG to Fuller, 19 Jan. 1853, in Fuller, *Reminiscences of Garfield*, p. 73 ("living grave").

48. *Diary of JAG*, I, 17 Feb. 1853.

49. JAG to Mary Hubbell, 27 Feb. 1853.

50. Ibid.; JAG to Mary Hubbell, 26 March 1853; JAG to Fuller, 9 April 1853, in Fuller, *Reminiscences of Garfield*, p. 77 (bleeding heart).

51. *Diary of JAG*, I, 31 Dec. 1853.

52. Ibid., 10 and 11 April and 31 Dec. 1853.

53. *Diary of JAG*, I, 27 March, 3 April, 1, 22, and 29 May 1853 (preaching), 25, 26, 27, and 30 April and 2 May 1853 (prowling), 7–8 June 1853 (expulsion).

54. *Diary of JAG*, I, 31 Dec. 1853.

55. Ibid., 28 Aug. 1853.

56. Henry Boynton, with postscript by Susan, to JAG, 7 Jan. 1855.

57. Henry Boynton, with postscript by Susan, to JAG, 18 Feb. 1856.

58. Cuyahoga Co. marriage records, Vol. 9, p. 130, Cuyahoga Co. Court House, Cleveland; *Cleveland Herald*, 2 Jan. 1863; JAG to Phebe Boynton Clapp, 28 Feb. 1863.

59. *Diary of JAG*, I, 28 June to 9 July 1853 (trip), 1–4 July 1853 (Bethany); JAG to Fuller, 19 July 1853.

60. *Diary of JAG*, I, 23 June 1854 (sit at the feet), 2 July 1853 (visit to the Campbells), 1 July 1853 (Munnell); JAG to Fuller, 16 May 1853, in Fuller, *Reminiscences of Garfield*, p. 79 (Munnell's illness).

61. *Diary of JAG*, I, 4 July 1853 ("southern dandyism"), 1 July 1853 (play).

62. Ibid., 23 June 1854.
63. Ibid., 25 March and 23 June 1854 (doubts about Bethany), 1 Jan. and 23 June 1854.
64. *Diary of JAG,* I, 20 April and 23 June 1853 (Hayden's offer), 1 Oct. and 28 Nov. 1853 (classes), 1, 6, 10, 18, 19, and 31 Oct., 29 Nov., and 26–31 Dec. 1853 (throat trouble and other illness), 14–15 Dec. 1853 (writing class); JAG to Fuller, 26 Dec. 1853, in Fuller, *Reminiscences of Garfield,* p. 103.
65. *Diary of JAG,* I, 27 Dec. 1853 ("madness"), 1 Jan. 1854 (intention of taking special care of his health), 3 March 1854 ("recruit and invigorate"), 27 Feb. to 16 March 1854 (trip to Blue Rock); JAG to LR, 2 March 1854 (throat), JAG to Fuller, 16 April 1854, in Fuller, *Reminiscences of Garfield,* p. 112; JAG to EBG, 1 May 1854 (improvement in health).
66. *Diary of JAG,* I, 23 June 1854.
67. Mark Hopkins to JAG, 7 June 1854. James construed the statement of Hopkins as "We shall be glad to do what we can for you." *Diary of JAG,* I, 23 June 1854.
68. JAG to Corydon Fuller, 26 June 1854.
69. *Diary of JAG,* I, 23 June 1854.

## Chapter 3. Lucretia

1. JAG to LR, 25 Feb. 1856. "B'hoys" was then a slang term for roistering and disorderly males.
2. LR, Diary, 1854–1856, 19 May 1854, and 4 Oct. 1855, and LR memorandum, 1 Jan. 1854, LRG Papers; LR to JAG, 1 March 1856.
3. *Diary of JAG,* I, 24 Aug. 1849, 7 May 1850, and 9 July 1853.
4. LR memorandum, 1 Jan. 1854, LRG Papers.
5. Fuller, *Reminiscences of Garfield,* pp. 54–55; Green, *Hiram College,* pp. 55–56; Treudley, *Prelude to the Future,* pp. 44–45, 52.
6. *Diary of JAG,* I, 23 April 1853; JAG to LR, 16 Nov. 1854; LR to JAG, 15 Dec. 1854; LR, Diary, 1854–1856, 24 June 1854, LRG Papers.
7. *Diary of JAG,* I, 25 June 1853 ("lottery business").
8. Ibid., 31 Dec. 1853.
9. JAG to LR, 16 Nov. 1854.
10. *Diary of JAG,* I, 24 June 1853 (Commencement program); Fuller, *Reminiscences of Garfield,* pp. 85–86.
11. LR to JAG, 31 Dec. 1855.
12. JAG to LR, 16 Nov. 1854.
13. B. A. Hinsdale, *Arabella Mason Rudolph, Her Ancestry, Life and Character* (Cleveland, 1879); genealogical records of the Rudolphs and Masons in JAG Papers.
14. LRG to Harry A. Garfield, 21 Feb. 1898, Harry A. Garfield Papers, L.C.; Arabella Rudolph to LR, 1 April 1849, LRG Papers; LR to JAG, 21 Nov. 1854.
15. JAG to LR, 28 Oct. 1854, LR to JAG, 21 Nov. 1854 and 10 Feb. 1856, LRG to Silas Boynton, 14 April 1870 (Lucretia's health). LRG to Harry A. Garfield, 21 Feb. 1898 (family kisses), Harry A. Garfield Papers, L.C.
16. LR to JAG, 18 Feb. 1856. See photograph of the Greek class in this book.
17. LR to JAG, 30 Nov. 1854.
18. JAG to LR, 30 Nov. 1853 (from Niagara Falls), LR to JAG, 30 Nov. 1854.
19. LR to JAG, 30 Nov., 14 and 28 Dec. 1853, 16, 26, and 31 Jan., 12 Feb. 1854; JAG to LR, 8 Dec. 1853 ("winter's empire"), 21 Dec. 1853 ("Dead Languages"), 4 Jan., ? Jan., 21 and 28 Jan., 11 Feb. 1854.
20. *Diary of JAG,* I, 31 Dec. 1853.
21. Ibid., 31 Dec. 1853 (relation between the sexes), 2 July 1854 (JAG's views on women

speaking in public); LR, Diary, 1854–1856, 23 July 1854 (Lucretia's approval of women speaking in public), LRG Papers.

22. JAG to LR, 11 Feb. 1854; *Diary of JAG,* I, 31 Dec. 1853.
23. LR to JAG, 23 Feb. 1855; *Diary of JAG,* I, Jan.–Feb. 1854. After making an entry for 1 Jan. 1854, Garfield neglected his diary for several weeks; he then made one entry covering the period from 2 Jan. to 23 Feb.—the date of his meeting with Lucretia.
24. Ibid.; JAG to LR, 2 March 1854.
25. LR, Diary, 1854–1856, 19 April to 18 June 1854, passim, LRG Papers.
26. JAG to LR, 16 Nov. 1854; LR to JAG, 31 Dec. 1854.
27. Philip Burns to JAG, 28 June 1854; *Diary of JAG,* I, 24 June 1854.
28. LR, Diary, 1854–1856, 17 and 19 June 1854, LRG Papers.
29. Commencement program of the Eclectic, 22 June 1854; LR, Diary, 1854–1856, 30 and 31 May, 5, 8, and 20 June 1854 (Lucretia's oration), 22 June 1854 (Commencement), LRG Papers.
30. Ibid., 23 and 24 June 1854, 24 June 1855; *Diary of JAG,* I, 24 June 1854.
31. LR, Diary, 1854–1856, 24 June 1854, LRG Papers.

### Chapter 4. Williamstown

1. *Diary of JAG,* I, 29 June to 11 July 1854; JAG to LR, 3 July 1854.
2. *Diary of JAG,* I, 11 July 1854; JAG to LR, 15 July 1854.
3. *Diary of JAG,* I, 17 and 22 July 1854; JAG to Corydon Fuller, 30 July 1854; JAG to LR, 30 July 1854.
4. JAG to LR, 14 Aug. 1854, and JAG to Corydon Fuller, 10 Aug. 1854 (illness); JAG to LR, 13 Sept. 1854, and JAG to Corydon Fuller, 14 Sept. 1854 (trip to Monterey); Daniel Garfield to JAG, 25 Feb. 1855, and Henry Garfield to JAG, 3 June 1855 (Daniel and the Know-Nothing Party); *Diary of JAG,* I, 23 Aug. to 5 Sept. 1854; *Williams Quarterly,* III (Sept. 1855), pp. 25–27 ("Sam").
5. JAG to Mary Watson, 16 Sept. 1854, in Fuller, *Reminiscences of Garfield,* p. 150 (sympathy for Streator); JAG to LR, 13 Sept. 1854; *Diary of JAG,* I, 6–12 Sept. 1854.
6. *Diary of JAG,* I, 24 June 1854, and JAG to EBG, 2 Aug. 1854 (Wilber); LR to JAG, 21 Aug. 1854.
7. LR, Diary, 1854–1856, 28 Aug. to 20 Sept. 1854, passim.
8. JAG to LR, 13 Sept. 1854.
9. Ibid.; LR to JAG, 20 Sept. 1854.
10. LR to JAG, 8 June 1855; LR, Diary, 1854–1856, 22 Sept. 1854 to 21 June 1855, passim.
11. *Catalogue of the Officers and Students in Williams College . . . 1854–55* (Williamstown, 1854); Frederick Rudolph, *Mark Hopkins and the Log: Williams College, 1836–1872* (New Haven, 1956).
12. Rudolph, op. cit.; JAG to LR, 7 and 21 April 1855 (novels, German); C. H. Hill to J. M. Bundy, 23 June 1880, in Bundy, *Garfield,* p. 34 (readings, Philologian Society); JAG to Corydon Fuller, 22 Aug. 1854 (readings) and 12 Nov. 1854 ("Chivalry").
13. Silas P. Hubbell to J. M. Bundy, 28 June 1880, in Bundy, *Garfield,* pp. 37–39; JAG to Corydon Fuller, 23 May 1855 (*Quarterly*); JAG to Corydon and Mary Fuller, 17 July 1855 (president of Philologians); 2 Nov. 1855 (prejudice against Westerners); JAG to LR, 6 March 1855 (revival); Charles Wilber to LR, 6 March 1855 ("boys"), LRG Papers.
14. Silas Hubbell to J. M. Bundy, 28 June 1880, in Bundy, *Garfield,* pp. 38–39; C. H. Hill to J. M. Bundy, 23 June 1880, ibid., p. 34; Fuller, *Reminiscences of Garfield,* pp. 236–237.

15. JAG to LR, 28 Sept. 1855 and 6 April 1856; Charles Wilber to JAG, 30 Sept. and 9 Dec. 1856.
16. Elijah Cutler to J. M. Bundy, 30 June 1880, in Bundy, *Garfield,* pp. 40–41 (Bundy erroneously has the name "Cutter"); *Diary of JAG,* I, 26 June 1874; *Williams Quarterly,* III (Dec. 1855), pp. 118–119. Tennyson's "The Charge of the Light Brigade" was published in 1854.
17. *Dairy of JAG,* I, 8 Nov. 1855; JAG to Harry Rhodes, 15 April 1859.
18. JAG to LR, 24 March 1855; JAG to Phebe Boynton, 24 April 1855; Thomas Garfield to JAG, 28 Feb. 1855.
19. JAG to EBG, 21 Dec. 1854, and 14 Feb. 1855.
20. JAG to Corydon Fuller, 23 May and 19 June 1855; JAG to EBG, 14 Feb., 30 May, 18 June, and 22 July 1855.
21. W. R. Bee (Baxter) to JAG, 9 Dec. 1855.
22. JAG to EBG, 11 March 1855, and Maria Learned to JAG, 6 March 1859 (Mary Jane). The date of the second letter is established by the letter's content; the L.C. *Index* to the Garfield Papers has the date as March 1858.
23. Myron Streator to JAG, 5 March and 8 March 1855; JAG to EBG, 11 March 1855; JAG to Mary Watson Fuller, 13 March 1855, in Fuller, *Reminiscences of Garfield,* pp. 181–182.
24. JAG to Corydon Fuller, 23 May 1855; JAG to EBG, 26 May 1855; JAG to LR, 12 May 1855.
25. Maria Learned to JAG, 1 Oct. 1856, 15 Jan. 1856, and 6 March 1859. "Prophet's Chamber" as a term for "spare bedroom" was in use during this period.
26. LR to JAG, 22 June 1856 ("perfect bliss"); Charles Wilber to JAG, 1 Aug. 1855; LR to JAG, 31 July 1856 (school).
27. JAG to Corydon and Mary Fuller, 20 Aug. 1855.
28. JAG to LR, 11 Aug. 1855; LR, Diary, 1854–1856, 27 Aug. 1855, LRG Papers.
29. Ibid., 19 Aug., 27 Aug. to 7 Sept., and 13 Sept. 1855.
30. Ibid., 6–7 Sept. 1855.
31. *Diary of JAG,* I, 10 Sept. 1855.
32. Ibid., 11 Sept. 1855.
33. LR to JAG, 3 Feb. 1856; JAG to LR, 28 Sept. 1855; E. N. Manley to J. M. Bundy, 8 July 1880, in Bundy, *Garfield,* p. 41 (Bible reading with Eliza).
34. LR to JAG, 12 Sept. 1855.
35. JAG to EBG, 18 Sept. 1855 (return trip); JAG to LR, 10 Nov. 1855 (metaphysics); JAG to Corydon and Mary Fuller, 2 Nov. 1855 (Hebrew); JAG to Corydon Fuller, 7 Sept. 1855 (Uncle Thomas).
36. Silas P. Hubbell to J. M. Bundy, 28 June 1880 (Philologian), in Bundy, *Garfield,* p. 38; Elijah Cutler to Bundy, 30 June 1880 ("lively glimpses"), ibid., p. 40; C. H. Hill to Bundy, 23 June 1880 (Longfellow), ibid., p. 34; Lavalette Wilson to Bundy, 28 June 1880 (political meeting), ibid., p. 39; JAG to LR, 11 Oct. 1855 (New York), 1 Nov. 1855 (Amherst); *Diary of JAG,* I, 2 Nov. 1855 (political meeting).
37. JAG to LR, 18 Sept. and 1 Nov. 1855.

## Chapter 5. Rebecca

1. LR to JAG, 12 Dec. 1855.
2. JAG to LR, 19 Dec. 1855.
3. JAG to LR, 8 Dec. 1855; Rebecca Selleck to JAG, 21 Aug. 1857.
4. Maria Learned to JAG, 1 Oct. 1857 (date established by contents of letter—L.C. *Index*

to Garfield Papers has 1856); Rebecca Selleck to JAG, 4 Jan. 1856 ("pedal telegraph").

5. Charles Wilber to JAG, 24 Jan. 1857. See photograph of Rebecca Selleck in this book.

6. William Edwin Selleck, *Selleck Memorial* (Chicago, 1916). Dates of birth and death have been taken from two monuments in the Berk Hill Cemetery, Lewisboro, New York.

7. Maria Learned to JAG, 13 Nov. 1857 (date established by contents of letter—L.C. *Index* to Garfield Papers has 1858).

8. Rebecca Selleck to JAG, 21 Aug. 1857 (beard), 11 Feb., 18 and 31 March 1856 (Lucretia).

9. Rebecca Selleck to JAG, 30 Dec. 1856.

10. JAG to Corydon Fuller, 11 Feb. (Troy, Hiram, winter), 18 March 1856 (college work), 16 Jan. 1858 (law); JAG to EBG, 3 March (health), 26 March and 8 April 1856 (money); *Williams Quarterly*, III (March 1856), pp. 207–208, 233–254.

11. JAG to LR, 16 March 1856; LR to JAG, 16 March 1856; JAG to LR, 23 March 1856.

12. JAG to LR, 13 April 1856.

13. Ibid.; JAG to LR, 20 and 26 April 1856; Rebecca Selleck to JAG, 30 April 1856.

14. JAG to LR, 13 April and 1 May 1856; Rebecca Selleck to JAG, 10 May 1856.

15. JAG to LR, 9 (teaching offers) and 15 June 1856; Rebecca Selleck to JAG, 8 and 21 June 1856; Maria Learned to JAG [written between late May and early June, 1856]; JAG to Corydon Fuller, 11 Feb. and 17 June 1856.

16. LR to JAG, 1 March, 11 May, and 1 June 1856; Rebecca Selleck to JAG, 10 and 17 May 1856; Rebecca Selleck to LR, 5 June 1856, LRG Papers.

17. LR to JAG, 22 June 1856; JAG to LR, 29 June 1856.

18. LR to JAG, 1 Sept. 1857.

19. Mary Maxon Hyde Field to JAG, 16 Aug. 1880; information about the Hyde family from Department of Manuscripts and University Archives, Cornell University Library.

20. Rebecca Selleck to LR, 6 Sept. 1856, LRG Papers.

21. Rebecca Selleck to JAG, 15 Aug. 1856 (fever), [9 Sept. 1856] ("crushing weight"); Fuller, *Reminiscences of Garfield*, p. 236, and Silas Hubbell to J. M. Bundy, 28 June 1880, in Bundy, *Garfield*, p. 39 (Commencement).

22. Rebecca Selleck to JAG, 4 Sept. 1856.

23. Rebecca Selleck to JAG, 17 Oct. 1856 (quoting LR's letter to Rebecca).

24. LR to JAG, 9 Nov. 1856; Rebecca Selleck to JAG, 31 Dec. 1856 and 17 Nov. 1857.

25. JAG to Corydon Fuller, 8 Sept. and 14 Dec. 1856; Charles Wilber to JAG, 24 Jan., 11 April, and 29 May 1857.

26. LR to JAG, 29 June 1856; JAG to LR, 6 July 1856.

27. Treudley, *Prelude to the Future*, p. 82 (factions).

28. Lizzie Atwood Pratt to LR, 23 May 1857, LRG Papers; JAG to LR, 18 May 1857.

29. Treudley, *Prelude to the Future*, pp. 82–83; Green, *Hiram College*, pp. 94, 382–383.

30. JAG to Corydon Fuller, 30 Aug. 1857, in Fuller, *Reminiscences of Garfield*, p. 256.

31. Ibid., p. 257; *Diary of JAG*, I, 1 Oct. 1857 to 20 April 1858, passim (JAG's lectures), and 4 May 1858 (charge against Garfield); Treudley, *Prelude to the Future*, pp. 83–84 (physical improvements).

32. Almeda Booth to Corydon Fuller, 24 June 1855, in Fuller, *Reminiscences of Garfield*, p. 195 ("tremendous smart"). In 1881 Harry Rhodes spoke at a Garfield memorial service at Hiram College. "For two years after his graduation at Williams, we roomed together at Hiram. The old office in 'the Orchard' is more hallowed to me by that

two years of companionship than any other temple made by human hands." See Hinsdale, *President Garfield and Education*, p. 127. *The Diary of JAG*, I, has many references to Rhodes.

33. Garfield, "Almeda A. Booth," in Hinsdale, *President Garfield and Education*, pp. 384–385 (Almeda's lost love); Fuller, *Reminiscences of Garfield*, p. 56 (description of Almeda).

34. Almeda Booth to JAG, 30 Jan. 1858 (trouble with James), 15 Aug. 1861 ("dreadful agony"); *Diary of JAG*, I, 1, 4, and 11 Feb. 1858 and note, p. 320.

35. EBG to JAG [Oct. 1856]. Garfield responded to this letter on 16 Oct. [1856]. The year is established by JAG's references to political debates during the campaign of 1856.

36. *Diary of JAG*, I, 1 and 11 Feb. 1858.

37. Rebecca Selleck to JAG, 25 Sept., 17 Oct., and 31 Dec. 1856 ("undisciplined heart"), 11 Nov. 1856.

38. LR to Rebecca Selleck, Oct. 1856, LRG Papers. Whether this is a copy or a first draft of a letter sent to Rebecca or a letter that was not sent is not known. Arabella Rudolph to LR, 14 March [1857 or 1858], LRG Papers.

39. LR to JAG, 9 Nov. 1856; JAG to LR, 13 Nov. 1856.

40. LR to JAG, 23 May 1857 ("not miserable"), 30 June 1857 (*Pickwick*), 19 Dec. 1857, and 17 Jan. and 18 Feb. 1858 (Crete's activities in Cleveland).

41. LR to JAG, 30 June 1857.

42. Maria Learned to JAG, 27 April 1857.

43. JAG to EBG, 10 and 23 July 1857; Rebecca Selleck to JAG, 2 July 1857; Myron Streator to JAG, 20 Oct. 1856 (return of Ebenezer); *Diary of JAG*, I, 28 July 1857 (phrenological analysis of James as recorded by Rebecca Selleck).

44. *Diary of JAG*, I, 28 July 1857 (Fowler's advice); Rebecca Selleck to JAG, 2 and 11 Aug. 1857.

45. Rebecca Selleck to JAG, 2 Aug. (after JAG's departure) and 21 Aug. 1857 ("awful parting moments").

46. *Diary of JAG*, I, 13 Aug. (arrival of Jonas) and 12 Nov. 1857 (*Ingomar*); JAG to LR, 24 Oct. 1857.

47. LR to JAG, 1 Sept. 1857; JAG to LR, 24 Oct. 1857.

48. Charles Wilber to Maria Learned, 26 Oct. 1857, JAG Papers; Charles Wilber to JAG, 27 Nov. 1857 and 22 April 1858; Rebecca Selleck, to JAG, 7 Nov. (Wilber's letter) and 17 Nov. 1857 (JAG's letters to Rebecca); Maria Learned to JAG, 13 Nov. 1857; LR to JAG, 19 Dec. 1857.

49. Lucretia Rudolph to Charles Wilber, undated draft, LRG Papers. Lucretia wrote, "You are no longer to assume any knowledge of me or my affairs or any right to farther interference." *Diary of JAG*, I, Dec. 1857, passim; William Letcher to JAG, 17 Nov. 1857.

50. *Diary of JAG*, I, 31 Dec. 1857.

51. Ibid., 1, 2, and 4–13 Jan. 1858. Rebecca Selleck to JAG, 26 Jan. 1858. Garfield arrived in Poestenkill on 9 Jan. and left on 11 Jan.

52. *Diary of JAG*, I, 14 April ("finalities") and 17 April 1858 ("try life in union"); JAG to Harry Rhodes, 4 Dec. 1858 ("isolating effects"), LR to JAG, 18 May and 4, 8, and 27 June 1858 (housing); JAG to LR, 30 May and 29 June 1858 (housing).

53. *Diary of JAG*, I, 15 June to 14 July 1858; JAG to LR, 29 June 1858; JAG to Harry Rhodes, 30 June and 19 July 1858; LR to JAG, 14 July 1858.

54. Rebecca Selleck to JAG, 30 Aug., 15 Sept., 5 Oct., and 9 Nov. 1858 (references to letters from JAG); *Diary of JAG*, I, blanket entry for 15–31 July 1858; LR to JAG, 19 Aug. 1858.

55. Frederick A. Henry, *Captain Henry of Geauga, A Family Chronicle* (Cleveland, 1942), pp. 191–192. Charles E. Henry ("Captain Henry"), the father of the author, was a student at Hiram during Garfield's principalship, a member of Garfield's Forty-second Ohio Infantry (his highest rank during the war was first lieutenant), and a close friend of Garfield thereafter. He entered the postal service as Congressman Garfield's protégé; in 1881 President Garfield appointed him U.S. Marshal of the District of Columbia. His mother attended Garfield's wedding, and the account in the book is her story of the event as recorded by her son. The book, a model of family history, is of great value for a reader interested in Garfield or in life in northern Ohio during the nineteenth century. *Diary of JAG,* I, 11 Nov. 1858: "Was married to Lucretia Rudolph by Pres. H. L. Hitchcock of Western Reserve College." This was Garfield's entire entry for the day. In a note to Garfield shortly before the wedding, Lucretia wrote, "*Joe* [Lucretia's seventeen-year-old brother] is very anxious that a special invitation be sent to you. Will you please attend a wedding party at Zeb Rudolph's on Thursday evening Nov. 11th."

## Chapter 6. Transition

1. Several weeks before the birth of her first child (Eliza, known as "Trot") Mrs. Garfield began a series of letters to the baby. Trot died on 1 December 1863. There were no other entries in the leather-bound volume until 26 July 1869, when Mrs. Garfield began a "mother's journal," a record of her children. Entries were made in 1871, 1873, and annually from 1874 to 1879. This volume will be cited as LRG, Letters to Trot and Children's Record, LRG Papers. The bedroom furnishings are described in LRG's letter to Trot, 16 Jan. 1861. JAG to Harry Rhodes, 8 Jan. 1859 ("We live in . . .").

2. Garfield, "Almeda A. Booth," in Hinsdale, *President Garfield and Education,* pp. 406–407 (Denton debates); JAG to Harry Rhodes, 3 Feb. 1859 (chess), 6 Oct. 1858 ("end of criticism"). During the chess controversy Garfield circularized a number of Ohio educators, asking for their views on the question.

3. LRG to JAG, 3 Feb. 1860; note of LRG to Harry Rhodes, in JAG to Rhodes, 8 Jan. 1859 ("family together").

4. LRG to Harry Garfield, 21 Feb. 1898, Harry A. Garfield Papers, L.C.; Almeda Booth to Harry Rhodes, in JAG to Rhodes, 4 Dec. 1858.

5. For the debates with Denton see JAG to Harry Rhodes, 4 Dec. 1858 and 8 Jan. 1859, JAG to Burke Hinsdale, 10 Jan. 1859, Garfield's notes preparatory to and during the debate, *Diary of JAG,* I, 31 Dec. 1858, and Treudley, *Prelude to the Future,* pp. 87–88, Hinsdale, *President Garfield and Education,* pp. 79–82, and W. W. Wasson, *James A. Garfield: His Religion and Education; A Study in the Religious and Educational Thought and Activity of an American Statesman* (Nashville, 1952), pp. 56–61.

6. JAG to Harry Rhodes, 8 Jan. 1859.

7. JAG to Harry Rhodes, 20 June 1859, JAG to LRG, 18 Jan. 1860, and LRG to JAG, 22 Jan. 1860 (barrel of beer); JAG to Harmon Austin, 22, 24, and 30 March 1859, JAG to Isaac Errett, 3 May 1859, in J. S. Lamar, *Memoirs of Isaac Errett,* 2 vols. (Cincinnati, 1893), p. 220, and Treudley, *Prelude to the Future,* pp. 94–95 (slavery); JAG to Harry Rhodes, 14 and 29 May 1859, Rhodes to JAG, 2 and 21 May 1859, LRG to EBG, 10 July 1859, JAG to Harmon Austin, 21 May 1859, Austin to JAG, 28 May 1859 (Dunshee); JAG to Harry Rhodes, 15 April 1859 ("dispense with Norman").

8. JAG to Harry Rhodes, 15 and 23 April 1859, and Rhodes to JAG, 18 April 1859.

9. JAG to EBG, 25 July 1859; Jonas Learned to JAG, 14 June 1859; Maria Learned to

JAG, 27 June [1859]–year established by context; L.C. *Index* of Garfield Papers has 1858.

10. Mark Hopkins to JAG, 2 June 1859; JAG to Harry Rhodes, 7 June and 8 July 1859; Rhodes to JAG, 10 June 1859. A draft of Garfield's oration, "Art an Educator," is in the JAG Papers. For the Williams Art Association see Rudolph, *Mark Hopkins and the Log*, p. 80.

11. *Diary of JAG*, I, 22, 23, and 30 Aug. 1859.

12. W. J. Ford to JAG, 30 Aug. 1859, quoting Symonds Ryder, Sr.; JAG to Corydon Fuller, 9 Nov. 1859; *Diary of JAG*, I, Sept.–Oct. 1859.

13. JAG to J. E. Jackson et al., 12 Sept. 1859; JAG to A. G. Riddle, 5 Dec. 1859; *Diary of JAG*, I, 2 Dec. 1859 (John Brown).

14. JAG to LRG, 31 Dec. 1859 ("nearly killed with kindness"); JAG to EBG, 1 Jan. 1860; JAG to Harry Rhodes, 1 Jan. [1860]; JAG to Corydon Fuller, 7 Jan. 1860, in Fuller, *Reminiscences of Garfield*, pp. 290–291.

15. JAG, Dictated Notes, 1880 (youngest member); J. D. Cox, "The Youth and Early Manhood of James Abram Garfield," in *Society of the Army of the Cumberland, Fourteenth Reunion, Milwaukee, Wisconsin, 1882* (Cincinnati, 1883), p. 96; W. D. Howells, *My Literary Passions* (New York, 1895), p. 192 ("The poet in a golden clime"), and *Years of My Youth* (New York, 1916), p. 151; JAG to Burke Hinsdale, 22 Jan. 1860, JAG to Harry Rhodes, 21 Jan. 1860, JAG to "Dear Friends," 24 Jan 1860; JAG Scrapbook (newspaper clippings), 1860.

16. JAG to Harmon Austin, 5 Feb. 1860, JAG to LRG, 3, 5, and 9 Feb. 1860 (illness); JAG to Hinsdale, 22 Jan. 1860. For difficulties of electing Chase, see JAG to J. H. Clapp, 21 Jan. 1860.

17. JAG to Harry Rhodes, 18 Feb. 1861 ("set speeches"); Rhodes to JAG, 18 and 24 Jan. and 17 Feb. 1860.

18. JAG to "My Dear Unresponsives" [Harry Rhodes, Almeda Booth, and Lucretia Garfield], 7 Jan. 1860 ("run of Legislative business").

19. JAG to Harry Rhodes, 9 Jan. 1860 ("aristocracy").

20. J. D. Cox to JAG, 4 April 1860 ("Bascom says . . .").

21. Wallace J. Ford to JAG, 25 Feb. 1860, and John H. Clapp to JAG, 26 Feb. 1860 (reports of Garfield's having been seen drinking with others in the Weddell House in Cleveland); E. S. Harmon to JAG, 5 March 1860 (writer associates Garfield with "the *big drunk*" at Columbus—probably a reference to the reception of the visiting Kentucky legislators); Almeda Booth to JAG, 22 Jan. and 2 Feb. 1860.

22. JAG to LRG, 11 Nov. 1862 ("sadness . . . despair"); LRG to JAG, 18 March 1860 (marriage a mistake); Harry Rhodes to JAG, 16 March 1860; LRG, Letters to Trot and Children's Record, 28 May 1860, LRG Papers.

23. Garfield's Ravenna speech, "The American Union," was published as a pamphlet, a copy of which is in the JAG Papers; JAG to Corydon Fuller, 3 Oct. 1860, in Fuller, *Reminiscences of Garfield*, p. 294 (Columbus speech and its consequences; either Garfield or Fuller erred in giving the month of the Wigwam speech as July instead of June); W. T. Bascom to JAG, 15 and 28 June, 7 July, and 13 Sept. 1860.

24. *Diary of JAG*, I, 23 July 1860 (beginning of trip); JAG to LRG, 24 and 25 July 1860; LRG to JAG, 29 July 1860; JAG to Harmon Austin, 23 Aug. 1860 (Garfield's sadness); JAG's notes for a series of lectures on his trip.

25. Maria Learned to JAG, 17 Oct. 1860; *Diary of JAG*, I, 20, 22, 23, and 30 Sept. 1860.

26. W. T. Bascom to JAG, 13 Sept. 1860; W. J. Ford to JAG, 27 and 30 July 1860 and 7 Jan. 1861 (horse).

27. In a letter to Corydon Fuller, 3 Oct. 1860, in Fuller, *Reminiscences of Garfield*, p. 294, Garfield said that he had made more than forty speeches in the previous two

months; during October and early November he made many more. There are many
brief references to speeches in the *Diary of JAG*, I, 1 Aug. to 5 Nov. 1860, passim;
Tuesday 6 Nov. was election day—see entry for that date.

28. *Diary of JAG*, I, 8 and 9 Nov. 1860; JAG to Harry Rhodes, 7 Jan. [1861], 26 Jan.
1861—L.C. *Index* of Garfield Papers has 26 June—18 Feb. 1861 and 3 March 1862;
Rhodes to JAG, 17 Jan., 9 Feb., and 11 March 1861 and 20 April 1862. There are
other letters bearing on the venture in the JAG Papers. *Cincinnati Daily Commercial*,
29 Jan. 1861; J. S. Newberry, "The Rock Oils of Ohio," in Ohio State Board of Agriculture, *Annual Report . . . for the Year 1859* (Columbus, 1860), pp. 605–618; Harold
F. Williamson and Arnold R. Daum, *The American Petroleum Industry: the Age of Illumination, 1859–1899* (Evanston, 1959), p. 102; George A. Whitney, "History of Oil Development in Ohio," *Derrick*, 7 Aug. 1924. The heavy oil found at Mecca was suited
for lubricants rather than illumination. Its value was not realized until after the Civil
War, when most of the early investors, Garfield among them, had disposed of their
holdings.

29. Harry Rhodes to JAG, 6 Feb. 1862 (supper table). Mrs. Garfield was called "the Lady
Kensington" and Almeda Booth "Queen Ann."

30. LRG, Letters to Trot and Children's Record, 8 Jan. ("as fearless as . . .") and 28 Jan.
1861 (David Copperfield), LRG Papers.

31. Ibid., 8 Jan. 1861; LRG to JAG, 9, 17, 21, and 24 Jan. 1861 (missing James).

32. JAG to Harry Rhodes, 26 Jan. 1861; JAG to Burke Hinsdale, 15 Jan. 1861 (slavery).

33. JAG to Burke Hinsdale, 17 Feb. 1861, and JAG to LRG, 17 Feb. 1861 (Lincoln at
Columbus). "Emasculates" or "emasculated Republicans" referred to fearful or conciliatory Republicans who sometimes sided with the Democrats. The quotation is
from the letter to Hinsdale.

34. JAG to LRG, 19 March 1861 (work for Dennison) and 14 April 1861 (military
science); JAG to Harry Rhodes, 13–14 April 1861.

35. JAG to Harry Rhodes, 17 April 1861, JAG to LRG, 5 May 1861, W. T. Bascom to
JAG, 11 June 1861, John Q. Smith to JAG, 15 July 1861 (Dennison's promise). John
Q. Smith and Garfield became friends when they were both Republican members of
the state senate, 1860–1861, and the friendship continued until Garfield's death.
Smith was a member of the U.S. House of Representatives, 1873–1875.

36. Erastus B. Tyler to JAG, 24 April 1861; Halsey R. W. Hall to JAG, 25 April 1861;
JAG to Harry Rhodes, 30 April 1861 (Illinois trip); JAG to Gov. Dennison, 3 May
1861 (draft of report on Illinois trip); JAG to LRG, 28 April 1861 (Seventh Regiment).

37. JAG to LRG, 28 April 1861 (Garfield at Cleveland); J. H. Clapp to JAG, telegram, 28
April 1861, and J. H. Clapp to W. T. Bascom, telegram, 1 May 1861. Clapp apparently did not know that Garfield had gone to Illinois.

38. JAG to LRG, 5 May 1861 (informal election of Tyler); Lyman W. Hall to JAG, 6 May
1861 (ill feeling against Garfield). Hall urged Garfield to step aside, assuring him
that if he did, he considered him "booked for Congress." The Seventh Ohio Regiment was part of Jacob D. Cox's brigade. It was routed on Aug. 26 at Cross-Lanes in
western Virginia. Although Cox treated him with consideration afterward, Tyler was
bitter toward Cox. In 1862 Tyler was made brigadier general; he was breveted major
general at the close of the war. Tyler was postmaster of Baltimore when Garfield became President, and Garfield soon asked for his resignation as a result of his involvement in a scandal.

39. JAG to LRG, 5 May 1861 ("bargains and brandy").

40. LRG to JAG, 2 May 1861; JAG to LRG, 5 May 1861.

41. Harry Rhodes to JAG, 26 Nov. 1861.

42. Bascom to JAG, 23 and 27 May 1861 (urging Garfield to act), Bascom to J. H. Clapp, telegram, 8 June 1861, and Bascom to JAG, 11 June 1861 (lieutenant colonelcy for Garfield); Bascom to JAG, 19 June 1861 (asking whether Garfield can accept), and 24 June 1861 (regretting Garfield's refusal); JAG to Gov. Dennison (copy), 18 June 1861 (rejecting offer). JAG to LRG, 14 June 1861, and JAG to Harmon Austin, 28 June 1861 (army question and trip to Virginia).

43. JAG to Harmon Austin, 28 June and 3 and 14 July 1861; LRG to EBG, 26 July 1861, Harry A. Garfield Papers; JAG to LRG, 30 July 1861; JAG to EBG, 15 Aug. 1861; Lamar, *Isaac Errett*, I, p. 246.

44. Dennison to JAG, 27 July 1861; JAG to Dennison, draft, 7 Aug. 1861; W. T. Bascom to JAG, 9 Aug. 1861; JAG to LRG, 14, 15, and 22 Aug. 1861; JAG to Harry Rhodes ("Dear Friends at Home"), 19 Aug. 1861; JAG to EBG, 30 Aug. 1861; Harry Rhodes to JAG, 16 Aug. 1861; C. P. Buckingham, adjutant general of Ohio, to JAG, 5 Sept. 1861 (appointment as colonel of the Forty-second); three-year commission signed by the governor, 14 Dec. 1861. The best of Garfield's Civil War letters are to be found in Frederick D. Williams, ed., *The Wild Life of the Army: Civil War Letters of James A. Garfield* (East Lansing, 1964), a splendidly edited volume.

45. JAG to LRG, Sept.–Dec. 1861, passim; F. H. Mason, *The Forty-second Ohio Infantry* (Cleveland, 1876), passim. Mason, a student at the Eclectic before the war, and a ' member of the Forty-second, was a longtime friend of Garfield. After a long period as a newspaperman in Cleveland he entered, with Garfield's help, the U.S. consular service. For Pardee, see Henry, *Captain Henry of Geauga*, pp. 100–104.

46. *Cincinnati Daily Commercial*, 25 Oct. 1861; JAG to Harry Rhodes, 26 Oct. 1861; Helen King to JAG, 4 Nov. 1861.

### Chapter 7. The War: 1862

Apart from Garfield's letters, the major sources for the Forty-second Regiment and the Sandy Valley campaign are: F. H. Mason, *The Forty-second Ohio Infantry* (Cleveland, 1876); Frederick A. Henry, *Captain Henry of Geauga, A Family Chronicle* (Cleveland, 1942); James A. Garfield, "My Campaign in East Kentucky," *North American Review*, 143:525–535 (Dec. 1886)—data prepared in 1880 for a campaign biography by Edmund Kirke (James R. Gilmore); *The War of the Rebellion: A Compilation of the Official Records of the Union and Confederate Armies*, 70 vols. (Washington, 1880–1901), Series I, Vol. VII (Since all the volumes of the *Official Records* cited in this book are in Series I, the series number will not be repeated in each citation.) See also Allan Peskin, "The Hero of the Sandy Valley: James A. Garfield's Kentucky Campaign of 1861–1862," *Ohio History*, 72:3–24, 129–139 (Jan. and April 1963), and Owen J. Hopkins, *Under the Flag of the Nation*, ed. by Otto F. Bond (Columbus, Ohio, 1961); Hopkins, seventeen when he enlisted, was a member of Company K of the Forty-second Regiment. He was mustered out in 1865 as first lieutenant.

1. Hopkins, *Under the Flag of the Nation*, pp. 13–14; Mason, *The Forty-second Ohio Infantry*, pp. 45–49; Henry, *Captain Henry*, pp. 109–110; JAG to LRG, 16 Dec. 1861.

2. JAG to LRG, 22 Aug. (Trot) and 16 Dec. 1861.

3. Rhodes to JAG, 27 Dec. 1861; JAG to Rhodes, 8 Oct. 1861. See also other letters of Rhodes to JAG during the summer and fall of 1861; Henry, *Captain Henry*, pp. 109–110.

4. JAG to LRG, 16 Dec. 1861.

5. Henry, *Captain Henry*, p. 110, quoting from an address by Charles E. Henry, 1901 (Hazen); JAG to Harry Rhodes, 17 Dec. 1861; Rhodes to JAG, 6 Nov. 1861 (sword).

6. JAG to Harry Rhodes, 17 Dec. 1861, JAG to LRG, 16 and 20 Dec. 1861; Garfield, "My Campaign in East Kentucky," p. 527.

7. Ibid., pp. 528–529; *Official Records,* VII, p. 32 ("a well disposed . . .").

8. Garfield, "My Campaign in East Kentucky," pp. 529–530.

9. Ibid., pp. 528 and 531 (Cranor); *Official Records,* VII, pp. 26–28; JAG to LRG, 1 Jan. 1862.

10. JAG to LRG, 13 Jan. 1861; Hopkins, *Under the Flag of the Nation,* pp. 17–18; *Official Records,* VII, pp. 27–29.

11. *Official Records,* VII, p. 542 (order to Sheldon); Garfield, "My Campaign in East Kentucky," p. 521; JAG to LRG, 13 Jan. 1861.

12. JAG to LRG, 13 Jan. 1861.

13. Ibid.; *Official Records,* VII, p. 30; JAG to F. A. Williams, copy, 23 March 1861 (Napoleon).

14. JAG to LRG, 13 Jan. 1861; *Official Records,* VII, pp. 30–31; Mason, *The Forty-second Ohio Infantry,* pp. 72–73.

15. JAG to LRG, 27 May 1862 (Jim); JAG to Harry Rhodes, 12 Feb. 1862 (slavery).

16. Henry, *Captain Henry,* p. 114, quoting note made 10 Jan. 1881 by Charles E. Henry.

17. *Official Records,* VII, p. 31 (return to Paintsville), p. 48 ("well whipped"), p. 33 (proclamation); a copy of the address to the troops is in the JAG Papers.

18. *Official Records,* VII, p. 24 (Buell), pp. 24–25 (McClellan); Harry Rhodes to JAG, 20 Jan. and 6 and 21 Feb. 1862; W. T. Bascom to JAG, 12 and 25 Jan., 3 and 23 Feb. 1862. W. T. Bascom's efforts at Columbus were abetted by Dr. Robison, who had been elected to the state senate. Early in February that body addressed to President Lincoln a recommendation that Garfield be promoted. According to W. J. Ford it was signed by all members of the senate except two who were absent because of illness. A copy of the senate's letter to Lincoln was enclosed in the letter of Ford cited above. The newly inducted governor, David Tod, a Union Democrat who had been opposed by Garfield and whose appointment of army officers had been subject to sharp criticism, was not inclined to be obstructive. See Harry Rhodes to JAG, 6 Jan. 1862—L.C. *Index* of Garfield Papers has 1861. In his diary entry for 25 Sept. 1862, S. P. Chase noted that Garfield had been made a brigadier general "at my instance." See David Donald, ed., *Inside Lincoln's Cabinet: the Civil War Diaries of Salmon P. Chase* (New York, 1954), p. 160.

19. JAG to LRG, 26 Jan. (on the river) and 15 Feb. 1862 ("special providences"); Mason, *The Forty-second Ohio Infantry,* pp. 78–79.

20. JAG to LRG, 15 Feb. 1862; JAG to W. J. Ford, 14 Feb. 1862, in Williams, *The Wild Life of the Army,* pp. 66–67 ("through the Cumberland Mountains"); JAG to J. Q. Smith, 15 Feb. 1862; *Official Records,* VII, p. 35 (railroad).

21. JAG to LRG, 23 Feb. and 10 March 1862; JAG to Harry Rhodes, 3 March 1862; Mason, *The Forty-second Ohio Infantry,* pp. 82–83; Henry, *Captain Henry,* pp. 118–119.

22. JAG to LRG, 19 March 1862; Mason, *The Forty-second Ohio Infantry,* pp. 83–87; JAG to C. P. Buckingham, adjutant general of Ohio, copy, 14 March 1862 (Sheldon and Pardee).

23. JAG to LRG, 2 April 1862; JAG to Augustus Williams, copy, 16 April 1862.

24. JAG to LRG, 2 and 4 April 1862.

25. JAG to LRG, 21 April 1862; JAG to Mary Larabee, 11 April 1862.

26. JAG to LRG, 21 April and 1 May 1862.

27. JAG to LRG, 21 April and 1, 4, 9, 12, and 27 May 1862; JAG to EBG, 8 May 1862; JAG to Almeda Booth, 20 May 1862, and JAG to Harmon Austin, 28 May 1862; LRG to JAG, 13 May 1862 (Plumb).

28. *Congressional Globe,* 38 Cong., 1 Sess., 28 Jan. 1864, p. 404 ("black phantom"); JAG to Harry Rhodes, 1 May (Wood and "Before God . . .") and 28 May 1862 (Wood).

29. In his letter to Rhodes, 1 May 1862, Garfield spoke of the "haughty tyranny of proslavery officers." See also JAG to Harmon Austin, 25 June 1862.

30. Rhodes to JAG, 9 May 1862; JAG to Rhodes, 19 May 1862.

31. JAG to George A. Wiswall, 9 June 1862 (Lake Huron, Port Austin, Williams), Harry A. Garfield Papers, L. C. Wiswall, of West Troy, New York, and Port Austin, Michigan, was a member of the Williams College class of 1859; he died in 1862 (information from Williams College Library).

32. Ibid.

33. Ibid. (Halleck's management and Garfield's dysentery); JAG to Harry Rhodes, 10 June 1862.

34. JAG to Harry Rhodes, 10 June 1862 (Congress); JAG to Harmon Austin, 25 June 1862 (fugitive slave).

35. JAG to Harmon Austin, 25 June 1862; LRG to JAG, 20 July 1862.

36. JAG to Harmon Austin, 25 June 1862 (unwillingness to have doubt thrown on his motives); JAG to LRG, 5 July 1862 (unwillingness to come home at this time); JAG to LRG, 17 July 1862 (Turchin court-martial); JAG to Harry Rhodes, 9 July 1862 (court-martial) and 24 July 1862 (illness); JAG to Corydon Fuller, 5 Sept. 1862, in Fuller, *Reminiscences of Garfield,* p. 330 (illness, presiding from cot, etc.).

37. JAG to LRG, telegram, 2 Aug. 1862.

38. LRG to JAG, 27 Oct. and 5 Nov. 1861 (moving) and 1 and 8 June 1862 (brother John); Zeb Rudolph to JAG, 24 March 1862 (John).

39. Eliza's short diary entries during 1861 and 1862 reveal some of her war-related activities. In EBG to JAG, 12 Jan. 1862—written on "garish Union stationery"—she described herself as his "anxious and Patriotic Mother." LRG to JAG, 22 June 1862.

40. LRG to JAG, 20 and 28 July 1862; Henry, *Captain Henry,* p. 125 (death of Augustus). In 1864 Charles E. Henry married Sophia Williams, sister of Augustus. In 1868, following the death of his first wife, Harry Rhodes married Adelaide Robbins.

41. LRG, Letters to Trot and Children's Record, 5 Oct. 1862.

42. JAG to Corydon Fuller, 5 Sept. 1862, in Fuller, *Reminiscences of Garfield,* p. 330 (Garfield's physical condition); Almeda Booth to JAG, 29 July [1862]—L.C. *Index* of Garfield Papers has 1860—(letter in *Herald*).

43. JAG to Harmon Austin, 14 Aug. 1862 ("political maneuver"); JAG to EBG, with note from Lucretia, 2 Sept. 1862; JAG to Burke Hinsdale, 12 Sept. 1862; JAG to Corydon Fuller, 5 Sept. 1862, in Fuller, *Reminiscences of Garfield,* p. 330 (Howland Springs); LRG, Letters to Trot and Children's Record, 5 Oct. 1862 (Howland Springs, Trot); JAG to LRG, 17 Sept. ("alabaster box"), 27 Sept., 31 Oct., and 11 Nov. 1862; LRG to JAG, 18 and 28 Sept., 26 Oct., and 16 Nov. 1862.

44. LRG to JAG, 19 Oct. 1862 (Rebecca); JAG to LRG, 11 Nov. 1862.

45. LRG to Harry A. Garfield, 21 Feb. 1898, Harry A. Garfield Papers, L.C.

46. Garfield's history of his military services, submitted to the adjutant general, 6 June 1873, a typed copy of fifteen pages; JAG to Ralph Plumb, copy, 2 Sept. 1862; Mason, *The Forty-second Ohio Infantry,* p. 15.

47. JAG to LRG, 20 Sept. 1862 (arrival in Washington). The battle of Antietam was fought on 17 September; on the night of 18 September General Robert E. Lee withdrew into Virginia.

48. JAG to Burke Hinsdale, 13 Oct. 1862, and JAG's remarks in Williams, *The Wild Life of the Army,* pp. 314-315 (McClellan); JAG to Harmon Austin, 25 Sept. 1862 (Emancipation Proclamation).

49. JAG to LRG, 20 Sept. 1862.

50. JAG to Harmon Austin, 25 Sept. and 14 Oct. 1862, JAG to Burke Hinsdale, 13 Oct. 1862, JAG to Harry Rhodes, 26 Oct. 1862 (Florida scheme); JAG to LRG, 20 Sept. and 7 Nov. 1862, JAG to Harry Rhodes, 10 Nov. 1862 (South Carolina).

51. JAG to LRG, 27 Sept. (invitation ·to live in Chase home) and 12 Oct. 1862 (Kate's nose); JAG to Harry Rhodes, 5 Oct. 1862 (weekend in the country).

52. JAG to LRG, 16 Nov. 1862 ("morbid fear"); Harry Rhodes to JAG, 28 Nov. 1862 ("polish of Washington life").

53. JAG to LRG, 16 Nov. 1862. For Chase's extravagance see Thomas Graham Belden and Marva Robins Belden, *So Fell the Angels* (Boston, 1956), pp. 80–81.

54. JAG to LRG, 14 Oct. (plan to visit Rebecca) and 24 Oct. 1862 (visit to Rebecca); LRG to JAG, 19 Oct. 1862.

55. JAG to Burke Hinsdale, 30 Oct. 1862.

56. JAG to Harry Rhodes, 7 Dec. 1862 (finance); JAG to Burke Hinsdale, 13 Oct. 1862, and Garfield's remarks in Williams, *The Wild Life of the Army,* pp. 314–315 (McClellan).

57. JAG to LRG, 7 Oct. (an interview with McDowell), 12 Oct. (enclosing the manuscript), and 31 Oct. 1862 (reference to the manuscript); these letters and the manuscript, together with Garfield's own "remarks," are in Williams, *The Wild Life of the Army. Official Records,* XII, Part 2, pp. 506, 507 (military commission and court-martial in Porter case).

58. JAG to LRG, 31 Oct. 1862; for an excellent statement on the Porter case and Garfield's anti-Porter bias, see Williams, *The Wild Life of the Army,* pp. 303–305; for later references by Garfield to the Porter case see JAG Diary, 17 Oct. 1879, 21 Jan., 5, 6, 8, 13, 16, and 29 Feb., and 1, 4, 5, 6, 8, 9, 10, and 11 March 1880, and JAG to J. D. Cox, 18 Feb. 1880, in Jacob D. Cox, *The Second Battle of Bull Run, as Connected with the Fitz-John Porter Case* (Cincinnati, 1882), pp. 119–120 ("stung"). As it happened, Garfield had no opportunity to debate the Porter case in the House.

59. JAG to Harry Rhodes, 5 Oct. 1862.

60. JAG to Harmon Austin, 25 Sept. 1862; JAG to Burke Hinsdale, 1 Dec. 1862; JAG to LRG, 2 Jan. 1863.

### Chapter 8. The War: 1863

1. Edwin M. Stanton to Rosecrans, copy, 14 Jan. 1863; JAG to Burke Hinsdale, 16 Dec. 1862.

2. LRG to JAG, Sept.–Dec. 1862, passim.

3. LRG to JAG, 16, 19, and 24 Nov. and 14 Dec. 1862; JAG to LRG, 20 and 25 Jan. 1863 (after his visit); LRG, Letters to Trot and Children's Record, 3 March 1863 (Trot).

4. JAG to LRG, 20 Jan. 1863 (contract, loans); Hinsdale, *President Garfield and Education,* p. 88; Garfield, Notes dictated for the use of biographers in June 1880. Hinsdale is the authority for the statement that Garfield paid $825 for the house; Garfield, in the 1880 notes, guessed that the cost was $1,200. Both set the cost of the enlargement and other improvements at $1,000.

5. JAG to LRG, 1 and 5 Feb., 28 March, 1, 21, and 25 April, 6 and 23 May, 2 and 14 June, 8 July, 23 Aug., and 1 Sept. 1863 (references to building). In 1872 Garfield sold the house to Burke Hinsdale. At present (1977) it is the home of Mr. and Mrs. John Zimmerman; Mrs. Zimmerman is the namesake and great granddaughter of Garfield's cousin, Phebe Boynton Clapp, who took over the house after the departure from Hiram of Burke Hinsdale in the early 1880s.

6. JAG to LRG, 25 Jan. 1863; James R. Gilmore, *Personal Recollections of Abraham Lincoln and the Civil War* (Boston, 1898), pp. 118–119 (room of Rosecrans). See James V. Mink, *The Papers of General William Starke Rosecrans and the Rosecrans Family; a Guide to Collection 663* (University of California Library, Los Angeles, 1961) for a drawing of Rosecrans's headquarters.

7. William M. Lamers, *The Edge of Glory: a Biography of General William S. Rosecrans, U.S.A.* (New York, 1961), pp. 244–247 (after Stone's River).

8. JAG to LRG, 26 Jan. 1863 ("unlike McClellan"); JAG to Harry Rhodes, 27 Jan. 1863.

9. JAG to LRG, 26 Jan. (first night), 1 Feb. (order from Rosecrans), and 13 Feb. 1863 (religion); JAG to Harry Rhodes, 27 Jan. (Rosecrans's religious history) and 14 Feb. 1863 (favorite topic). On 22 March 1863 Garfield wrote to his mother from Murfreesboro, "General Rosecrans . . . has Catholic service in his room or mine every few days. I sometimes attend, and as I can understand the Latin service it is not altogether unmeaning to me. I hope you are not alarmed about my becoming a Catholic. You ought to be glad that I take time to think and talk about religion at all. I have no doubt the Catholics have been greatly slandered."

10. JAG to LRG, 5 and 13 Feb. 1863 (horses, delay); JAG to Harmon Austin, 18 Feb. 1863 (short acquaintance).

11. For comments on and characterizations of Rosecrans, see Jacob Dolson Cox, *Military Reminiscences of the Civil War,* 2 vols. (New York, 1900), I, pp. 111–112, *Memoirs of Henry Villard, Journalist and Financier,* 2 vols. (Boston, 1904), II, p. 66, and Whitelaw Reid, *Ohio in the War: Her Statesmen, Her Generals, Her Soldiers,* 2 vols. (Cincinnati, 1868), I, p. 349. Garfield described Rosecrans as "kind and genial" (JAG to LRG, 1 Feb. 1863).

12. JAG to LRG, 28 Feb. 1863, and Lamers, *Edge of Glory,* pp. 232–233 (death of Garesché); JAG to Harry Rhodes, 14 Feb. 1863 ("almost alone").

13. JAG to Harry Rhodes, 14 Feb. 1863.

14. JAG to LRG, 26 Feb. 1863; *Official Records,* XXIII, Part 1, p. 92; Kirke [Gilmore], *Garfield,* p. 19.

15. JAG to LRG, 26 Feb. and 3 March (Harry's visit), 14 March (own mess), and 28 March 1863 (late hours, Swaim); JAG to EBG, 22 March 1863 (late hours); JAG to Corydon Fuller, 4 May 1863 (late hours), in Fuller, *Reminiscences of Garfield,* p. 336.

16. JAG to LRG, 10 and 21 April, 2 and 12 May 1863; JAG to S. P. Chase, 5 May 1863, in Williams, *The Wild Life of the Army,* p. 266; *Official Records,* XXIII, Part 1, p. 281 (Rosecrans's report of the capture of Streight's force), pp. 281–282 (Garfield's instructions to Streight), pp. 285–293 (Streight's report, 22 Aug. 1864). The enlisted men under Streight were soon exchanged, the officers held in prison. In February Streight and four of his officers escaped; when he made his report more than six months after his escape, he said that the rest of his officers were still confined or had died of disease. For a sharply critical comment on the Streight expedition and on Garfield, see *Personal Memoirs of Major-General D. S. Stanley, U.S.A.* (Cambridge, Mass., 1917), pp. 131–132. General Stanley was in command of the cavalry of the Army of the Cumberland.

17. JAG to S. P. Chase, 5 May 1863, in Williams, *The Wild Life of the Army,* p. 266; JAG to Corydon Fuller, 4 May 1863, in Fuller, *Reminiscences of Garfield,* p. 337.

18. See Halleck's Report, 15 Nov. 1863, in *Official Records,* XXIII, Part 1, p. 9 ("our last reserve"—letter of Rosecrans, 21 June 1863; Rosecrans to Halleck, 10 June 1863, on deferring advance until end of Vicksburg campaign). Rosecrans's desire for more mounted troops is shown in his letters, ibid., Part 2, pp. 31, 147, 154, 245 (to Halleck), pp. 34, 270–271 (to Stanton), and pp. 271, 320–321 (to Quartermaster General Montgomery Meigs).

19. Lamers, *Edge of Glory,* pp. 159–180, passim, and Bruce Catton, *Grant Moves South* (Boston, 1960), pp. 313–320 (Grant and Rosecrans); Hartsuff to Rosecrans, 8 Jan. 1863, Rosecrans Papers, UCLA Library.

20. *Memoirs of Villard,* II, pp. 65–67.

21. Ibid., pp. 65–66.

22. Donald, *Inside Lincoln's Cabinet,* pp. 25–26, and Belden and Belden, *So Fell the Angels,* pp. 102–104 (Chase and patronage); Gilmore, *Recollections,* pp. 95–103; A. G. Riddle, *The Life, Character and Public Services of Jas. A. Garfield* (Cleveland, 1882), p. 69. Riddle, who lived in northern Ohio for many years before moving to Washington, D.C., was a well-known lawyer and writer and a friend of Garfield, from whom he heard of Gilmore's mission. In May 1863 Garfield sent to his wife a copy of Gilmore's "new book," *My Southern Friends. Down in Tennessee* (1864) has a description of Garfield as Gilmore first saw him in May 1863; a chapter, "The Ohio Boy," in *Patriot Boys and Prison Pictures* (1866), is an account of Garfield's life; *On the Border* (1867) includes a fictionalized account of Garfield's eastern Kentucky campaign—described by Garfield as "almost perfectly accurate history." Gilmore's *Personal Recollections* and his life of Garfield cannot be similarly described.

23. Gilmore, *Recollections,* pp. 118–136, passim; JAG to LRG, 23 May 1863.

24. Gilmore, *Recollections,* pp. 145–146.

25. JAG to John Russell Young (managing editor of the *New York Tribune*), 31 March 1867, J. R. Young Papers, L.C. This statement seems to support the claim made by Riddle that Garfield had given Gilmore's scheme "emphatic discouragement" (Riddle, *Garfield,* pp. 69–70).

26. JAG to Harry Rhodes, 11 June 1863; *Official Records,* XXIII, Part 1, p. 8 (Rosecrans to Halleck, 11 June 1863).

27. JAG to Harry Rhodes, 11 June 1863; JAG to LRG, 14 June 1863.

28. JAG to Harry Rhodes, 11 June 1863; *Official Records,* XXIII, Part 2, pp. 420–424 ( JAG to Rosecrans, 12 June 1863)—the letter is also in Williams, *The Wild Life of the Army,* pp. 277–282; JAG to LRG, 24 June (army in motion), 27 and 29 June and 8 July 1863 (rain).

29. *Official Records,* XXIII, Part 1, pp. 403–409 (Rosecrans's report); Lamers, *Edge of Glory,* pp. 279–289.

30. *Official Records,* XXIII, Part 2, p. 518 (Stanton to Rosecrans, 7 July 1863, and Rosecrans's sarcastic reply, same date), pp. 552–592, passim (communications between Halleck and Rosecrans); Lamers, *Edge of Glory,* pp. 296–298.

31. *Official Records,* XXIII, Part 1, p. 409.

32. JAG to LRG, 17 July, 23 July (telegram concerning visit by Crete), and 1 Aug. 1863.

33. John P. Sanderson Diary, 21 July (Rousseau reveals plan), 24 July (Sanderson calls on Rosecrans), 25 July (Rosecrans in Sanderson's room), and 26 and 30 July 1863 (Rosecrans and the documents, departure of Sanderson and Rousseau, and a reference to a speech in Louisville by Rousseau), 4, 5, and 9 Aug. 1863 (references to political activity of Rousseau and Sanderson), Ohio State Historical Society, Columbus; the dates of Sanderson's entries are not always the dates of the events being described. *Official Records,* XXIII, Part 2, pp. 599–600 (Rosecrans to Stanton, 26 July 1863), pp. 598–599 (Rousseau to Stanton, 7 Aug. 1863).

34. JAG to S. P. Chase, 27 July 1863, in Williams, *The Wild Life of the Army.*

35. *Official Records,* XXIII, Part 2, p. 592 (Halleck to Rosecrans, 4 and 5 Aug. 1863—peremptory order), p. 593 (Halleck to Burnside, 5 Aug. 1863).

36. Rosecrans to Alexander McD. McCook, copy, 8 Nov. 1879, Rosecrans Papers, UCLA Library; *Official Records,* XXIII, Part 2, p. 594 (Rosecrans to Halleck, 6 Aug. 1863), p. 597 (Halleck to Rosecrans, 7 Aug. 1863).

37. JAG to Chase, 27 July 1863, in Williams, *The Wild Life of the Army;* JAG to John Russell Young, 31 March 1867, Young Papers, L.C.
38. See Lamers, *Edge of Glory,* pp. 298–299.
39. Roy Basler, ed., *The Collected Works of Abraham Lincoln,* 9 vols. (New Brunswick, N.J., 1953–1955), VI, pp. 337–378 (Lincoln to Rosecrans, 10 Aug. 1863).
40. JAG to LRG, 1, 14, and 23 Aug., 1 and 6 Sept. 1863.
41. *Official Records,* XXX, Part 1, pp. 52–53 (Rosecrans's report), Part 3, p. 479 (telegram to Halleck); Lamers, *Edge of Glory,* pp. 306–310.
42. *Official Records,* XXX, Part 1, pp. 53–54 (Rosecrans's report); Emerson Opdycke, "Notes on the Chickamauga Campaign," in R. V. Johnson and C. C. Buel, eds., *Battles and Leaders of the Civil War,* 4 vols. (New York, 1884–1887), III, p. 669; Vincent J. Esposito, ed., *The West Point Atlas of American Wars,* 2 vols. (New York, 1959), I, map 110 and accompanying text; *Memoirs of Villard,* II, pp. 90–91; Lamers, *Edge of Glory,* pp. 308ff; Benjamin P. Thomas and Harold M. Hyman, *Stanton: the Life and Times of Lincoln's Secretary of War* (New York, 1962), p. 285.
43. Charles A. Dana, *Recollections of the Civil War: with the Leaders at Washington and in the Field in the Sixties* (New York, 1898), pp. 61–77 (sketches), 103–108 (Dana's mission to the Army of the Cumberland and first meeting with Rosecrans); Gordon Granger to Rosecrans, 6 June 1864, Rosecrans Papers, UCLA Library; Charles Vincent Spaniola, "Charles Anderson Dana: His Early Life and Civil War Career" (Ph.D. dissertation, Michigan State University, 1965), p. 157 (unpopularity of Dana).
44. John P. Sanderson Diary, 9, 16, and 24 Aug. (Rousseau and Sanderson in Washington) and 19 Oct. 1863 (Sanderson's revelations to Rosecrans), Ohio State Historical Society; Dana, *Recollections,* pp. 107–110; *Official Records,* XXX, Part 1, pp. 35–36 (Halleck), pp. 184–185 (Dana to Stanton, 12 Sept. 1863), pp. 186–187 (Dana to Stanton, 14 Sept. 1863).
45. JAG to LRG, 16 Sept. 1863.
46. Emerson Opdycke, "Notes on the Chickamauga Campaign," in *Battles and Leaders,* III, p. 670. Opdycke commanded the 125th Ohio Infantry. Frederick D. Williams has said of General Burnside's defiance of orders from Washington to aid Rosecrans, "Burnside's performance throughout the campaign is a sorry chapter in the nation's military history." See *The Wild Life of the Army,* p. 296, note 60. Orders sent by Halleck nearly a week before the battle of Chickamauga to commanders on the Mississippi to send aid to Rosecrans were not delivered until after the battle.
47. *Official Records,* XXX, Part 1, pp. 54–56 (Rosecrans's report), pp. 605–606, 248–249, 487 (reports of Crittenden, Thomas, and McCook, respectively); Lamers, *Edge of Glory,* pp. 318–324; Vincent Esposito, ed., *West Point Atlas,* I, maps 112 and 113 and accompanying text.
48. John P. Sanderson Diary, 19 Sept. 1863 (the Widow Glenn's), Ohio State Historical Society; *Official Records,* XXX, Part 1, pp. 56–57 (Rosecrans's report); Emerson Opdycke, "Notes on the Chickamauga Campaign," in *Battles and Leaders,* III, p. 670; W. F. G. Shanks in the *New York Herald,* 29 Sept. 1863, quoted in Theodore Clarke Smith, *The Life and Letters of James Abram Garfield,* 2 vols. (New Haven, 1925), I, p. 324 (at the Widow Glenn's on 19 Sept.).
49. *Official Records,* XXX, Part 1, pp. 59–60 (Rosecrans's report); Cox, *Reminiscences,* II, pp. 9–10 (Garfield's account as given to Cox of the aftermath of the withdrawal of a division from the Union line); Reid, *Ohio in the War,* I, pp. 343, 349–350 (the fatal order). The "fatal order" was written not by Garfield but by Major Frank S. Bond, Rosecrans's senior aide; thus Garfield was not involved in the bitter controversy that ensued concerning the order and the responsibility of its recipient, General Thomas Wood.

50. Tyler Dennett, ed., *Lincoln and the Civil War in the Diaries and Letters of John Hay* (New York, 1939), pp. 109-110 (Garfield's account to Lincoln); John G. Nicolay and John Hay, *Abraham Lincoln, A History*, 10 vols. (New York, 1890), pp. 226-227; *Memoirs of Villard*, II, p. 157 (Garfield's account to author); Cox, *Reminiscences*, II, pp. 9-10 (Garfield's account to author; "listlessly"). Cox was summing up Garfield's account and did not claim to be giving Garfield's exact words.

51. Henry M. Cist, *The Army of the Cumberland* (New York, 1882), p. 226 (Rosecrans). General Thomas reported that Garfield had arrived "with Lieutenant-Colonel Thruston, of McCook's staff, and Captains Gaw and Barker, of my staff, who had been sent to the rear to bring back the ammunition, if possible." G. P. Thruston later wrote, however, that he and Garfield had probably reached Thomas about the same time but that they had come from different directions (*Battles and Leaders*, III, p. 665). Captain J. D. Barker testified that he had ridden from a mile south of Rossville to Thomas's line, but he did not mention Garfield. In his first dispatch to Rosecrans after he had reached Thomas, Garfield reported that Captain Gaw's horse and an orderly had been killed as his party had turned off the Rossville road to Thomas's line (*Official Records*, XXX, Part 1, p. 141).

52. *Official Records*, XXX, Part 1, p. 141 (Garfield's dispatch to Rosecrans, 3:45 P.M., from Thomas's headquarters), p. 140 (Rosecrans to Thomas, about 4:15 P.M.—for question of time see pp. 245, 256); JAG to EBG, 13 Oct. 1863 (loss of orderly and wounding of Billy).

53. *Official Records*, XXX, Part 1, p. 140 (Rosecrans to JAG—order for Thomas and Granger), p. 145 ( JAG to Rosecrans, 8:40 P.M.—"thoroughly whipped" and receipt of order); JAG to Rosecrans, letterpress copy, 14 Dec. 1870 ("strenuously urged"); Archibald Gracie, *The Truth about Chickamauga* (Boston, 1911), pp. 153-156. Rosecrans himself considered his order to Thomas as discretionary: "General Thomas, considering the excessive labors of the troops, the scarcity of ammunition, food, and water, and having orders from the general commanding to use his discretion, determined to retire on Rossville, where he arrived in good order." *Official Records*, XXX, Part 1, p. 61.

54. *Official Records*, XXX, Part 1, p. 145 ( JAG to Rosecrans, from Rossville, 8:40 P.M.), p. 146 ( JAG to Rosecrans, 1:30 A.M., 21 Sept. 1863), p. 147 ( JAG to Rosecrans, 7:45 A.M., 21 Sept. 1863).

55. JAG to LRG, 25 Sept. 1863; Garfield, "Gen. George H. Thomas: His Life and Character," in Burke A. Hinsdale, ed., *The Works of James A. Garfield*, 2 vols. (Cleveland, 1882), I, pp. 664-665.

56. *Official Records*, XXX, Part 1, pp. 157-158 (orders to Thomas, 21 Sept.), pp. 158, 255 (defenses), pp. 885-886 (withdrawal from Lookout), p. 215 (Dana's comments to Stanton on withdrawal from Lookout and opposition of Garfield and Granger).

57. *Official Records*, XXX, Part 1, p. 163 (Rosecrans to Lincoln), pp. 197-198 (Dana to Stanton), Part 3, p. 792 (Garfield to Chase). All three dispatches were prepared on the morning of Sept. 23—Garfield's at 10:30, Dana's at 11:30, and Rosecrans's at 11:40; all were received in the evening of the same day—Dana's at 9:45, Garfield's at 10:30, and Rosecrans's at 12:40. The time of receipt is on the telegrams of Garfield and Rosecrans in *Official Records;* according to Thomas and Hyman, *Stanton*, p. 286, Dana's message was received at the time indicated.

58. Tyler Dennett, ed., *Diaries and Letters of John Hay*, p. 93 (Stanton's sneer); Donald, *Inside Lincoln's Cabinet*, pp. 201-203 (the midnight conference); Thomas and Hyman, *Stanton*, pp. 268-288 (the midnight conference and the "wartime miracle").

59. JAG to LRG, 25 Sept. 1863; J. P. Sanderson Diary, 15 Oct. 1863; *New York Sun*, 26 Nov. 1879 (Steedman); *Memoirs of Villard*, II, pp. 185-186. Villard, a newspaper cor-

respondent, was in Chattanooga shortly after the battle of Chickamauga to gather material for a review of the battle.

60. Lamers, *Edge of Glory*, pp. 370–379, passim; Dana, *Recollections*, pp. 126–127; Johnson and Buel, *Battles and Leaders*, III, pp. 676–678 (river transportation).

61. *Memoirs of Villard*, II, pp. 184–185; *Official Records*, XXX, Part 1, p. 62 (Rosecrans's report).

62. JAG to Rosecrans, 23 Oct. 1863 to 23 March 1867, passim, Rosecrans Papers, UCLA Library.

63. *Official Records*, XXX, Part 1, p. 60; Dana, *Recollections*, pp. 121–122.

64. *Memoirs of Villard*, II, pp. 157, 185–186.

65. Ibid., p. 211; *Official Records*, XXX, Part 1, p. 204 (Dana to Stanton, 30 Sept. 1863); Rosecrans to Alexander McD. McCook, 8 Nov. 1879 (warning of Thomas), drafts in Rosecrans Papers, UCLA Library.

66. For Dana's reports to Stanton on Rosecrans, see *Official Records*, XXX, Part 1, pp. 198–221 (23 Sept. to 18 Oct. 1863), passim. Dana's recommendation of Thomas is in his dispatch of 30 Sept. (pp. 204–205); in his dispatch of 8 Oct. (p. 211) he said that Rousseau had reported to Thomas that Stanton had inquired how the army would like to have Thomas in the chief command. See Dana, *Recollections*, pp. 125–126, for an account of Stanton's request to Dana and the reaction of Thomas to Dana's visit and to other rumors.

67. *Official Records*, XXX, Part 1, p. 1051 (removal order), pp. 214–215 (Dana's dispatch); Dennett, *Diaries and Letters of Hay*, p. 93 (Stanton on Rosecrans); JAG to Rosecrans, 12 Dec. 1863, Rosecrans Papers UCLA Library, and *Memoirs of Villard*, II, p. 211 (Lincoln).

68. *Personal Memoirs of U.S. Grant*, ed. by E. B. Long (New York, 1952), pp. 308–309; JAG to Rosecrans, 12 Dec. 1863, Rosecrans Papers, UCLA Library; Thomas and Hyman, *Stanton*, p. 291.

69. *Cincinnati Commercial*, 21 Nov. 1879 (interview with Steedman by "F.D.M.").

70. *Official Records*, XXX, Part 4, pp. 248–249 (relieving Garfield), pp. 389–390 (instructions), pp. 415, 435–436, 436–437, 479 (Garfield's reports—the last has quotation).

71. This statement differs somewhat from Grant's own account (*Personal Memoirs*, pp. 308–309, 312), usually followed by historians. Grant says that Stanton received a dispatch from Dana "informing him that unless prevented Rosecrans would retreat, and advising peremptory orders against his doing so" and that this message led, late in the evening, to the dispatch to Rosecrans of the order by which Grant assumed command and of orders relieving Rosecrans, placing Thomas in command, and directing Thomas to hold Chattanooga. No such telegram is in the *Official Records*, and John Hoffman, assistant editor of *The Papers of Ulysses S. Grant*, states that "there appear to be no contemporary copies of such a telegram and Grant makes no specific reference to it at that time." (Hoffman to Harry Brown, 29 Nov. 1976). Dana (*Recollections*, p. 129) claims that he sent such a telegram just before he left Chattanooga on the morning of 19 October. One must bear in mind that Ida Tarbell put together *Recollections* and that Grant's book was published more than a decade before Dana's. It may well be that Stanton received on the evening of 19 October a dispatch sent by Dana on 18 October and that this made him more nervous about Chattanooga. The order to Thomas to hold Chattanooga was not sent at the same time as the other orders. This order was dispatched at 11:30 P.M., 19 October (*Official Records*, XXX, Part 4, p. 479). Grant's assumption of command occurred on 18 October (*Official Records*, XXX, Part 4, pp. 450–451). The dispatches relieving Rosecrans and placing Thomas in command were sent on 18 October (*Official Records*, XXX, part 4, pp. 478, 480;

XXXI, Part 1, p. 666). Rosecrans found his order on his table when he returned about dusk on 19 October after a day of inspection.

72. *Cincinnati Commercial,* 21 Nov. 1879 (interview with Steedman by "F.D.M."); *Official Records,* XXXI, Part 1, p. 684 (Stanton to P. H. Watson—"more than confirm the worst").

73. JAG, Dictated Notes, 1880; JAG to David Swaim, 16 Nov. 1863, Western Reserve Historical Society; Dennett, *Diaries and Letters of Hay,* pp. 109–110.

74. JAG to Rosecrans, 23 Oct. ("great wrong" and "great mistake") and 2 Nov. 1863 ("power among the people"), Rosecrans Papers, UCLA Library.

75. Goddard to Rosecrans, 7 Dec. 1863, Rosecrans Papers, UCLA Library; *Congressional Globe,* 38 Cong., 1 Sess., 17 Feb. 1864, pp. 713–714; Rosecrans to JAG, 12 March 1864.

76. JAG to Rosecrans, 18 Dec. 1863, Rosecrans Papers, UCLA Library; Lamers, *Edge of Glory,* pp. 415–439 (Missouri).

77. Smith, *Garfield,* II, pp. 845–885 ("Garfield, Rosecrans and Dana"); *Memoirs of Villard,* II, p. 211. In Dana's *Recollections,* completed in 1897 shortly before his death and published in book form in 1898, there are no derogatory references to Garfield nor is there any suggestion that Garfield had anything to do with the removal of Rosecrans. Dana presents an unflattering description of Rosecrans and leaves the reader with the impression that he should have been removed, but he does not claim credit for the removal. The *Recollections* were put together by Ida Tarbell, "constructed . . . primarily around Dana's dispatches and letters. Generally she used these in such a way that Dana was permitted to speak for himself." During interviews with him, Tarbell found Dana "unenthusiastic about having his memoirs written. He seldom offered information unless it was in response to some specific question." See Spaniola, "Dana," p. 293.

78. Rosecrans to JAG, 20 Dec. 1879; JAG to Rosecrans, 19 Jan. 1880, Rosecrans Papers, UCLA Library.

79. Two newspaper clippings (Rosecrans's "card" and an editorial comment) were enclosed in a letter to JAG from Channing Richards, 27 Aug. 1880; Frank Darr to Rosecrans, 28 July, 2 and 7 Aug., and 16 Sept. 1880 (Garfield's "treachery"), Rosecrans Papers, UCLA Library; Rosecrans to JAG, undated, received by JAG 23 Dec. 1880; JAG to Rosecrans, letterpress copy, 28 Dec. 1880. The newspaper referred to is the *Alta California* (San Francisco).

80. *New York Sun,* 8 March and 12 June 1882; Schuckers to JAG, 12 Nov. 1859 to 25 April 1881, passim; for a more detailed discussion of the publication of Garfield's letters to Chase, see Smith, *Garfield,* II, pp. 868–873. On 17 March 1882 Rosecrans wrote to Dana that he had always thought that he was the cause of his removal, but that he was now beginning to think that he had done Dana injustice. Charles A. Dana Papers, L.C. Eight years after this letter was written Rosecrans was able to read in the *Official Records* Dana's dispatches from the Army of the Cumberland.

81. *New York Sun,* 12 June 1882 (letter of J. W. Schuckers).

82. *Congressional Globe,* 38 Cong., 1 Sess., 17 Feb. 1864, pp. 713–714; letters of JAG to Rosecrans, passim, Rosecrans Papers, UCLA Library.

83. JAG to Rhodes, 26 March 1865.

### Chapter 9. Congress

1. J. D. Cox, "The Youth and Early Manhood of James Abram Garfield," in *Society of the Army of the Cumberland, Fourteenth Reunion, Milwaukee, Wisconsin, 1882* (Cincinnati,

1883), pp. 100–101; JAG, Dictated Notes, 1880 (Lincoln); JAG to LRG, 6 Dec. 1863 (secretary of war).

2. JAG to Corydon Fuller, 13 Dec. 1863, in Fuller, *Reminiscences of Garfield,* pp. 344–345.

3. JAG to LRG, 6 Dec. 1863.

4. George Alfred Townsend, "President Garfield and his Cabinet," *Frank Leslie's Popular Monthly,* 11:514 (April 1881) (description of Blaine); Riddle, *Garfield,* p. 75; JAG to Burke Hinsdale, 4 April 1876 (Blaine as politician).

5. Charles Henry's associations with Garfield are fully treated in Henry, *Captain Henry of Geauga;* see also James D. Norris and Arthur H. Shaffer, eds., *Politics and Patronage in the Gilded Age: the Correspondence of James A. Garfield and Charles E. Henry* (Madison, 1970).

6. A very large amount of correspondence between these men and Garfield is to be found in the Garfield Papers. See letters of Garfield to William Cooper Howells and Victoria Howells in this volume.

7. *Dictionary of American Biography,* Vol. 4, p. 472 (Cowles); *Diary of JAG,* III, footnote p. 255 (Mason). In 1880 Garfield secured the appointment of Mason as U.S. consul in Basel; he continued in the consular service for more than thirty years.

8. *Ashtabula Sentinel,* 24 August 1864, quoted in Smith, *Garfield,* I, pp. 378–379; James S. Brisbin and William Ralston Balch, *The Life and Public Career of General James A. Garfield . . .* (Chicago, preface 1881), pp. 247–248; Riddle, *Garfield,* pp. 106–108.

9. JAG to Harmon Austin, 31 Jan. 1870.

10. J. D. Cox to William Henry Smith, 14 July 1885, W. H. Smith Papers, Ohio Historical Society. I am indebted to Michael Burlingame for sending me a copy of a portion of this letter.

11. JAG, Dictated Notes, 1880; Bundy, *Garfield,* p. 122; JAG to Harmon Austin, 13 Dec. 1865; JAG to Burke Hinsdale, 5 Dec. 1867. In the letter to Hinsdale, Garfield also said that Colfax hoped to conciliate Schenck, who did not like him and frequently abused him.

12. Blaine to JAG, 10 Nov. 1868 and March 1869; JAG to Blaine, draft?, 11 March 1869; Dawes to Blaine, 3 Dec. 1871, copy, Dawes Papers, L.C.; JAG to Burke Hinsdale, 3 Dec. 1871. The second letter of Blaine is an answer to Garfield's of 11 March; in it Blaine tells Garfield that he is giving him an assignment to Appropriations, the chairmanship of the Census Committee and a place on the Rules Committee. The subsequent decision to appoint Garfield chairman of the Committee on Banking and Currency must have resulted from a private conference between the two men.

13. *Congressional Globe,* 42 Cong., 2 Sess., 23 Jan. 1872, pp. 536–540; *Diary of JAG,* II, 12 June 1872.

14. E. V. Smalley, "Characteristics of President Garfield," *Century Magazine,* XXIII:168 (Dec. 1881); Hinsdale, *Works of Garfield,* I, p. 451 (Hinsdale's introduction to a speech on the census delivered by Garfield on 16 December 1869), II, pp. 185–217 (census article); JAG to LRG, 30 May, 4, 9, 10, 13, 15, 16, 18, and 29 June, 1 July 1869; JAG to Carl Schurz, draft, 20 Jan. 1881 (Walker's appointment).

15. JAG to W. C. Howells, 18 June 1864 (in this volume).

16. JAG to Burke Hinsdale, 1 Jan. 1867 (in this volume); *Congressional Globe,* 42 Cong., 1 Sess., Appendix, 4 April 1871, pp. 149–155 (speech on Ku Klux bill), 41 Cong., 2 Sess., 24 June 1870, p. 4784 (anomalies, whirlwinds).

17. JAG to Burke Hinsdale, 30 Dec. 1880 (in this volume); JAG Diary, 25 Jan. 1881.

18. The Boston speech, the Chicago speech, and the *Atlantic* article are in Hinsdale, *Works of Garfield,* II, beginning pp. 586, 610, and 246, respectively.

19. *Congressional Globe,* 39 Cong., 1 Sess., 10 July 1866, p. 3720.

20. J. L. Hayes, "General Garfield and his Services to the National Wool Industry," *Bulletin of the National Association of Wool Manufacturers,* 11:284–285; House Report No. 1400, Part 2, 46 Cong., 2 Sess., Serial 1937; W. A. M. Grier to JAG, 7 June 1880.

21. Garfield, "Some Tendencies of American Education," a speech delivered in Washington, D.C., 5 Feb. 1879, in Hinsdale, *President Garfield and Education,* p. 342.

22. JAG to S. C. Armstrong, letterpress copy, 27 Sept. 1870, and to the Joint Committee on Schools and Colleges of the Virginia legislature, letterpress copy, 17 Dec. 1870 (Armstrong letter in this volume); *Congressional Globe,* 39 Cong., 1 Sess., 8 June 1866, pp. 3049–3051 (Bureau of Education); 42 Cong., 2 Sess., 6 Feb. 1872, pp. 859–860 (public lands). See also Allan Peskin, "The Short, Unhappy Life of the Federal Department of Education," *Public Administration Review,* 33:572–575 (Nov.–Dec. 1973).

23. *Congressional Record,* 45 Cong., 3 Sess., 11 Feb. 1879, pp. 1209–1210.

24. Joseph Stanley-Brown, "Memorandum" (Geological Survey); *Diary of JAG,* II, 7 April (Henry) and 15 Aug. 1872 (Hayden), 17 Jan. 1873 (Nantucket); JAG to Simon Newcomb, 30 March 1872, Newcomb Papers, L.C.; William J. Rhees to JAG, 29 Dec. 1880 (quoting Asa Gray); Board of Regents, Smithsonian Institution, *Annual Report* for 1873 (Washington, D.C., 1874), pp. 148–151.

25. JAG to Reid, 9 Dec. 1868, Whitelaw Reid Papers, L.C.; JAG to E. C. Stanton, letterpress copy, 9 Jan. 1872; JAG to S. B. Anthony, letterpress copy, 24 Aug. 1880. The Reid and Anthony letters are included in this volume.

26. For the visit to Louisiana see *Diary of JAG,* III, 10 Nov. to 5 Dec. 1876; JAG to LRG, 15–26 Nov. 1876; *Senate Executive Documents,* Doc. No. 2, Serial 1718, 44 Cong., 2 Sess. (report to the President by Garfield and other Republicans).

27. *Diary of JAG,* III, 17 Jan. to 1 March 1877, passim, (electoral commission); *Congressional Record,* 44 Cong., 2 Sess., 25 Jan. 1877, pp. 968–973; JAG to R. B. Hayes, 19 Jan. 1877, R. B. Hayes Library; JAG to Harmon Austin, 16 Feb. 1877. The Hayes letter is included in this volume.

28. The so-called Compromise of 1877 has been the subject of much research and considerable controversy. The most influential modern work on the subject is C. Vann Woodward, *Reunion and Reaction* (Boston, 1951). For a more recent view see Allan Peskin, "Was There a Compromise of 1877?," *Journal of American History,* 60:63–75 (June 1973); Woodward's response, "Yes, There was a Compromise of 1877," ibid., pp. 215–223. Garfield's views and activities are revealed in part in *Diary of JAG,* III (see entry for 26 Feb. 1877 on the Wormley Conference), and in his letters (see JAG to R. B. Hayes, 12 Dec. 1876, R. B. Hayes Library, in this volume).

29. *Diary of JAG,* III, 17 Feb., 29 March, 3, 6, and 9 April 1877 (Speakership), 5 March 1877 (Senate); JAG, Dictated Notes, 1880; Hayes to JAG, copy, 9 March 1877 (Senate), R. B. Hayes Library.

30. JAG Diary, 3 March 1878; JAG to Howells, 1 March 1878; see also JAG to Harmon Austin, 3 March 1878. For an excellent study of the Hayes administration see Kenneth E. Davidson, *The Presidency of Rutherford B. Hayes* (Westport, Connecticut, 1972).

31. JAG, Dictated Notes, 1880.

32. William Henry Smith, "Personal Memoranda," 25 May 1879, typescript of original in the R. B. Hayes Library. Smith, a close friend of Hayes, was manager of the Western Associated Press and collector of the port of Chicago. For a very interesting comparison of Garfield and Hayes, see John Thomas Houdek, "James A. Garfield and Rutherford B. Hayes: A Study in State and National Politics," Ph.D. dissertation, Michigan State University, 1970, Chapter 1.

33. See JAG Diary, 18 March to 1 July 1879, passim, for the special session; JAG, Dictated Notes, 1880.

34. *The Nation*, 32:216 (31 March 1881); E. V. Smalley, "Characteristics of President Garfield," *Century Magazine*, 23:168 (Dec. 1881); James G. Blaine, *Eulogy on President James Abram Garfield Delivered before the Senate and the House of Representatives of the United States, February 27, 1882* (Boston, 1882), p. 29. Memoirs of Thomas Donaldson, typescript, p. 76, R. B. Hayes Library—the original is in the library of the Indiana Historical Society, Indianapolis.

35. Blaine, *Eulogy on Garfield*, pp. 31-32.

36. Donaldson, Memoirs, typescript, Hayes Library, p. 75 (moral courage); *The Capital*, 30 Aug. 1874 (rabbit—attributed to J. S. Black; exasperating manner); George F. Hoar, *Autobiography of Seventy Years*, 2 vols. (New York, 1903), I, p. 399 (lurch); John Sherman, *Recollections of Forty Years in the House, Senate and Cabinet*, 2 vols. (Chicago, 1895), II, p. 807; Charles Richard Williams, ed., *Diary and Letters of Rutherford Birchard Hayes*, 5 vols. (Columbus, Ohio, 1922-1926), IV, p. 110.

37. Hoar, *Autobiography*, I, pp. 399-400.

38. Captain F. H. Mason, *The Life and Public Services of James A. Garfield* (London, 1881), pp. 131-132.

39. *Cincinnati Commercial*, 22 March 1880.

40. *Diary of JAG* and JAG Diary are the best sources of information on Garfield's public speaking. Smalley, "Characteristics of President Garfield," pp. 171-172.

41. Ibid., p. 172; *Diary of JAG*, III, 9 Feb. 1876 (Cox).

42. Ibid., 9 March 1876.

43. JAG Diary, 1 and 2 Sept. 1879; *Diary of JAG*, 8 Sept. 1876.

44. Riddle, *Garfield*, p. 229 (statement authorized by Garfield and printed in the *Cincinnati Gazette*).

45. House Report No. 77, "Crédit Mobilier Investigation," 42 Cong., 3 Sess., Serial 1577, pp. 21, 28 (Dec.), pp. 295-298 (Jan.), p. 461 (Feb.).

46. Ibid., p. 129.

47. Chaffee to Dawes, 9 March 1881, Dawes Papers, L.C.

48. House Report No. 77, "Crédit Mobilier Investigation," pp. vii, viii.

49. Black to JAG, 29 Sept. 1872, original or copy, J. S. Black Papers, L.C.; Black to Blaine, 15 Feb. 1873, in Garfield, *Review of the Transactions of the Crédit Mobilier Company* (1873), p. 14; *New York Sun*, 28 Sept. 1880 (letter of Black to the editor).

50. *New York Sun*, 28 Sept. 1880 (letter of Black to the editor); Black to JAG, 29 January 1873.

51. "Remarks of Hon. James A. Garfield to his Constituents, at Warren, Ohio, September 19, 1874, in Reply to Attacks upon his Official Character," in *The Republican Campaign Text Book for 1880* (Washington, D.C., 1880). In April 1873 Garfield published a broadside "To the Republican Voters of the Nineteenth District" after a Republican convention in Trumbull County had adopted a resolution calling upon him to resign.

52. *Diary of JAG*, II, 4, 11, 12, and 16 Dec. 1873 and 13 Jan. 1874.

53. Senate Report No. 453, 43 Cong., 1 Sess. (DeGolyer investigation); the statement of Parsons in regard to Garfield is on p. 1075.

54. *Diary of JAG*, II, 2, 13, 17, 18, and 19 June 1872. In the speech at Warren (cited in note 51) Garfield said that he had heard of the DeGolyer matter for the first time on 8 June, two days before the adjournment of Congress. The testimony of Parsons before the investigating committee (note 53) suggests that Parsons had first contacted Garfield earlier than 8 June. If he had not done so, Garfield's visit to Shepherd on 2 June must have been for reasons unrelated to DeGolyer pavement.

55. *Diary of JAG*, II, 15 April 1874; 3 May and 11 June 1872.

56. Garfield's Warren speech (note 51); JAG to Burke Hinsdale, 30 April 1874.

57. *Diary of JAG*, II, 15 April 1874; see also JAG to Harmon Austin, 27 April 1874.

58. LRG to JAG, 11 June 1879.

59. *Diary of JAG*, II, 15 Jan. 1873 (shadow); JAG Diary, 16 March 1878; *Washington Post*, 15 March 1878.

60. Rose is mentioned many times in Garfield's diary, and he seems to have been responsible for Garfield's beginning on 1 January 1872 to keep a regular diary after the lapse of many years. A large part of the diary from 1872 to 1880 is in Rose's hand; Garfield sometimes dictated entries to him and sometimes gave him entries to be copied into the diary. Letters relating to Rose's services and payments for them are in the LRG Papers.

61. Joseph Stanley-Brown, "Memorandum." Joseph Brown's paternal grandfather's surname was Stanley; when he came to the United States from Scotland he changed his name to Brown. In the 1880s Joseph Brown, at Mrs. Garfield's suggestion, changed his name to Joseph Stanley-Brown; he married Mollie Garfield in 1888, after Mrs. Garfield had put him through college.

62. Brisbin and Balch, *Garfield,* p. 332 (Garfield's books).

63. *Diary of JAG*, II, 23 Nov. 1873 (Mill) and 13 Nov. 1874 (26 volumes), III, 11 June (Swiss) and 24 June 1875 (gypsies), 19–30 April and 1–6 May 1876 (Trevelyan); JAG to Burke Hinsdale, 4 Jan. 1874 (Goethe) and 29 April 1876 (delighted with Trevelyan).

64. *Diary of JAG*, III, 18 June to 31 July ·1875, passim.

65. Ibid., II, 23, 24, 26, and 27 Nov. 1874 (Holmes), III, 30 March (New Britain), 8 Sept. (Defiance), and 9 Sept. 1875, 8 Sept. 1876 (history of Maine), 17 Sept. 1877 (*Chuzzlewit*).

66. *Diary of JAG*, II, 21 Nov. 1874.

67. *Diary of JAG*, II, 1 Jan. 1872 (*Divorce*), 12 Dec. 1873 (Jefferson); JAG Diary, 1 Feb. 1878 (Sothern), 18 April and 12 and 24 May (*Pinafore*), and 6 Dec. 1879 (breakfast).

68. *Diary of JAG*, III, 26 Dec. 1876.

69. Riddle, *Garfield,* pp. 51, 358–359 (study of law); JAG, Dictated Notes, 1880 (Black).

70. 71 U.S. 2; for Garfield's argument, see pp. 42–61.

71. *Diary of JAG*, III, 14 and 15 Oct. 1875; Cox to William H. Smith, 14 July 1885, W. H. Smith Papers, Ohio Historical Society. I am indebted to Michael Burlingame for sending me a portion of this letter.

72. *Diary of JAG*, II and III, passim; JAG Diary, 16 May 1879 (Lynch) and passim.

73. An extract from a letter of JAG to Rhodes, 8 Dec. 1867.

74. JAG, Dictated Notes, 1880.

75. Ibid.; JAG to W. C. Howells, 23 Dec. 1869 (in this volume). For details of the building of the house, see letters of Garfield to Swaim, spring and summer of 1869, Western Reserve Historical Society, and Swaim to JAG, for the same period. There are letterpress copies of letters from Garfield to Swaim in the JAG Papers.

76. EBG to Alpha Boynton, 13 Jan. and 1 May 1868, EBG to Phebe Boynton Clapp, 20 Feb. 1868; JAG to EBG, 24 March 1864 (Garfield's answer to Eliza's charge).

77. EBG to sister and niece, 18 Jan. 1872 (stuffed chair); EBG to nieces, 8 Dec. 1873.

78. *Diary of JAG*, III, 4 May 1876; Brisbin and Balch, *Garfield,* p. 330.

79. Diary of Mollie Garfield, 27 Sept. 1883, in the possession of Mrs. Herbert Feis, daughter of Mollie. The part quoted was sent to M.L. by Mrs. Feis.

80. LRG to JAG, 26 Nov. 1876; John Q. Smith to wife, 4 Jan. 1873; *Diary of JAG*, III, 24 Aug. 1875; LRG, Letters to Trot and Children's Record, 16 Dec. 1877, LRG Papers.

81. LRG to JAG, 5 June 1877.

82. *Diary of JAG*, II, 13 Nov. 1873.

83. LRG, Letters to Trot and Children's Record, 16 Dec. 1877, LRG Papers.

84. *Diary of JAG,* III, 6, 10, and 13 Nov. (Audubon) and 4 Dec. 1875 (*Macbeth*), 30 Aug. 1876 (Laurel Hill), 18 Oct. 1877 (*Henry V*); JAG Diary, 3 Dec. 1879 (Irvin), 25 Sept. 1880 (word book); JAG to children, 19 April 1875.

85. JAG Diary, 6 Sept. 1879.

86. Ibid., 20 and 21 Dec. 1879.

87. *Diary of JAG,* I, 4 Aug. 1867 (Spurgeon), II, 3 Aug. 1873 (on going to church), III, 19 Dec. 1875 (Moody). The Garfield pew is in the National City Christian Church on Thomas Circle, a short distance from the site of the Vermont Avenue church attended by Garfield.

88. Hinsdale, *President Garfield and Education,* p. 74; *Diary of JAG,* III, 5 Dec. 1875. For an excellent short study of Garfield's religious history see W. W. Wasson, *James A. Garfield: His Religion and Education* (Nashville, 1952).

89. *Diary of JAG,* III, 27 Aug. 1875.

90. *Diary of JAG,* III, 31 Oct. 1876 and 14 and 16 April 1877. The description of the farm is from footnote 110, p. 473, of *Diary of JAG,* III, an item from the *Geneva (Ohio) Times,* 24 March 1877.

91. EBG to Alpha Boynton, 2 June 1877; for life on the farm see *Diary of JAG,* III, 1877, and JAG Diary, 1878–1881, passim.

92. Ibid., passim. See also Brisbin and Balch, *Garfield,* pp. 314ff, and Bundy, *Garfield,* pp. 217–224.

93. The very large number of letters between James and Lucretia constitute the best source for a study of their relations and their feelings for each other.

94. LRG to JAG, 7 July 1867; JAG to LRG, 8 July 1867.

95. LRG to JAG, 7 July 1867; JAG to LRG, 6 July (wronging her) and 8 July 1867.

96. JAG to LRG, 2 Dec. 1867.

97. LRG to JAG, 28 July 1876.

98. JAG to LRG, 31 July 1876.

99. LRG to JAG, 18 May 1879 (notorious woman), 20 May 1879, enclosing draft of a letter to Mrs. Henry Spencer, who was reported to have been the source of the story; *The Independent,* 27 March 1879; Jeremiah Chaplin to JAG, 24 April 1879; JAG to Chaplin, 30 April 1879, R. B. Hayes Library; JAG Diary, 27 and 29 April 1879.

100. LRG to Harry A. Garfield, 21 Feb. 1898, H. A. Garfield Papers, L.C.

101. EBG to JAG and LRG, 11 Aug. and 8 Sept. 1867.

102. Lieber to JAG, 10 July 1867; *Diary of JAG,* I, 13 July to 6 Nov. 1867.

103. *Diary of JAG,* I, 29 July and 8 Aug. 1867 (Parliament).

104. Ibid., 26 Sept. to 1 Oct. 1867.

105. LRG to JAG, 20 Nov. 1867; JAG to LRG, 24 Nov. 1867.

106. JAG to Harmon Austin, 2 March 1868.

107. JAG Diary, 6 Aug. to 14 Oct. 1879, passim; Garfield's comment is in the entry for 14 Oct.

108. Ibid., 21–23 and 25 Oct. 1879.

109. Ibid., 23 July 1878; JAG to Eugene Cowles, draft, 30? July 1877. Eugene was the son of Edwin Cowles.

110. JAG Diary, 1 July and 23 Nov. 1879.

111. Henry, *Captain Henry of Geauga,* pp. 288–290; Norris and Shaffer, *Politics and Patronage in the Gilded Age,* pp. 219–266, passim; JAG Diary, 6 Jan. 1880. Houdek, "James A. Garfield and Rutherford B. Hayes," pp. 400, 405–406 (Sherman).

112. Henry, *Captain Henry of Geauga,* p. 291; JAG Diary, 14 Jan. 1880; *Painesville Telegraph,* 22 Jan. 1880 (speech).

113. JAG Diary, 16–31 Jan. 1880, passim.

114. *Cincinnati Commercial,* 7 Jan. 1880.

## Chapter 10. The Presidency

1. Gail Hamilton (Mary Abigail Dodge), *Biography of James G. Blaine* (Norwich, Connecticut, 1895), pp. 396–399 (Ingersoll).
2. For a brief discussion of factionalism within the Republican party in the three states mentioned see Robert D. Marcus, *Grand Old Party: Political Structure in the Gilded Age, 1880–1896* (New York, 1971), pp. 29–34.
3. R. A. Horr to JAG, 20 Jan. 1880; JAG Diary, 25 Jan. 1880; JAG's letter to Horr, 26 Jan. 1880, is in Henry, *Captain Henry of Geauga*, pp. 292–293; JAG to Charles E. Henry, 8 Dec. 1879 ("exceedingly anxious") and 26 Jan. 1880 (comment on letter to Horr).
4. *Saline County* (Nebraska) *Standard*, 15 Jan. 1880, *Duluth Tribune*, 16 May 1880, and *Reno Evening Gazette*, 14 Feb. 1880 (clippings in JAG Papers scrapbook); William W. Thompson to JAG, 24 Jan. 1880 (thane of Cawdor); John J. Williams to JAG, 29 Jan. 1880 (Garfield Club); Rhodes to JAG, 12 Feb. 1880; Barker to JAG, 2 Feb. 1880.
5. JAG Diary, 18 Feb. and 24 April 1880 (Barker); letters of Barker to JAG—eight between 12 Jan. and 18 May 1880.
6. JAG Diary, 11 Feb. 1880.
7. Sheldon to JAG, 30 Jan. 1880 (anti-Sherman sentiment).
8. JAG Diary, 26 Feb. 1880; *Cincinnati Inquirer* (Washington dispatch), 3 March 1880.
9. JAG to Hinsdale, 21 April 1880; Hinsdale to JAG, 23 April 1880; Charles Foster to JAG, 4 May 1880 (Sherman's choices); Sherman, *Recollections*, II, p. 771.
10. JAG Diary, 30 April 1880.
11. Harry Rhodes saw the nominating speech as an opportunity for Garfield. In a letter to Garfield, 14 May 1880, he said, "I have been intending to write you for some time to say what you probably fully appreciate, that in making a speech at Chicago in behalf of Mr. Sherman, your own golden hour may have struck. Do your level best, with all the heartiness and power you can command."
12. JAG to Gen. T. J. Wood, letterpress copy, 12 April 1872 (Grant).
13. JAG Diary, 18 Feb. 1880.
14. Ibid., 28 and 29 May 1880.
15. Ibid., 29 May 1880.
16. Ibid., 29 and 31 May 1880.
17. *Proceedings of the Republican National Convention . . . 1880* (Chicago, 1881), pp. 179–182 (Conkling's speech), pp. 184–186 (Garfield's speech); Brisbin and Balch, *Garfield*, p. 492 (quoting reporter).
18. Conkling to JAG, 2 June 1880. Writers have assigned various dates to this note. The note in the JAG Papers, L.C., has "June 2 2½ P.M." It is not clear whether the day and hour were noted by Conkling himself. The note is signed "R.C." The name "Roscoe Conkling" in someone else's hand is also on the sheet. The *Index* of the JAG Papers does not assign a date other than "1880" to the note. The case for 2 June is strengthened by a statement in Ferris Jacobs (Williams College classmate of Garfield who was a New York delegate to the convention) to JAG, 18 June 1880: "I thought that note Roscoe wrote you the first day amiable, almost angelic for him . . . I asked you when you showed me the note whether there was any bone between you. I felt better when you said there was not."
19. *Utica Herald*, 9 June 1880.
20. Wharton Barker, "The Secret History of Garfield's Nomination," *Pearson's Magazine*, 35:435–443 (May 1916).
21. *Proceedings of the Republican National Convention . . . 1880;* details of the balloting may also be found in Brisbin and Balch, *Garfield*, pp. 464–481. Conkling's Grant

medal is shown in Conkling, *Conkling,* opp. p. 609. The obverse includes a portrait of Grant and a listing of the votes cast for him on each of the thirty-six ballots. The reverse has this inscription: "Commemorative of the 36 ballots of the Old Guard for Ulysses S. Grant for President. Republican National Convention Chicago June 1880." Below the inscription is the name "Roscoe Conkling."

22. William Walter Phelps to JAG, 24 Oct. 1880 (L.C. *Index* of JAG Papers has misdated the letter 24 Nov.); Henry, *Captain Henry of Geauga,* p. 296.

23. Edward C. Smith to A. F. Rockwell, 22 June 1880, JAG Papers, has a long excerpt from a letter of Jacobs to Smith about the convention and the telegram to Hopkins.

24. William Dennison to John Sherman, 8 June 1880, Sherman Papers, L.C.

25. Thomas C. Reeves, *Gentleman Boss: the Life of Chester A. Arthur* (New York, 1975), p. 180.

26. John Sherman to Warner Bateman, 9 June 1880, Bateman Papers, Western Reserve Historical Society.

27. *Washington Star,* 15–19 June 1880; T. Harry Williams, ed., *Hayes: The Diary of a President, 1875–1881* (New York, 1964), pp. 279–280. Garfield made no entries in his diary from 2 June to 23 July 1880.

28. JAG to Conkling, 17 June 1880, Conkling Papers, L.C.; Reid to JAG, 26 June 1880; JAG to Reid, letterpress copy, 29 June 1880; Conkling, *Conkling,* p. 611.

29. The most recent and best biography of Conkling is David M. Jordan, *Roscoe Conkling of New York, Voice in the Senate* (Ithaca, 1971).

30. Ibid.; Eugene H. Klempell, "James M. Comly, Journalist-Politician," Ph.D. dissertation, Ohio State University, 1936, p. 288, footnote (smell of cowyard); *Albany* (New York) *Evening Journal,* 18 April 1888, p. 46.

31. Jordan, *Conkling,* pp. 309–312 (noisy confrontation); Belden and Belden, *So Fell the Angels,* pp. 306–309; *The Independent,* 31:4–5 (26 June 1879).

32. JAG to LRG, 13 Aug. 1879.

33. Katharine Chase Sprague to Arthur, Convention, Friday [June 1880], Arthur Papers, L.C. Friday was the third day of the Convention.

34. Hinsdale, *Works of Garfield,* II, pp. 782–787; Thomas Nichol to JAG, 18 Nov. 1880.

35. Hinsdale, *Works of Garfield,* II, p. 786. Garfield explained and defended his civil service statement in a letter to Schurz, letterpress copy, 22 July 1880.

36. Marshall Jewell to JAG, 29 July 1880, quoting a letter of JAG "to another gentleman" ("dummy"); JAG Diary, 24 July to 2 Nov. 1880, passim; Riddle, *Garfield,* pp. 462–465 (group visits); C. S. Carpenter, comp., *James A. Garfield. His Speeches at Home, 1880* (Oneonta, N.Y., 1880).

37. JAG Diary, 24 July to 2 Nov. 1880, passim; Joseph Stanley-Brown, "Memorandum," Stanley-Brown Papers, L.C.

38. JAG Diary, 24 July to 2 Nov. 1880, passim.

39. Dorsey to JAG, 25 and 26 July 1880; Dorsey to JAG, telegrams, 24 and 25 July 1880; Dorsey to Charles Foster, 28 July 1880, JAG Papers; Jewell to William E. Chandler, 21 July 1880, Chandler Papers, L.C.; Jewell to JAG, 29 and 30 July 1880; William E. Chandler to JAG, 24 and 28 July 1880; Frank Hiscock to JAG, 25 July 1880; William E. Chandler to JAG, 17 Feb. 1881 (Dorsey).

40. Hinsdale to JAG, 30 July 1880.

41. JAG Diary, 5 Aug. 1880; Louis J. Lang, comp. and ed., *The Autobiography of Thomas Collier Platt* (New York, 1910), pp. 129–133.

42. JAG Diary, 6 Aug. 1880; Garfield, "The Future of the Republic: Its Dangers and its Hopes," in Hinsdale, *Works of Garfield,* II, pp. 46–69; Whitelaw Reid to JAG, 31 Aug. 1880 (Supreme Court).

43. JAG Diary, 6 and 9 Aug. 1880; Conkling, *Conkling,* pp. 612–613 (statement by unnamed gentleman); Platt, *Autobiography,* pp. 130–131.
44. It is possible that Platt, Arthur, Crowley, and Morton, in their eagerness to get Conkling to participate in the campaign, gave their leader a more specific report, as far as Garfield's assurances were concerned, than the facts warranted.
45. Whitelaw Reid to JAG, 13 Aug. 1880.
46. *New York Times,* 18 Sept. 1880.
47. JAG to Harmon Austin, 6 Oct. 1880 (in this volume).
48. Joseph Stanley-Brown, "Memorandum," Stanley-Brown Papers, L.C.
49. JAG Diary, 28 Sept. 1880; *Painesville* (Ohio) *Telegraph,* 30 Sept. 1880.
50. Platt, *Autobiography,* p. 135.
51. Dorsey to Swaim, 1 Sept. 1880, JAG Papers; Pound to JAG, 9 Oct. 1880; Hinsdale to JAG, 5 Oct. 1880; Marshall Jewell to JAG, 15 Oct. 1880.
52. *New York Sun,* 27 Sept. 1880.
53. John I. Davenport, *History of the Morey Letter* (New York, 1884). Davenport, a Republican federal office holder in New York, was active in the campaign of 1880.
54. JAG Diary, 20–23 Oct. 1880; Davenport, *History of the Morey Letter,* pp. 59–63.
55. T. H. Williams, ed., *Hayes: The Diary of a President,* pp. 278–279.
56. *Garfield and Arthur Campaign Song Book 1880* (Washington, D.C., 1880), p. 20.
57. JAG Diary, 2 Nov. 1880 to 3 March 1881.
58. JAG, "Memorandum Diary," 27 Nov. 1880; Blaine to JAG, 20 Dec. 1880. Although Garfield's memorandum of his conversation with Blaine is separate from his regular diary, it will be included in Vol. IV of the printed diary.
59. JAG Diary, 13 Dec. 1880, 29 Jan. (invitation to Conkling), 11 Feb. (letter from Conkling), and 16 Feb. 1881 (Conkling's visit); JAG to Conkling, letterpress copy, 31 Jan. 1881; Conkling to JAG, 8 Feb. 1881; JAG to Morton, 26 Feb. 1881; Morton to JAG, telegram, 28 Feb. 1881. Morton's reply, couched in terms suggested by Garfield, read, "Your suggestion approved but hope the amendment suggested to Swaim is in your mind." The idea of having Conkling in the cabinet originated with Blaine, Reid, and William E. Chandler. After thinking the matter over, Blaine concluded that the appointment of Conkling was out of the question. See Whitelaw Reid to JAG, 26 Jan. 1881, Chandler to JAG, 26 Jan. 1881, and a statement by Blaine, 5 Feb. 1881 (the statement, unsigned and not in Blaine's hand, is probably a copy of an original statement, perhaps enclosed in a letter of Blaine to JAG, 5 Feb. 1881). When Cornell and Platt visited Mentor on 29 January, Garfield asked them what they thought of Conkling and Blaine for the first two places in the cabinet. "They thought," Garfield noted in his diary, "C. could not be spared from the Senate."
60. Small notebook in which Garfield made notes concerning cabinet appointments.
61. JAG Diary, 20, 21, and 22 Dec. 1880, 8, 15, 20, 26, 27, and 28 Feb. 1881.
62. On a separate sheet in JAG Papers.
63. JAG to Rhodes, 16 Nov. 1880 ("bleak mountain"); JAG to Austin, 7 Feb. 1881; Hinsdale, *President Garfield and Education,* p. 106–108.
64. *Washington Star,* 1 March 1881, and *New York Times,* 2 March 1881 (arrival in Washington); JAG Diary, 1 March 1881; LRG, Diary, 1 March 1881, LRG Papers.
65. JAG Diary, 1 March 1881.
66. Ibid., 2 March 1881.
67. Ibid., 3 March 1881; Joseph Stanley-Brown, "Memorandum."
68. JAG Diary, 4 March 1881.
69. Ibid.; LRG, Diary, 4 March 1881, LRG Papers; EBG, Diary, 4 March 1881, Western Reserve Historical Society.

70. Hinsdale, *Works of Garfield,* II, pp. 788–795.

71. JAG Diary, 4 March 1881.

72. Ibid., 5 March 1881; *The Nation,* 32:216 (31 March 1881).

73. JAG to Hal and Jim, 18 Dec. 1880, Harry A. Garfield Papers, L.C.; Lucretia G. Comer, *Strands from the Weaving* (New York, 1959), pp. 25–26; Ruth Feis, *Mollie Garfield in the White House* (Chicago, 1963). Harry Garfield and Mollie Garfield were the parents, respectively, of Mrs. Comer and Mrs. Feis.

74. JAG to Whitelaw Reid, copy, 7 Dec. 1881; Hay to JAG, 25 Dec. (quotation) and 31 Dec. 1881; Swaim to JAG, 23 Feb. 1881 (Blaine); JAG Diary, 25 Dec. 1881 (importance of appointment).

75. Joseph Stanley-Brown, "Memorandum." The strain on Joe was so great that Mrs. Garfield suggested that he be given a rest by being sent to England to deliver some government bonds. He left Washington on 1 June and was back on 1 July. President Arthur invited him to stay on as secretary, but he left the White House a few months after Garfield's death to work on the papers of the late President.

76. See note 61 for Chapter 9; Comer, *Strands from the Weaving,* p. 44.

77. JAG Diary, 15 March 1881; Rose to JAG, 14 March 1881; Hinsdale to Rose, 28 Aug. 1882, JAG Papers. See also LRG Papers for correspondence of Rose with Mrs. Garfield. H.B. called on Lucretia Rose in Lanham, Maryland, on two occasions in the late 1950s and early 1960s; her father lived into the 1930s.

78. Of the close friends of Garfield mentioned, only Sheldon continued active in the office to which Garfield had appointed him until the end of the Garfield–Arthur administration.

79. JAG Diary, 7, 8, 14, 16, and 26 March 1881.

80. Ibid., 20 March 1881; George S. Boutwell, *Reminiscences of Sixty Years in Public Affairs,* 2 vols. (New York, 1902), I, p. 273 (quoting Conkling).

81. Conkling to JAG, and JAG to Conkling, letterpress copy, 21 March 1881. Conkling has only "Monday Morn" on his letter; at the top of the letter someone has written "April/81," and the *Index* of the Garfield Papers has perpetuated this error. The date is established by the contents of the letter.

82. JAG Diary, 22 March 1881; *Journal of the Executive Proceedings of the Senate of the United States of America,* XXIII (Washington, 1901). The volume contains the proceedings from 5 March 1881 to 3 March 1883. A handwritten copy of the Executive Journal for the period from 5 March to 20 May 1881 is in the JAG Papers.

83. LRG, Diary, and JAG Diary, 22 March 1881.

84. LRG, Diary, 22 March 1881.

85. Ibid., 23 March 1881.

86. Sherman to JAG, 23 Jan. 1881.

87. Joseph Stanley-Brown, Record of statements made to Stanley-Brown and James R. Garfield by Thomas L. James, 11 Feb. 1889, James R. Garfield Papers, L.C.

88. Ibid.; JAG Diary, 25 March 1881.

89. Ibid. (both references in note 88). For a somewhat different account from that of James as reported by Stanley-Brown, see T. B. Connery, "Secret History of the Garfield–Conkling Tragedy," *Cosmopolitan,* 23:145–162. According to Connery, James and Platt left a hotel together to go to see Conkling, picking up MacVeagh on the way. Connery also says that James went alone to the White House to report Conkling's refusal to the President and that Garfield was disgusted and indignant at the news. Garfield's diary does not mention an evening visit from James.

90. JAG Diary, 31 March (Merritt), 1 April (cabinet), 2 April ("test of friendship"), 3 April 1881 (Sherman).

91. Ibid., 4 April 1881.

92. Henry L. Dawes, "Garfield and Conkling," *Century Magazine*, 47:343–344.
93. Ibid.; JAG to Hubbell, copy in J. S. Brown's hand, 22 Aug. 1880.
94. JAG Diary, 29 April 1881; Dawes, "Garfield and Conkling," p. 344.
95. JAG Diary, 30 April 1881.
96. JAG Diary, 4–5 May 1881.
97. Ibid., 5 May 1881.
98. Ibid., 9–10 May 1881.
99. The letter is in a box of family papers which H.B. saw when it was in the possession of the late Carle Robbins, grandson of Phebe Boynton and grandnephew of Silas Boynton. The papers are now in the possession of the family of Mr. Robbins.
100. JAG Diary, 19 May 1881; JAG to Jacob Dolson Cox, letterpress copy, 22 May 1881.
101. Rhodes to Henry, 18 May 1881, in Henry, *Captain Henry of Geauga*, pp. 309–310; EBG to Alpha Boynton, 19 May 1881.
102. Grant to JAG, 24 April 1881.
103. JAG to Grant, copy, 15 May 1881 (in this volume).
104. JAG Diary, 24 and 25 June 1881.
105. House Report No. 2165, 48 Cong., 1 Sess., Serial 2259, pp. 1–12; Earl J. Leland, "The Post Office and Politics, 1876–1881: The Star Route Frauds," Ph.D. dissertation, University of Chicago, 1964; *The Nation*, 32:288 (28 April 1881).
106. House Report No. 2165, pp. 1–12.
107. Chandler to JAG, 17 Feb. 1881.
108. Blaine to JAG, 20 Jan. 1881.
109. House Miscellaneous Report No. 2165, Part 2, 48 Cong., 1 Sess., Serial 2234, "Testimony Relating to the Star-Route Cases," pp.1–2.
110. Dorsey to JAG, 17 Feb. 1881.
111. House Miscellaneous Report No. 2165, "Testimony," p. 2; *National Republican*, "Thomas J. Brady," an editorial, 20 June 1881.
112. JAG Diary, 22 June and 1 July 1881; EBG, Diary, 22 June to 1 July 1881, Western Reserve Historical Society.
113. Samuel J. Kirkwood, quoted in *New York Times*, 3 July 1881 (Washington dispatch of 2 July).
114. JAG Diary, 1 July 1881. Garfield does not mention a cabinet meeting in the diary.

## Epilogue II. A Hot Saturday Morning in Washington

1. W. T. Crump, "Callers at the Executive Mansion, March 4–July 2, 1881," (includes list of those present at meals), JAG Papers; W. T. Crump's memoranda of the morning of 2 July and later, LRG Papers; A. F. Rockwell, "Account of Assassination," written 9 July 1881, A. F. Rockwell Papers, L.C.; Joseph Stanley-Brown, "Memorandum."
2. *Proceedings in the Supreme Court of the District of Columbia, in the Case of Charles J. Guiteau*, 3 vols. (Washington, 1882), I, pp. 704–705. Hereafter cited as *Trial of Guiteau*.
3. *Trial of Guiteau*, passim; the quotations are in I, p. 307.
4. *Trial of Guiteau*, I, pp. 583–585; *New York Times*, 7 Aug. 1880. On the evening of 6 August, Garfield was serenaded in front of the Fifth Avenue headquarters of the Republican National Committee. He and a number of other Republicans made short speeches. According to the *Times*, Guiteau was one of the speakers; his remarks were not reported. Guiteau had returned to the city on 1 August.
5. Guiteau to JAG, 16 Oct. and 31 Dec. 1880.
6. *Trial of Guiteau*, I, p. 660 (Guiteau's arrival), p. 586 (first call at White House), pp. 207–208 (Guiteau at the White House—J. S. Brown's testimony), p. 631 (room-

ing houses); Guiteau to JAG, printed copy, 8 March 1881, JAG Papers. Several of Guiteau's letters to Garfield were removed from the Garfield Papers for the trial and replaced by printed copies.

7. *Trial of Guiteau,* I, pp. 120–123.

8. Ibid., p. 665.

9. Guiteau to JAG, printed copy, 29 April 1881.

10. *Trial of Guiteau,* I, p. 593; Guiteau to JAG, printed copy, 23 May 1881.

11. *Trial of Guiteau,* I, pp. 224–225 (O'Meara's testimony), pp. 636–637 (Guiteau's testimony).

12. Ibid., pp. 697, 701 (jail), p. 640 (book), pp. 694–695 (church), pp. 215–216 (Address), p. 703 (Mrs. Garfield).

13. Ibid., pp. 692–693 (Blaine episode); JAG Diary, 27 and 29 June 1881 (Long Branch, carriage ride); H. G. and C. J. Hayes, *A Complete History of the Trial of Guiteau, Assassin of President Garfield . . .* (Philadelphia, 1882), pp. 19–20 (carriage episode—statement of district attorney), pp. 433–434 (carriage episode—statement of Guiteau); *Trial of Guiteau,* I, pp. 692–693 (Blaine episode); Harriet S. Blaine to "Dear M.," 8 July 1881, in Harriet S. Blaine Beale, ed., *Letters of Mrs. James G. Blaine,* 2 vols. (New York, 1908), I, p. 215.

14. *Trial of Guiteau,* I, pp. 704–706 (testimony of Guiteau).

15. Rockwell, "Account of Assassination"; *Trial of Guiteau,* I, pp. 225–227 (Rockwell's testimony), pp. 186–191 (Kearney's testimony).

16. *Trial of Guiteau,* I, p. 121 (Blaine's testimony), pp. 140–141 (Sarah White's testimony); Rockwell, "Account of Assassination"; Diary of James R. Garfield, 2 July 1881, James R. Garfield Papers, L.C.

17. *Trial of Guiteau,* I, pp. 186–191 (Kearney), pp. 215–216 (letter to White House), p. 217 (letter to Sherman).

18. Ibid., pp. 228–235 (Dr. Bliss); Rockwell, "Account of Assassination."

19. Rockwell, "Account of Assassination."

20. Joseph Stanley-Brown, "Memorandum."

21. Ibid.; Harriet S. Blaine to "Dear M.," 3 July 1881, in Beale, *Letters of Mrs. James G. Blaine,* I, pp. 210–211; Mrs. Blaine's narrative of events of 2, 3, and 4 July, James G. Blaine Papers, L.C.

22. Rockwell, "Account of Assassination." Harriet S. Blaine to "Dear M.," 3 July 1881, in Beale, *Letters of Mrs. James G. Blaine,* I, p. 211.

23. For a day-to-day account of Garfield's illness, with the bulletins issued by the doctors and some of Blaine's dispatches to James R. Lowell, see John Clark Ridpath, *The Life and Work of James A. Garfield . . . embracing . . . the Tragic Story of his Death* (Cincinnati, 1881), pp. 517–645; information about Silas Boynton was obtained by H.B. from the late Carle B. Robbins, grandson of Phebe Boynton and grandnephew of Dr. Boynton; *Trial of Guiteau,* I, p. 383; W. T. Crump's memoranda (holy water), LRG Papers.

24. Albert Gallatin Riddle, *Garfield* (1881), p. 534 (Rockwell's statement), p. 535 (Dr. Edson's statement); Theodore Clarke Smith, *Garfield,* II, p. 1196 (Ohio and Conkling), p. 1198 (Mrs. Garfield); JAG to EBG, 11 Aug. 1881 (in this volume).

25. Riddle, *Garfield,* pp. 524–525 (Lincoln and Garfield); Reeves, *Gentleman Boss,* p. 242 (Arthur); Jordan, *Conkling,* p. 407 (Conkling). The subscription list for the fund for Mrs. Garfield is in the JAG Papers. The total amount subscribed was a little more than $361,000. Under the terms of the gift, the money was to be invested in government bonds, the income from which was to be paid to Mrs. Garfield; after her death the principal was to be divided among her children. Congress awarded her about

$25,000 and an annual pension of $5,000. She was thus able to live in comfort and to educate her children; she died in 1918.

26. Ridpath, *Garfield,* pp. 610–624.

27. Ibid., pp. 624—639 (at Elberon; includes cables to Lowell and Swaim's account of Garfield's death).

28. Brisbin and Balch, *Garfield,* pp. 709–710; Reeves, *Gentleman Boss,* pp. 246–247.

29. Ridpath, *Garfield,* pp. 646–672; Brisbin and Balch, *Garfield,* pp. 712–760. Newspapers, of course, carried detailed accounts of the funeral ceremonies.

# INDEX